Embodiment of a Nation

EMBODIMENT OF A NATION

Human Form in American Places

Cecelia Tichi

HARVARD UNIVERSITY PRESS
CAMBRIDGE, MASSACHUSETTS
LONDON, ENGLAND
2001

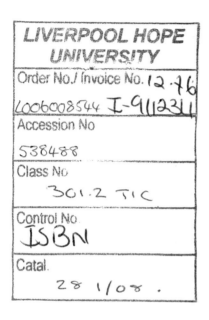
Chapter 4's fourth epigraph is from *The Moon Is Always Female* by
Marge Piercy, copyright © 1980 by Marge Piercy. Used by
permission of Alfred A. Knopf, a division of Random House, Inc.

Library of Congress Cataloging-in-Publication Data
Tichi, Cecelia, 1942–
Embodiment of a nation : human form in American places / Cecelia Tichi.
p. cm.
Includes bibliographical references (p.) and index.
ISBN 0-674-00494-9 (alk. paper)
1. United States—Intellectual life. 2. United States—History, Local. 3. United
States—Environmental conditions. 4. National characteristics, American.
5. Human body—Social aspects—United States—History. 6. Anthropomorphism.
7. Landscape—United States—Psychological aspects—History. 8. Landscape—Social
aspects—United States—History. 9. Historic sites—United States. I. Title.

E169.1 .T543 2001
973—dc21   00-069711

For Bill, Claire, and Julia

There is no endowment in man or woman that is not tallied in you,
There is no virtue, no beauty in man or woman, but as good is in you.

—WALT WHITMAN, *Birds of Passage,* 1881

Contents

Illustrations

Acknowledgments

Books are collaborative endeavors, proving that "colleague" and "friend" are synonymous. This project has been no exception. At the very beginning, Amy Lang saw possibilities in the topic and encouraged its pursuit. At Vanderbilt University, I am greatly indebted to my colleague Teresa Goddu, who has been consistently encouraging and critical, reading drafts and offering advice at every point. Late in the project, in addition, Thadious Davis proposed a valuable direction of inquiry and particular references. I thank her for the timeliest of advice. Helen Vendler's suggestion of a Robinson Jeffers poem and Ann Cook's festive gift of the ceramic "flower power" planter (Figure 13) are much appreciated also.

This project has benefited substantially from institutional research support. Vanderbilt University provided sabbatical leave and funds for research, including travel to the Newberry Library, the National Archives, and the Hot Springs (Arkansas) National Park, where archivist Sharon Shugart generously aided my research. I am indebted, too, to the staffs of the Jean and Alexander Heard Library and of the Historical Collections of the Eskind Biomedical Library of Vanderbilt University, especially Mary Telo and James Thweatt, for their help. I also much appreciate the research assistance of Jill Anderson and Alison Piepmeier.

The project was enriched by my month-long stay at the Rockefeller Foundation Study Center at Bellagio, Italy, whose staff provided ideal conditions for writing. I especially thank Gianna Celli, assistant director of the center, for her warmth and support. The scholars in residence that fall of 1997 offered numerous helpful suggestions, and I am particularly grateful to Alix Kates Shulman and Brenda Silver. Along the way, faculty and graduate students have posed important questions in response to presentations I have made of various portions of this work, and I thank the Departments of English at Brandeis University, Case Western Reserve University, and the California Institute of Technology in addition to the American Studies Association of Israel and the Dibner Institute of the Massachusetts Institute of Technology. A portion of Chapter 3 appeared in "Pittsburgh at Yellowstone: Old Faithful and the Pulse of Industrial America," *American Literary History* 9, no. 3 (Fall 1997): 522–541, and I appreciate the permission of Oxford University Press to reprint it here in revised form.

Finally, outside reviewers have contributed much to this undertaking, which is the better for their efforts. I also wish to express my appreciation to Lindsay Waters, Kim Steere, and Elizabeth Gilbert of Harvard University Press, who have guided the project at every step.

Embodiment of a Nation

Introduction

This project began on a cross-country drive late in the summer of 1965. I had reached South Dakota's Black Hills and was on a two-lane blacktop winding among the area's signature pines and granite peaks. For a split second that afternoon, a particular mountain range seen through the Ford windshield caught my attention because it looked so bizarre, so deformed. Somehow the AAA guidebook had not quite prepared me for the actual encounter, its abruptness, its incongruity. It took an instant for the name of the tourist site to mesh with the resolution of rocks into human heads.

Of course, Mt. Rushmore.

At the time, it did not occur to me, as a young graduate student in literary studies, that Mt. Rushmore connected substantively with canonical American literature or that it might prove central to a project on environmental nationality. Encountered on a road trek toward a Ph.D. program in California, the outdoor presidential sculpture offered a mere transitory moment, an excuse to pull over, get out, and stare upward along with my fellow automobile tourists, most of them vacationing families, all eyes on Gutzon Borglum's monumental sculpture of U.S. presidents Washington, Jefferson, Theodore Roosevelt, and Lincoln. Like the vacationers, I slipped a quarter into one of the coin-operated binoculars, a George Washington quarter to better view the gargantuan Washington and his presidential cohorts of the mountain. Most everyone on the shoulder gravel at that moment seemed respectful both of the heads and of the auto mileage clocked just to get there. The visitors wanted to feel themselves at a site of national symbolic commemoration, not a P. T. Barnum sideshow of the kind Karal Ann Marling later dubbed the "Colossus of Roads."

It was, above all, an uncomplicated moment for me, a white female graduate student in that era dominated by formalist New Criticism, for politics was not yet understood to be inherent to all literature and art. More than a decade into the future were the sociocultural arguments to be raised by literary theory and cultural studies in the United States. In August 1965, Mt. Rushmore viewed through roadside binoculars was not a contested site, at least not to a mainstream white. Those lenses did not show a sculptural ideological message of white male authority over minority groups or women. The quarter's worth of magnification was not enough to focus Mt. Rushmore's link, say, to the civil rights movement with its sit-ins and marches by Negroes, or to mark a horizon line of the women's liberation movement then in the offing.

Nor did the huge heads show the extent to which Mt. Rushmore could be considered an imperialist project, since white mainstream America knew nothing of the monument's violation of the sacred ground of the Oglala Sioux (and might well have been indifferent had it known, since the Native American rights movement had not yet organized its civil rights initiatives). The Vietnam War, at that time, had not intensified sufficiently to trouble a large segment of the citizenry and implicate the patriarchal arrogance expressed in the mountaintop carving. The binocular moment was therefore "innocent"—and also brief, just a few minutes' duration. There wasn't much rush from Rushmore, though no tourist said so aloud as the car doors clunked shut and the lot of us hit the road again.

The incident might have become a minor entry in memory's scrapbook except for two crucial other "lenses" that soon appeared and, years later, proved crucial to this project. These were two book-length compilations considered required reading both in and out of the mid-1960s graduate seminar room. Each cast a long shadow in literary-cultural analysis for decades: Perry Miller's *Errand into the Wilderness* (1956; rpt. 1965) and Norman O. Brown's *Love's Body* (1966). Miller's book is a gathering of essays mainly on American colonial literature, and Brown's a series of meditations or *pensées* on the centrality of the human body to personhood, social organization, acts of documentation, and history. Conjoined, these works would become foundational for this study.

To be sure, when Perry Miller included "Nature and the National Ego" in *Errand into the Wilderness,* he was not thinking of Mt. Rushmore or Hot Springs, Arkansas, or Yellowstone's Old Faithful geyser. Miller did not anticipate the Sixties counterculture's embrace of Thoreau and Walden Pond. He did not live to ponder the moon of the Apollo space project. He could not have foreseen that an obscure waste canal in upstate

New York would become notorious in the late 1970s—Love Canal, a national symbol of environmental contamination. He certainly did not foresee the momentous role that gender would soon play in literary-cultural studies.

What interested Miller, principally a scholar of New England Puritanism, was an environmental crisis he perceived in the American nineteenth century. He found a deep social anxiety underlying America's celebration of civilization advancing under the ax of deforestation. Miller found that, when faced with the crisis of hastening environmental transformation, the American writers and artists of the first half of the nineteenth century toiled mightily to identify the Republic with timeless "virtues of pristine . . . 'romantic' Nature," and hastened their efforts to record that nature in print and paint before it fell to the ax and disappeared (207). In the face of a much-feared "European"-style civilizing of the New World wilderness, Miller realized, the cohort of American writers and artists "identified the health, the very personality of America with Nature" (207).

Miller identified "Nature" (versus civilization) as the great subject of American literature, political discourse, and visual art in the first half of the nineteenth century. This romantic "veneration" of capital-N Nature, he found, was pervasive in print and visual texts. If American character exists, Miller said, it was molded by the salutary natural world and the "impositions of geography" (210). It perceived all virtue to be "inherent" in the natural environment, and thus it made America "Nature's nation" (209).

In this model of nationality, nature itself imparts virtue rather like an irradiating force from a geologic moral core. Geography is the active agent in moral and ethical suasion.[1] In terms of historicity, the key term in Nature's nation is "inherent," which not only locates the moral excellence of the nation in its natural environment but categorizes that moral state as phenomenal. As such, it is not developmental, and its etiology is not knowable. Nature's nation self-evidently manifests itself in the very topography and geomorphology of America. And it is timeless, transcendent of the vicissitudes of historical process through years, decades, centuries, millennia.

Bodies form the conceptual complement to this project, and it was Miller's contemporary, Norman O. Brown, who produced the crucial antecedent body project, *Love's Body*. This was the ur-text for the "body" scholarship that would flourish in the later twentieth century, though claim its paterfamilias in the French theorists, notably Michel Foucault.

The author of *Life against Death* and other books, Brown chose an experimental form for *Love's Body* (1966), a dazzling and puzzling nonlinear pastiche, a kind of diary-collage of meditations and blunt assertions: "knowledge is carnal knowledge," "to explore is to penetrate; the world is the insides of mother," "the body is a body politic" (249, 36, 126). Absent footnotes, the text quotes from and refers to myriad sources, its argumentation largely Freudian psychoanalytic. Above all, Brown showed the extent to which the human body operates as homology and synecdoche in every social, personal, and governmental organization. Brown's book demonstrates on every page that "knowledge is carnal knowledge."

Indeed, back in 1965, Brown's chapter "Head" might well have prompted rethinking of my own recent Mt. Rushmore moment. At that time, however, I failed to grasp the connection and returned to *Love's Body* only after many years of repeated literary encounters with tropes of the American environment embodied. These are tropes extending from the era of discovery to the contemporary moment, tropes of Nature's nation.

Tropes of bodies, of course, have been commonplace in representations of the earth for millennia, and in one sense American texts have simply resumed the tradition in which geophysical features had been likened to parts of the human body: foothills, headwaters, mouths of rivers, snowy mountain breasts, and so on, with mountains as "bones of the world" and water flowing in the veins of earth, and the human head writ large in the very globe itself (Nicolson, *Mountain,* 162, 170; Nicolson, *Breaking,* 40). As conceptions of cosmology changed with the development of modern science, with the belief in actual correspondences between the human body and the earth discredited, literature of the New World nonetheless exhibited a remarkably stubborn pattern of geomorphological bodily incarnation—the Continental Divide as national backbone, the Grand Tetons as female breasts, a rock formation in New Hampshire's White Mountains as the Old Man of the Mountain.

The American pattern dates at least from Christopher Columbus's "Letter to the Sovereign on the Third Voyage" (1492), which represents the world as a "very round ball, on one part of which something like a woman's teat were placed" (18). That image was taken up again in the twentieth century with erotic overtones in F. Scott Fitzgerald's *Great Gatsby* (1925), whose narrator imagines the sailors in Henry Hudson's exploration of the "fresh, green breast" of the New World (182).

The trope of environment-as-body crosses gender lines and extends through the nineteenth century. In an essay in *Natural History of Intellect,* Emerson, echoing Scripture, urges geographical exploration because "Nature . . . is bone of our bone, flesh of our flesh, made of us" ("Country Life," 1858, *NHI*), while Henry David Thoreau opens *Cape Cod* (1855) with an extended trope of the state's geography as a female pugilist: "Cape Cod is the bared and bended arm of Massachusetts; the shoulder is at Buzzard's Bay, the elbow, or crazy-bone, at Cape Mallebarre, the wrist at Truro, and the sandy fist at Provincetown . . . like an athlete protecting her bay" (4).

Other examples of geographic embodiment include the turn-of-the-century historian Frederick Jackson Turner, remarking that "civilization in America has followed the arteries made by geology," and Mark Twain, commenting in *Life on the Mississippi* (1883) on "the Mississippi [River] . . . always changing its habitat bodily" (Turner, 14–15; Twain, 8). Harriet Beecher Stowe exclaimed in *Uncle Tom's Cabin* (1852) on the Mississippi's "bosom," bearing unprecedented "wealth and enterprise" (Stowe, 226). In the twentieth century Langston Hughes reprised the same image in the poem "The Negro Speaks of Rivers," in which the poet claims riparian African-American ancestry in a Mississippi whose "muddy bosom turn[s] / all golden in the sunset" (Hughes qtd. Lewis, 257).

Such twentieth-century embodiment continues, not only in Fitzgerald's famous figure of the "fresh, green breast" but in the quasi-epic poem of William Carlos Williams, *Paterson* (1948–1963), which represents the hill and valley of the northern New Jersey geographic site of the poem as a male-female couple: "Paterson lies in the valley under the Passaic Falls / its spent waters forming the outline of his back. He / lies on his right side, head near the thunder / of the waters filling his dreams! . . . . . / And there, against him, stretches the low mountain. / The Park's her head, carved, above the Falls, . . . / facing him, his arm supporting her, by the *Valley of the Rocks*, asleep" (*Paterson*, 6–7, 8).

All these tropes exhibit what Walt Whitman, in his preface to the 1855 edition of *Leaves of Grass*, called incarnation. The American bard, he wrote, responds spiritually to his country's own spirit. He "incarnates its geography and natural life and rivers and lakes" (713). Whitman's statement works two ways, both to make the poet the physical incarnation of the country and, in the reverse, to obligate the poet to the literary incarnation of America's geography. It was as if Whitman worked inferentially, ratifying the practices of his predecessors, and also prescriptively in requiring that very incarnation as a national literary mandate for the present and future. To think seriously about the foregoing tropes is to take Whitman's statement as a guideline.

It is also to broaden the notion of "bard" to include producers of the

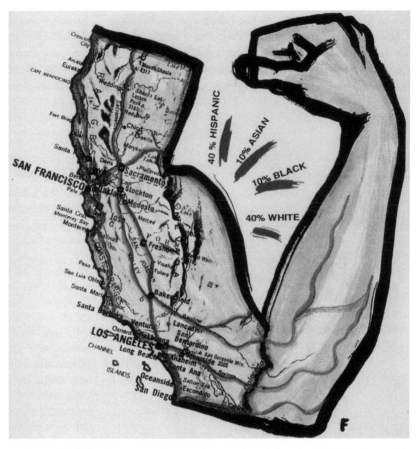

1. State of California as muscular arm in map-based drawing by Filip Pagowski, 1998.

multifarious texts that incarnate America. This project operates within the framework of environmental studies, history, and visual and literary texts. Among recent studies, this one might be linked with William Cronon's edited collection, *Uncommon Ground: Rethinking the Human Place in Nature* (1996), and Simon Schama's *Landscape and Memory* (1995), both volumes that show the extent to which nature and culture are enmeshed through history, which is conceived as public memory.

Embodiment of a Nation operates similarly, but with two provisos as it addresses historical change and the constitution of environmental studies at the turn of the twenty-first century. This is to say, first of all, that this book proceeds under the assumption that certain subject areas are so culturally compelling that they persist through periods of marked social change.[2] The very persistence of geographical embodiment in diverse texts representing America over five centuries indicates a continuity that is profitably analyzed historically. "Nature's nation" is Miller's own formulation of a sociohistorical pattern enduring over a long period of time. Spanning the nineteenth and twentieth centuries, the present discussion seeks to disclose the basis on which a cultural concept—of a geomorphically embodied Nature's nation—persists through historical shifts in sensibility, mentality, and changed social conditions.

Although the elegance of the term "Nature's nation" suggests a critical loftiness of conception, in fact the bodily expression of Miller's phrase has been overlooked because its central motive principle—anthropomorphism—is distinctly unfashionable in academic study.[3] "Landscapes . . . suggest humanity," insists Stewart Guthrie in a recent study of anthropomorphism and religion. Guthrie's statement that the external environment is innately suggestive of the human being is the premise of any work on bodily identity within the natural world. Anthropomorphism, he

2. Athlete as embodied map on *Sports Illustrated* cover, 1996.

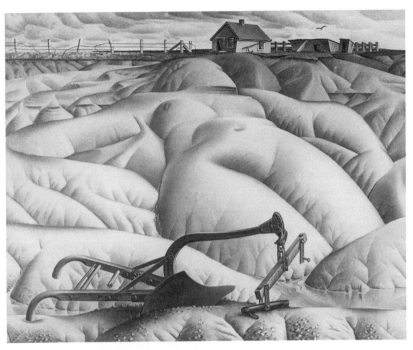

3. Topography as female embodiment in *Erosion No. 2: Mother Earth Laid Bare,*
by Alexander Hogue. Oil on canvas, 1936.

argues, is the persistent, involuntary cognitive process underlying environmental bodily figuration. Guthrie's *Faces in the Clouds: A New Theory
of Religion* identifies several anthropomorphized sites in North America—
two peaks in Arizona known to the Papago Indians as the Twin Sisters,
the Grand Tetons or big breasts in Wyoming, Sleeping Ute Mountain in
Colorado, considered by the Ute Indians to be "the feet, knees, and folded
arms of a reclining man" (117). (The trope of nature as a mother, he suggests, is currently so common as to be "almost invisible" [118].)[4]

As a scholar of religion, Guthrie's outsider relation to literary and cultural studies enables him to chide colleagues for viewing the anthropomorphic as a critical strategy rather than as a primal response to the
world. Contemporary scholars "find personification artificial, as a deliberate figure of speech for a literary purpose": "They call it variously a 'technique,' a 'trope,' a 'metaphor,' a 'conceit,' a 'move,' or a 'literary mode,'
and treat it solely as a phenomenon of language and especially of rhetoric.
Few scholars think personification either spontaneous or part of a broader
worldview, and fewer still identify it as a form of anthropomorphism"
(Guthrie, 124).

To be sure, literary studies' status claims of civilized sophistication militate against a self-identification with animistic primitivism linked to anthropomorphism. Yet the bodies of Nature's nation must be understood within anthropomorphic motives.[5] *Faces in the Clouds* concludes that "because no clear line separates models of humans and models of other things and events, we are able to find, with no sense of incongruity, all manner of humanity in the nonhuman world" (194). Guthrie had earlier stated that "because a human presence is so important, we superimpose widely different human forms on widely different phenomena" (140).

Anthropomorphism, however, need not involve the entire body. Thoreau's trope of the pugilist Massachusetts is unusually morphologically thorough, with left and right arms, shoulder, breast, and feet in a defensive stance of guardianship. Much more often, as we have seen, the body is signified solely by a part, for example, the Continental Divide as the nation's backbone. As the above-cited texts reveal, it is not necessarily the entire body but a part or a feature presented to stand for the whole or to be privileged as the physical feature so important that it becomes the dominant bodily identity. This apparent isolation of body parts is not an act of bodily dismemberment or figurative amputation so much as it is an act of synecdoche, in that certain parts of the human body stand for national traits socially prized and authenticated precisely because these traits are thought to inhere in the body and to manifest themselves in the natural world of the nation state.

It must be argued that anthropomorphism actually makes the mythic Nature's nation possible. The anthropomorphic America is ahistorical, really history-proof. Anthropomorphism collapses temporal and spatial boundaries, as between historical periods and between primitives and sophisticates, and thus lends itself to the formulation of "Nature's nation" as a prevalent paradigm.

Yet the bodies do vary over time, their meanings redirected under the pressure of social change. Under the aegis of "the embodiment of a nation," then, this project examines not a single body but several. We are directed toward such plurality in the tropes surveyed above. Just as Columbus' female "teat" indicates a New World of maternal nurture, so *Paterson's* recumbent male-female figures emphasize erotics, while Thoreau's pugilist Cape Cod is a staunch shoreline defender-sentinel. The bodies are diverse, subject to authorial decision motivated by shifting sociopolitical conditions even as the paradigm of Nature's nation governs them all.

This book does not strive, however, for comprehensiveness. It is not about a complete body count, to use a baleful term from the Vietnam era. The bodies under discussion here are not the sum total of the corporeal in the corpus of public discourse in the United States over two centuries. The point of *Embodiment of a Nation* is not to provide an exhaustive inventory of bodily identities but to demonstrate the way in which a national paradigm expresses itself in variation, contrariety, statement, and counterresponse.

Most of the sites considered here, in fact, are more or less familiar through media images if not personal encounter. They belong to tourism and popular culture. Mt. Rushmore, Old Faithful, Love Canal, and the other sites have been socially constructed through promotional materials, television and motion pictures, journalistic accounts, scientific and pseudoscientific literature, narratives, tracts, fiction, and verse. One recalls, for example, the climax of Alfred Hitchcock's *North by Northwest* as Cary Grant and Eva Marie Saint scramble over the huge presidential faces at Mt. Rushmore, or the NASA footage of the Apollo 11 astronauts planting the U.S. flag on the surface of the moon, samples of which were retrieved for display around the country. The presidential heads of Mt. Rushmore appear in greeting card parodies and on postage stamps, while Walden Pond, with a caption from *Walden,* is a recurrent image for nature calendars. Old Faithful is perennially a favorite western tourist site.

As for Hot Springs, Arkansas, it is perhaps better known outside the southeastern United States as the boyhood home of President William Jefferson Clinton than as the first national park, famed from the nineteenth century for its natural thermal springs which continue to draw vacationers and health seekers from the South and Midwest today. And Love Canal is memorable to much of the public from the intense national media attention focused in the late 1970s on the upstate New York suburban subdivision whose land had been contaminated by chemicals from a nearby landfill in an "ecotastrophe."

Discussion of these sites here is structured in pairs under rubrics revealing the particular historical relation of the bodies over two centuries. The analyses include, in Part I, Crania Americana, a consideration of ways in which mental autonomy and authority in America are geomorphically embodied, with Mt. Rushmore as representative of nineteenth-century headship and Walden Pond—"earth's eye," as Thoreau called it—expressive of the twentieth-century Sixties countercultural effort to renegotiate the democratic basis of authority and consciousness.

Part II, Frontier Incarnations, addresses the ways in which the American frontier, a key term in the identification of national character extending at least from Frederick Jackson Turner to Disneyland, is embodied in the later nineteenth century and again in the twentieth, seemingly as nature's own ratification of hegemonic technologies. These technologies span the era of steam and rocket propulsion, and the frontiers paired here are the male West of railroad-era Yellowstone and the female moon of the Apollo project, begun in the early 1960s as part of the Kennedy administration's New Frontier. Interestingly, these frontier sites are both male, in the masculine frontier pulse of the West, and female, in the erotic frontier incarnation of La Luna.

Part III, Bon Aqua (a title taken from a town in the state of Tennessee), concerns the female aquatic embodiment of health in Nature's nation. Tracking the course of an American Hygeia, goddess of health, the discussion considers the terms on which Hot Springs, Arkansas, is the locus of the female aquatic embodiment that is found in numerous texts of nineteenth-century America. In the late twentieth century, the Hygeian obversion appears in the scandal of Love Canal, which is figured as a body infected, malignant, contagious, though subject to healing in the mythic terms of an ecofeminism that upholds the paradigm of Nature's nation.

As this project works to show historical change within the ahistorical paradigm of Nature's nation, so it also operates under a second proviso. *Embodiment of a Nation* defines environmental history as a history of collective memory that is produced by the continuous textual mediation of sites and places. By this model, Mt. Rushmore, for example, is defined historically only in part by the factual data of its key personnel, its financing, its construction in South Dakota, and so on. The greater understanding of its position in U.S. history requires analysis of the antecedent texts that make the very conception of such a project possible—texts from the late eighteenth century identifying mountains as male rulers, texts featuring heads themselves as a synecdoche of the human body, texts celebrating corporate heads as business leaders. Add to these the texts making use of Mt. Rushmore that continue to produce meanings and thus add to the collective sociocultural memory—including postcards, Hitchcock's film, and comic-strip parodies that substitute outer-space alien heads or those of pop culture stars such as Elvis or Marilyn Monroe. Add to these, too, such coinage as "Rushmoritis" and proposals that additional presidents' heads be carved on the South Dakota granite skyline, notably Ronald Reagan's.

This is to say that site-specific environmental study per se is too limited, not only for Mt. Rushmore but for the other places discussed here. To be site-specific is to block adequate appreciation of the complex cultural identification of geographical *loci*. It is to prevent understanding of the extent to which environments, including Mt. Rushmore and all other places under discussion here, circulate through mixed media hundreds or many thousands of miles from the site itself.

Indeed, this is to argue that the very term "environment" must widen as natural-world places are increasingly experienced via photographic and electronic replication. The environmental historian Richard White has remarked on the exclusivity of the term "nature" as used by certain interest groups, and he represents himself as someone whose workday is spent at a computer screen but whose work is nonetheless integral to the natural world (184–185). Indeed the omnipresence of the screen in late twentieth-century America makes it an environment in and of itself as we move from the televisual environment to that of the World Wide Web. Television, as I have elsewhere argued, became an American environment from the 1950s onward, just as the Web is an environment at the turn of this century. Those unable to venture to Yellowstone National Park to experience an eruption of Old Faithful can click to the web site where a fixed WebCam broadcasts a new shot of the geyser hole every thirty seconds. Such onscreen reception may displease some environmentalist constituencies, but this electronic Old Faithful in cyberspace, a geyser mediated by camera and screen, is only the newer version of the geyser as represented on railroad flyers or in line drawings in early twentieth-century magazines.

To conclude and also to begin: national embodiment must be examined as a strategic process or program of natural-ization by which the nation is defined and redefined in critical historical moments. We need to ask how sites of the natural world are representationally constructed as bodies, how phenomena of nature gain national bodily identity at crucial points of technological or political change, and through whose agency and advocacy. We must ask what interests are served by this identity formation.[6] How and why might certain sites, at certain specific moments in time, prompt the cultural work of geographic embodiment? How might they disclose hegemonic interests and social dislocations too? What happens when bodily geo-identity is not stable but subject to reinterpretation and to new invention, in the root meaning of *invenire,* to come upon, to encounter? How is the mythology of the exceptionalist Nature's nation sustained in the face of historical challenge? This book responds to these and other questions. It is a case study of social memory, revealing lines of contention between national myth and historical intervention.

I

Crania Americana

1

Mt. Rushmore: Heads of State and States of Heads

I couldn't and wouldn't have started to drill on that mountain if I hadn't known that the portrait of Washington had been there for forty million years and I had to find it. And that of Jefferson and Lincoln, who saved our country, and finally Teddy Roosevelt.

—GUTZON BORGLUM, sculptor of Mt. Rushmore

The "Shrine of Democracy" versus the "Patriarchy Fixed in Stone"[1]— these are the competing readings of the Mt. Rushmore presidential sculpture in the Black Hills of South Dakota. The site attracts between 2 and 2.5 million visitors annually, in part because travel magazines regularly feature articles with titles like "Giants in Granite" and "Mount Rushmore: Shrine of Democracy." The rhetoric typically exalts the sculptural achievement of "cutting into the crust of the earth America's shrine of democracy" (Smith, "Shrine," 41). Visitors can buy postcards featuring the Stars and Stripes superimposed over the presidential heads along with the words "Freedom: More than a Dream" or, if they prefer, cards with a photographic view of the mountain and a verse printed to the left, as if inscribed in the very clouds:

> Hail the shrine of Democracy!
> May its spirit ever reign
> And bring the strength of our leaders great
> into our hearts again!

This verse, by Violet May Paulson, goes on to celebrate the heroes who "conquered stress and strife," who "paved the road to peace and joy" and

"foretold" the "greater" democracy to prevail, God willing, "forevermore."
On the back of the cards purchasers and recipients are informed that the
Mount Rushmore National Memorial commemorates freedom and is "an
inspiration to every American." As a signifier of democracy, the monu-
ment's image is thus reproduced in numerous contexts. During the presi-
dential campaign of 1996, for instance, the Cable News Network opened
its series "Democracy in America '96" with a graphic design featuring the
Mt. Rushmore monument on parchmentlike paper reminiscent of the
Declaration of Independence, the Constitution, and the Bill of Rights.
The monumental image is meant to be the imprimatur of democracy.

In the late twentieth century, however, the academy and journalism
have unmasked the patriarchal and racist dimensions of the monument.
Its sculptor, the Danish-American John Gutzon Borglum (1867–1941),
celebrated on the postcards as "the American patriot who visualized a
dream," has been revealed as an anti-Semite, an anti-Catholic, a 1920s
member of the Ku Klux Klan, and a racialist celebrant of the Anglo-Saxon
and Nordic peoples over and against those from the Mediterranean or Africa (Shaff and Shaff, Heard). The four heads of Washington, Jefferson,
Theodore Roosevelt, and Lincoln, blasted and chiseled from a granite
mountain range between 1924 and 1941, are exposed as "four Great
White Fathers [who are] all intellect and logic, disembodied and soulless"
(Boime, 143).

Some contemporary analysts cite the popular culture parodies of the
sculpture ("the great white elephant of American monuments") in deconstructive ridicule, and even *Smithsonian* magazine weighs in with this
1992 coinage, "*Rushmoritis, n.,* a condition of inherent outrageousness"
(Montgomery, 252; Jackson, 65). While one student of popular culture
identifies Mt. Rushmore as a public shrine comparable to the Baseball
Hall of Fame at Cooperstown, the art historian Albert Boime interprets it
in the context of the United States' violent aggression against Native
Americans. The Mt. Rushmore monument is located on Oglala Sioux sacred land in violation of treaty agreements dating from 1868–69, and
Boime finds the sculptured presidents' "magisterial gaze" to be recurrent
in American art as the embodiment of the expansionist idea of Manifest Destiny, just as he exposes the monument as a masquerade for "authoritarian impulses and imperialist politics," especially as the monumental heads "stare down from the lands of their victims, the vanquished
native Americans" (143, 156–165; Combs, 72). One Native American,
the Sioux chief Crazy Horse, who defeated General George Custer at
the Battle of Little Bighorn in 1876, is currently emergent in an eques-

4. Mt. Rushmore, South Dakota, presidential sculpture by Gutzon Borglum of (left to right) George Washington, Thomas Jefferson, Theodore Roosevelt, and Abraham Lincoln.

trian statue some ten times larger than the Mt. Rushmore memorial and located near it on Thunderhead Mountain as a deliberate pro–Native American statement of pride and a rebuke to Borglum and to the U.S. government for its shameful treatment of the native peoples (Grogan and Phillips).

With racism and imperialism as keywords, then, hymns to the sublimity of Mt. Rushmore sound complicitous with a patriarchal mentality bent on its own reproduction. Franklin Delano Roosevelt's 1936 comment on the monument's "magnitude, its permanent beauty and its importance," reads like a solipsism, as does a 1949 hymn on "the Mount Rushmore Memorial [which] will stand in proud dignity through wind and sunlight and dark, to say 'God Bless America' to all of future generations" (Dean, 75, 128). In 1993 a South Dakota–based computer company, Gateway, featured a color spread of the monument with reverential copy: "Mount Rushmore salutes American ideals and values, and recognizes that hard work can indeed make dreams come true." The link between the sculpture and commerce, however, seems a chauvinistic business strategy to sell computers as patriotically American. The presidential stone quartet has come to be recognized as a conspicuous expression of patriarchal nationalism.[2]

Brain Feeders

Yet this status obscures the historic fact of the heads themselves—heads qua heads—carved at a time when business organization and industrial automation were changing ideas about the ideal male body. Back in the mid-nineteenth century, the minister Lyman Beecher had argued that a strong mind must be matched by a body of equal strength. "To the action of a powerful mind, a vigorous muscular frame is . . . indispensable," wrote Beecher. "The mental action and the physical reaction must be equal" (380). Much analysis of the American male physique through the late nineteenth and early twentieth centuries seems in agreement with Beecher, calling attention to the nationalistic male athleticism evinced in such images as Theodore Roosevelt posed as a western ranchman with rifle, in western buckskins. At the same time, such nationally identified sports as baseball, football, and bare-knuckle boxing were lauded for their expression of physical force and rugged individualism (Bederman, Gorn, Mrozek). The prevalent middle-class male ideal was indeed the Rooseveltian Anglo-Saxon man, rough riding in the rugged outdoors with intermittent military adventurism abroad or in the American West. Borglum, born in the West, proclaimed of himself, "I do everything, boxing, fencing, wrestling, horseback riding" (Smith, *Carving*, 54). The sports historian Donald J. Mrozek identifies the turn-of-the-century belief that "human health was at its greatest when the body expressed itself in action" and that "sport was proof of health" (190). The muscular man living a strenuous life is thus often thought to be the male American bodily paradigm.

Another masculine bodily ideal, however, was insurgent from the late nineteenth century. The work of the head, or brain work, as it was termed in the 1890s, so gained in prestige that conceptions of the male physique underwent radical change. Vast fortunes had been amassed in the United States by men whose power came from strategic cunning, not physical courage. Andrew Carnegie never charged up San Juan Hill, nor did John D. Rockefeller or J. P. Morgan. The polio-stricken Franklin D. Roosevelt, photographed from the waist up, was largely confined to sofas and chairs. These men manipulated the levers of power with their intellect. The genteel heroine of Louisa May Alcott's *Work* (1873) proclaimed her worldly resources to be a triad of head-heart-hands, as did Booker T. Washington in his Atlanta Exposition Address of 1895, but Theodore Dreiser's novel *The Financier* (1912), based on the career of the Chicago financier Charles T. Yerkes, features a protagonist and cohorts whose masculine audacity is purely cerebral, not corporeal or subject to sentiment. The Yerkes cohort are "men with shrewd ideas, subtle [and] great mental resources . . . nerve, ideas, aggressiveness." The Yerkes-like protagonist is ever "thinking, thinking, thinking . . . his brain was his office" and his sole safety "the magnificent subtlety of his own brain" (27, 42, 60, 72, 240, 291–292).

The new ideal male body was thus a "brain feeder," as one educational text of 1894 put it: "Every day the demand becomes more explicit for a body that is the best possible brain and nerve feeder." The body of Hercules had been perfect for the age of forests, wild beasts, and crude weaponry like the cudgel. The body of Richard the Lion Heart had been "ideal" for the work of "chivalry, armor, battle-axes, superstition, tyranny." The newest bodily ideal, however, was the head, its exemplar the railroad magnate Jay Gould: "When engaged in intense thought, the veins on his forehead would so swell, that observers say the very skull seemed to distend with the volume of blood that was passing through his brain" (Durell, 121–127).

In addition to the valorization of cerebral power, the development of industrial technology in a world of push buttons and levers was also steadily shifting the masculine ideal from brawn to brain. "Mere muscular development no longer adds particularly to a man's privileges or efficiency," said one late nineteenth-century text, which argued that even Samson would not be a contemporary hero because mere physical strength has been supplanted by the forces of technology. Dynamite, bullets, artillery, and hydraulic engines had obviated the need for powerful muscle and bone. "Every day physical labor becomes more and more a pressure of levers and buttons and less a matter of dead lift and carry. . . . Man is becoming less a direct physical worker himself, and more a manager of work. Almost all work is done by machines and tools" (Durell, 124). Thus the Herculean heavyweight boxer John L. Sullivan was now an anachronism, a curio. As one text, *Brain and Personality* (1907), put it, "In a former age men worshipped the body . . . [for] bodily strength and beauty," as the "savage tribes" had continued to do, but modern civilization properly privileged the mind: "we are living in an age in which mental gifts are estimated above all else" (Thomson, 264–265). The prominent woman physician Mary Putnam Jacobi observed in 1882 that "the idea of mental training as a means of developing force is rather new to the world," while the feminist writer Charlotte Perkins Gilman, no friend of this new masculinist ideal herself, nonetheless wrote that "the brain's ultimate use is that of . . . a transmitter of power into action" in a periodical series, "Our Brains and What Ails Them" (1912) (Jacobi, "Shall," 370; Gilman, 219). Gilman cited a historical precedent extending through millennia, wherein a priesthood "strove to monopolize the brains of the world and the training of them" along the lines of "class power and class aggrandizement" (220). In bodily terms, then, both friendly and hostile analysts agreed that the new man was the mastermind, his body a glorification of the head.

This is the new male body that became enshrined at Mt. Rushmore. This was the body as cerebral mastermind geographically "incarnated," in Myra Jehlen's sense of the term, in the Oglala Sioux sacred ground of South Dakota. In this regard, the history of the Mt. Rushmore monument is not only an imprint of U.S. imperialism but, in addition, the record of a changing concept of the white American male body.

Current parlance phrases this relation as a mapping of that body onto American geography. Contemporary supporters and admirers of the Mt. Rushmore project, however, understood the relation in reverse. For them the sculpture was a geomorphic manifestation of the American body inherent in the nation's terra firma. According to this view, the nation's geomorphic body was thought to correspond perfectly with the best bodies of the nation and thereby once again to prove America to be the exceptionalist Nature's nation, its geographic space a correlate with its paradigmatic American human figures.

The geomorphology of the United States was thus shown to disclose the presence of this new body. In these terms, the great male American heads had been present all along, foreordained by the very concept of America as Nature's nation and emergent in the propitious moment.[3] Borglum himself said, "Sculptured work on a mountain must *belong* to the mountain as a natural part of it"; "I couldn't and wouldn't have started to drill on that mountain if I hadn't known that the portrait of Washington had been there for forty million years and I had to find it. And that of Jefferson and Lincoln, who saved our country, and finally Teddy Roosevelt" (Smith, *Carving*, 158; Dean, 89–90). Here Borglum's sculpting becomes an act of location and disclosure. His statement expresses that part of American exceptionalism in which the very continent was understood to embody and, in due course, to manifest the body type of the most powerful Americans. Enmeshed in his own historical moment, Borglum revealed the heads which he argued had been present throughout geological time. It is thus significant that the base of Mt. Rushmore is strewn with the rubble from the blasting and carving by Borglum and his crews. More than refuse, the rubble stands as testimony to the embedded presence of the presidential heads over the millennia preceding the actual carving.

It is the geomorphic correspondence with model Americans that interests us here, including the terms under which those paradigmatic heads were established. True, it is valuable to historicize the Mt. Rushmore monument as a statement of early twentieth-century imperialism in what Henry Luce brazenly called "the American century." Such a framing, however, excludes the broader cultural history of the homology developed between American spatial sites and Americans themselves—all in terms of the body. The cultural history of Mt. Rushmore is a history of the construction of a homologous relation between white male Americans and the American environment.

5. Scaffolding and ladder visible during sculpting of Lincoln at Mt. Rushmore, 1938.

It is also a chapter in the history of American bodies excluded from the homology, bodies declared ineligible because they have the "wrong" bodily identity. Those excluded either possess inferior heads in a gendered and racialized hierarchy, or else they are thought to have no heads at all. The nineteenth-century textile mill worker Harriet Robinson recalled that factory operatives "were not supposed to be capable of social or mental improvement" and that public discourse did not admit the possibility that workers "could be educated and developed into something more than work-people" (60–61). In terms of occupation and class, the laborer was most susceptible to this headless bodily construction. From the 1910s, Frederick Winslow Taylor scientized the headless worker when he configured the body of the immigrant "Dutchman" worker, one Schmidt, into an efficient robotic machine. Under the tutelage and total control of the efficiency engineer, the ironworker increased his tonnage of hoisted iron by a factor of nearly four. In the Taylorist formulation, the body-as-machine or as-machine-part is a figure precluded from Rushmorean, brain-feeder status. In the industrial age, such a figure could become a machine cog—but never a head. In the cultural production of ideal male heads, the very heads of Mt. Rushmore, such bodies as Schmidt's were by definition socioculturally decapitated.

The heads at Mt. Rushmore, of course, are not to be experienced as severed from their bodies. The presidential heads, on the contrary, *are* the bodies, brain feeders every one. The Mt. Rushmore project can thus be seen as a cultural production of a highly industrialized American moment in which huge fortunes were amassed by individuals and by corporations whose own corporate heads—presidents and CEOs—represent the idea of the powerful, modern cerebral male ideal. "For the manufacturer no identification of the company could be more personally gratifying than one that united his visage, in a . . . portrait or marble bust" (Marchand, 31). In this sense the Mt. Rushmore sculpture merits discussion in terms of the social history of American business and technology.

But there is more to it than this. During the Mt. Rushmore project, Gutzon Borglum identified himself intermittently with Prometheus, "bound to the rock," but he more properly belonged to a tradition originating in the late eighteenth century. As text, that is, the South Dakota sculpture is just one among several expressions of a homology extending back into antebellum and even colonial America. The narrator of Dreiser's *Financier* points us toward the antecedents of the Mt. Rushmore homology when he remarks on "men who were getting rich and famous. . . . Such towering figures as Cornelius Vanderbilt, Jay Gould, Daniel Drew,

James Fish, and others in the East, and Fair, Crocker, W. R. Hearst, and Collis P. Huntington, in the West." These men, writes Dreiser, "were already raising their heads like vast mountains" (436).

Monuments-in-Waiting and the Moment of Phrenology

The image of heads as mountains leads us to the source of the Mt. Rushmore mentality. The "towering" phallic aristocracy of robber barons figured as mountainous heads directs us to the tradition of geographic naming, as the names of North American promontories were anglicized to accommodate the cultural advance of the colonists.

In this tradition, Mt. Rushmore originates in the eastern United States, specifically in the White Mountains of New Hampshire, the Granite State. The White Mountain range is composed of varieties of gneiss, crystalline schist, and granite, and was named in 1672 by John Josselyn (*"White Mountains* upon which snow lieth all the year"), who anglicized the Indian word "Waumbekketmethna," referring also to the whiteness of the mountains (Anderson and Morse, 235). The entire range also bore the Native American name "Agiocochook," meaning the place of the Spirit of the Great Forest.

In 1792 Jeremy Belknap effaced Native American geography in his *History of New Hampshire,* in which he recorded of a certain mountain, "It has lately been distinguished by the name of *Mount* Washington." This is the first appearance of the name in print. It may be that Belknap's own mountaineering party, ascending the mountain in 1784, named it on the spot. The other peaks of the Presidential Range were named on July 31, 1820, by a party of "seven gentlemen," one of them John W. Weeks, of Massachusetts, a congressman, senator, and secretary of war, who is credited with naming the several peaks: [James] Madison, [John] Adams, [Thomas] Jefferson, and [James] Monroe. Other peaks were assigned "great man" names—[Daniel] Webster, [Andrew] Jackson, [DeWitt] Clinton, [Benjamin] Franklin, [Henry] Clay. "They gave names to several peaks, and then drank healths to them—[a beer-and-rum concoction dubbed Black Bett or O Be Joyful]—in honor to the great men whose names they bore" (Anderson and Morse, 196). The practice of naming presidential mountains was thus in place by the so-called Era of Good Feelings. The peak and the head of state were related as correlates, and the idea established of worthy cohorts—of mountains, of American statesmen—which are counterparts of one another.

6. *The Mount Washington Road,* 1872.

Social critique of this honorific naming came from Nathaniel Haw-thorne in an 1835 travel sketch, "The Notch of the White Mountains," in which he wrote that Mt. Washington "looked near to heaven," was "white with snow a mile downward, and had caught the only cloud that was sail-ing through the atmosphere to veil his head." Touring the area in mid-September 1832, Hawthorne un-named the other Presidentials: "Let us forget the other names of American statesmen that have been stamped upon these hills, [which] never should be consecrated to the mere great

men of their own age and country." Only Mt. Washington deserved its
name—more precisely, its consecration—because Washington alone was a
figure of universal glory "whom all time will render illustrious." Hawthorne makes a crucial statement: "Mountains are Earth's undecaying
monuments" (Weber, Lueck, and Berthold, 29).

His words argue that because mountains transcend history, they ought
to be named only for those rare greatest of great men who transcend historical vicissitude. Just as Hawthorne's "Custom House" preface to *The
Scarlet Letter* would expose elderly Revolutionary War officer-heroes as se-
nile dodderers, and just as *The Marble Faun* critiqued the mid-nineteenth
century's high-volume production of marble portrait busts of egoistic
"blockhead[s]," so "The Notch of the White Mountains" warned against
a chauvinistically profligate and premature naming of mountain peaks
honoring those whose status over time is uncertain (*Marble Faun*, 95–
96).[4] Mere popularity is a liability, ephemeral notions of greatness a trap
for officials eager to exploit natural grandeur in order to monumentalize
American political history. Hawthorne, who was to enjoy political patron-
age from his authorship of an 1852 campaign biography of his Bowdoin
College classmate Franklin Pierce, would learn firsthand about political
puffery; he understood that a mountain mismatched with the name of a
hero manqué could expose American political history as the mock heroic.
(Indeed, the figure of Theodore Roosevelt has served this deconstructive
function at Mt. Rushmore.)

To Hawthorne, the New Hampshire peaks were so many monuments-
in-waiting, transcendent geomorphological entities awaiting transhis-
torical personages commensurate with them. In this Hawthorne establishes the ideological position that found material statement in the Mt.
Rushmore monument. (Indian mountain names had no claim to credibil-
ity, in his view. Just a few paragraphs following his comment on Mt.
Washington, he wrote of his inability to see any romance or poetry, grandeur or beauty in the Indian character and added, "I do abhor an Indian
story" [33].)

Hawthorne's cautionary sketch, together with the anglicized naming of
the Presidential Range, might seem solely a historical preface to the era of
the Mt. Rushmore sculpture and the valorized white male brain-feeder
heads. Yet at mid-nineteenth century there occurred a remarkable production of textual heads from New England male literati, the very "classic"
writers who were establishing reputations for their own cerebral productions. In 1850–51, Hawthorne, Herman Melville, and Ralph Waldo Emerson all produced "head" texts in the literary tale, the novel, and the

essay, in Melville's *Moby-Dick,* Hawthorne's "Great Stone Face," and Emerson's "Napoleon, Man of the World" from *Representative Men.* In different genres, all three writers propounded the strengths and virtues of white, male, American heads, and in this sense they too are antecedent to the Mt. Rushmore project.

More than antecedent. It is tempting to situate the Melville-Hawthorne-Emerson texts solely as precursors or as part of a Rushmorean "long foreground." But the mid-nineteenth-century literary heads, contextualized with the Mt. Rushmore project, divulge yet another layer of the history of the environmental and bodily American homology. By looking closely not only at Mt. Rushmore but also at the textual heads of the New England male writers, we can read both manifestos and also clear distress signals about leadership, power relations, and white male identity in the United States.

To begin with, the nineteenth-century New England writers had an important quasi-intellectual source for the valorizing of the white male head. As scholars of "scientific" racialization have revealed, Samuel G. Morton's treatises, including *Crania Americana* (1839), his study of aboriginal skulls of North and South America, not only separated science from fundamentalist Christianity but also established racial hierarchies privileging the heads of white males (Horsman, 125–132; Nelson, 109–123; Otter, 102–118). In addition, the pseudoscience of phrenology was pervasive among the mid-nineteenth-century American intelligentsia and had a powerful impact on the legitimization of the Anglo-American head as constantly "improving in morals and intelligence" (Spurzheim, 47). These movements, especially phrenology, strongly influenced the Mt. Rushmore sculpture, even though phrenology was a discredited movement by the time Borglum began his artistic career.

The impact of phrenology in nineteenth-century America has lately been revealed in literary and fine arts studies, notably in Charles Colbert's *Measure of Perfection* (1997) and Samuel Otter's *Melville's Anatomies* (1999). Phrenology reached the United States in 1832, when a German physician, Johann Spurzheim, delivered a series of lectures at the Boston Athenaeum on the new science, which had originated in Vienna and was named from a combination of Greek terms meaning "discourse on the mind." In Europe, Spurzheim had visited prisons and identified "the organ of theft," "of murder," and "of the propensity to steal" in cranial examinations of inmates (Spurzheim, 26, 29). He insisted on the *science* of phrenology as distinct from and antithetical to "fortune telling" or palm reading (7). By the time he arrived in America, Spurzheim had published six books on phrenology in London and would soon, in 1833, publish for the American market.

Spurzheim's reception in the United States has been termed "electric." Harriet Martineau commented, "When Spurzheim was in America, the great mass of society became phrenologists in a day, wherever he appeared . . . all caps and wigs [were] pulled off, and all fair tresses disheveled, in the search after organization" (qtd. Stern, xiv). Phrenology's major U.S. proponents were the Fowler family—Orson, Samuel, Almira, and Edward—who moved from upstate New York to Baltimore and St. Louis. Madeleine Stern writes, "They went to Providence (where they examined Margaret Fuller), to Hawthorne's Salem, somewhat later to Mark Twain's Hannibal, feeling a multitude of heads, analyzing the foibles of a nation, and giving its writers a new vocabulary" (19).

During the years of its greatest popularity, 1840–1880, phrenology flourished in terms set forth in Orson S. Fowler's *Phrenological Chart* (1836): "Phrenology professes to point out a connection between certain connections of the brain and certain manifestations of the mind. . . . The brain is the organ of the mind . . . the mind is a plurality of innate and independent faculties . . . these different faculties are possessed, originally, in different degrees of strength, by the same individual, and also by different individuals . . . The brain consists of as many different organs as the mind does of faculties. . . . The exercise of any corporeal organ, of which the brain is one, augments its size. . . . The increase of one portion of the brain more than of another, must proportionately elevate that portion of the skull above it: for the shape of the brain determines the shape of the skull, and . . . corresponds with it. . . . If then we can ascertain what portions of the brain are employed by the various faculties, and also how much larger one portion is than another, we can also ascertain even the *minutiae* of a person's character and talents" (Davies, 177–182).

Or as Madeleine Stern put it, "Phrenology postulated that since the brain was the organ of the mind and shaped the skull which neatly compressed the brain, there was an observable concomitance between man's mind—talents, disposition, character—and the shape of the head. To ascertain the former, one need only examine the latter" (x). Phrenology, not surprisingly, found ample evidence to support its claim that a "world of physical facts" proves that all "powerful and profound thinkers, all deep, original reasoners are possessed by European heads," a point elaborated in Reginald Horsman's *Race and Manifest Destiny* (Davies, 177–180; Horsman, 116–157).

As a science, phrenology claimed its expertise and findings extended to

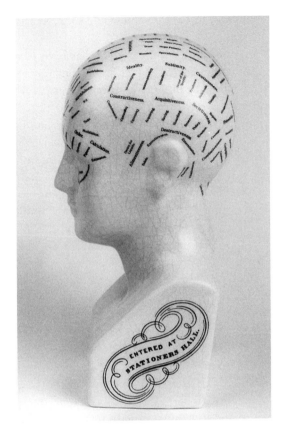

7. Nineteenth-century ceramic phrenology model
showing cranial areas considered to be centers of
human traits of personality and intelligence.

the past as well, and its popularity is in large part attributable to its
scientized validation of received opinion codified along lines of racial hierarchy and nationalism. Spurzheim had decreed that a "specimen of the
ancient Greek" skull showed such intellectual and moral excellence that it
"became a model for other nations to follow" (46). Skulls of "barbari-
ans"—a Brazilian cannibal, a Wabash savage, a Hindu—exhibited their
supposedly innate racialized depravity, as did the cranial topography of
the malefactors of Western civilization, such as the Roman emperor
Caracalla and Cardinal Richelieu (46).

Spurzheim and other phrenologists lost no time in evaluating their
American counterparts. The founding fathers, not surprisingly, were re-

vealed to be figures of sterling character when phrenological analyses were conducted on extant portraits, busts, and sculptures. Because it was crucial that these be verified as accurate renderings, anecdotal verification was sought from living links to the late eighteenth century. The prominent Scottish phrenologist, George Combe, traveled and lectured in the United States in 1838–1840, and saw a portrait of Benjamin Franklin in the hall of the American Philosophical Society, "a portrait of Franklin in the act of reading" that represented Franklin's face differently from other portraits and busts and phrenologically was said to indicate "more concentration of mind." One Mr. Vaughan personally testified to Combe that this was "a faithful representation" of Franklin—and therefore that Combe could

8. Bust of Washington, a phrenological ideal head as represented in *The Image Peddlar*, by Francis W. Edmonds. Oil on canvas, c. 1844. © Collection of The New-York Historical Society, Detail.

read the head in full confidence (Combe, 1:329–330). Likewise, Combe was assured by Rembrandt Peale, the portraitist of George Washington, that he, the artist, was personally acquainted with the president and that the "likeness [was] faithful" (1:339, 341–342).

Phrenology indeed provided a new vocabulary, not only for the visual arts but for American writers, who exploited it for the iconic characterization that would redefine bodily masculinity by the end of the century. Emerson, Hawthorne, and Melville each relied upon phrenological conventions, though for differing purposes. As intellectuals, they were doubtless attracted to the idea of the valorized head per se, a formulation appealing to men of a sedentary intellectual life in a utilitarian activist culture, in which manual labor seemed a model for robust masculinity. The keyword in Ann Douglas's study *The Feminization of American Culture* (1972), based on the nineteenth-century alliance between women and the New England ministers, would expose the self-identification most fraught with anxiety for Emerson and, perhaps to a lesser extent, for Hawthorne, Melville, and others. The figure of a writer-intellectual, pen in hand and seated at his desk in his study, approximated the image of the woman seated with her needlework, each enclosed in domestic space. Emerson agonized as he saw the "literary class" becoming "sickly" and "enervated" because of "their too great fineness, effeminacy, and melancholy" (*Collected Works,* 6:153). Nicholas Bromell has shown the great efforts by which antebellum male American writers sought to enact worker activism in their texts and thus promote themselves as creative, hearty, and sexually potent. Phrenology, however, offered these intellectuals a bodily paradigm free of the feminine other, unshadowed by the physicality of the manual worker and, better yet, concomitant with their primary cerebral identity. Phrenology permitted a revaluation of the male body, according privileged status to males most closely identified with intellectual acumen.

For Melville, phrenology served the "corporeal fascinations" that drove him "to know the racial body," the "face, skin, and head [which] became invested with world historical meanings" (Otter, 3). Indeed, so many phrenological books were published in the United States between 1822 and 1850 (at least twenty-eight) that phrenology furnished writers of fiction a standard vocabulary for physical description indicative of character, as when in *Billy Budd* Melville says of the malevolent Claggart, "His brow was of the sort phrenologically associated with more than average intelligence" (314).

More important, Melville understood phrenology as a hermeneutic by which to pose the ontological problems of the source(s) of inscrutability and mystery and, in addition, to challenge the very hierarchical racial categories phrenology itself had established. In *Moby-Dick* (1851), Melville first puts his reader on a kind of phrenological alert by recounting the cannibal Queequeg's sojourn along the Nantucket streets, attempting to sell embalmed aboriginal heads. These were heads which, as Michael T. Gilmore has shown, served as a trope for the mid-nineteenth-century writer struggling with publishers and readers in a competitive marketplace. The writer's head was for sale, to be sure, but phrenology also turned the head into a site for the discernment of degrees of civility and savagery. Otter notes, "In *Moby-Dick*, Melville gives access to the excess of the extraordinary nineteenth-century quest for bodily knowledge. He offers an anatomy of anatomies, a viscerally immanent critique of nineteenth-century efforts to get inside the body, and to gauge and rank its character" (102). The Fowlers' publications from the 1830s featured drawings of aboriginal heads and skulls, and phrenologists' cabinets typically contained hundreds or even thousands of models and specimens. Queequeg's sackful of shrunken heads would have been marketable for the phrenology trade, as students and practitioners of the newest "science" would have known.

Thus Melville's reader would not be surprised to find Ishmael, in *Moby-Dick*, reading Queequeg's head "phrenologically," even if Ishmael's analogy proved startling when Queequeg's head, "an excellent one . . . [reminded him] of General Washington's head, as seen in the popular busts of him." Ishmael concludes, "Queequeg was George Washington cannibalistically developed," which would be a disjunctive observation had the text not already deployed ethnic and racial inversions in the mock heroic and the burlesque, literary forms that deliberately inverted familiar categories (here, the savage and the civil) for a comic response that essentially reaffirmed the categorical status quo.

Phrenology also authorized Melville's metaphysical dissection on a colossal scale that otherwise could have echoed Swift's Gulliver confronting the corpus of a Brobdingnag. The pseudoscience authorized Melville's meditations on the whale's enormous head, which, as Otter finds, reveals "the incommensurability between outer form and inner contents," since the whale's head is all forehead. (The Fowlers explicitly authorized such speculation, for they included animal skulls in their phrenology cabinets and incorporated the bestiary in their analyses of temperament.) With a phrenological heuristic, Ahab inquires into the mystery of the decapitated sperm whale whose head is hoisted against the side of the *Pequod* and buoyed by the water lest it capsize and sink the ship. "Speak, thou vast and venerable head," commands the captain, though the head is as speechless as the cosmopolitan third-world crew. "O head! thou hast seen enough to split the planets and make an infidel of Abraham, and not one syllable is thine" (417–418).

The pseudoscience fails as hermeneutic in *Moby-Dick* but thereby proves consistent with Melville's baffled interrogation of all systems of knowledge from pantheism to Christianity. The "Sphynx" episode reiterates Ahab's thwarted quest to strike through the world's many masks, just as Ishmael's overtly phrenological query about the head of Moby-Dick yields up one of his confidence men. "To the phrenologist," says Ishmael, Moby-Dick's brain seems "that geometrical circle which it is impossible to square. . . . Phrenologically the head of this Leviathan . . . is an entire delusion. . . . The whale . . . wears a false brow to the common world," which is to say that the false-browed whale becomes yet another Melvillean confidence man, just as the riddle of the "Sphynx" is but another of Melville's unsolvable metaphysical puzzles.

Melville's phrenological forays exploited the terms of the pseudoscience and valorized the head itself. Phrenology legitimated his recurrent reversion to heads, including heads of the "other"—of the savage, of the whale. If these, however, are maddeningly impenetrable, the very terms of the impenetrability devolve from other heads, Ishmael's, Ahab's, above all Melville's. Shrunken heads, savage heads, decapitated whale heads, and the head of the legendary Moby-Dick are ultimately subordinated to the head of the writer who masterminds all others. To read the novel is to read the authorial head. The harpooneer, Tashtego, dives into the head of a captured whale to rescue his officer, Stubb, and yet the dive yields no knowledge of the mind of the whale (nor of the third-world harpooneer). The double opacity of the scene nonetheless reminds one of Melville's favorite phrase of admiration—deep diving—applied to the man of questing intellect, a man, no doubt, like Herman Melville, whose colossal novel stands as the phrenological paradigm of the white American man in the mode Melville most admired.

In this sense, the reader becomes Melville's phrenologist, and *Moby-Dick* Melville's head. The novel is populated by inscrutable Madagascars, Malayans, Africans, Indians, and so on, but they are no match for an American captain, who in turn is at the command of the novelist. Herman Melville's ancestry could be traced to Hungary, Norway, and Holland, and he therefore qualified phrenologically as a superior European "powerful and profound thinker" and "deep, original reasoner." As he wrote in *Moby-Dick,* the non-Americans provide the "muscles," while the "native American," like himself, "liberally provides the brains" (216). Melville, the grandson both of a Massachusetts militiaman who participated in the Boston Tea Party and of a Revolutionary War general, was the very type of a certified, first-rate native American brain. (In 1999 the performance artist Laurie Anderson, in a production entitled *Songs and Stories from Moby-Dick,* suggested that the novel "is really about head size" [Rothstein].)

The year prior to the publication of *Moby-Dick* saw Hawthorne, too, exploit the colossalism of a white male human head. His short tale "The Great Stone Face" was far more modest than Melville's literary leviathan, and yet Hawthorne's sociopolitical focus put the tale at the center of the debate about the viability of popular democracy in the United States. If Melville valorized reasoning and anticipated the "thinking, thinking, thinking" protagonist of the turn-of-the-century business text of white male power, Hawthorne's "Great Stone Face" explicitly delineated the geophysical model that Borglum reprised at Mt. Rushmore.

In "The Great Stone Face," the gigantic head manifests itself not in the high seas but on the terra firma of a mountain, specifically a granite outcropping in Franconia Notch, New Hampshire, which in the 1840s rivaled Mt. Washington as a major visitors' attraction. Approached from the valley, the towering rock formation presented an uncanny profile of a human face. Known as the Old Man of the Mountain, the facial rock formation seemed a *genius loci* of the area.

"The Great Stone Face," first published in *National Era* on January 24, 1850, explicitly reverts to the Franconia Notch Old Man of the Mountain. "The Great Stone Face" is a fable about a credulous and fickle public and the development of ethical individual character in a democracy. The tale engaged crucial national issues of democratic republicanism and the threat of popular deception that might derail the nascent nation politically. Like Melville, Hawthorne cast his critique in a fable that resorted to phrenology, but unlike the author of *Moby-Dick,* Hawthorne used phrenological thought to further the homology he located in the relationship between George Washington and the New Hampshire mountain bearing his name. This is Hawthorne's representation of the geologic formation, which he terms:

> a work of Nature in her mood of majestic playfulness, formed on the perpendicular side of a mountain by some immense rocks, which had been thrown together in such a position, as, when viewed at a

proper distance, precisely to resemble the features of the human countenance. It seemed as if an enormous giant, or a Titan, had sculpted his own likeness on the precipice. There was the broad arch of the forehead, a hundred feet in height, the nose, with its long bridge, and the vast lips, which, if they could have spoken, would have rolled their thunder accents from one end of the valley to the other. True it is, that if the spectator approached too near, he lost the outline of the gigantic visage, and could discern only a heap of ponderous and gigantic rocks, piled in chaotic ruin one upon another. Retracing his steps, however, the wondrous features would again be seen, and the farther he withdrew from them, the more like a human face, with all its original divinity intact, did they appear; until, as it grew dim in the distance, with the clouds and glorified vapor of the mountains clustering around it, the Great Stone Face seemed positively to be alive. (27)

Hawthorne proceeds with a tale of the citizens in the New England valley who grow up and live in full view of the benign, "noble" presiding presence of the stone visage. The entire valley knows of the legend, extending back into the prehistoric mists of Indian times (and so much for Hawthorne's repudiation of Native American narratives, which he utilizes here to locate an origin in narrative rather than in geology). The legend has prophesied the birth of one destined to be born in the vicinity of the valley and to become the "greatest and noblest personage of his time." His "countenance, in manhood, should bear an exact resemblance to the Great Stone Face" (28).

In the course of the tale, a fickle public in the valley thrice deludes itself into believing briefly that the prophecy has been fulfilled. By turns, the villagers celebrate the coming of Gathergold, a rich and greedy merchant, then General Blood-and-Thunder, a veteran warrior, and finally an opportunistic politician, Old Stony Phiz (doubtless the nickname for stone-cold physiognomy). Herein lies Hawthorne's fable of human foibles, for misinterpretation is a public liability, and history's wayward turnings are those of a misled, popular herd without moral compass.

Resisting these mercenary-military-political fads is clear-sighted young Ernest, a fatherless, modest valley boy who sees no resemblance whatsoever between these self-interested opportunists and the Great Stone Face. Ernest grows up projecting onto the rock outcropping the values of benevolent paternity that guide his life and give him strength. Indeed, Ernest's lifelong filial devotion to the ideals he projects onto the Face leads him to become—and at last, in his own old age, to be recognized in the

9. *The Old Man of the Mountain,* illustration by
Henry Fenn for *Picturesque America* (vol. 1, 1872),
edited by William Cullen Bryant. The text, by Susan
N. Carter, explains: "The rocks of which it is formed
are three blocks of granite so set together as to form
an over-hanging brow, a powerful, clearly-defined
nose, and a chin sharp and decisive" (168–169).

valley to be—the figure who fulfills the prophecy. We, the readers, have understood this all along. Ernest is the true son of the mountain.

This tale is interesting in psychoanalytic terms as one encounters the invention of the father, self-fashioning, surrogacy, and the totemic imputation of personality to the inanimate mineral formation, all of which provide rich interpretive directions and point as well to Mt. Rushmore, especially because of Hawthorne's physical description of the face. Its features are "noble, its expression was at once grand and sweet, as if it were the glow of a vast, warm heart that embraced all mankind in its affections, and had room for more. It was an education only to look at it" (27).

The education derives emphatically from phrenology as Hawthorne sculpts the "brow, with its massive depth and loftiness" and writes that "all the other features, indeed, were boldly and strongly hewn, as if in emulation of a more than heroic, of a Titanic model." The face exhibits "sublimity and stateliness, the grand expression of a divine sympathy" (41).

Listen, now, to phrenological wisdom: "Great men have great foreheads . . . the Caucasian race has more brain above and before the ears than any of the other races, and proportionally more of the mental powers Phrenology locates there . . . the really great men of the [Caucasian] race have foreheads as much larger than ordinary men as they have more intellectual calibre" (O. S. Fowler, 177).[5] As father of the nation, George Washington is cited as the exemplification of "a well-balanced organism." "Such persons unite cool judgments with intense and well governed feelings; great force of character and intellect with perfect consistency; scholarship with common sense; far-seeing sagacity with brilliancy; and have the highest order of both physiology and mentality. Such a temper had the immortal Washington, and his character corresponded" (O. S. Fowler, 273–274). Hawthorne, of course, approved of the New Hampshire peak bearing Washington's name and positioned himself to act mimetically in his representation of the Old Man of the Mountain.

Hawthorne's "Great Stone Face" relies on phrenological characterization in presenting its manifestation of white, male American greatness. Paired with citizen Ernest, the Face enables the tale to present a homology conveying a message on exemplary democracy (though based in a world in which women and nonwhites are ineligible). Greatness, the tale says, can take local forms. It need not be recognized and celebrated nationwide (even when its geological homologue is a major antebellum American tourist attraction, "a sign hung out by the Deity in New Hampshire," in Daniel Webster's term) (qtd. Keyes, 65). There are local, lowercase Washingtons, Hawthorne's tale suggests, and the nation can thus be repeatedly fathered at the local level by those Ernests who are rock-solid, rock-steady figures of the highest character throughout their lives—if only the populace will recognize and rely on them. This provision, this *if,* haunts the tale as Hawthorne indicates it haunts the nation, whose popular political judgment often errs.

"The Great Stone Face" bids to be a fable about disclosure of national character, and it promotes the American character at its democratic best as phenomenal, not developmental. Militarism, greed, and tyranny threaten the nation throughout history, but nobility of character, if unimpeded by these corruptive forces, can prevail. At its best, time will tell, but what is told is really *fore*told in the geography of the North American continent. The Great Stone Face is a geomorphic *genius loci* presiding benevolently, and this is as it ought to be.

Hawthorne's homology supports the foreordination of a democratically ethical America. Even in periods of backsliding, however, America is led by familiar versions of the white male heads as phrenology interpreted them and as Hawthorne (and his literary cohorts) portrayed them. His stentorian militarist is a distortion of the proper soldier as guardian, his greedy merchant a perversion of enterprising prosperity, his cold tyrant a deviant version of leadership. All are warped versions of the ideal male head of the Great Stone Face, but the warping indicates and reinforces the image idealized in the rock formation and in Ernest too. The exemplary and the deviant all operate within the same terms, creating a closed system that excludes those heads that might truly represent alternative conceptions of the individual and society. In "The Great Stone Face," social critique and national inspiration are correlates as the white male head prevails.

While Hawthorne's tale presents the gargantuan rock head as a political fable and *Moby-Dick* allies the outsize head with colossal intellect, the enormous head in Emerson means masculine activist power—"pure act," to borrow Henry Adams's trenchant critique of Theodore Roosevelt. Emerson complements Hawthorne and Melville in his selection of a cerebrally masterful Napoleon Bonaparte as one of his *Representative Men* (*Essays and Poems,* 611–761), the volume a hagiography of an Emersonian Plato, Emmanuel Swedenborg, Montaigne, Goethe—the philosopher, the mystic, the skeptic, the writer. The fifth figure, Napoleon Bonaparte, is the worldly exponent of force defined and legitimated as destiny, as indicated in Emerson's title: "Napoleon; or, the Man of the World" (*Essays and Poems,* 727–745).

Emerson exclaims upon the "capacious head" of the French emperor, a head "revolving and disposing sovereignly trains of affairs, and animating such multitudes of agents" (739). And Emerson's Napoleon is a panopticon in the Benthamite sense of a phallic tower beaming its light of surveillance, which Emerson celebrates as the penetrant Napoleonic "eye, which looked through Europe" (730) (and which reprises the eye of his "phallic mother," Aunt Mary Moody Emerson, who had an eye that "went through & through you like a needle" [qtd. Newfield, 142]). Emerson continues to extol "this prompt invention; this inexhaustible resource" (*Essays and Poems,* 739). Above all, Napoleon represents the quotidian activism announced in the introductory chapter, "Uses of Great Men," meaning those whose names "are wrought into the verbs of language" (615).

Emerson captures Napoleon's verbal imperative, worldly action, in this prose rhyme: "He gains the battle; he makes the code; he levels the Alps; he builds the road" (729). The notion of leveled Alps might come as a surprise to those who live amid or visit the craggy peaks of France, Italy, Austria, and Switzerland, but Emerson was rapt at the idea of one man's personal force or will dominating the social and material worlds. The Emerson who in "The American Scholar" deplored the sociocultural dismemberment of whole human beings in a "divided" age is satisfied to exploit a divisive bodily hierarchy in order to exalt Napoleon. Bonaparte, he said, "renounced sentiments and affections, and would help himself with his hands and his head" (730).

Napoleon's head, however, is vastly different from those of mere artisans: "To be sure there are men enough who are immersed in things, as farmers, smiths, sailors and mechanics," but "these men ordinarily lack the power of arrangement, and are like hands without a head" (730). Emerson quotes Napoleon's statement: "My hand of iron was not at the extremity of my arm, it was immediately connected with my head" (731). The grotesque image is meant to convey a sense of thought translated instantaneously into worldly action. The emperor's "power of arrangement" (730) is the mastermind's master plan for a world of which he is lord and master.[6]

One might point out that Napoleon is not an American and therefore is outside the nationalistic homologic project. But Emerson, perhaps anticipating such demurral and eager to claim the emperor's American identity, actually transplants him and his deeds without a continental or oceanic qualm: "The old, iron-bound, feudal France was changed into a young Ohio or New York" (737). Napoleon Bonaparte, in short, is in reality temperamentally American and reinvents Europe in the youthful mold of the new States.

This notion of the sovereign, outsized, activist male head has recently been analyzed conceptually by Christopher Newfield, who argues that Emerson's readers have been shortsighted, heeding his injunctions to individual self-reliance but failing to register the rest of the Emersonian paradigm, which expresses the necessity to yield to a "transcendent destiny." Newfield comments, "Defiance turns into obedience with such thoroughness that they become the same thing" (23). Newfield identifies a pattern in Emerson's thought in which "the transcendentality of the law [appears] . . . as the rule of superiority, that which compels obedience" (23). The Emersonian male, Newfield argues, "both desires the comrade and defines him as his superior. . . . The brother Emerson seeks is a big brother, he who can be imagined as a father" and whose superiority is thus fraternal and paternal, even patriarchal (125).

The need for obedience explains why Emerson would proclaim Bonaparte "never weak and literary," since the weaker, literary man stands in proper awe of the patriarch (730). (A despotic Napoleonic father figure has perhaps so embarrassed Emerson's recent readers that only Larzer Ziff among the post–World War II scholar-editors includes "Napoleon" in a miscellany of Emerson's writing. The emperor has probably been too resonant of Hitler and Mussolini for inclusion in volumes of the American philosophical proponent of individual freedom. Even Robert D. Richardson's recent intellectual biography of Emerson, subtitled *The Mind on Fire,* avoids discussion of "Napoleon," perhaps because the imperial cerebral flames would approach the incendiary.)

Phrenology plays its part too in the Emersonian formulation of Bonaparte. The intellectual lobe is "very large" in Napoleon, says the phrenology textbook, which sees the emperor as the manifestation of "Intellect," a faculty of governance and command, of monarchic and dictatorial power: "*Thou,* O Intellect, and especially O *Reason,* art the *crowning* gift of God to man. . . . Its frontal position proves that its office is to guide and govern all. The pilot-house is above, and in front of all, that it may command all. There is an inherent *fitness* between this position and its directing function. Who but must see that the location of this intellectual lobe proclaims its sovereign dictator and absolute monarch of man!" (O. S. Fowler, 275–277). Emerson's "Napoleon" supports the basis for such claims, and the Sage of Concord gave credence to the pseudoscience even when it came under attack. Emerson would say in his *Historic Notes of Life and Letters in New England* that phrenology was "coarse and odious to scientific men" but "had a certain truth in it; it felt connection where the professors denied it, and was leading to a truth which had not yet been announced" (*Lectures and Biographical Sketches,* 318).[7]

Emerson, moreover, enforces the homologous relation expressed in Hawthorne's Great Stone Face and in the material world of the South Dakota sculpture in the twentieth century. He wrote this of Napoleon Bonaparte's origination: it is "as if the sea and land had taken flesh and begun to cipher. Therefore the land and sea seem to presuppose him" (730).

A presuppositional American geography per force legitimates Napoleon as its very geologic offspring. The route from Concord, Massachusetts, to the Black Hills of South Dakota—via France and a Europe youthfully renewed à la Ohio and New York—is explained homologically. The American-Napoleonic heroic head inheres in the planet's geomorphology and is begotten by it. The very presuppositional term of its appearance settles the vexing question of history that so troubled Hawthorne in "The Great Stone Face." That tale revealed the authorial angst that immoral historical interventions might damage the foreordained noble America, that the homology of American nobility expressed in the mountain face might be falsified by mistaken public embrace of self-interested imposters, masked and false faces of corrupt and corruptive heads.

Emerson, however, set terms that foreclosed such anxiety. The land and sea incarnated in Napoleon left Emerson the tasks of celebratory exegesis, tempered only briefly with a critique of the emperor's lethally orgasmic, masturbatory "absorbing egotism" (745). Because the land and sea, the firmament, have begotten their true American scion, Napoleon, Emerson need not morally assay his actual earthly deeds acted out in time. His historical interventions are irreproachable, given his genesis, and inevitably "men give way before such a man, as before natural events" (732). An awestruck Emerson need only gloss the Napoleonic-American "capacious head."

Chronological sequence leads us from the capacious heads of Emerson, Melville, and Hawthorne, abetted by the phrenology movement, to the twentieth-century South Dakota of Mt. Rushmore. Over the course of a century, the discursive heads of a literary culture did indeed transpose themselves to the environmental materialism of the Black Hills' *crania Americana*. In between, however, we find an identifiable agency in the case of the environmentalist and proponent of national parks, John Muir. Muir, born in Scotland in 1838, grew to maturity in rural Wisconsin and attended the University of Wisconsin, where a professor gave him access to the work of Emerson and Thoreau. Following a brief career in industrial production, Muir committed himself to the study of nature through walking and camping trips, especially in the West, where he developed a new theory of the Yosemite glaciers and began in the 1870s to write articles eventually published in eastern seaboard periodicals such as the *Atlantic Monthly, Harper's,* and *Scribner's.*

In *Our National Parks* (1901), John Muir says that in his first years in the Sierra, he beckoned "everybody within reach" to come and admire the forests but found no one "warm enough" until Ralph Waldo Emerson came. "I had read his essays," Muir writes, "and felt sure that of all men he would best interpret the sayings of these noble mountains and trees." Emerson did not disappoint: "He seemed as serene as a sequoia, his head in the empyrean" (131–132). Muir proposes a "camping trip back in the heart of the mountains" because "up there lies a new heaven and a new earth." Alas, laments Muir, it is too late, "too near the sundown" of Emerson's life, and the Sage of Concord is subject to his handlers, indoor philosophers who "held Mr. Emerson to the hotels and trails," fearing that he might catch cold (132).

"You are yourself a sequoia," Muir reports saying to Emerson. "Stop and get acquainted with your big brethren" (135). The extravagant kinship claim is important. Muir's representations of the sequoia "brethren" and of other, analogous natural forms renew the homologic relation between the American environment and the nation's white male exemplary heads. Muir anthropomorphizes trees and rocks in terms that glorify the white male body and privilege the head. In Muir, Emerson's own head becomes the figure study for the American West. Personified by Muir and refracted through Emerson's essays, the sequoia brethren have "regularity of form" and "finely modeled . . . sculptural beauty" with "strong limbs" and "the magnificent dome head" (271). They are "awfully solemn and earnest," yet not "alien" in looks (272). The sequoia "hold[s] the best right to the ground as the oldest, strongest inhabitant." They are "lonely, silent, serene, with a physiognomy almost god-like." Procreative in springtime, the sequoia embodies "Nature's immortal virility. . . . When the storm roars loudest, they never lose their god-like composure, never toss their arms or bow or wave . . . but only slowly, solemnly nod and sway, standing erect, making no sign of strife . . . too calmly, consciously noble and strong to strive with or bid defiance to anything. . . . As far as man is concerned they are . . . emblems of permanence" (283–285, 269).

Muir did not confine such language to the sequoias. His representation of the rock formations of Yosemite corresponds directly to that of the great tree. The rock formations come in for personification as a kind of group of sculptural forms: "Every rock in its walls seems to glow with life. Some lean back in majestic repose; others, absolutely sheer . . . for thousands of feet, advance beyond their companions in thoughtful attitudes,

. . . seeming aware, yet heedless, of everything going on about them. Awful in stern, immovable majesty, how softly these rocks are adorned, and how fine and reassuring the company they keep: their feet among beautiful groves and meadows, their brows in the sky" (8).

Muir renders the full figure here, not only the head. The suprahuman form inheres in the rock formations, which are cast in the plural. The sculptural grouping is here as it would be at Mt. Rushmore, each form with its companions, though Muir evidently draws heavily on Emerson's "Society and Solitude," which defines the genius as solitary and necessarily "lonely," inhabiting a world of social "isolation." Emerson's essays helped to provide Muir the words by which the rocks and trees of the Sierra and Yosemite could be monumentalized in terms of the white male body with "dome head" and "brows in the sky." However powerful the storms, these figures retain their "god-like composure." Thoreau had complained in *Walden* that men "have the St. Vitus's dance, and cannot possibly keep our heads still," but Muir knew better (76). His figuration emphasizes the *gravitas* surely appealing to eastern seaboard readers of *Scribner's, Harper's,* the *Atlantic Monthly,* and *Century* magazines in which these passages first appeared. If Easterners considered the West as an exotic site of savage Indians, deadly deserts, desperados, polygamous Mormons, even Chinese, its geomorphic forms were reassuringly noble in terms referent to the white male bodily ideal of European, especially Anglo-Saxon, descent. Muir moved the "head" texts west but did so in terms which the Anglo-European could approve. (In this regard, it is interesting to notice that in 1997, the discredited presidential advisor Dick Morris recalled in his political memoir that President Bill Clinton loomed over him "like a sequoia" [qtd. Dowd, E17].)

Domain of the Masterminds

Gutzon Borglum knew John Muir's work (Dean, 17). His foursome of presidential brain feeders in the Mt. Rushmore carving is arguably a multiplication of the solitary Emersonian individualist brought forward with Muir's agency. (To examine the sightlines of the four heads is to see that although they may appear to be a cohort, their gazes never intersect, so that each gazes into his own domain.) To the extent that the monument manifests this ideal of the American male body, the Mt. Rushmore sculpture is also ahistorical. It putatively celebrates the history of the nation from Washington's presidency to that of Theodore Roosevelt—including the moments of the Declaration of Independence, the Revolution, and Constitution, the preservation of the Union, and the completion of the Panama Canal linking East with West. Conceptually, however, the monument collapses history into one atemporal moment governed and defined by the cerebral male bodily ideal. The facial features may differ, with the clean-shaven classicism of Washington's and Jefferson's eighteenth century contrasted to the nineteenth-century hirsute masculinity of Roosevelt and Lincoln. These kinds of distinctions, however, are merely superficial because each of the four is a mastermind in the mold of the others. The four presidents represent not diversity but sameness. They are essentially one ur-head of state, the distinctions in their presidential eras elided as they become replicants of one another.

That, finally, is the reassurance of the grouping, that all four presidents are reproductions of one another, that each head, as head, replicates the others in its essential definition as male American mastermind. It does not matter that Roosevelt's placement between Jefferson and Lincoln breaks chronology, for each presidential masculine mastermind replicates the others, and America itself is thus led and governed by a supreme standard that guarantees an unchanging headship into perpetuity.

Borglum is reported to have gazed across Harney Peak and exclaimed, "Here is the place! American history will march along that skyline!" (Smith, *Carving*, 33). The real inspirational message of the sculpture, however, is that heads may march, but not history. There is yet additional mountainous rock to Lincoln's right, and subsequent presidents may be revealed embedded in that rock, foreordained to appear in due course. Their emergence, facilitated by a latter-day Borglum, would only show an identical essence of cerebral masculinity and serve to ratify American exceptionalism in geography. Emerson's "patient rocks" will yield their lode of presidential heads, but each head manifests the essence of its predecessors and its successors ("The Farmer"). The interpretive act predates the revelation of the heads in the rock.

Capitation and Decapitation

Throughout this discussion, I have used the customary terms of temporal location—"antecedent to" or "precursor of," and the like—the usual casting forward and backward in scholarship, the from–to organizational model. In one sense, this enables survey-style breadth, so that recurring phenomena can be tracked over a long time period: *from* the naming of

Mt. Washington *to* the blasted and chiseled presidential heads of Mt. Rushmore and back again. This rhetorical convention, however, can block important questions. We must ask, What preserves this particular homology from one epoch to another? Why do these white male heads reappear with culturally obsessive frequency (presidential candidate Pat Buchanan posing before Mt. Rushmore in a *New York Times* front-page photo during the 1996 Republican primary campaign)? What is the motivation for the relentless textual production of the same bodily identity?

An insistence on racial and sexual supremacy is the obvious answer, and recent analysts have noted the blatant hypocrisy in Borglum's democratic utterances vis-à-vis his racist mentality and the contemporary American sociopolitical context of the Mt. Rushmore construction years. It has been pointed out, for instance, that the post–World War I era of the Mt. Rushmore construction was notable for its intolerance of foreigners, as white, Protestant Americans of Anglo-Saxon and Teutonic origin displayed hostility toward Catholics and Jews, Asians and African Americans. This era marked the apex of the Ku Klux Klan, and in the very year when Borglum accepted the Mt. Rushmore commission, 1924, President Calvin Coolidge signed into law the Johnson-Reed Act, better known as the National Origins Act, which prohibited Japanese immigration and severely restricted European immigration, especially from southern and eastern Europe (Boime, Heard).

As Borglum's crews developed their procedure for scaling the rock face and blasting the head of George Washington, nativists were rejoicing at the results of the new law. By 1926 the president of the Nordic League declared that the Johnson-Reed Act had put several American cities "into the Nordic column," and the commissioner of immigration at Ellis Island reported that most immigrants now looked just like "Americans" (Boime, 152; Higham, 324–325). (In 1927 President and Mrs. Calvin Coolidge visited the Mt. Rushmore construction site and, with trousers stuffed into new cowboy boots, the president who signed Johnson-Reed dedicated the South Dakota mountain: "We have come here to dedicate a cornerstone that was laid by the hand of the Almighty. On this towering wall of Rushmore in the heart of the Black Hills is to be inscribed a memorial which will represent some of the outstanding events of American history" [Smith, *Carving,* 147, 150–155].)

So much for the 1920s, but what about the mid-nineteenth century of Hawthorne, Melville, and Emerson? What was happening during the production of *Moby-Dick,* "The Great Stone Face," and "Napoleon"? Notably, theirs was an era that saw an unprecedented influx of immigrants and the reaction against them in nativist politics, which had been on the rise

since the 1830s. The New York civic leader George Templeton Strong remarked that "our Celtic fellow citizens are almost as remote from us in
temperament and constitution as the Chinese" (Tindall and Shi, 465). In
1854 the nativist Know-Nothing party won all but two seats in the lower
house of the Massachusetts legislature, their platform calling for the exclu-
sion of Catholics from public office and the extension of the naturalization period from five to twenty-one years.

This political movement was largely a response to immigration and its
demographics. From 1783 to 1819, new arrivals had numbered some
250,000 (just under 7,000 per year), and thereafter the figures rose
steadily (10,199 in 1825—23,322 in 1830—84,066 in 1840). After
1845, however, the numbers increased strikingly. The 1840s saw 1.7 million, and another 2.6 million in the 1850s. Between 1845 and 1854, the
years when Hawthorne, Melville, and Emerson produced their "head"
texts, the United States experienced the greatest proportionate increase in
immigrants in its history.

These numbers represent many, many bodies—a mere half-million
British, but 1.2 million German and 1.6 million Irish. The Transcendentalist Theodore Parker had called such Irish "the worst people in Europe
to make colonists of" (Tindall and Shi, 465). Their bodies are ethnically
identified as those of uneducated, poor servants and manual laborers for
the docks, the kitchens, the whorehouses, the warehouses, the canals, the
railroads, and the textile and iron mills. Such bodies were "hands" in
Dickens's *Hard Times* (1854) and appeared in *Walden* worked to death
and interred as railroad cross-ties. They surface in Hawthorne's travel
sketches as diabolical "wild Irish . . . condemned to keep alive the flame of
their own torment" (Weber, Lueck, and Berthold, 49). They emerge in
Rebecca Harding Davis's *Life in the Iron Mills* (1861) as stoop laborers
who "skulk along like beaten hounds [with] . . . dull, besotted faces . . .
sharpened here or there by pain or cunning" (15, 12). These are bodies
abysmally paid, wretchedly housed and fed, propertyless, stupefied by toil.

But these immigrants and others were also the bodies of potential and
actual strikers, of rioters and street fighters, of angry mobs. These were, in
short, potentially rebellious bodies swarming into the United States in
huge numbers. On a steamboat on Lake Ontario in 1832, Hawthorne
saw them as "foreign vice . . . the scum which every wind blows off the
Irish shores—the pauper-dregs which England flings out upon America."
From his first-class self-styled "aristocratic" spot on an upper deck, he
looked down to identify them as a "Mob" contained only by the boat's se-
vere spatial class divisions (Weber, Lueck, and Berthold, 54, 49).

Emerson, meanwhile, worried about the enervation of the self-reliant, civilized white male, a property holder who nonetheless "has lost his aboriginal strength" and is defenseless against the "savage with a broad axe" (*Selections,* 48). To Emerson, a certain human "ferocity" justifies the "arming of the [heroic, white] man" who must "dare the gibbet" and—shades of Hawthorne—"the mob" ("Heroism," in *Natural,* 148).

For his part, Melville, in *Benito Cereno* (1855–56), warned of the jeopardy of white male American obtuseness in a factually based tale of a cunning, murderous shipboard slave revolt that nearly succeeds. Orson Fowler's phrenology textbook, *Human Science,* provided assurance that African-American heads show a "love of hilarity, song, and dance, without much wit" (184–185), but *Benito Cereno* says otherwise. Melville arguably critiques the mental deficiency of the white, male authoritative head—the American ship captain—whose stupidity nearly causes the massacre of his crew and himself, together with that of their counterparts on the Spanish ship on which the revolt has occurred. At the end of the tale, readers learn that the head of the black slave leader of the revolt, "that hive of subtlety," is impaled on a pole in the plaza of Buenos Aires and meets "unabashed, the gaze of the whites." His is a gaze that challenges the white man's power, for it is the head of a black "whose brain, not body, had schemed and led the [slave] revolt" (*Benito Cereno,* 258). (Notice that the phrenology text mentions the "rapid increase" of African Americans [184–185].)

Ethnic mobs, savage killers, cunning plotters, bodies black and primitive and naturally rhythmic but cunningly cerebral too. Defined by white male writers, these representations suggest a deep anxiety on the part of those self-identified with the white, cerebral male authority. Add to them the Indians, whom the phrenology text defines according to "an extreme development of Destruction," meaning "that cruel, bloodthirsty, and revengeful disposition common to that race" (180). (And consider that the Crazy Horse Memorial, ten times larger than the presidential heads of Mt. Rushmore, is intended to dwarf the presidential heads and remind all white males of their vulnerability to defeat in battle.)

Factor in all *other* bodies, say, those of the women whose commercial literary success so appalled Hawthorne that he lashed out at these rivals as "a d——d mob of scribbling women," while Thoreau immobilized "womankind" as "slumberers" in his essay "Walking" (1861), in which Thoreau's "out and erect" phallic architectural columns stand to guard— or is it imprison?—the women whom the essayist figuratively puts to sleep each afternoon, their bodies as immobile as the expeditionary Thoreau's is ambulant (Hawthorne, *Letters,* 303–305; Thoreau, "Walking," 596). In 1841 Catherine Beecher, in her *Treatise on Domestic Economy,* bemoaned the sedentary "prevailing system of female education" in which girls are "deprived of the sports and exercise . . . which strengthen the muscles of boys" and were thereby "enfeebled" (113–114).

Women's "intellects," argued Margaret Fuller in *The Great Lawsuit* (1843), "need developing," and the New England contemporary of Hawthorne and Emerson, of Melville and Thoreau, advised women to "lay aside all thought . . . of being taught and led by men" (in E. Davis, 370, 371, 373). In 1848, the year of revolution, politically activist women, of course, met at Seneca Falls, New York, to begin agitating for constitutional rights, launching the decades-long suffragist movement which resulted in the 1920 ratification of the Nineteenth Amendment granting women voting rights. Meanwhile, Thoreau's image of narcoleptic women conjoined a nineteenth-century culture of female illness and invalidism, fostered by a patriarchal medical establishment which operated to immobilize middle-class female bodies (their working-class counterparts already virtually immobilized by exhaustion from wage-earning work, childbearing, and the child care of their own offspring and also those of the class of women whom Thoreau anesthetized in "Walking").

Affluent American female bodies, presumed to be illness-prone, were also aestheticized and spiritualized in an ideal of disembodiment, which, it has been argued, became nonetheless a source of female power (see D. Herndl). Charlotte Perkins Gilman's best-known text, "The Yellow Wallpaper" (1891), which described a woman going insane while confined by her physician-husband to bed rest in an attic room, fixed the nineteenth-century image of patriarchal medical-legal authority which immobilized the body of the very affluent female apt to seek education and to commit her thought to written form. By the 1910s, however, in "Our Brains and What Ails Them," Gilman gave voice to the women demographically identifiable with her "Yellow Wallpaper" narrator and also resumed Margaret Fuller's argument, adding to intellectual imperatives those of bodily activism by calling for bodily-intellectual stimulation on the part of women (as well as men). Gilman's argument was premised upon the "psychic demand for association, specialization and interchange" which would strengthen "the [human] race-brain—the common inheritance of us all" and necessarily release women into physical-intellectual activism in every male-occupied cultural site (220, 226–227).

The ratio of white male heads to all these bodies is tremendous, incalculable. Gender as well as race apply to Benedict Anderson's observation that "nationalism thinks in terms of historical destinies, while racism dreams of eternal contaminations" (149). Racism, Anderson adds, originates in "ideologies of *class,* rather than in those of nation" (149). For those of male Anglo-Saxon stock, the numbers were terrible. "When the storm roars loudest," wrote John Muir, the sequoias never lose their "god-like composure." What loud roaring storm? If not the suffragists' clamor, perhaps the Great Railroad Strike of 1877, when wage cuts, together with the ongoing depression from the panic of 1873, prompted the rail workers of Martinsburg, West Virginia, to walk out and block the tracks, then to become a mob that burned and plundered railroad property and led to sympathy walkouts and demonstrations from Maryland to Chicago to San Francisco. That strike engulfed the nation coast to coast, and federal troops were mobilized to stop it after local militiamen proved sympathetic to the strikers and joined them. Although the strike did not succeed, the looting, burning, rioting, and destruction of railroad company property ("miles of ties turned into glowing coals and tons on tons of iron car skeletons and wheels almost at white heat") prompted speculation that another civil war was at hand, this one between labor and capital (Tindall and Shi, 793–795).

Or, in terms of this discussion, the war would be between the white, brain-feeder heads and the brawny, angry bodies that so outnumbered them. Events correlative with the Great Railroad Strike make up a long miscellany in the nineteenth and twentieth centuries, and Howard Zinn's *People's History of the United States, 1492–Present* records a consistent pattern of insurgent efforts to claim rights on the part of the disaffected, the dispossessed, the marginalized—the tenants, minorities, women, the Okies, and many others.

The white male heads are crucial to this numbers game and to the "people's history." The essential message of "The Great Stone Face," *Moby-Dick,* "Napoleon," phrenology, John Muir's sequoias and Yosemite rocks, and Mt. Rushmore is one of cerebral control over the vast hordes. In and of themselves, the iconic heads argue that mere numbers will not matter as long as the masterminds outwit and outfox all others. Vastly outnumbered, the heads nonetheless need not be toppled. Heads will not roll if they can keep cool (as in Muir's "god-like composure"), can keep their very heads, their cerebral control. Theodore Roosevelt said it explicitly: "The prime requisites are cool judgment and that kind of nerve which consists in avoiding being rattled . . . What a man needs is . . . nerve control, cool-headedness" (*Autobiography,* 34). This is the fundamental reassurance of the brain-feeder head—and also the measure of its anxiety, lest it not be quite brainy enough to maintain control and supremacy over the long term.

The homology, however, provides incentive and ideological motivation for these heads. As long as the nation's geomorphic body is thought to correspond with the best, brain-feeder bodies of the nation, then the Rushmorean head is not about greed or power or disregard for the rights of others, but about the foreordained order of Nature's nation, America. The homologic relation between American terra firma and its paradigmatic bodies provides assurance that the social order is as it ought to be.

The Rushmorean stone heads have come forward satirically in recent years, probably starting with Alfred Hitchcock's *North by Northwest* (1959), a comic spy-thriller with a climactic chase scene in which Cary Grant and Eva Marie Saint scramble over the face of George Washington. The sculptor Marisol has executed a granite head of Richard Nixon (this at the National Portrait Gallery in Washington, D.C.), and Colgate-Palmolive advertises toothpaste on television with a computer-graphic brushing of Teddy Roosevelt's Rushmorean teeth. A sports reporter for the *New York Times* identifies football coaches Tom Landry and Don Shula as two great Mt. Rushmore-profile icons, while the religion editor of the Nashville *Tennessean* calls Madalyn Murry O'Hair "the Mount Rushmore of atheism," and *The New Yorker* calls former New York City mayor Ed Koch "ready for some Jewish Mt. Rushmore" (Traub, 47). Cartoonist Gary Larson draws a Rushmore-esque monument with space aliens who resemble Jim Henson's Muppet Honkers. A merchandise catalog offers a "Rushmore" wall print in which the presidents are replaced by the pop icons Marilyn Monroe, Humphrey Bogart, James Dean, and John Lennon. Country music vocalist and song writer Emmylou Harris has etched the monument in acidic satire in her quasi-autobiographical album, *The Ballad of Sally Rose* (1986), in which the protagonist grows up on a South Dakota Sioux reservation under the oppressively statist shadow of "Roosevelt's nose."

Mt. Rushmore, in fact, seems as susceptible to parody as the Iowa farm couple in Grant Wood's *American Gothic,* the variations being an endless play of whimsical defamiliarizations. It might be argued, however, that the additions and substitutions in the images of Mt. Rushmore are efforts to disempower the heads, either to deconstruct the very conception of "greatness" or to democratize the notion in terms of popular culture and a meritocracy based upon criteria different from corporate-statist control—based, for instance, on the movies or popular music. (And it is well to recall that the origins of Mt. Rushmore involve popular culture, since its South Dakota sponsors hoped to lure automobile tourism to the state.)

10. Mt. Rushmore caricatured in a Sony advertisement of 1996.

For indeed, the tradition of the agency of the presidential power heads continued apace with the satire well into the twentieth century and beyond. Cartoonists and song writers may satirize, but Ayn Rand's best-selling novel *The Fountainhead* (1943) earnestly celebrates the master "head" architect named Howard Roark, loosely modeled on Frank Lloyd Wright, whose vision is monumental and uncompromising. The advertising copy for the 50th Anniversary Edition (1993) represents the story as the "desperate battle" of an architect "whose integrity was as unyielding as granite." His buildings are quotidian versions of Roark's body. He wields a blowtorch with such ease that the metal seems cut from his very hand, and a steel rock drill becomes an extension of his arms (92, 201). As a quarryman, he drills the rock in an orgasmic "convulsive shudder": "to feel the drill and his body gathered into the single will of pressure, that a shaft of steel might sink slowly into granite—this was all of life for Howard Roark" (201). Rand's novel urbanizes the Mt. Rushmore head, objectifying it in the phallic high-rises of the twentieth-century American city. The master architect's posture, including his head and stance, "gave to his body the structural cleanliness of his own building" (550).

11. President George H. W. Bush swimming off Honolulu, Hawaii, October 1990—a casual moment far from Rushmorean formality.

One can feel contemptuous of the sophomoric fascism of *The Foun-tainhead* and, in the opening years of the twenty-first century, easily scornful of the imperialism of the Mt. Rushmore monument, joking about its status as kitsch. But if one feels a certain disdain, together with the certainty that one is not at all self-identified or complicitous with the brain-feeder heads, it might be worthwhile to pose a kind of personal test. One might gaze upon the blurry wire service news photo of President George Bush falling ill at a state dinner in Japan on January 12, 1992, when the president, the head of state, leaned over to vomit into the lap of the Japanese prime minister. Macabre? Funny? Or does the image evoke a slight sense of unease, just a tremor on some nationalistic, patriotic Rich-ter scale? If so, that tremor is the legacy of culture in which certain Ameri-can men "raised their heads like vast mountains."

2

Walden Pond: Head Trips

So let freedom ring from the prodigious hilltops of New Hampshire.
Let freedom ring from the mighty mountains of New York.
Let freedom ring from the heightening Alleghenies of Pennsylvania.
Let freedom ring from the snow-capped Rockies of Colorado.
Let freedom ring from the curvaceous slopes of California.
But not only that.
Let freedom ring from Stone Mountain of Georgia.
Let freedom ring from Lookout Mountain of Tennessee.
Let freedom ring from every hill and molehill of Mississippi, from every
mountainside, let freedom ring.

—MARTIN LUTHER KING, JR., "I Have a Dream," 1963

At the heart of everything is what we shall call a change of consciousness. This means a 'new head'—a new way of living—a new man. This
is what the new generation has been searching for, and what it has
started achieving. . . . If a history of Consciousness III were to be written, it would show a fascinating progression. The earliest sources were
among the exceptional individuals who are found at any time in any society: the artistic, the highly sensitive, the tormented. Thoreau . . .

—CHARLES REICH, *The Greening of America,* 1970

A lake is the landscape's most beautiful and expressive feature. It is
earth's eye; looking into which the beholder measures the depth of his
own nature.

—HENRY DAVID THOREAU, *Walden,* 1854

Standing before the Lincoln Memorial on August 28, 1963, Martin
Luther King, Jr., delivered his nationally televised "I Have a Dream"

speech, the keynote address of the March on Washington. In his conclusion to what has been called "one of the most memorable speeches of the century," King quoted lyrics from the song "America the Beautiful"—"from every mountainside, let freedom ring"—and then explicated the line to his audience of two hundred thousand blacks and whites who had marched down the Mall singing "We Shall Overcome" and who constituted the largest civil rights demonstration in American history (Tindall and Shi, 1339).

King offered a lesson in American geopolitics. In tones of both indictment and inspiration, he moved systematically across the topography from which the Mt. Rushmore presidential heads began to be objectified in the late eighteenth century—the very topography familiar to generations of the nation's schoolchildren—from New England's White Mountains, including its Presidential Range, through New York's Adirondacks and the Alleghenies of the Middle Atlantic states, then on to the western Rockies and California's Sierra. King then swept around to the South, the Appalachians and Smokies and every "molehill" of the Mississippi Delta. From "sea to shining sea," he argued, America was not yet "America the Beautiful." Its African-American population did not enjoy the "inalienable rights to life, liberty, and the pursuit of happiness" promised in the Declaration of Independence (M. L. King, 217). Freedom did not yet ring out from every—indeed, from any—mountainside of the nation.

King did not explicitly name South Dakota's Black Hills or Mt. Rushmore, but his panorama was meant to include all peaks and promontories named for national founders and for American great men from the late eighteenth century onward, from Mt. Washington in New Hampshire to Alaska's Mt. McKinley. Spiritually, he said, blacks experienced these peaks as a "mountain of despair" that left them in a "valley of despair," and "I Have a Dream" thus sent the message that those mountains, embodying great white American men, were not as yet geomorphic monuments to freedom (219). The white male leadership had failed to live by the democratic values set forth in the nation's scriptural documents, and by extension the landmarks named for these men bore their honorific identities hypocritically, even fraudulently. Nearly two centuries into the American experiment in democracy, the leading white heads so far had failed, and the topography identified with them was thereby a travesty of the nation's ideals.

The Sixties project of which King was a part included not only a denunciation of the Rushmorean brain-feeder heads but also, environmentally, a bid to supplant the South Dakota site with a different bodily manifestation of the head of Nature's nation. The figure of Henry David Thoreau, influential in King's thought, became crucial in this shift, first of all because in "Civil Disobedience" (1849) Thoreau had denounced the typical Rushmorean "legislators, politicians, lawyers, ministers, and officeholders" as mere putative "good citizens" who "serve the state chiefly with their heads." Thoreau identified these "heads" as racists and imperialists who, bereft of conscience, rarely made moral distinctions and "are as likely to serve the devil . . . as God" (*Portable Thoreau,* 112).

For King's Sixties—an era extending well into the 1970s—Thoreau was crucial to the decanonization of the Rushmorean *crania Americana* and equally important to the concomitant sacralizing of a different site. The newer countercultural consciousness found expression in Walden Pond, which Thoreau saw as the "earth's eye," a trope that cast the whole earth as the realm of consciousness and which objectified the "greening of America" (*Walden,* 435). The pond became the manifestation of the "new head" of unprecedented enlightenment modeled on what were thought to be Thoreau's insights and on his demonstration of "a new way of living" beyond the era of libertarian individualism and of repressive industrial and bureaucratic hierarchies.

Although the presidential *crania Americana* embedded in a South Dakota granite mountain range was not, after all, a sculptural disclosure of the bodily identity of freedom and democracy, a different American environmental site might certainly manifest these values. The failure or mistake of Mt. Rushmore did not invalidate the concept of an authentic Nature's nation and the conviction that its geomorphology must express the quintessential America in bodily terms. If Mt. Rushmore was a misbegotten undertaking—cruel in its authorized exploitation of the nonwhite population, imperialist in its disregard for sacred Sioux land, chauvinist in its symbolic hypermasculinity—nonetheless a corporeal America was still ideologically operant. The bodily expression of the valorized America could be found elsewhere in the territory of Nature's nation. An enactment of American ideals was surely possible in a site constituted as antiimperial, anticapitalist, antihierarchical, and instead politically inclusive, communal, spiritual, even mystical. The Sixties, accordingly, reconceived Nature's nation in ways that shifted the environmental bodily locus—and its identity—from the cunning masterminds disclosed on the South Dakota mountain ridge to the visionary self as expressed in what Alan Watts termed "the inner world, the world of imagination and fantasy and the unconscious" (*Zen and the Beat Way,* 24).

The pathway from Mt. Rushmore to Walden Pond can be located, in fact, in Christian terms in "I Have a Dream," which shows the basis on which, in the Sixties, the rocky peaks gave way to fresh waters, which is to say that the mountain gave way to the lake. First, King invoked biblical geographic language to call for equality: "I have a dream that one day every valley shall be exalted, every hill and mountain shall be made low, the rough places shall be made plain, and the crooked places shall be made straight" (219).

In the New Testament passage (Luke 3:4–5) on which King's words are based, John the Baptist enjoins the faithful to make preparations for the coming of Christ, to "Prepare ye the way of the Lord," to "make his paths straight" (3:4). King's rhetoric brings the New Testament millennial vision into American history by turning a mandate of topographic change into the trope for the attainment of civil rights for all. The very topography must be made level for the attainment of social equality. The place or site must be a smoothed, leveled plane. No great stone faces ought to peer from on high, and no peoples should bow their heads in submission to such idols.

King went further. His vision included a multiracial "symphony of brotherhood" and "table of brotherhood," but also a smoothed and level place so free and just that King called it an "oasis," a fertile place in the desert due to the presence of water (219).

King imagined the oasis in Mississippi, not in Thoreau's Massachusetts. But considering the civil rights leader's pan-American survey of mountainous oppression, the designated site could transcend region and state. If the "molehill" in the Deep South was as much a "mountain of despair" as, say, New England's Mt. Washington, then the "oasis" in Mississippi would be as liberating as a pond denoting freedom near the village of Concord, Massachusetts.

King's was one voice in a complex public discourse calling for a radical rethinking of America, which Charles Reich's influential *Greening of America* (1970) defined as nothing less than a mandate for a "change of consciousness" which "means a 'new head'—a new way of living" (5). Sixties "head" talk seemed everywhere. America, said Norman Mailer, "was mighty but headless" (*Fire on Moon,* 67). The developing counterculture, of course, embraced the very term "head," and the hippies, one journalist said, advocated "changing people's attitudes and values, by changing the heads of men" (MacDonald, 152). As Andrew Kopkind has said, "Private head trips seemed to be adjuncts or companions of social movements" (qtd. Chapman, 207).

At issue were the personal and sociopolitical uses of thought and the ways in which consciousness might be radically altered in order to engender a more egalitarian and benign social order and a deepening of personal experience. By 1968 Kenneth Keniston could sum up the Sixties shift in consciousness in his study *Young Radicals,* identifying a counterculture who "tended to agree that American society is dominated by a loose combine of industrial, corporate, and military interests, a 'power elite' that is economically and militarily imperialistic and more concerned with maintaining its own power and containing the 'Communist menace' than with implementing the creedal values" of the country (130). To the Sixties counterculture, the United States desperately needed a radical greening because the entire nation seemed to be a kind of "Mississippi" desert, benighted, oppressive, locked in the grip of a Rushmorean white male oligarchy. The very idea of the *greening* of America was precisely the transformation of a sociopolitical Great American Desert of oppression, militarism, and technocracy into a fertile oasis of luminescent justice, equality, and freedom. King's image of the oasis proved crucial for a transposition of the Sixties head from the mountain to the lake. The green pastures and still waters (Psalm 23) of the new oasis would restore the soul of America, albeit in psychedelic terms beyond the Judeo-Christian tradition in which King framed "I Have a Dream."

The American Mind, Moloch, and Uncle Sam

It is important to recall how prodigious was the deconstructive work that enabled the "green" project to emerge, how pervasive and persistent the ideological typology of the Mt. Rushmore heads even as the sculpture itself was satirized in film, cartoons, and greeting cards. The American patriarchal masterminds continued to be socioculturally powerful, their hierarchical status tenaciously reinscribed in visual and print texts. After all, *The Greening of America,* which was based on events of the Sixties, was not published until 1970 (underscoring the way in which the historical moment called the Sixties extended well into the 1970s). The movement, including the civil rights initiatives that King referred to as a "marvelous new militancy," must be seen against the mainstream representations legitimating patriarchal male power still very much in circulation well into the 1960s (218). The counterculture's revisionism can best be appreciated by a look at the kind of Rushmorean educational structures of knowledge dominant even in that decade.

At mid-century, to cite one major example, a sort of American phrenology emerged in the field of intellectual history in Henry Steele Commager's "head" text, *The American Mind,* subtitled *An Interpretation of American Thought and Character since the 1880s* (1950). Issued in paperback in 1959 and used in college and university classrooms well into the 1960s, *The American Mind,* reprinted thirty-five times, expresses an authoritative conception of a national mentality and thereby shows how difficult the radical challenge to it would be.

The son of a journalist, the historian Henry Steele Commager was born in Pittsburgh at the turn of the century and educated at the University of Chicago (Ph.D. 1928). He taught at New York University and rose through the ranks from instructor to full professor before joining the faculty at Columbia University in 1939. He collaborated with eminent academicians such as Samuel Eliot Morison and Allan Nevins and, singly and with others, produced some twenty-five books, of which the best known and the most influential is *The American Mind.* Commager's biographical profile in the *Dictionary of Literary Biography* defines his work as an act of civic duty: to make readers "more informed and responsible participants in the great experiment launched in the eighteenth century to make a free, democratic, and bountiful society a reality on the North American continent . . . his articles demand[ed] that Americans live responsibly and prove worthy of their heritage" (Cobb, 117, 118; see also Jumonville).

The title *The American Mind* comes from Jefferson's 1825 reference to the Declaration of Independence as "an expression of the American mind," and though Commager conceded that his subject was "vast and amorphous" and "elusive" of statistical data, his "major premise . . . is that there is a distinctively American way of thought, character, and conduct" ("Jefferson to Henry Lee"; Commager, vii). Commager professed himself concerned with "ideas that illuminate *the* American mind," an entity conceived as unitary and entire (viii, emphasis added).

The ideas were found in politics, religion, material culture, and literature, but *The American Mind* assures readers of the continuity of the American mind via its premise that the founders—the Mt. Rushmore fathers—were national paragons, in proof of which the text opens with a primer on the foundational America of the late eighteenth century.

In fact, Commager's Rushmorean heads are intact as the paradigmatic American mind. Although George Washington is too remote and "formidable" a figure to endear himself to the American people, readers are reminded that Washington furnished a plethora of enduring images for civic emulation by the young. "Every child carried with him a number of images of the father of his country: the boy George with his hatchet—

12. U.S. postage stamp reinforcing belief in presidential authority.

'Father, I cannot tell a lie' . . . Washington crossing the Delaware; kneeling in prayer at Valley Forge" (32).

As for Lincoln, he is "the very apotheosis of the American, too homely for idolatry, too inscrutable for mere history, a legend before the [Walt Whitmanesque] lilacs bloomed again" (33). The Lincoln of *The American Mind* is a "hero" brought forth in the crisis of the Civil War as the spokesman of the "deepest feelings" of the "people of the North" (345–346).

Thomas Jefferson, however, is Commager's preeminent embodiment of America, its consummate philosopher-statesman. A self-proclaimed Jeffersonian, Commager had written *Majority Rule and Minority Rights:*

A Study in Jeffersonian Democracy and Judicial Review (1943), its argument the applicability of Jefferson's philosophy and practice to twentieth-century America. Commager's "theses always revolved around Jeffersonian liberalism" (Cobb, 119).

Throughout the history of the Republic, Commager wrote, the nation's major political philosophers had been statesmen, so it is consistent that another of the Mt. Rushmore presidents, Theodore Roosevelt, was in Commager's view "the instrument chosen by destiny for the implementation of a reform movement . . . the most fit instrument for achieving the positive state" (348). And Commager extends his Rushmorean figures. Woodrow Wilson is a "moral crusader," while Franklin D. Roosevelt understood that "much of the meaning of American history was to be found in the steady enlargement of the concept of liberty and the expansion of self-government" (354).

The pantheon of white male authority, evinced from the past, becomes the prognosticator for the future. America will remain intact and will prevail because its foundational leadership is intact over centuries. Commager employs the ideological tactic used by Borglum, in that his parade of white male leaders represents, not historical change, but replication and perpetuation of an essentialist authority. Woodrow Wilson and Franklin Delano Roosevelt prove the lineage. Disappointing presidencies such as that of "silver-plated" William McKinley are but pauses or brief interruptions in a phrenological American manifest destiny (346). The white male paradigm remains in place, including its coefficients of democracy: the American work ethic, optimism, youthfulness, utilitarianism, inventiveness, a meritocracy, passion for fairness, versatility, geniality, class barriers felled by love and talent (3–40). Despite the acknowledgment of a twentieth-century decline in creativity, individualism, and eccentricity, a recent "moral flabbiness," the deskilling of work, and a standardization that pervades American life from chain stores to country clubs, *The American Mind* affirms an inventive and practical "genius" that "made the two-party system work, achieved reforms by evolution rather than revolution, produced able leaders in times of crisis, and maintained liberty and republican institutions in times of war" (412–416, 410). The American "still professed faith in democracy, equality, and liberty and practiced that faith as well as any other people" (411).

Commager concluded *The American Mind* with a series of sermonic exhortations cloaked as open-ended questions (for example, Americans "had created an economy of abundance; could they fashion a political mechanism to assure equitable distribution for that abundance?" [442–443]).

The questions, however, are essentially rhetorical. Commager, who acknowledged the discontinuities of nineteenth- and twentieth-century political practices vis-à-vis eighteenth-century principles of the Constitution and Declaration, nonetheless held the founders and their "heirs" to be democratically exemplary.[1] Oxymoronic as it sounds, his position can be said to represent a kind of positivist stasis. In fact, the essentialist panegyric of *The American Mind* meant that Commager's text could neither engage nor rebut the kind of charge made by disaffected African Americans such as Chester Himes and Eldridge Cleaver in, respectively, *If He Hollers, Let Him Go* (1947) and *Soul on Ice* (1968), that for blacks, the notion of George Washington as the country's "father" was only "jive," that these founder-statesmen were the "architects of systems of human exploitation," and that the generations of schoolchildren taught to revere them were not educated but indoctrinated (Himes, 151; Cleaver, 73). Structurally, *The American Mind* could not show democratic principles as compromised and flouted from the beginning, or counterargue against those who felt they were. The limits of Commager's argument lay in his totalizing, his positivism, his masculinist white "phrenology" which was poised for the rejection that would come from a younger generation of students and social activists of the Sixties.

It is, however, important to recognize that the very limitations of *The American Mind* are, conversely, its strengths—or, rather, its power. Univocal in its position, it is a virtually unassailable rhetorical fortress. Its totalizing terms mean that efforts to pose a radical critique of it would necessarily be regarded as iconoclastic attacks based upon motives of insanity, extremism, subversion, sedition, radicalism, communism—all charges leveled at the counterculture through the 1960s.

Conceptually, the shift from a Rushmorean hegemony to a Thorovian "'new head'—a new way of living" thus required a tremendous sociopolitical realignment redefining the basis of human development, of social interaction, and of the relation between human beings and the environment (Reich, 5). George Lipsitz remarks, "The value placed on altered consciousness in counterculture reflected a belief that social change had to start with self-knowledge" (218). That knowledge, cautioned Alan Watts, a student of Eastern thought, necessitated an understanding of one's own culture at such depth as to make one impervious to its premises, even unconsciously (*This Is It*, 90).

A cursory survey of the Sixties shows the counterculture's development via an eclectic mix of Easternism, Native Americanism, black power, Christian elements, psychedelics and the drug culture, outlawry, even youthfulness per se, which became an identifier over and against the older generation held responsible for American society's failings. The terms by which these were aggregated—"alternate," "counter," even "underground"—all indicate positionings separate from a hegemonic "mainstream" or "center" of U.S. culture and society, and even the most casual students of the period can enumerate the counterculture's heuristic positionings.

Self-identified alterity, found, for example, in the outsider status of the criminalized, proved to be heuristically effective, in this case in Eldridge Cleaver's prison memoir, *Soul on Ice,* which directly rejected the phrenological antecedents at Mt. Rushmore by exposing "the great white statesmen whom school children are taught to revere" as the "architects of systems of human exploitation." Paired with religious leaders and educators, they are seen as a brainwashing and whitewashing clique complicitous in condoning and justifying "evil deeds" (73).

Cleaver, in fact, provides a good case in point of the deconstructive uses of an alternative heuristic. He takes issue directly with the Rushmorean head: "The ideal white man was one who knew how to use his head, who knew how to manage and control things and get things done" (80). This, in Cleaver's view, was the mind that "administered the plantation, doing all the thinking, exercising omnipotent power over the slaves," and never conceiving the reversibility of their positions (80). Citing the crucial failure of the powerful to consider a dislocation that might invert the top and bottom of the social order, Cleaver exposes the elites' naturalization of the white male hierarchy and the presupposition widely disseminated in the educational system, in the media, and elsewhere, that intellect and administrative power are centered by nature in the white male head and thereby socially legitimated.

Politically, Nature's nation, in these terms, depends on "never conceiving the reversibility" of social positions. In the postwar era of nuclear threat and of white flight to the suburbs of split-level houses, Cleaver cites the newest manifestation of these authoritative whites' "split-level heads" and of their "squinting bombardier eyes" (30). Their president is "Lyndon Strangelove," in which Lyndon Johnson merges with the demonic cold warrior of the Stanley Kubrick film (27). (The alternative newspaper *International Times* asked in 1967, "How long will it be before [Lyndon B.] Johnson decides to straighten out HIS head?" [Wilcock, 2]). As Cleaver demonstrates, alterity was crucial to the reimagining of America. The "new head" could only be conceptualized from a site alternative to that of received knowledge and custom.

The countercultural canon would include numerous texts that, like Cleaver's, assailed the position of *The American Mind,* among them novels, memoirs, poetry, self-help books, and works of social theory.[2] Two figures, nonetheless, born within a year of each other and extraordinarily different in background, are essential to the formulation of the new countercultural head : Allen Ginsberg and Malcolm X. Both used public discourse, poetry and speeches respectively, to conduct a frontal assault against "the American Mind" as such postwar consensus analysts as Commager defined it. Both made the attack on the heads of nonelites a central critical focus. Both understood the ways in which the head was the point of both vulnerability and greatest strength and therefore subject to relentless attack by statist power. Both deployed the figure of the human head to delegitimate "the American mind." In terms of the project to supplant the Rushmorean paradigm with a new one, their task was simultaneously deconstructive and reconstructive, in that the communitarian "new head" was instated even as the white male head was discredited.

Malcolm X, born Malcolm Little in 1925, was one of eight children of a West Indian mother and a Georgian itinerant preacher committed to the message of Marcus Garvey's United Negro Improvement Association. Malcolm spent his early years in Lansing, Michigan, and recalled quietly intense meetings in Negro homes at which his father spoke of "Africa for the Africans," the continent to be run entirely "by black men" (*Autobiography,* 6–7). By the 1950s, however, he was a former self-styled Harlem street hustler who, from his teens through his early twenties, had supported himself through gambling, drug dealing, prostitution arrangements, and burglary. He served ten years in prison, where he read voraciously and became an adherent of Elijah Muhammad's racially separatist Nation of Islam, upon his release recruiting and becoming instrumental in the formation of a series of temples in Philadelphia, Detroit, and New York City. He spoke publicly and wrote short newspaper features and a column for the *Amsterdam News* in Harlem and the *Herald Dispatch* in Los Angeles before founding *Muhammad Speaks,* the Nation of Islam newspaper. In numerous speeches at colleges and universities, he offered his educational credentials: "I finished the eighth grade in Mason, Michigan. My high school was the black ghetto of Roxbury, Massachusetts. My college was in the streets of Harlem, and my master's was taken in prison" (*Autobiography,* 288).

On the East Coast, Irwin Allen Ginsberg (b. 1926) was the son of radical leftist Russian immigrants, including a poet and high-school teacher father who recited aloud the poetry of Dickinson, Milton, and the English Romantics around the Paterson, New Jersey, household during Allen's boyhood. He was subject, also, to the fervid communist beliefs of his mother, who took him to party cell meetings and to a communist summer camp. An excellent student, Allen planned to study labor law at Columbia University and to work on behalf of labor unions and the working class. Drawn to the study of literature, however, he became a protégé of Lionel Trilling and a friend of Jack Kerouac (whose football scholarship at Columbia had been revoked as the result of an injury). Ginsberg also was attracted to the study of Zen Buddhism. At a time when a college served in loco parentis, Ginsberg ran afoul of college officials for infraction of rules, both for consorting with "disreputable" sorts like Kerouac and William Burroughs and also for scrawling obscenities in graffiti on his dorm windows, which led to a suspension. Columbia's deans seemed unaware that Ginsberg was homosexual, a fact the poet understood from about age ten. He served in the merchant marine and moved to the San Francisco Bay Area when he left Columbia. His *Howl and Other Poems* appeared in 1956, just six years after the publication of Commager's *American Mind.*

Both Ginsberg and Malcolm X were outsiders to what has been called a postwar "official culture based on middle-class notions of propriety and success" (Jamison and Eyerman, 153). The official culture was normatively heterosexual, thus excluding Ginsberg, and it was racialized as white, thereby excluding Malcolm. (In a postwar society also increasingly idealized for its nuclear family, both Ginsberg and Malcolm X had mothers institutionalized for insanity.)

Malcolm emphatically rejected the Negro version of the official culture, inveighing against "complacent and misguided so-called 'middle-class' Negroes—the typical status-symbol-oriented, integration-seeking type of Negroes" both the *haute bourgeois* of sycophantic professionals dissembling to the white power structure and those "belowstairs" whose occupation as waiters, janitors, and bootblacks only revealed their oppression and their false consciousness as they filled the roles whites set for them (*Autobiography,* 5). He denounced the black professional class as a collective "Uncle Thomas," a "*professional* Negro for the white man. . . . Black bodies with white heads!" (*Autobiography,* 248).

Ginsberg, politically on the left, was a gay man who acknowledged his Jewish identity at a time when others tried to pass as gentile-unto-genteel aesthetes. One must recall that the literary presiding presence at Ginsberg's Columbia University was Lionel Trilling, a Jew of whom it has been said that "gentility reigned supreme" (Gitlin, 49). Literary study at Columbia, to quote Todd Gitlin, "emphasized cool distance, teeth-gritting irony, the decorous play of literary reference" (49). Indeed, Trilling's response to *Howl* was negative. He termed it "dull" prose, "all rhetoric without any music," and lacking in "voice." "Im afraid I have to tell you," wrote Trilling to his former student, "that I don't like the poems at all" (Schumacher, 239).

Perhaps this response was predictable, since Ginsberg "turned the images and traditions of high culture against itself . . . challeng[ing] the traditional view of American literature at Columbia, taking [his] cue from the culture found on the streets of New York" (Jamison and Eyerman, 143, 152). As numerous readers have recognized, he reached more toward Whitman's "barbaric yawp" updated to the New York streets of the 1940s–1950s. The anti-obscenity trial that ensued charged the publisher of *Howl* with "willfully and lewdly" printing, publishing, and selling "obscene and indecent writings," and the American Civil Liberties Union defended Lawrence Ferlinghetti, the publisher, and Ginsberg (Schumacher, 254–255, 259–264). As for the terms of the poem, *Howl* directly challenged a hypocritical civility: "America, go fuck yourself with your atom bomb" (39).

Howl rejected the "narcotic tobacco haze of Capitalism" and declared, "Your machinery is too much for me. . . . It's true, I don't want to join the Army or turn lathes / in precision parts factories" (13, 39, 43). Commager's American mind—its very reassuring strength its fundamental endurance—was Ginsberg's Moloch, a version of the god of the ancient Phoenicians and Ammonites to whom children were sacrificed by burning—hence a god demanding terrible sacrifice.

Howl decries an American Sphinx—surely a Rushmorean figure of imperial enigma—as a monster of cement and aluminum that destroyed the creatively deviant—that is, the best—American heads. It "bashed open the skulls and ate up" the "brains and imagination" of "the best minds of [the poet's] generation" (21, 9). This sphinx is an American Moloch of soulless jailhouses, "Ugliness!," "Ashcans and unobtainable dollars," militarism, capitalism, machine technology, "monstrous bombs" (21–22).

But the poet cannot simply take an oppositional stance against the modern American Moloch. The poet of Ginsberg's *Howl* complained, in the first person, that Moloch had "entered my soul early! Moloch in whom / I am consciousness without a body" (22).

Why no body?—because the "best minds of [the poet's] generation . . . broke their backs lifting Moloch to Heaven!" (22). Body and soul, they participated in a Molochian America and paid the sacrificial price. The putative American mind of Commager's formulation was a sham, according to *Howl* and to the Beat and psychedelic writers who followed, and was destructive, deadening, and irremediable.

Malcolm X, too, had identified a Moloch, and it was Uncle Sam, destroying successive generations of African Americans by deforming them into the false consciousness of dejected Uncle Toms, with Harriet Beecher Stowe's figure of Christian stoicism debased into a type of servility, useful only for self-interested role-play ("For two bits, Uncle Tom a little—white cats especially like that" [*Autobiography*, 49]). Malcolm repudiated a "corrupt" and "criminal" system "that in 1964 still colonizes . . . [and] enslaves . . . 22 million African-Americans" (50). Uncle Sam had created Uncle Tom, and "his hands are dripping with the blood of the black man in this country" (35).

Bodily figuration of bloody violence—especially of violence to the head—pervades Malcolm X's speeches and his *Autobiography*, in which a series of crucial moments show the bind of the African-American male with the graphic clarity of a medieval morality play. The black male who loses to a white in sport is publicly humiliated, with his head hung in shame (*Autobiography*, 25). The black aspirant to the intellectual professions suffers trauma to the head when advised to redirect his ambitions to his hands (as was the onetime head-of-the-class Malcolm, whose eighth-grade teacher dismissed his ambition to become an attorney, saying, "A lawyer—that's no realistic goal for a nigger" [*Autobiography*, 37–38]).

Alternately, the black man seeking a proximate white identity is left "deaf, dumb, and blind, mentally, morally, spiritually . . . mentally dead," and emblematically so in submission to a caustic hair process by which the "conked" head is itself a sign of relentless cultural brainwashing (*Autobiography*, 203, 228). (Malcolm admits to having once marveled at the "transformation" of his own hair when it became as "straight as any white man's," an act he later reflected on as one of "self-degradation" [*Autobiography*, 56].)

Finally, a black male who spoke out publicly—as did Malcolm's father, Earl Little, who carried the political message of racial pride—put himself in mortal danger. A searing early memory was the story of Malcolm's mother taken by the police to the Lansing, Michigan, hospital to see the mangled body of her dying husband, Malcolm's preacher-father, whose "skull, on one side, was crushed in" by the white supremacists who had threatened, harassed, and assaulted this "uppity nigger" before finally killing him and laying his body across trolley tracks to make his death appear accidental (*Autobiography*, 10). (This moment is echoed in the autobiographical account of a Muslim brother, failing to obey a patrolman's order to "move on," then "attacked with nightsticks": "His scalp was split open . . . blood had bathed his head and face and shoulders" [*Autobiography*, 238].)

Malcolm X's speeches, accordingly, are filled with images of the black body under constant assault, especially the center of thought. Anesthetized by whites, the very jaws of blacks are smashed and bleeding—"blood running all down your jaw, and you don't even know what's happening because someone has taught you to suffer—peacefully" (12). And white society approves this bodily image, for media representations of blacks are acceptable only when "you get your head busted," an image evoking pity and guilt but conveying the message that racial-social hierarchy will be maintained even if agents of the status quo are brutes wielding batons (93). Whites have become specialists, moreover, in how to "psycho the American Negro" (173, 175). Just as Moloch broke the backs and devoured the brains of young whites, so have racist whites "brainwashed" black Americans into a loathing of their own bodies: "We hated our heads, we hated the shape of our nose, we wanted one of those long doglike noses . . . we hated the color of our skin, hated the blood of Africa that was in our veins. And in hating our features and our skin and our blood, why, we had to end up hating ourselves" (168–169). Self-hatred engendered and instilled by the racialization of America was, Malcolm discovered, the root cause of African Americans' feelings of inferiority, inadequacy, helplessness, and victimization (169).[3]

It has been argued that the black militants and the white counterculture were politically antithetical, the whites disenchanted by—and exiting—the very consumerist, materialistic, corporate culture that blacks aspired to join in order to enjoy the sense of sociocultural participation, status, and material comforts so long denied them. A sociologist differentiated blacks from hippies in the 1960s in these terms, writing that hippies had "voluntarily dropped out" while blacks "[bought] *the American Dream* . . . a 'piece of the action' that include[d] the Cadillac and the white picket-fenced house" (Yablonsky, 26). One journalist observed in 1968, "The hippies are not really on the Negroes' side, for they interpret the Negroes' demand for a better life as crassly materialistic and hopelessly middle-class" (MacDonald, 151).

The emphasis on race-based ideological mismatch, moreover, leads to another problematic issue, namely, the terms by which one model can supplant another. Critical efforts to discredit the one risks its replication. One set of revered—or feared—heads could be substituted inadvertently for another. For instance, Elijah Muhammad, founder of the Nation of

Islam, propounded a human creation myth in which a black satanic figure, said to have loosed on earth a race of white devils, is himself a figure of "unusually large" head, a "big-head scientist" (*Autobiography of Malcolm X,* 168). Here oppressive power is demonized, but in Rushmorean terms of the giant heads of state as updated for the nuclear era.

Readers of the speeches and *Autobiography* of Malcolm X may notice his reinscription of the very kind of heads he denounces. His account of travels to the Middle East and Africa includes joyful, awed announcement of appointments and "private audiences" with world-famous personages, including some "heads of [African] nations" (*Autobiography,* 200, 378). Malcolm, a relentless and caustic critic of statist authority, shows only reverential admiration for a roster of presidents of Egypt, Tanzania, Nigeria, Ghana, Guinea, Kenya, and Uganda. Even an effort to account for centuries of oppression of dark-skinned peoples promotes the notion of the powerful head.

It is useful, nonetheless, to recognize the apposition between Allen Ginsberg's Moloch and Malcolm X's Uncle Sam because they form an allied countercultural heuristic operating to crack open the unitary *The American Mind* and its production of cultural meanings. This mind is a Moloch that cannibalized its children, cracked their skulls and ate up their brains and imaginations. They died mad, starved, hysterical, and naked, and Ginsberg's *Howl* is a kind of "Kaddish" for them. Similarly, Uncle Sam bashed the heads and bloodied the jaws of African Americans, fomented their self-hatred by fostering a loathing of their own heads and denied them the birthright of their own intelligence. What Malcolm X termed whites' "psycho" of blacks found its counterpart in the counterculture's fear of and anger at "mindfucking." Ginsberg and Malcolm X both worked to read "the American Mind" down to what Roland Barthes called "degree zero," rejecting its terms and its forms, its fixed connections, its monolithic key words, its whole "totality of meanings, reflexes and recollections" (47). In so doing, they helped to open the public discursive space by which other texts could produce the American "new head" that replaced the Rushmorean mountain with the Thorovian lake.[4]

The Greening of America

The preoccupation with powerful heads seems to militate against a contrasting vision of the pastoral Walden Pond, which appears, initially at least, insipid, perhaps (to use a Sixties byword) "irrelevant." As a Sixties alternative to the granite heads of Mt. Rushmore—of Moloch and Uncle Sam—the pond seems inert, quiet, utterly passive. How can the "oasis" of a greening America possibly weigh in as a counterclaim against the granite *crania Americana?* How can a limpid eye outshine the piercing gaze of the "giants in granite"? Does Thorovian agency emerge at the reminder that Allen Ginsberg cited him in defense of free speech, lauded "Ecologist Thoreau," and at one point contemplated withdrawing to an "isolated spot for the solitary life, where he could exist like Thoreau"? (Schumacher, 317, 471, 476, 529). Does it advance knowledge one iota to find Malcolm X, in his *Autobiography,* recalling that while in prison, a knowledgeable fellow inmate taught him about Thoreau, even when we find Malcolm silent on what he learned or what he made of it? [157].

To understand the transition from Mt. Rushmorean authority to that of a green oasis, it is perhaps useful to recognize a certain sense of crisis about the accommodation to the new era and to acknowledge one of the major texts of the Sixties, *The Greening of America* by Charles Alan Reich. Reich (b. 1928), the son of a physician father and an educator mother, had graduated from Oberlin College in 1949 and proceeded to take a law degree from Yale in 1952, after which he worked as an attorney in several New York and Washington, D.C., firms. He joined the faculty of Yale University as professor of law in 1960, increasingly spending time with his students and reevaluating his prior career, realizing its rigidity and his own alienation from a materialistic and repressive society. Reich found in his Yale students a new consciousness that afforded hope for the future, and accordingly he wrote *The Greening of America* (1970), which argues that "the creation of a new consciousness is the most urgent of America's real needs" (351). The new heads of a green America "do not want to stand head and shoulders above the crowd" as did those of the hierarchically benighted Rushmorean past. That past encompassed the era of colonization and of pioneering characterized by individualist libertarianism and of the succeeding industrial technocracy that became the "Corporate State" from the late nineteenth century to the Sixties (Reich, 227).

Now poised on the verge of a green era which Reich called Consciousness III, society can proclaim "wholeness of self" as the ethos that rejects "hierarchy, security, money, possessions, power, respect and honor" as "not merely wrong" but "*unreal*" (Reich, 235, 239). Oppression and its concomitant elitism based on race, ethnicity, job status, money, and material goods are to vanish. The alleged meritocracy, exposed as specious, will make way for the green mentality of Consciousness III in which all identities are valued and a new, truly democratic social organization can emerge.

The new ideology of a green America and its Walden bodily expression may best be approached by realizing that the Sixties counterculture emerged just as leading social theorists in America were predicting an imminent era of technological automation so productive of consumer goods that it was thought certain to produce a civilization of unprecedented leisure. Sociologists such as David Riesman (*The Lonely Crowd,* 1950) and C. Wright Mills (*White Collar: The American Middle Classes,* 1951), together with the popular press, argued that tedious, grueling and repetitious work would soon vanish in a new age of leisure. As Mills said, "The old middle class work ethic—the gospel of work—has been replaced . . . by a leisure ethic" (236). The inner world of creative loafing had been propounded in the mid-nineteenth century, of course, by Walt Whitman, but the Sixties additionally embraced Thoreau and Walden, enshrining them as saint and sacred site within a kind of "leisure" tradition of pastoral harmony. From the viewpoint of Eastern thought, Alan Watts cautioned, "We are deliberately creating an economy in which machines do our work for us, so we have got to learn to loaf," lest a "vicious cycle" of production and consumption continue, fueled by a social propaganda machine motivating people to "buy up the surplus production" (*This Is It,* 36–37). *The Greening of America* presumed that technological production would inaugurate an era heretofore only dreamed of by prophets and philosophers: "If machines can take care of our material wants, why should not man develop the aesthetic and spiritual side of his nature?" (352). Watts called the real "New Frontier" the "inner world, the world of imagination and fantasy and the unconscious" (*Zen and the Beat Way,* 23–24).

Cultural indices of the new leisured green era included clothing styles and music, considered central to the new aesthetics and spirituality. The "full range of electric instruments and the technology of electronic amplifiers" enhanced and simulated the psychedelic experience in multimedia presentations in San Francisco "Bay Area Ballrooms, the Fillmore, the Avalon, or Pauley Ballroom at the University of California, the walls covered with fantastic changing patterns of light" (Reich, 233, 244).

"Often music was played out of doors, where nature—the sea or tall redwoods—provided the environment" and drug use "heightened the whole experience" (Reich, 233, 244). Musically, the green America was of Bob Dylan, the Beatles, Janis Joplin, and such bands as Jefferson Airplane, the Grateful Dead, Quicksilver Messenger Service, the Byrds, Cream, the Eagles, Sly and the Family Stone, all producing music that "rocks the whole body, and penetrates the soul" (Reich, 246). The Byrds' "Eight Miles High" attempted an aural enactment of the LSD rush, Bob Dylan's

"Visions of Johanna" showed "the infinitesimal focus of acid-time compression," and John Cipollina's guitar on Quicksilver Messenger Service's "Pride of Man" was "as metallic as that acid taste in your mouth" (Henke, 190, 191, 194). (In 1997, the thirtieth anniversary of the 1967 Summer of Love, a Rock and Roll Hall of Fame and Museum exhibition catalogue accompanying an exhibit on the psychedelic era profiled "The Psychedelic 100" songs, 1965–1969 [Henke, 190–199].)

Green-era clothing styles also attempted to break with the past and enter into the realm of the green pastoral playfulness and naturalness. Movement people flouted militarism by costuming themselves in braided uniforms and chose psychedelic tie-dyed cottons, and they proclaimed affinity with the natural world with the denims and twills and earth shoes thought to be "earthy and sensual," like "architecture that does not clash with its natural surroundings but blends in" (Reich, 234–235). "To the extent that clothes can do it," wrote Reich, "people have the opportunity to meet one another as real, total persons, mind, face, and body" (239).

Green America's identification with the natural world was primal. *The Greening of America* asserts that "contact with the open spaces of nature [is] a basic need" (168) and puns on the term "new generation," referring to Sixties youth culture and its vivification, as it bonds mind and body to the natural environment:

Perhaps the deepest source of consciousness is nature. Members of the new generation seek out the beach, the woods, and the mountains. . . . They do not go to nature as a holiday from what is real. They go to nature as a source. The salt water of the sea is the salt in their blood; the freedom of the sea is their freedom. The forest is where they came from, it is the place where they feel closest to themselves, it is renewal. . . . Nature is not some foreign element. . . . Nature is them. (262)

Nature is them. The statement is Emersonian, sacralized by and for the Sixties in Thorovian terms. In this passage, the green America is not only the map of a nation in its latest evolutionary development but also a blueprint for a utopia imminent but not yet fully in place, and therefore developmentally somewhat at risk. The green America, nonetheless, whether conceptual or attained, is the American consciousness as Nature's nation on a continental scale with "heads in the same place at the same time" (251). It is the pan-American oasis, the "new head" of "higher, transcendent reason." This "this-worldly mysticism [is] an ecstasy of the body and of the earth" (Roszak, 129). As Roszak put it in *The Making of a Counter Culture,* "The 'psychedelic revolution' comes down to the simple syllogism: change the prevailing mode of consciousness and you change the world; the use of [psychedelic drugs] changes the prevailing mode of consciousness; therefore, universalize the use of [these drugs] and you change the world" (168).

Thoreau, Walden Pond, and "Earth's Eye"

Thoreau was the prophet, saint and confrere of this green America, and Walden Pond its shrine. Lawrence Buell's meticulous account of the "formation of American culture" via "the environmental imagination" shows how historically well prepared were Thoreau and Walden Pond for the kinship claims of the Sixties counterculture, so successful had been the production, since the late nineteenth century, of a "Saint Thoreau" and a sacred Walden that meshed perfectly with the agenda of the Sixties counterculture. Indeed, Thoreau's "environmental sainthood" made possible

13. The idea of the Sixties counterculture as a psychedelic "new head" of flower power as represented in cranial flower pot.

Walden Pond's resonance from the oasis both of Martin Luther King, Jr.'s address and of the psychedelic Sixties and its green movement. "Thoreau himself initiated the tradition of viewing Walden through green spectacles" (Buell, 321). His two-year stay at the pond (1845–1847) culminated in *Walden* (1854), whose sales were dismal for decades. By the 1870s, nevertheless, a process of sacralizing the author and his subject was well under way. Although Walden Pond by the late 1860s had become a "pleasure resort," Thoreau's Walden was steadily subjected to the sacralizing that engendered what Buell terms "Environmental Sainthood," "Thoreau as Cultural Icon," and "The Thorovian Pilgrimage" (324, 322, 309, 311, 313, 338).

The "mythification" of "Saint" Thoreau occurred, for instance, with the accretion of statements such as that of an 1870s nature writer: "Every student of nature . . . as exemplified in life and action" ought to visit Walden Pond, "the spot which was made sacred by the two years' solitary residence of Henry D. Thoreau" (324). In the 1890s John Muir became one of those visitors whose "pilgrimage" to Concord moved him to invoke Thoreau's own image of Walden Pond in a letter to his wife: "a beautiful lake . . . fairly embosomed like a *bright dark eye* in wooded hills of smooth moraine gravel and sand" (317; emphasis added). (Muir's "eye" image is all the more remarkable considering that he had not read *Walden*.)

Indeed, it was through print culture—a series of editions of Thoreau's writings, of biographies, of literary scholarship, of anthologies of selections for school textbooks, and for seasonal gift books exploiting Thoreau's own seasonal design in *Walden*—that the author and the pond were elevated to sacred status. As of the turn of the twentieth century, Buell finds, "Walden was being transformed from Thoreau's sacred place into the reading community's sacred place," and the idea of a pilgrimage to Walden was one "of an American apotheosis of green retreat from urban entanglements" (324, 328). Prominent twentieth-century nature writers who have subsequently focused on other sites, from Wisconsin to Utah to Virginia, also contributed to the mythification. They may have "decentralized" Walden (even as King's oasis would centralize Mississippi), but thereby they maintained its paradigm of a redemptive, sacred nature (236–237). By the 1960s Thoreau virtually awaited the counterculture, having been thoroughly historicized as a " 'green' writer" and environmental hero," and Walden Pond formulated as a "spiritual center . . . an oasis of pastoral felicity," its visitors really pilgrims embracing its "liminoid, sacralized vision" (315, 323, 321).

This, then, was the Thoreau and Walden Pond ready for the Sixties counterculture to take its own turn in sacralizing Walden Pond and "re-canonizing" Thoreau in such texts as *The Greening of America, The Making of a Counter Culture,* and *Walden II,* all of which cite his precocity, his modeling of social reorganization along lines of ecological economy (Reich, 222; Roszak, 101; Skinner, xiv, 7).

It must be noted, however, that Walden Pond in the Sixties was not the province solely of the counterculture. Other special-interest constituencies were active on its behalf. In 1961, a committee of ad hoc volunteers called the Save Walden Committee gained a state superior court order enjoining the commissioners permanently from "violating any more of the provisions of the deeds in which Walden Pond and its environs were left to the [Massachusetts] Commonwealth"—this after an acre of trees, two hundred by some counts, was bulldozed in 1958 to make way for a service road to a swimming beach where Red Cross lifesaving classes were held (Fenton). (The court order required the replanting of the bulldozed acre.)

The administration of the pond became a political zoning issue again in 1967, when a committee of the Massachusetts House of Representatives proposed that the legislature pass a bill shifting control of the pond from the Middlesex County commissioners to the state Department of Natural Resources, which at the time managed a three-hundred-acre portion of the site (which also included sixty-four pond acres, plus one hundred forty-five additional acres, these managed by the county commissioners) (Fenton). The proposal advocated the acquisition of additional land at the site, and the Thoreau Society, chartered in 1941, weighed in in favor of the Commonwealth's taking over the administration of the entire area, which ultimately was unified as the Walden Pond Reservation.

Not all representations of Walden Pond in the Sixties involved such politics. For instance, in 1971, Eugene H. Walker, a geologist and Concord resident, published an essay, "Tracing the Source of Walden Pond's Waters," in *Man and Nature,* a publication of the Audubon societies of several New England states. Walker quoted from Thoreau's Journal and, on the basis of the pond's glacial origins, theorized about the reasons for its water-level fluctuations. Were one to read *Man and Nature* and to keep track of the administration of Walden Pond by Massachusetts county and state authorities, one would not necessarily know that Thoreau and Walden Pond had become sacred to a new counterculture.

Nor would one grasp that connection from reading reviews in the "straight" press of the remarkable 1971 reprinting of Thoreau's writings. On July 4, the *New York Times Book Review* featured a review essay by the Columbia University professor Quentin Anderson of two editions of

Walden and two volumes of selections from Thoreau's Journal (Anderson, sect. 7:1, 16–18). These four volumes arguably constituted an academic sacralizing of Thoreau and Walden Pond, whose links to the counterculture were but obliquely present in the review's passing notice of the "passionate attention" directed at Thoreau in the years of the late 1960s–early 1970s, together with the suggestion that a national "cult" might be "still vigorous in 1971" (1).

Thoreau's countercultural identity and its relation to Walden Pond, however, were explicitly acknowledged elsewhere in public discourse. Just as a pre-Sixties array of texts served to sacralize Walden Pond and Thoreau, so the Sixties produced its own new countercultural sacralizing version. This is to say that just as pre-Sixties readers of the various gift-book editions of Thoreau's writings could come to feel they knew the pond and Thoreau intimately if they read portions of *Walden* and made vicarious pilgrimages to the Pond, so the Sixties counterculture on a similar basis enshrined Thoreau as their own hippie and the pond as a sacred site.

Instead of parlor table editions, counterculturists were apt to encounter Walden Pond and its author in the 1966 W. W. Norton paperback *Walden and Civil Disobedience,* which was widely used in college courses and slipped easily into students' rucksacks or the hip pockets of jeans. Reich may typify these readers, for in *The Greening of America,* we find the following entry reportedly originating in a list on his yellow tablet. Under a heading called "aspects of the human experience either missing from our lives or present only in feeble imitation," Reich wrote, "*Nature* The experience of living in harmony with nature, on a farm, or by the sea, or near a lake or meadow, knowing, using and returning the elements; Thoreau at Walden" (112).

The *Walden* that had served earlier in the twentieth century as a model of experimental living in idealized "green retreats" gained new Sixties urgency as measured by the proliferation of guides for Walden life and narratives of those attempting it. Such efforts include *My Walden,* by Susan Baumgartner, and the nickname "Walden South" (referring to ex-newspaperman Charles Seib's retreat in the Virginia woods, complete with cabin and a half-acre pond) (Owings, 198, 25). A recent study of the American "country book," entitled *Quest for Walden* (1997), provides an annotated survey of nearly twenty "green retreat" titles of the Sixties, together with a compilation of a dozen "Country-Life Guides" published in those years under such titles as *How to Live on Almost Nothing and Have Plenty, How to Make It on the Land, Homesteading,* and *The Complete Homesteading Book* (Owings, 198–247).

The Sixties counterculture and its sympathizers claimed as their contemporary "the Now Thoreau," a man who "belongs more to the 1970s
than to the age in which he lived," according to the 1970 play *The Night
Thoreau Spent in Jail*, by Jerome Lawrence and Robert E. Lee, also the coauthors of *Inherit the Wind* (vii). The play, based upon "Civil Disobedience," was set against the increasingly unpopular Vietnam War, and it
centers on the night Thoreau spent in the Concord jail rather than pay
taxes to a government conducting an unpopular war against Mexico. Between seventy-five and eighty sold-out productions of the play were performed on college and university campuses in 1970, including UCLA and
Ohio State University, before it opened for a two-month run at the Arena
Stage in Washington, D.C., in November of that year. "Audiences are responding as if Thoreau were their contemporary," wrote Howard Taubman, "which in the large sense he is" (16).

The Night Thoreau Spent in Jail features Walden Pond as Thoreau attempts a courtship of Ellen Sewall, rowing her onto the pond in a boat, at
which point the stage directions state, "The background trembles with the
wavering pattern of sunlight reflected from water," whereupon Thoreau
anthropomorphically denounces a shoreline scene of deforestation "making the poor earth bald before her time" (33). Momentarily, he says, "here
is life in front of us, like the surface of this pond, inviting us to sail on it.
A voyage, an experiment" (37).

The contours of that experiment were so culturally familiar that the
cartoonist Garry Trudeau developed a Walden Pond sequence in *Doonesbury* in 1971–1973, published in book form as *I Have No Son* (1973). In
the sequence the countercultural Mark Slackmeyer, when presented by his
disaffected bourgeois father with an invoice for the costs of his upbringing, decides to leave home and join with Michael to lease a country house
for communal living with a "bunch of friends" (n.p.). The leased twelve-
room house and a porch on forty acres includes, as they discover, a spring-
fed puddle. The group's hippie, Zonker, proclaims, "Well, of course! All
the great communes have overlooked small bodies of water!" and he gives
theirs a name: "Walden Puddle."

Zonker is the Thorovian figure who elevates the puddle to global significance when he identifies himself with Magellan and Cortés ("You
know, I'll bet I'm the first human-type to lay eyes on that puddle! What a
puddle! Wet and Wild, and unpolluted to boot!"). Trudeau's sequence
parodies Thoreau's style in Zonker's Thorovian declamations as he snor-
kels underwater in the puddle-pond, surfacing to announce himself as
maritime explorer "Zonker [Jacques] Cousteau," then dives to fantasize
about a submariner's life commanding a World War II German U-boat.

14. Early 1970s *Doonesbury* comic strip, by G. B. Trudeau, features countercultural embrace of Walden Pond ("Walden Puddle").
© G. B. Trudeau. Reprinted with permission of Universal Press Syndicate. All rights reserved.

Trudeau, himself a counterculture figure who began antiestablishment cartooning as a Yale undergraduate, satirizes the movement's simultaneous rejection of, yet dependence upon, upper-middle-class American material comforts and conveniences. His Thorovian Zonker is less the questing hero than a self-centered recreationist, and Walden Puddle is a diminishment of the pond just as the cartoon commune represents a debased Thorovian identity. Similarly, the titles of the Sixties' Waldenesque narratives tended to spoof their authors' failed attempts to re-create an ideal life as set forth in *Walden,* for example, Jerry Bledsoe's 1975 *You Can't Live on*

Radishes: Some Funny Things Happened on the Way Back to the Land or Peter Matson's 1977 *A Narrative of the Imperfect Art of Homesteading and the
Value of Ignorance* (Owings, 199, 220).

The success of Trudeau's satire of Walden Pond depends upon a readership familiar with the Thorovian values of the pond and with Thoreau's
rhetorical moves and literary style. Trudeau's national newspaper syndica-
tion attests to the broad readership presumed to grasp the system of values
by which the humor of Walden Puddle comments on Walden Pond. As
one reporter wrote in coverage of a three-day symposium on Thoreau in
May 1967, Thoreau "made a half-mile pond famous over the planet"
(Lask).

Indeed, the hippie Zonker's naming of the puddle underscores Thoreau's Sixties counterculture identity as ur-hippie, with the pond accordingly the counterculture's shrine. The artist Leonard Baskin's portrait of a
thin, bearded Thoreau for a first-class, five-cent U.S. postal stamp issued in the summer of 1967 became a benchmark of divisiveness over
who "owned" Thoreau, the hippies or the straights, the counterculture
communards or the traditionalist "huge audience among lovers of bird
and bush," as Richard Ruland described them in 1968 (1). Even as the
Thoreau Society held its annual meeting in mid-July in Concord in 1967
and visited Walden Pond, the stamp was appearing on the front page of
New York City's underground newspaper, the *East Village Other,* and
drawing queues of hippies to buy fifty-stamp sheets at postal windows
while several Thoreau societies lodged protests. That fall, on the West
Coast, in the classified ads of the alternative *Los Angeles Free Press,* amid
personals in search of "pretty young bisex fem" and "broadminded" couples, there appeared an enlarged reproduction of the Thoreau stamp (October 20, 1967: 31). The point both camps agreed upon was that Baskin's
Thoreau was a portrait of a hippie ("Postal 'Hippie' Art Is Going Over Big
with Hippies Here"). "Idolized by hippies," said a journalist of Thoreau,
while a *New York Times* reviewer fumed that *The Night Thoreau Spent in
Jail* made him "the first hippie" (Fenton, Barnes).

The identity involved much more than the beard and the informal
clothing. This hippie Thoreau, sacralized by the counterculture and its
sympathizers, becomes the figure entitled to identify Walden Pond as
"earth's eye." Thoreau's trope originated in a mind—a head—considered
to be precociously in synch with the Sixties counterculture, starting with
the eye itself. Emerson, in his essay "Nature," had deployed the figure
of the transcendently visionary "transparent eyeball" of a self through
whom "currents of the Universal Being circulate" and thereby attempted

15. Henry David Thoreau as Sixties "hippie" on U.S. postage stamp, designed by the artist Leonard Baskin, 1967.

to unify the human being with the outer world (*Selections,* 24). Additionally, from the late nineteenth century, a series of anthropologists had propounded the myth of a Native American devotion to Mother Earth whose "eyes are the lakes and ponds" (Gill, 132). In the mid-1940s, in his poem "The Eye," Robinson Jeffers, the poet of the Pacific shore, proclaimed the innocence of a Pacific oceanic "eyeball of water . . . the staring unsleeping / Eye of the earth" (123).

By the Sixties, the Thorovian "earth's eye" of Walden Pond received

recurrent and elaborated iterations that fit the era's preoccupation with illumination, dawning, and the ocular-visionary. One commune believed
all members could see into their fellow members' spirit with the " 'third
eye,' the center of spiritual insight located in the forehead" (Houriet,
354). *The Greening of America* proclaimed that "everything, from political
affairs to aesthetics" was now seen with "new eyes" (261). Psychedelic
posters featured the visionary eyeball, as in Rick Griffin's poster for Jimi
Hendrix, as did psychedelic art, such as Ernest Fuch's *Moses and the
Burning Bush*. A favorite crafts project was the construction of "god's eyes"
out of brightly colored yarn. (Fittingly, the term "the one I love" was a
psychedelic Sixties phonetic rendering of "the one-eye love.")

The Sixties thereby embraced the Thorovian optical epiphany reported
in "Civil Disobedience," when, released from prison after refusing to pay
his poll tax in support of a war-mongering U.S. government, Thoreau reported that "a change had to my eyes come over the scene." He now "saw"
clearly the oppression of the state and the fecklessness of his American village community (*Portable Thoreau*, 129–130). To the Sixties, this was the
Thorovian eye seeing clearly the injustice of the Vietnam War and America's racial inequality.

To the Sixties, moreover, Thoreau's was the head possessing an empa-
thetic knowledge of Native American ways. The alternative newspaper
Indianhead discussed environmental exploitation under this line: " 'Many
things I prize are being civilized off the face of the earth'—Thoreau"
(Van Zandt). Thoreau's was the head, in addition, that studied Eastern
thought. *The Shores of America*, Sherman Paul's study of Thoreau's "Inward Exploration," published in 1958, fostered a Sixties emphasis on
Thoreau's Easternism, including the development of his concept of spiritual heroism: "the Brahmin, merging with [Thoreau's] notion of the poet-
as-seer, became Thoreau's spiritual hero" and taught "the way of piety, the
activity of contemplation that directed one to a union with the spirit"
(Paul, 71, 74–75). The editor of the alternative paper the San Francisco
Oracle recommended Thoreau as "guru," the Hindu term for a preceptor
giving personal religious instruction (MacDonald, 154).

For a generation officially suspicious of anyone over the age of thirty,
this was a head identified as "*Young* Man Thoreau" (to cite Richard
Lebeaux's 1977 book title) who took up life at Walden Pond at age
twenty-eight. A 1967 *Saturday Review* article directed readers to the Norton edition of *Walden and Civil Disobedience*, advising "older people who
want to know what the younger generation is up to . . . [to] take a second
look at these publications, which many probably have not read since high

school days" (Woodring). To the generation rebelling against bourgeois customs and the industrial system, this was a head of clear diagnostic insight: "Men have become the tools of their tools. . . . Let us not be upset and overwhelmed in that terrible rapid and whirlpool called a dinner" (*Walden*, 350, 292). A 1967 *Time* magazine cover story on "The Hippies" emphasized this head that rejected consumerism: "The hippie philosophy borrows heavily from Henry David Thoreau, particularly in the West Coast rural communes, where denizens try to live the Waldenesque good life on the bare essentials . . . thus refusing the consumerism of 'complicating wants' of the U.S. economy" (20).

To a counterculture believing that a leisure society was just in the offing, it was Thoreau's head that saw an alternative to careerist entrapment and found a pathway for self-educational enlightenment. The stay in a cabin at Walden Pond was a paradigm for the future ("In warm evenings I frequently sat in the boat playing my flute" [174]). And this was a selective and excerptable Thorovian head, to be sure, not the writer obsessed by the polarities between work and labor as identified in recent criticism by Nicholas Brommel, or the writer Michael T. Gilmore has shown to be complicitous with the capitalist marketplace, or the writer surrounded by brutal dislocations of industrial capitalism of the earlier nineteenth century as mapped by Caroline Porter. To the counterculture, Thoreau was an anticapitalist American exemplar from an ideal rural past, and his name was invoked in terms of reverential approbation from the alternative press to the monographs of social theorists.

There is yet another, crucial reason why the Sixties counterculture claimed Thoreau, and this involves his psychedelic consciousness in its ability to identify a pond as the eye of the earth. Thoreau rejected medicinal "quack vials" and celebrated "undiluted morning air!" as his daily exhilarant, but to the Sixties, the air of Walden Pond was demonstrably psychedelic (138). Any counterculture reader could find in *Walden* the textual proof of Thoreau's psychedelic experience and thus verify his credentials as countercultural authority through whose agency the green movement could be advanced and its visionary center designated as "earth's eye."

A particularly useful text in this regard, perhaps ironically, is a social science study which was explicitly skeptical of the very "messianism" of Timothy Leary and the counterculture. The coauthors of *The Varieties of Psychedelic Experience* (1966) (the title a clear invitation to link it with William James's *Varieties of Religious Experience,* which it cites) assert a main interest "in exploring the full range of the consciousness-*changing*

16. Walden Pond—"earth's eye"—seen from Thoreau's Cove.

aspects of the psychedelic experience and in recording the phenomenology of that experience," which they describe in sum as "the apprehension of a world that has slipped the chains of normal categorical ordering" (Masters and Houston, 5).[5]

To approach *Walden* by way of the reportorial narratives in *The Varieties of Psychedelic Experience* is to encounter passages virtually identical to those of the Sixties psychedelics—for instance, Thoreau's statement that "if you stand right fronting and face to face to a fact, you will see the sun glimmer on both its surfaces, as if it were a [s]cimeter, and feel its sweet edge dividing you through the heart and marrow, and so you will happily conclude your mortal career" (98). A consuming rhapsody, this, to be sundered by the sun itself in an erotic, ecstatic moment.

Framed by Sixties psychedelic reports, the springtime sandbank episode in *Walden* becomes a singular and supreme moment of psychedelic transcendental ecstasy. The scene serves as the culmination of the year at Walden Pond. In it, Thoreau notices that the sandy clay of a railroad embankment, frozen all winter long, now has begun to thaw. "Few phenomena," he begins, "gave me more delight than to observe the forms which thawing sand and clay assume in flowing down the sides of a deep cut on the railroad through which I passed on the way to the village" (304). The bank, we are told, measures from twenty to forty feet high and extends for a quarter of a mile.

In a Sixties context, Thoreau's description of the thawing embankment can be approached via the narrative of a psychedelic "trip" taken by a forty-one-year-old musician and former journalist who first described "patterns of rich hues and abstract design," and then, following a series of disjunctive images, experienced "foliage [which] appeared to be a lush tropical garden, the wax-like leaves and blades of grass taking on a deep olive hue. It seemed as if I could distinguish every blade of grass" (Masters and Houston, 159). Another subject reported the "undescribable beauty of nature" experienced under the influence of LSD: "Leaves of the trees become as intricately patterned as great snowflakes and at other times resembled webs spun by God-inspired spiders of a thread of unraveled emeralds" (Masters and Houston, 11).

Thoreau, similarly, in the mid-nineteenth century had extended his range of imagery as if in free association in what the Sixties called psychedelic or "tripping." The sand on the railroad embankment "flows down the slopes like lava," then "takes the forms of sappy leaves or vines, making heaps of pulpy sprays a foot or more in depth," after which "you are reminded of coral, of leopards' paws or birds' feet, of brains or lungs or bowels, and excrements of all kinds." True to the disjunctive, nonlinear quality of a "head trip," Thoreau then becomes fascinated with the colors—"iron colors, brown, gray, yellowish and reddish" (307). He freely mixes images of earth and of the human body ("What is man but a mass of thawing clay? . . . Is not the hand a spreading palm leaf with its lobes and veins?" [548]). The references move the reader across the planet in a kind of strobe-light disjunction which flouts the very notion of a spatially orderly geographic itinerary presented in linear prose.[6]

Thoreau's psychedelic project was also of the mimesis of the head, not only in his self-portrait as intellectual cleaver and burrowing hands and feet ("my head is hands and feet . . . for burrowing" [98]) but as a perception of the earthly environ manifesting its own sculptural human face. Once again, the scene is the sandbank episode in springtime:

The ear may be regarded, fancifully, as a lichen, *umbilicaria,* on the side of the head, with its lobe or drop. The lip—*labium,* from *labor* (?)—laps or lapses from the sides of the cavernous mouth. The nose is a manifest congealed drop or stalactite. The chin is a still larger drop, the confluent dripping of the face. The cheeks are a slide from the brows into the valley of the face, opposed and diffused by the cheek bones. (307–308)

Here one encounters the green America ideal of the body-as-earth and earth-as-body, with Thoreau's vocabulary for the one interchangeable with the other. The sandbank sculpture is neither the Mt. Rushmore head of state nor Great Stone face but the earthly evocation of a generic human face in a kind of earth portrait insistent that each facial feature is of the earth and thus distinctly different from Mt. Rushmore, in which the heads come from the stone, emerge from the earth. Bear in mind, too, that Thoreau's earth-face demonstrates Alan Watts's injunction to gain "a respect for the external world as one's own body." And here, too, Thoreau is a compatriot of the Sixties psychedelics in feeling their "inner body as consisting of trees and vines, streams and waterfalls, hills and valleys" (Masters and Houston, 88). Subjects feel the "body as partaking of the substance of the earth or stone or grass on which [it] stands" (166). The researchers into psychedelic experience identify this as a "body-nature empathy or synonymity" (166). The subject, they find, may feel that his or her bodily substance now is "the same as that of some part of the environment . . . that his [or her] body or some part of it feels as if it has become the stone or clay upon which he [or she] stands, or that his [or her] hands have become like the water into which they were dipped" (166–167). (Alternatively, the experience can be one of the outside environment experienced as a bodily being, as in "the silver-surfaced river, bathed in fresh dawnlight, reflected trees reaching down as if yearning toward the heart of the earth" [11].)

Thoreau's appeal to the psychedelic Sixties is entirely understandable in this context. The counterculture claimed him as a Sixties contemporary because Thoreau so amply displayed his credentials as a psychedelic. It was not solely that he performed an act of civil disobedience to protest an immoral war or that he simplified life by retreating to a cabin in the woods, but that his intense sensate experiences were directly comparable to—even identical with—those of a hallucinogenic.

To read *Walden* as a psychedelic text in Sixties countercultural terms is thus to double its sacral identity. Just as Thoreau and Walden Pond were sacralized, so too was the realm of psychedelic drugs. "Both LSD and 'grass' are viewed by many hippies as the sacraments of their religion" (Yablonsky, 22). The texts are themselves a conflation of prayer and poetry (for example, in Timothy Leary's *Psychedelic Prayers,* many of which are formatted as poems). The idea of the sacred, combined both in Thoreau and in psychedelic drugs, made *Walden* an American Scripture for the Sixties and the pond a psychedelic ideal as "earth's eye." (Even the geologist Eugene Walker, who hypothesized the glacial causes of Walden Pond's fluctuating surface level in the Audubon Society magazine in 1971, could not resist anthropomorphizing the pond, which "rises and falls, as if breathing, in perfect harmony with its surroundings" [4].)

This, then, is the mentality locating the environmental identity of the head in America. Claimed as a *genius loci* of the Sixties counterculture, Thoreau provided in *Walden* the new homology which reverted not to the Americanized Napoleonic imperial gaze of Emerson's inscriptions but to the Thorovian embrace of Eastern thought in which the body, the mind, and the earth are experienced as one. The sandbank face is but one expression of this. Thoreau's trope of Walden Pond as earth's eye and, additionally, of its mouth and pulse and breast gave the Sixties counterculture a stable, enduring environmental model consonant with the newer politics of communitarianism and inward journey (*Walden,* 294, 181, 188). Unlike the springtime sandbank face, which is ephemeral, the pond is a stable geographic entity. Proof of Nature's nation, it participates in the tradition of spiritualization yet is measurable in physical terms (depth, length, width). Its ice is cut and harvested in winter, and it bathes Thoreau daily and floats his boat for evening pleasures. It is present in all weathers and seasons and in every year. The pond expressed the Sixties ideal of the expanded consciousness, allowing the "mind to descend into [the] body and redeem it" (*Walden,* 186, 222). The pond shows "circling dimples, in lines of beauty," these being the "gentle pulsing of its life, the heaving of its breast" (188). The pond is framed for earth's own personification as head: "A lake is the landscape's most beautiful and expressive feature. It is earth's eye; looking into which the beholder measures the depth of his own nature. The fluviatile trees next the shore are the slender eyelashes and cliffs around are its overhanging brows" (186). Thoreau meditates on the tonal colors of the "iris" of the Walden eye. Conditions of atmospheric light change it from sky blue to slate gray, to a yellow-tinged green "which gradually deepens to a uniform dark green in the body of the pond" (176). Unlike the Mt. Rushmore heads, imperiously distant in a stony gaze impossible to meet, the liminal pond-eye reciprocates the onlooker's gaze in an ever-deepening relationship commensurate with the depth of the gazer's own nature and abolishing the boundaries between them. The antithesis of the heads in authoritarian granite, the Thorovian embodied

earth and its visionary eye became the Sixties paradigm for communal human habitation on earth. Thoreau's inscription of Walden Pond validated
the green America mantra on identity, that "Nature is not some foreign element. . . . Nature is them" (Reich, 262).[7]

Minorities, Elites, Vegas, and the Marketplace

The Sixties green consciousness is nonetheless problematic. Despite the
ideality of "earth's eye" and the unity of self and the world beyond, the
green movement was implicated in racism (and has proved subject to a
corporate capitalist culture ever eager for marketplace appropriation). In
addition, it was vexed by a sexism disclosed in the development of the
women's movement. As Timothy Miller writes, the Sixties movement was
"male-defined"; a pronounced gap existed between "egalitarian hippie
rhetoric and male hippie actions," as indicated in the chauvinist dismissal
of women as "chicks" or "old ladies." "At least at first," Miller says, "the
male hippies were as disinclined as males elsewhere in society to allow
women equal rights and privileges" (15–16). It has been acknowledged
that the women's movement of the later twentieth century got its impetus
from the political skills learned by these same "chicks" and "old ladies"
who gained "the intellectual ammunition—the language and ideas—with
which to fight their own oppression," oppression institutionalized in
structures of capitalism and patriarchy (Echols, 153, 157). It can readily
be argued that the green America over whom Thoreau, the unitary male,
presides is one of males at liberty to seek gratification in an environment
consenting to male desires. In this sense, "earth's eye" is implicitly embodied in the female form which Annette Kolodny, in her study of American
literary texts, recognized as subject to subjection, including rape and con-
cubinage.

In racial terms, additionally, Malcolm X shows why Walden Pond was
not to be shared by blacks and other minorities. Quite simply, in a culture
based on the principle of privately owned property, a sense of partici-
patory ownership is crucial. Robert Frost's poem "The Gift Outright"
(which he read at the 1961 inauguration of President John F. Kennedy)
opens with the line "The land was ours before we were the land's," but an
African-Americanist viewpoint exposes the identity of the "ours" and the
"we" to show how much of the population, African Americans and other
residents of color, was excluded from that presumptive first-person plural
pronoun. Politically, the "we" is "a shortcut to authority that precludes an

honest relationship to existing traditions," as Marianna Torgovnick has observed. It "allows the writer to speak for the culture." It "coerces and assumes the agreement of the 'you' it addresses" and "masks the multifaceted complexity of group identities" (264).

Malcolm X puts the case in terms of ownership in a capitalist world in which whites owned African Americans' housing and sites of employment. The Nation of Islam was in part compelling to him and others precisely because it advocated African-American ownership of businesses and other property. In his *Autobiography,* when Malcolm envisions an African-American environmental site expressive of an autonomous human head, it is located, not surprisingly, far offshore, either in an idealized Muslim Middle East or in an idealized Africa, which was Malcolm's own self-identified place of origin.

Malcolm X's environmental expression of the African-American head, the "Holy World hilltop," is a spiritualized mountain similar to Martin Luther King's mountain from which Moses saw the Promised Land (*Autobiography,* 372). "I've been to the mountaintop," King said in his last speech, meant to rally striking sanitation workers in Memphis and delivered in 1968 on the eve of his assassination (*Essential Writings,* 286). But in "A Testament of Hope," published posthumously, King had also articulated the sociohistorical conditions blocking actual possession of that land and keeping it spatially and spiritually elusive:

> It is time that we stopped our blithe lip service to the guarantees of life, liberty and the pursuit of happiness. These fine sentiments are embodied in the Declaration of Independence, but that document was always a declaration of intent rather than of reality. There were slaves when it was written; there were still slaves when it was adopted; and to this day, black Americans have not life, liberty, nor the privilege of pursuing happiness, and millions of poor white Americans are in bondage that is scarcely less oppressive. (*Essential Writings,* 315)

The historical indictment couples here with King's acknowledgment of the ways in which racialization conceals class oppression across racial lines. The white leadership selects the manipulable black "leader" who is but a "figurehead," wrote King in "Black Power Defined" (*Essential Writings,* 308). He dismissed such a pseudo-leader as an irrelevant anachronism. Although Martin Luther King's methods of nonviolent protest have been traced to Gandhi by way of Thoreau's "Civil Disobedience," the site of the actual pond as represented in *Walden* itself forms no particular part of the African-American identity (Epps, 6–7). But though King, Malcolm X, Cleaver, and other African-American public figures did not participate directly in the siting of the Sixties "new head" environmentally, and though Malcolm X was severely critical of King, these leaders rejected the identity of "white heads on black bodies" and proved repeatedly how they took possession of their own heads.

Another problem of representation of the luminous green consciousness lay in its debasement—or rather its profanation. The mind-altering drugs through which Thoreau and Walden Pond were sacralized in terms of a new consciousness were also celebrated as part of a recreational hedonism, especially in Tom Wolfe's *Electric Kool-Aid Acid Test* (1968), an account of the journey of novelist Ken Kesey and his Merry Pranksters, made up of the author's friends and family, on a bus painted psychedelic colors traveling coast to coast while its occupants tripped on LSD, "speed or grass, or so many combinations thereof that they couldn't keep track" (69). Wolfe's narrative gestures toward the idea of "the experience of the holy" or "ecstatic" as a component of every world religion, but the "ecstasy" or "flash" of the Pranksters in *The Electric Kool-Aid Acid Test* is one of constant, unending, presentist carnival (113–116).

The scene in which the Pranksters encounter Timothy Leary's League for Spiritual Discovery sharply divides the psychedelic sacred from its profane, parallel universe. Titled "The Crypt Trip," the scene presents the Prankster bus arriving, uninvited, at the upstate Millbrook, New York, estate provided as a respite and study center for the families, followers, and associates of Leary, Ralph Metzner, and Richard Alpert (who later took the Hindu name Baba Ram Dass), coauthors of *The Psychedelic Experience: A Manual Based on The Tibetan Book of the Dead* (1964).

"Jumping off the bus yahooing . . . and going like hell," the Pranksters are received by "cool," "distant," and "dour" Learyites appalled by the Pranksters' "parody rendition of *The Tibetan Book of the Dead* . . . one of the Learyites' most revered texts" (93–95). Leary's own sequestering for a three-day drug trip, the text implies, signals a snobbish aloofness. Wolfe's tone, allied with the Pranksters' project, dismisses the Leary cohort and the Millbrook estate as "sepulchral and Gothic," its meditation centers "little sanctums," its atmosphere a "freaking frostiness . . . one big piece of uptight constipation" (94–95). The text exploits and adheres to the notion of psychedelic substances as agents of hilarity, uproariousness, "a creamy groove machine . . . good and noisy" (97, 195). The sacral, the tradition claimed by *Psychedelic Prayers* and by the green Walden, is dismissed in contempt.

But in fact Tom Wolfe's *Kandy-Kolored Tangerine-Flake Streamline Baby* (1965) had already veered far from the sacred in claiming psychedelia for the carnivalesque and capitalist profane. The counterculture, of course, heard Alan Watts teach that the Eastern way was a Buddhist path toward illumination, that "clarity—the disappearance of problems—suggests light" and that "in moments of such acute clarity there may be the physical sensation of light penetrating everything" (*This Is It,* 19).

American religious thought had shown an important precedent for this view a half century earlier, in *The Varieties of Religious Experience* (1902), in which William James, whom Alan Watts cited and quoted, pronounced the mystical experience as "*super*-lucent, *super*-splendent, *super*-essential, *super*-sublime, *super* everything that can be named" (417). In citing lucence and splendor, James approaches the key terms of illumination which Leary, Metzner, and Alpert offered as indices to the kind of psychedelic expression engaged in by writers, visual artists, designers of the psychedelic. The expanded consciousness would be one of "liberation, illumination, enlightenment" (Leary, Metzner, and Alpert, 12). It would be, in sum, of the light.

Yet Tom Wolfe, a charter member of the personalized new journalist school of writing, also understood that the psychedelic consciousness was emerging, not in the precincts of sociopolitical revolution or reformation or mysticism, or in the Beats' sacrosanct free American road, or even in the utopian communes, such as Morning Star Ranch north of San Francisco, in which peace and love were embraced in ambient drugs. Wolfe understood, instead, that psychedelic America was emerging in the crass, gangster-built vulgarian desert oasis of Las Vegas, and that its vocabulary was rooted in commerce and business.

Here is Wolfe's effort to evoke and represent Las Vegas, which the architects Robert Venturi, Denise Scott Brown, and Steven Izenour would decode in their classic *Learning from Las Vegas: The Forgotten Symbolism of Architectural Form* (1972). Indeed, the architects endorse Tom Wolfe as a "Pop" art writer (52). I quote him here as an avatar of the psychedelia of commerce, his *Electric Kool-Aid Acid Test* a bid to site the psychedelic head in the material culture of Las Vegas:

Such shapes! Boomerang modern supports, Palette Curvilinear bars, Hot Shoppe Cantilever roofs and a scalloped swimming pool. Such colors! All the new electrochemical pastels of the Florida littoral: tangerine, broiling magenta, livid pink, incarnadine, fuchsia demure, Congo ruby, methyl green, viridine, aquamarine, phenosafranine, incandescent orange, scarlet-fever purple, cyanic blue, tessellated bronza, hospital-fruit-basket orange. And such signs! Two cylinders rose at either end of the Flamingo—eight stories high and covered from top to bottom with neon rings in the shape of bubbles that fizzed all eight stories up into the desert sky all night long like an illuminated whisky-soda tumbler filled to the brim with pink champagne. (11)

The colors sound like cosmetic manufacturers' lipstick names, like chemical compounds, poisons, diseases, and a still-life version of the orchard now in thrall to agribusiness ("fruit-basket orange"). The prose, deliberately echoing Whitman's celebration of America ("The Shapes arise!") is also deliberately "psychedelic," Wolfe's attempt to capture in prose the consciousness altered by mind-altering drugs.

Wolfe's representation flouts the mystical, spiritual dimension of the new head. Blatantly tied to corporate culture in its most flagrant form, Las Vegas, the gambling casino desert oasis built by mobsters, is the shrine to greed and what Malcolm X scorned as American "Dollarism." In psychedelic terms, it is the Buddhist "Clear Light" debased and ridiculed. It is a capitalist psychedelia.[8] Tom Wolfe's Las Vegas is a site solely of sensate stimulation unredeemed by spiritual luminescence at any level.

And as the century drew to a close, Tom Wolfe's version of the profane, recreational psychedelia appeared increasingly in corporate America. Nightly for twenty years, 1976–1996, visitors to Disneyland lined up for the Main Street Electrical Parade, featuring parade floats illuminated by thousands of colored lights showing Disney characters and outlines of flags, locomotives, and a dragon referent to "Puff, the Magic Dragon" of the Peter, Paul, and Mary song, which has been doubly interpreted as a children's fable and as a reference to marijuana. Among the Disney light creatures were mushrooms, a sanitized echo of the Sixties psychedelic mushrooms depicted on the side panels of Janis Joplin's handpainted Porsche.

Although the Disney Electrical Parade has ceased, its "psychedelia" has spread in recent years and developed into the idea of the "retail entertainment complex" in the mid-South, the upper Midwest and the West Coast, in the Mall of America in Bloomington, Minnesota; the Forum Shops at Caesar's, Las Vegas; Ontario Mills, Ontario, California; Opry Mills in Nashville, Tennessee; and Downtown Disney at Lake Buena Vista, Florida. All feature "psychedelic" simulation of the kind Wolfe identified in the mid-1960s. Sixties psychedelia, in fact, submits to a theme-park Disney-fication in plans under way since Jerry Garcia's death for a "psychedelic interactive theater/theme park called *Terrapin Station*,"

17. Disneyland's Main Street Electrical Parade showcases
"Puff, the Magic Dragon."

named for a Grateful Dead song and album and sponsored by surviving
band members. As a project organizer says, "The technology available today makes the psychedelic light shows of the '60s look like, well, it's the
difference between an old fashioned stereo slide viewer and an Imax thea-
tre. . . . You'll walk in and things will happen to you that will blow your
socks off" (Schmitt; Strauss, B6).

   Corporate psychedelia extends beyond the theme park mall. Air trav-
elers passing through Chicago's O'Hare Airport via United Airlines'
"Terminal for Tomorrow" experience another corporate version of post-
Sixties psychedelia. Designed by architect Helmut Jahn (of Murphy/Jahn)

to recall the great European rail stations of the nineteenth century, the glass-vaulted terminal includes a psychedelic people-mover, a corridor of New Age music, and hallucinogenic lighting of a kinetic light sculpture entitled "The Sky's the Limit," commissioned from the California artist Michael Hayden, who designed the 744-foot sculpture composed of mirrors and of hundreds of neon tubes programmed in sequence to provide continuously changing patterns of light in colors ranging from indigo to blue, green, yellow, red and orange. The airline commissioned the composer William Kraft to write music to "highlight the transition from one sculptural environment to another."

We might go one step further, to suppose some of the United Airlines passengers to be businessmen wearing bright, colorful neckties, reproductions of the youthful psychedelic art of the Grateful Dead's Jerry Garcia, the neckties licensed from the late musician's estate and retailed nationwide in the late 1990s. We might guess that as their luggage clears the security scanner, the screen would reveal some high-status Birkenstock sandals, "earth shoes" for the affluent in their casual off-hours. We might suppose that the businessmen and their Brooks Brothers–suited women colleagues occasionally snack on Cherry Garcia ice cream or frozen yogurt, the name licensed to the Ben & Jerry Co. for its line of premium, expensive frozen dessert products.

This is not to denounce the neckwear per se, nor comfortable footwear, nor to impugn United Airlines' aesthetic judgment by which, as architect Jahn said, passengers were to be excited and pleased rather than "pushed through some basement-like concourse."[9] Nor is it to censure an ice cream manufacturer. It is, however, to point out that the incorporation of—and sales of—the psychedelic mentality in commercial products signals an end of countercultural political agency. It is to recognize, in addition, that the commercialization involves for-profit recreation and aesthetics available only to the more affluent segment of the population. The incorporation of the psychedelic really measures the demise of the democratizing green movement toward a new, liberated consciousness invitationally open to all. Psychedelia in this context is reduced to the category of the vestigial and nostalgic attainable in a commercial transaction.

In 1968 Kenneth Keniston identified the "post-modern" style as incorporative, inclusive and open to what he called "the alien" or otherness of every kind (278–279). Yet he observed that the counterculture was "highly dependent on national and international history" and that "they have put their personal fates more directly in the hands of politics and history than are the fates of most of their contemporaries" (217–218).

Politics and history, in a striking irony, are not at work to automate industrial production in order to enable the emergence of a spiritually profound leisure society, but rather to deindustrialize the United States and to relinquish or to relocate industrial production to the so-called developing areas of Asia and across the Mexican border in the name of "globalization." At the turn of the twenty-first century, Las Vegas contends for the public's disposable dollars with the green movement, Greenpeace, the Sierra Club, and various land trusts, and the environmental justice movement is stalled in the courts.

"Earth's eye," meanwhile, arguably continues in artifactual form in Montgomery, Alabama, at the memorial for Martin Luther King, designed by Maya Lin, the architect of the Vietnam Memorial on the Mall in Washington, D.C. Lin's design for the civil rights memorial features a granite wall glazed with flowing water and bearing an inscription—"Until justice rolls down like waters and righteousness like a mighty stream"—taken from King's address "The American Dream" (1961). In it King called for a worldwide, transnational moral consciousness, and he cited "the poet Thoreau" as an authority on the errant direction of the so-called civilized world (*Essential Writings*, 211, 216).

Visitors—or pilgrims—to the Montgomery memorial not only read these words inscribed on a granite wall behind the shimmering waters but, in addition, tend to gather round to touch with outstretched palms the equally smooth-flowing water coating the polished granite circle which is positioned in front and to the side of that wall. As if reading Braille, the visitors feel the very words on that circle with their fingertips, apparently absorbing the import of the radial print lines which commemorate the crucial political and legislative events in the struggle for the attainment of civil rights: "BLACK STUDENTS STAGE SIT-IN," "MEDGAR EVERS ASSASSINATED," "PRESIDENT JOHNSON SIGNS CIVIL RIGHTS ACT OF 1964."

Lin calls the surface a "water table" and the inscriptions "a time line over which water flows" *(Maya Lin)*. These words and phrases are not linear but radiate, irislike, from the center of the circle in a tactile monument formally denoting sight and vision and its bodily expression. Lin's design, which features water as a "primary element," pays homage to the oasis, its granite fashioned not into the Rushmorean head but the Waldenesque lake, earth's eye.

It must be recognized, however, that the very fact of the memorial conveys a message of containment, of memory enshrined but safely relegated to the past. The interests served by this commemoration are not only those of civil rights supporters but those of collective established authority

18. Civil Rights Memorial, designed by Maya Lin,
Montgomery, Alabama.

in a capitalist political economy. Lin herself referred to the Montgomery
project as one in which "you begin to memorialize history." In this context, the very material of the Montgomery Civil Rights Memorial is inadvertently ironic, the granite form of earth's eye serving the ideological
interests of those paying tribute to a new consciousness that is not dy-
namically engaged but, on the contrary, is historically petrified. It gives a
particularly ironic twist to King's desire, expressed in "The American
Dream," that "with this faith we will be able to hew out of the mountain
of despair a stone of hope" (219).

As for Walden Pond in the post-Sixties turn of the twenty-first century,
it continues as a touchstone of an idealized, pristine America, which per
force critiques social trends, as in the oppositional juxtapositioning of "the
mall . . . *vs.* Walden Pond" (Raeburn, 14). It continues, too, as the "decen-

tralized" yet sacred version of itself, as when a New Yorker writes, "I suspect that Central Park in winter is for me what Walden Pond was for Thoreau" (Ascher). At the pond itself, between 1984 and 1986, a Thorovian classroom teacher from Nevada, David Barto, donned corduroys and a muslin shirt and pocketed a wood flute to act the role of Thoreau for tourists, reciting lengthy passages verbatim from *Walden* (categorized by sunrise, dogs, civil disobedience, and so on), convinced that "Thoreau is the highest form of teaching you can do" (Goldberg). When funds for his seasonal performances at the pond were depleted, Barto took his Thoreau act to the Cape Cod National Seashore.

The pond continues its recreational usage, with walking trails and a swimming beach. In the summer of 1999 park rangers waved people away from parking lots that were full by mid-morning in a summer heat wave. The following fall, middle schoolers took history field trips by bike to the pond, while seasonal employees of the Walden Pond State Reservation awaited wages owed to them but unpaid as the Massachusetts legislature debated the state budget.

One notable Sixties-related Walden episode bears notice here. In May 1989, the National Trust for Historic Preservation put Walden Woods, a twenty-five-acre tract near the pond, on its list of Eleven Most Endangered Places. Together with business partners, the developer Mortimer Zuckerman, then publisher of the *Atlantic Monthly,* had proposed the construction of a 139-unit residential condominium complex on the site of Walden Woods. Conservation groups nationwide voiced opposition, including the Thoreau Country Conservation Alliance. The months-long dispute was settled when rock and roll star Don Henley, formerly of the Eagles, assumed co-chairmanship of the Walden Woods Project and led a drive to raise funds to purchase the tract for a permanent land trust, while an alternate site was sought for the construction of moderate-income housing. Benefit concerts organized by Henley featured Sixties musicians Arlo Guthrie, Jimmy Buffett, and Bonnie Raitt. It is fitting that the energy and initiative for the preservation effort should have come from high-profile figures of the Sixties, those most self-identified with Thoreau as counterculture confrere ("Saving Thoreau's Pond").

The scriptural *Walden* of the psychedelic Sixties, however, had become the mere screed of the late twentieth century, a source more of piety than of sociocultural activism. The Thorovian head rebukes Mt. Rushmore but does not, finally, supplant it. And the socioeconomic conditions under which white American elites of the late nineteenth century feared insurrection by the violent, dark bodies of immigrants and strikers provoke periodic racial violence in the increasingly poor black cities from which whites and affluent people of color, male and female, remove themselves to take shelter in gated suburban subdivisions in which the green America is serviced by Chem-Lawn.

Some of Allen Ginsberg's poems anticipated this direction in terms of the eye—or "Eye." While still in college, studying Buddhism, he wrote of beginning to understand "the vastness and intelligence" of Asian mentalities (Schumacher, 153). Figures of eyes and eyeballs recur throughout his poems, and on the verge of the Sixties, in "American Change" (1958), Ginsberg read the nation's coins and bills as indices of its values, singling out the 1935 one-dollar bill with its "holy outstaring Eye sectioned out of the aire" and comprising "the Great Seal of our Passion, Annuit Coeptis, Novus Ordo / Seclorum" (*Collected Poems*, 187).

From Ginsberg's viewpoint, it was not "earth's eye" that prevailed, then, but the head trip of the Foucaultian panopticon of money and power which the poet disclosed in "Television Was a Baby Crawling toward That Deathchamber" (1961), featuring a

. . . . money-center of the mind
whose Eye is hidden somewhere behind All mass media—what makes reporters fear their secret dreamy news—behind the Presidential mike
& all its starry bunting, front for some mad BILLIONAIRES
who own United Fruit & Standard Oil and Hearst the Press and Texas
NBC and someone owns the Radios owns vast Spheres of Air—
(*Collected Poems*, 276–277)

In this context, the mystical oceanic pond of Robinson Jeffers's Pacific seems prophetic as a site actually of transpacific commerce, the very air mapped and sold for passenger and cargo "service." As for the new "earth's eye" of the green America, it would not be modeled on Walden Pond but centered in the symbol of commerce, trade, and material things—as Ginsberg foretold, on the American dollar bill. The ideal American green "eye" of Nature's nation would not be of the earth but of finance. It would be accorded value in an Argus of infinite arithmetic multiples of itself controlled and deployed to set the terms of power, status, rights and privilege. At the turn of the twenty-first century, it would not be the visionary oasis but a signifier, instead, of the global economy.

II

Frontier Incarnations

3

Pittsburgh at Yellowstone: Old Faithful and the Pulse of Industrial America

Moving westward, the frontier became more and more American. . . . The unequal rate of advance compels us to distinguish the frontier into the trader's frontier, the rancher's frontier, or the miner's frontier, and the farmer's frontier.

—FREDERICK JACKSON TURNER, "The Significance of the Frontier in American History," 1893

Looking down over the forests as you approach [the geysers], you see a multitude of white columns, broad reeking masses, and irregular jets and puffs of misty vapor . . . entangled like smoke . . . suggesting the factories of some busy town.

—JOHN MUIR, "The Yellowstone National Park," 1898

When the historian Frederick Jackson Turner delivered his address to the American Historical Association in Chicago in 1893, he used the 1890 national Census to argue the demise of the frontier era of American history. The nation's demographics showed a "broken" frontier line which, according to Turner, proved the conclusion of the American frontier settlement period ("Frontier," 1). Turner's address thereby relegated the entire territorial expanse of the United States—including Yellowstone National Park and its geysers—to postfrontier status.

Turner's tone was more celebratory than elegiac as he emphasized that American history—frontier history—was principally a story of the great

West, of nation building, and of democracy. The frontier, he asserted, had been "productive of individualism" and had promoted "the expansive character of American life" (30, 37). It enabled "escape from bondage of the past" and "furnish[ed] a new field of opportunity" (38). Nonetheless, he said, "the frontier has gone" (38).

John Muir's statement on Yellowstone geysers' resembling "the factories of some busy town" seems in full accord with Turner, who had characterized the frontier as a scene of birch canoes, hunting shirts and moccasins, not of foundries and manufacture. The notion of a factory in the forests of Yellowstone seems thus to corroborate Turner's argument that "this first period of American history" had "closed" (38).

Although the frontier episode of which Turner wrote could be declared closed, the term itself, however, was to continue to circulate vigorously in American culture. *Frontier* would be reprised endlessly in the future, revivified at every point to certify a robust and venturesome American character. Indeed, to the trader's, rancher's, miner's, and farmer's frontiers of Turner's mantra, one might add the national park tourist's frontier.

The eastern-affiliated industrial city and the natural western "Wonderland" seem geographically worlds apart in late nineteenth-century America, and it is startling to see them joined, especially by John Muir, the writer most closely identified with the American wilderness and its preservation. Industrial Pittsburgh, which a travel writer in 1883 called the "iron city" of the "outer edge of the infernal regions" (Glazier, 332) was ordinarily represented as a polar opposite of Yellowstone National Park, which became a tourist "Wonderland" after the 1870s, when a mix of writers, photographers, illustrators, publishers, and corporations, notably the Northern Pacific Railroad, repositioned its public identity so that it became what John Muir called "a big wholesome wilderness" ("Yellowstone," 37). As a naturalist, a proponent of the national park system, and founder of the Sierra Club, John Muir helped establish the park's new identity with his profile "The Yellowstone National Park" (1898).

While Pittsburgh was profiled as "the domain of Vulcan" (Glazier, 333), Muir usually avoided such references to Yellowstone, mainly portraying it as the site of wonders and delights, a scene where fountains splash, lakes shine, and rivers sing as the conservationist's language exhibits the assonance and alliteration that unify the natural features of the park and verify the initial designation of the area as benignly "wholesome" ("Yellowstone," 37, 70).

In Muir's Yellowstone, "the greatest of American rivers take their rise . . . [to] a densely forested and comparatively level volcanic plateau . . .

surrounded by an imposing host of mountains" ("Yellowstone," 37). Muir reassuringly conflates the shocks of "earthquakes, volcanoes, geysers, storms" with "the pounding of waves, the uprush of sap in plants" and confides to his reader that "each and all tell the orderly love-beats of Nature's heart" ("Yellowstone," 70). The "heavy pall of smoke," typical of American industrial cities such as Pittsburgh (Glazier, 332), was by no means the central descriptor in Muir's essay on Yellowstone, which celebrated a doubly gendered national park of both "Mother Earth" and "Nature working . . . like a man," a park in which weather, geothermal eruptions, and seasonal botanic cycles all evince cardiovascular health and beneficence to humankind ("Yellowstone," 50, 73).

In bodily terms of the "orderly love-beats of Nature's heart" (70), Muir discloses the apparent cardiovascular system of America. The heads of Mt. Rushmore were excavated from the granite peaks of South Dakota in order to attract automobile tourism to the state, and, as we have seen, Muir's strong-limbed sequoias, with their domed heads and god-like composure, together with rock formations in "majestic repose," promoted the idea of white male supremacy manifest in the Rushmore sculptures as if it were inherent in the very rock of Nature's nation. Muir took a position largely consonant with that of Frederick Jackson Turner, who identified the western frontier as "stalwart and rugged," strong, practical, and masterful (*Frontier,* 15). This, Turner argued, is the quintessential America (15, 37). Muir's sequoias and majestic rocks embody those values.

Muir, however, actually invoked a different bodily center when he invited visitors to Yellowstone to feel those "orderly love-beats of Nature's heart." The presidential heads would signify white male American leadership foreordained both naturally and nationally, but Yellowstone exhibited a complementary and equally foreordained bodily identity. Its geyser, Old Faithful, became the beating heart of Nature's nation, the very pulse of a paradoxically pristine yet industrial America, one which allied Pittsburgh and similar industrial cities to the far west.

We must recall that Yellowstone's earlier identity was as not a wonderland but a hell on earth. It was Frontier-as-Inferno. A significant part of Yellowstone's shift to the new geophysical identity involved representation of the human body, as Muir's essay indicates in its male and female images. In the latter decades of the century, as Yellowstone and its geyser region became identified as an American Wonderland, texts supporting the newer identity proliferated.

In part, the bodily terms in texts on Yellowstone operated as a familiarizing stratagem whereby the distant alien land of rocky mountain ranges, erupting geysers, mud volcanoes, boiling springs, and the like became more conceptually accessible, enticing visitors to a friendly frontier accessible by rail. Some 5,438 traveled there in the summer of 1895, 9,579 in 1899, the increase due largely to the easing of economic conditions following the panic of 1893 and the heavy promotion in railroad flyers. (The Northern Pacific printed the words "Yellowstone National Park Route" on each page of its brochures.) One visitor of 1887, Francis Sessions, positioned Yellowstone this way: "Nearly as large as the state of Connecticut, situated in the heart of the Rocky Mountains, about one thousand miles from St. Paul on the east and about the same from Portland, Oregon, on the west" (Sessions, 435).

Sessions's reference to the "heart" of the Rockies fits Muir's reference to "the very heart-joy of earth" in "the wild parks of the West" (*Our*, 282, 1– 36). The heart, in fact, is but one of the bodily terms pervasive in the discourse of the new Yellowstone, though attention to the role of figuration of the human body in texts on Yellowstone from the 1870s to the 1920s reveals the "double discourse of the natural and the technological" (Selt-

19. Yellowstone National Park visitors of the 1910s set out from Gardner Station for day trips by coach to geysers and other sights.

zer, 152). This discourse, especially focused on the geyser Old Faithful, produced an icon of industrial America. To recognize this is to see the basis on which the geyser area also became a text on the sociocultural disjunctions of the new industrial order.

Prior to a series of explorations beginning in 1869, the Yellowstone area was known as "Colter's Hell," a tall-tale scene of "burning plains, immense lakes, and boiling springs" encountered by a few white trappers, hunters, and mountaineers dating back to John Colter's foray in the area in 1807–1808, when he split off from the Lewis and Clark expedition and ventured into Yellowstone (Kinsey, 45–46). Colter was not alone, for another of the first white male explorers of the region, James Bridger, had called it "a place where hell bubbles up" ("Yellowstone Park as a Summer Resort," 248).

Such descriptions fit earlier nineteenth-century fables of the Far West as a Great American Desert, including "scenes of barrenness and desolation," of "the most dismal country" riddled with man-eating grizzlies, of "dismal and horrible mountains," of the "desert," of endless plains "on which not a speck of vegetable matter existed" (Lawton-Peebles, 224–225). In order for the Yellowstone area to become credible as a national park and tourist "Wonderland," as it was called by the *Helena Daily Herald* in 1872, it was necessary that it be assigned a new public identity.

This was achieved, as we shall see, in part by bodily images appearing in both travel and expeditionary texts. But the whole process of Yellowstone's reidentification has been documented as a part of the larger post–Civil War project by which the trans-Mississippi West, heretofore understood to be the Great American Desert, now became a pathway to the "Edenic civilization that would occur as Americans entered the region, settled there, exploited its natural resources, and made the West over in their desired image" (Hales, 46–47). In the case of Yellowstone, "Wonderland" replaced the inferno in expeditionary reports by Nathaniel P. Langford (1871) and especially by Ferdinand V. Hayden (1872), who extolled the beauty and "magnificent features" of the area (Kinsey, 83). These were augmented by guidebooks describing Yellowstone's majesty, beauty, enchantment, and by travel writing in the following decades in middle-class magazines such as *Harper's New Monthly Magazine, Scribner's, National Geographic,* and the *Atlantic Monthly,* whose essays recounted inspiring visits and beckoned readers to visit the park for health, adventure, and edification. Throughout, one finds a rhetorical strategy using bodily figures to emphasize maternal succor and masculine guardianship.

Yellowstone's new identity was also achieved by visual media, such as the Hayden party's expeditionary photographs by William Henry Jackson. These showed male, shaft-like rock formations and female valleys, along with canyons and waterfalls in compositional terms that "continued the Romantic landscape tradition" (Hales, 50). Alan Trachtenberg, discussing the work of Timothy O'Sullivan, another postbellum photographer of the West, remarks that such photographs belong to the tradition of landscape art as a particular genre of academic painting (128).

Painting also played a major role in establishing the new identity of Yellowstone. The painter Thomas Moran, also with the Hayden group, sketched scenes that provided illustrations for essays in *Scribner's* on "The Wonders of Yellowstone" and for James Richardson's *Wonders of the Yellowstone* (1872). Probably more important, Moran became nationally known for his huge (7 × 12 feet) oil painting, *The Grand Cañon of the Yellowstone* (1872), which was publicly exhibited in the U.S. Capitol and instrumental in the creation of the park by an act of Congress signed into law by President Ulysses S. Grant in March 1871, setting the region aside as "a great national park or pleasure ground for the benefit and enjoyment of the people."[1] In the painting, as in a series of his watercolors, Moran's compositional exploitation of arches, towers, rocks and trees, together with his adaptation of the aesthetic principles of John Ruskin and the painterly techniques of J. M. W. Turner in capturing atmospheric effects and color, enabled Moran to translate Yellowstone as a landscape of the American sublime, a response codified earlier in the century in relation to America's first icon of nature, Niagara Falls (Kinsey, 20–40; McKinsey, 30–36, 99). In Moran's painting, shafts of rock and tree trunks frame a wide deep valley from which a central column of white mist rises skyward. In bodily terms, one recalls Perry Miller's statement on late nineteenth-century representations of steam as "the pure white jet that fecundates America," inseminating the "body of the continent" (qtd. Seltzer, 27).

Business, too, was centrally involved in the transformation of Yellowstone from "a place where hell bubbles up" to the new Wonderland. *Scribner's* evidently funded the exhibition of Moran's huge canvas in Clinton Hall on New York's Astor Place, just as it published numerous Moran-illustrated essays on the area, including John Muir's. In addition, executives and financiers of the Northern Pacific Railroad understood the advantages of a sublime, enticing Yellowstone to generate income from passengers, freight, and stockholders (Kinsey, 64). Subliminally, at least, that phallic shaft of steamy white mist central to Moran's *Grand Cañon of the Yellowstone* looked enough like locomotive steam to appeal to such groups. The financier Jay Cooke was instrumental in the promotion of the new image of Yellowstone as an example of western grandeur, and

20. *The Grand Cañon of the Yellowstone,* by Thomas Moran. Oil on canvas, 1872.

after the collapse of his empire in 1873, the reorganized company continued its public relations campaign on behalf of the area. Joni Louise Kinsey writes of this group of businessmen, artists, and explorers: "Through their collective efforts, [Yellowstone] was transformed from a remote hell on earth into America's wonderland in the public imagination. . . . By 1890 the demonic perceptions of the place . . . were thoroughly transformed. Yellowstone had become, to the eager tourists and the corporations, a wonderland that promised unlimited rewards" (58, 78).

The vocabulary of the human body consistently figured in the transformation of the West and of Yellowstone in particular. One may presuppose that the rock shafts and deep ravines and gorges visually represented in photographs, woodcuts, and oil canvases conveyed a sexualized message of phallic and yonic forms. But an explicit bodily vocabulary can be found in the numerous print texts on Yellowstone. Incongruous as it may seem that texts sustaining the landscape tradition should revert to bodily figuration, the centuries-old practice of delineating geographic traits in bodily terms served the purposes of travel and expeditionary writers, who also followed rhetorical convention from the previous century, such as one typical late eighteenth-century verse on the American continent "where Oregon foams along the West, / And seeks the fond Pacific's tranquil breast" (Lawton-Peebles, 239; see Kolodny).

Breasts, faces, and the other physical features recurring regularly in the production of Yellowstone-as-Wonderland in middle-class American magazines from the 1870s to the 1920s for the most part do so in heterosexually normative terms. The mountains, like sentinels (presumably male bodies in military posture), "keep watch and ward over this bewilderingly beautiful handiwork of Nature's own" (Armstrong, 562). The object of the sentinels' vigilance is in part the adjectivally female Yellowstone Lake, "a beautiful body of water" (though elsewhere, in another text, the lake is depicted as shaped like the wounded hand of a German army veteran [Dale, 6]).

Some writers feminized the park in terms of maternal succor and the production of a milk-white snow: "The headwaters of the Missouri, Colorado, and Columbia rivers are all suckled here from the same breast of snow" (Comstock, 48), and Lake Yellowstone is "nestled in the bosom of the Rocky Mountains" ("Washburn Expedition, 2," 489). Late nineteenth-century texts also codify Yellowstone National Park as a sentient being expressive of feelings. The "mood" of Yellowstone Lake, for instance, "is ever changing." It "laughs" and then turns "angry" ("Washburn Expedition, 2," 490).

John Muir feminizes the park in terms of "Mother Earth" but moves anatomically inside the body when he says park visitors are "getting in touch with the nerves of Mother Earth" ("Yellowstone," 50, 2). Muir's image is significant for its anatomical internalization, a direction that other writers also followed. In 1893, in *The Significance of the Frontier,* Frederick Jackson Turner remarked that "civilization in America has followed the arteries made by geology . . . like the steady growth of a complex nervous system for the originally simple, inert continent" (14–15). Ferdinand Hayden explicitly linked the railroad's utilitarian relation to this geological arterial system: "The multitude of rivers that wind like arteries through the country . . . excavate the avenues for our railroads" (Hales, 69).

This textual mapping of the area in terms of internal organ systems is significant because it enables the production of certain social meanings that devolve from the traits of those organs, including arterial blood flow and cardiac pulse. The arterial rivers conjoin, in cardiovascular terms, with the heart, and not surprisingly, the April 5, 1873, *Harper's Weekly Magazine* included an article entitled "The Heart of the Continent: The Hot Springs and Geysers of the Yellow Stone Region" (273–274).

The heart-as-center was, of course, a centuries-old convention but gained a certain agency from the dictum of Ralph Waldo Emerson, whose American scholar is not only "the world's eye" but "the world's heart"

("American Scholar," 73). Cardiac vitality is correlatively located at the center of the Emersonian universe: "The heart at the centre of the universe with every throb hurls the flood of happiness into every artery, vein and veinlet, so that the whole system is inundated with the tides of joy" (*Society and Solitude,* 306–307). In "The Yellowstone National Park," Muir, the self-proclaimed student and admirer of Emerson, asserted, "The shocks and outbursts of earthquakes, volcanoes, geysers, storms, the pounding of waves, the uprush of sap in plants, each and all tell the orderly love-beats of Nature's heart" (70).

The health of that heart was measured in a pulse manifested by Old Faithful geyser. In his essay on Yellowstone, Muir describes "a hundred geysers," though Old Faithful was, then as now, preeminent. Named by Nathaniel P. Langford and Gustavus C. Doane, who had written of the Yellowstone area prior to congressional action establishing the park in 1871, Old Faithful is repeatedly singled out as exemplary.

It is the "most instructive" geyser, wrote Hayden in 1872: "When it is about to make a display, very little preliminary warning is given. There is simply a rush of steam for a moment, and then a column of water shoots up vertically into the air, and by a succession of impulses is apparently held steadily up for the space of fifteen minutes" (Hayden, "Hot Springs," 175). In 1878, Joseph Le Conte identified the trait—punctual regularity—for which Old Faithful is best known. " 'Old Faithful,' " he wrote, "is so called from the frequency and regularity of its eruptions, throws up a column six feet in diameter to the height of 100 to 150 feet *regularly every hour* and plays each time fifteen minutes" (412, emphasis added).

Like Le Conte's, numerous texts from the 1870s cite the unvarying regularity of Old Faithful, always in terms of approval and admiration. It is "the only reliable geyser in the park. You can always bet on seeing him every sixty-five minutes" (Francis, 34). "There has been no appreciable difference in its eruptions for over thirty years" (Hague, "Yellowstone," 523). "It always displays the same graceful, slender column . . . *the* geyser of the park" (Weed, "Geysers," 294). Old Faithful sets "a noble example to his followers . . . and [is] punctual [as] a tall, old-fashioned clock" (Rollins, 886). It is "the perfect geyser," the "model geyser" (Hague, "Yellowstone," 517). "Old Faithful is a friend to every tourist. . . . With the regularity of a clock, he pours out his soul toward heaven every sixty minutes and then sinks back to regain new strength" (F. King, 597).

The very name—*Old* Faithful—connotes the cherished, familiar, and dear. The geyser becomes an object of affection because of its very predictability, its punctuality. The hotel beside it would be named the Old Faithful Inn, as if hospitality itself were linked to the geyser, as if it performed intentionally for the visitors who had endured the inconvenience of travel here and elsewhere in order to experience what John Sears has called the "sacred places," the sacralized tourist sublime associated throughout the century with such sites as Niagara Falls, Kentucky's Mammoth Cave, and Yosemite. More than one writer said the road traveled to the geysers was "dull, dusty, glaring, and disappointing," but if Old Faithful failed to meet expectations, no one but Rudyard Kipling said so in print (Rollins, 872). This cherished, sacred Old Faithful is clearly central to Emerson's and Muir's idea of the organic, benevolent heart of the natural world.

Yet texts from the 1870s–1920s indicate that the sociocultural definition of Old Faithful changed radically from the version embraced in the rhetoric of Emerson and Muir. Pulse itself becomes a crucial term in this change. Numerous commentators characterized geyser eruptions as pulsations. *"The geyser,"* said one writer in 1890, "is a pool of limpid, green water whose surface rises and falls in rhythmic pulsations . . . at every pulsation, thick white clouds of steam came rolling out." A group in 1882 observed "nine successive pulsations" of the geyser named simply Grand. Many of the "springs . . . rise and fall every second or two . . . with each pulsation, [by] . . . steady impulses, . . . regular pulsations" (Weed, "Geysers," 291; "Washburn Expedition, 1," 437; Francis, 35; Hayden, "Hot Springs," 163, 174).

The pulse in these statements reverts to the arterial pulse, which in medical history is both mechanistic and organic. Texts such as Muir's ally the geysers' rhythms with those of waterfalls, storms, and avalanches, and thus position them with the rhythms of nature (54). The mechanistic, however, reverts to the many references to the steady, regular, clocklike pulsations and eruptions affirmed in the tributes to Old Faithful quoted above. In regard to Old Faithful, the relation of the organic-mechanic is neither a binary division nor an antithesis but a conjunction. The geyser operates as nature's own clockworks.

The regularity of Old Faithful's pulse had a crucial connection to medical history linking the body to the clock. Since the early eighteenth century the arterial pulse had been measured by the clock, when Sir John Floyer published *The Physician's Pulse Watch* (1707), an account of his invention of a mechanical watch with a second hand subsequently standard in timepieces. The sixty-second minute thus became the standard for pulse measurement. Floyer measured patients with "exceeding and deficient pulses," and these he worked to reregulate. Those that beat too fast or too slowly, according to the measurement of the pulse watch, were treated with medical regimens involving heat and cold. Life consists,

Floyer theorized, "in the Circulation of blood, and that running too fast or slow, produces most of our Diseases" (Clendening, 573–574). The healthy body was that whose pulse throbbed in synchrony with the measurement of the pulse watch.

By the late nineteenth and early twentieth centuries, medical experts agreed that "changes of the pulse are important" and recognized a normative range of healthy pulsations even as they named irregularities or arrhythmias, separated the arterial from the venal and hepatic pulses, and devised new instruments for measurement, such as the sphygmograph, which showed the pulse in a series of curves (Barwell, 89; Osler, *Principles,* 650–651). One specialist wrote in 1902, "The rate of the pulse is the most simple of all signs" and "variations in rhythm are usually readily recognized," though "the timing of the various events in a cardiac revolution . . . can only be acquired by careful practice . . . with the radial pulse as a standard" (Mackenzie, 6, viii).

Old Faithful, as we have seen, was celebrated for its hourly pulse measured radially. It met the standard of the sixty-second minute encapsulated within the sixty-minute hour. Its health was proven by its very regularity over decades.

Yet the pulse regularity of Old Faithful involved more than the apparent synchrony of nature with human horology. Muir tries to adhere to the organic model of the Emersonian "heart at the centre of the universe with every throb hurl[ing] the flood of happiness into every artery, vein and veinlet," but other writers, and even Muir himself, were responding to a new model of the body as machine (see Seltzer, Banta).

As Mark Seltzer has shown in *Bodies and Machines* (1992), ideology was convertible into biology in the late nineteenth and early twentieth centuries, with the previous distinction "between the life process and the machine process" now collapsed (159). This new body-machine conflation is evident, for instance, in the writings of William Osler, the preeminent physician-teacher-researcher at the University of Pennsylvania and the Johns Hopkins medical school, one of the founders of modern clinical medicine, and author of a major, much reprinted medical textbook, *The Principles and Practice of Medicine* (1895). Osler wrote extensively on the cardiovascular system in terms of mechanization and focused on the very kind of privileged white male bodies responsible for the new capitalist economic and industrial system. His patient, a "man of great vigor" who "lived a business life of the greatest possible intensity," the "hustling life of Wall Street," who "regarded himself as 'hard as nails,' " nonetheless failed to realize "that he is a machine" (5).

As such, Osler insists, his heart is a "pump," while the small arteries act as "stopcocks" or "taps" which, stimulated, become "sluice-gates to be open or shut." Each cell is a "factory." Diet should be temperate, says Osler, food intake "just enough to keep the engines running at steady speed" (13).

The physician extends a cardiovascular analogy to an irrigation system with supply pipes, pump, and sluices. Symptoms such as vertigo, head-aches, anginal attack, palpitations, and sclerotic arteries are attributable to "difficulty in clearing of ashes and cinder [from] the furnaces which keep up the fires of life in every unit of the bodily frame," as if "the engines are stoked for the Glasgow express . . . but put to work shunting empty trucks in the station yard" (7). Osler worried that the relentless "high pressure" pace of business and the professions (presumably including his own) gave the bodily "engines no rest" so that bodies at age fifty were "only fit to be scrapped" (8). Osler does compare cardiovascular obstructions to "weedy channels" in the farm fields and urges the patient with high blood pres-sure to "cultivate his garden," but the garden is technologically structured as a site of agricultural engineering.

The mechanistic body as produced by Osler converges conceptually with the pulse mechanism of Old Faithful. But the repositioning of Yel-lowstone as the U.S. Wonderland included such technologizing not only of the body but, additionally, of the material environment that was thought to be correlative with it. The post–Civil War decades not only redefined the body but witnessed the transformation of the Northeast and Midwest into industrial centers. This transformation, too, is important to the specific ways in which bodily identity produced Old Faithful as a bodily icon of industrial America.

The industrializing American scene is acknowledged in Muir's "Yellow-stone National Park" despite the preponderance of pastoral and domestic terms that bid to identify Yellowstone as a designed park on the order of Frederick Law Olmsted's Central Park or Fenway or Philadelphia's Fairmount Park. Muir's terms are organic, the very mineral formations turned into flowers.

Abruptly, however, Muir invokes a radically different environment as he describes the geyser basin. It is as if "a fierce furnace fire were burning beneath each" geyser, "hissing, throbbing, booming," writes Muir. "Look-ing down over the forests as you approach [the geysers]," he adds, "you see a multitude of white columns, broad reeking masses, and irregular jets and puffs of misty vapor . . . entangled like smoke . . . suggesting the fac-tories of some busy town" (43).

The factories of some busy town. So the "fierce furnace," the noises of hissing, throbbing, and booming recall the industrial landscape thousands of miles east of Yellowstone, which, ironically, is the very landscape preserved in its natural splendor from the encroachment of industrialism. The sublime Yellowstone of William Henry Jackson's photographs, of Thomas Moran's huge painting, of the railroad guidebooks and flyers, for that matter of Muir's own crafting, suddenly is challenged by an apparently incongruous, even antithetical, overt image of industrial America.

Comparing the geyser area to "the factories of some busy town," Muir's diction collapses the boundaries between the two worlds of nature's Wonderland and technological industrialism. The writer whose name had become synonymous with naturalism and conservation, with appreciation

21. Geyser-like vapors from industrial chimneys of Pittsburgh, Pennsylvania. Detail from postcard, 1910s.

22. Old Faithful, one of the Yellowstone geysers likened by John Muir to "the factories of some busy town."

of wilderness *qua* wilderness, who speaks of mineral formations as bouquets of flowers, who writes that the geyser visitors "look on, awe-stricken and silent, in devout, worshipful wonder," seems inadvertently to reveal a major disjunction in consciousness (53, 54). The geysers look like a factory, and the most visited site in Yellowstone National Park turns out to be Pittsburgh.

Others, in fact, explicitly named the city identified with steel and coke magnates Andrew Carnegie and Henry Clay Frick in their descriptions of Old Faithful. The "rising smoke and vapor" reminded one writer "of the city of Pittsburgh," and another observed that "a view of the city of Pittsburg [*sic*] from a high point would convey some idea of the appearance of this valley [of geysers and hot springs], except that in the former case the dense black smoke arises in hundreds of columns, instead of the pure white feathery clouds of steam" (Koch, 503; Hayden, "Hot Springs," 173). In 1889 S. Weir Mitchell, the physician known for his immobilizing "rest cure" for disordered women, described the area of "mud volcanoes" as comparable to "the exhaust of a steam-engine, and near it from the earth come the rattle and crash and buzz and whirring of a cotton-mill" (701). Significantly, it was another nature writer, John Burroughs, who compared the geyser area to an industrial site when he wrote in 1907 that "as one nears the geyser region, he gets the impression from the columns of steam . . . that he is approaching an industrial centre" (63).

In part, such comments are utilitarian, measuring wastefulness against a norm of efficient usage. The geysers emit steam "in extravagant prodigality . . . enough steam is wasted here to run all the Western railways" ("Editor's Study," 320). A writer in *The Nation* observed that enough geyser water shot into the air "to run all the factories of Pennsylvania for a week" ("Yellowstone Park as a Summer Resort," 249). Burroughs "disliked [seeing] so much good steam and hot water going to waste" because "whole towns might be warmed by them, and big wheels made to go round" (64).

Technological analogies providing easily accessible lessons to the read-

23. Industrial "geyser" field of Pittsburgh, Pennsylvania. Postcard, 1910s.

ing public also show the extent of middle-class familiarity with mechanistic thinking, as when a geologist in 1898 explained that some geysers "have been formed by explosion, like the bursting of a boiler," or when steam vents are said to "keep up a constant pulsating noise like a high-pressure engine on a river steamboat," or when geysers are termed "natural steam-engines," their vapor likened to "the smoke of the . . . locomotive" (Tarr, 1575; Hayden, "Hot Springs," 164; Weed, "Geysers," 299; Rollins, 883).

Whether used as a utilitarian measure of usage or wastefulness, or as a term of explanation or description, however, these references to machine technology, heavy industry, and the industrial city provide a context in which the bodily identity of Old Faithful becomes clearer. Although Muir grouped geophysical eruptions, wind-and-wave hydraulics, and botanic cycles as the percussive "orderly love-beats of Nature's heart," the industrial context produced a different cardiac model. The clockwork regularity of Old Faithful's pulse, when set within the context of an industrializing America, defines the geyser as an industrial-age bodily icon. If, as Osler argued, a man must realize "that he is a machine," then the geophysical expression of that machine body becomes Old Faithful geyser (Osler, *Collected Papers,* 5).

Old Faithful in this sense is a synecdoche of the valorized body of the industrial era—a body understood as a machine whose pulse must be regular as clockwork. This body is male, in that the realm of heavy industry was gendered masculine (despite the female operatives in textile mills), and its eruptions encompass the ejaculative in the arterial. Indeed, Muir emphasizes that geysers sometimes erupt for periods of nearly one hour, "standing rigid and erect . . . seeming so firm and substantial and permanent" ("Yellowstone," 42, 54).

Such expression of male virility is fully consonant with the new industrial ethos of the later nineteenth century, and Old Faithful thus exemplified the ideals of an industrial society organized for maximal rationalized production. Like the railroads and well-run industrial plants, Old Faithful produced on schedule. (The *Practical Guide to Yellowstone* included "Geyser Time Tables," as if the eruptions were naturally scheduled like trains.) True, Old Faithful's eruptions varied by a few minutes, but the concept of hourly regularity was intact, as the numerous tributes to the geyser as reliable, punctual, and regular as a clock all indicate. Old Faithful reassuringly enacted the unvarying, relentless rhythms of an industrial system and thus seemed to be the "American incarnation," in Myra Jehlen's term, of the capitalistic social order of industrial, technological production. Its pulse could be measured by the clock, its very arterial rhythm seeming to be nature's own expression of the American modernity manifest in the industrial system.

"Nature's nation" thus was validated by nature's own industrial pulse. The very geophysical heart of America beat the rhythms of mechanization. Those seeing the geyser basin as a version of Pittsburgh or a similar "industrial centre" thus could appreciate Old Faithful as the paradigmatic pulse of that very system. Presumably, those responding with approbation also felt their interests well served by the new industrial order. A mutually reinforcing triad emerges—of Osler's Wall Street white male engine, of the industrial environment devised and financed by it, and of the natural expression of the engine pulse of Nature's nation at Yellowstone. The three pulses are one, and they were represented by those who gathered in May, 1872, to view Moran's Yellowstone painting—as one railroad executive described them, "the press—the literati—the rich people" (Kinsey, 73).

Muir's essay on Yellowstone supports the class position of those most favorably situated to benefit from the new industrial system. Rhetorically, the essay confirms the natural order of the monied cosmopolites whose fortunes originated in industry. Along with hymns to the wild, Muir characterizes Yellowstone in terms of the country estate and of European travel. At Yellowstone, the rock and mineral formations resemble "ruined castles," classical ruins, and Gothic cathedrals (46, 60, 67). Muir's Yellowstone is also an architecturally distinguished and beautiful estate. There are "smooth silky lawns" and "travertine . . . pavements" and "low terraces," with certain features "adorned on a grand scale" (41, 46). The "mountain mansions" include a library with "a wonderful set of volumes" (59–60). Guests are met by Nature, who is the "generous host" offering "brimming cups in endless variety, served in a grand hall . . . decorated with glorious paintings and enlivened with bands of music ever playing" (56). The guests come to a ball. The geysers sing and perform a "fairy rhythmic dance," and the guests, too, join that dance (38, 42, 58). Nature-as-host is simultaneously Nature as the laborer and artisan who built and now maintains the estate, working as smith, carpenter, farmer, gardener "doing rough work and fine work," and finally exhibiting as painter and sculptor (73–74). It is Nature-as-owner, however, with whom Muir's reader-guests are identified. The Yellowstone estate and mansion are theirs to enjoy at their leisure. They appreciate the art and artisanry without the obligations of the construction crews or custodial staff.

In part, Muir's use of such terms as ruined castles and Gothic cathedrals shows reliance on stock European references deployed throughout the nineteenth century to situate American scenery in terms of the Old World. Such terms positioned the American West as a compensatory analogue to Europe, as the castles and other ruins of ancient civilizations supposedly found their counterparts in the marvelous, geologically ancient sites of the American West (Kinsey, 20–40). (Note the very name, *Castle* geyser, at Yellowstone.)

The lexicon of European travel, moreover, could be both explanatory and prestigious when applied to the western park, luring travelers with the assurance of gratification at least equal to that of a tour of the Old World. When Francis Sessions wrote that the Yellowstone geyser named the Fountain reminded one of "some of the large fountains in Versailles" and a contemporary visitor decided that the Giantess bubbled like champagne in hollow stemware, both identified themselves as affluent worldly travelers and implied that their peers, too, owed themselves a sojourn in the grand American West (Sessions, 438; Francis, 35).

Muir's usage, however, carries particular contemporary American resonance for the estates and mansions of those whose fortunes came from industrial plants producing iron, steel, coke, and so on. His description of Yellowstone's lawns, library, ballroom, and the like positions the park as a version of the Europeanized American mansions and estates emerging in the new industrial cities of Cleveland and Pittsburgh and along Fifth Avenue in New York City, "palaces," as Horatio Alger called them, "occupied by the wealthier classes" (43). They emerged at Newport, too, and even Asheville, North Carolina. Muir's terms suggest private estates such as The Breakers or the Marble House in Newport, or George Vanderbilt's Biltmore estate overlooking the Blue Ridge Mountains near Asheville. The names of owners and guests would be recorded in socialite Ward McAllister's roster of the socially elite "400," among them the names Vanderbilt, Astor, Carnegie, and Morgan.

The American elite or those aspirant to their class position would be pleased by the Yellowstone of Muir's evocation. Experientially, of course, the harried industrial city and its factories and mills are as far from Newport as from the precincts of Yellowstone. Muir invites visitors for western travel according to the seasonal migrations of the rich. His references to the mansion, its staff, its grounds, and the leisured life of balls and the arts, together with the travel to the Europe of Gothic cathedrals and picturesque ruins—all argue that the industrial pulse naturally produced an expression of great wealth in a Euro-American material culture. In Muir, the estate named Yellowstone proved the rectitude of the industrial pulse which was producing the material wealth of Nature's nation.

And those in the middle-class managerial and professional world were also positioned to find Old Faithful and their culture mutually reinforcing. For the steam pulse of Old Faithful beat steadily to power the machinery that produced the consumer goods of their material lives. That steam-powered industrial order was displayed proudly in the world's fairs, such as the Centennial Exposition in Philadelphia, 1876, and the Columbian Exposition in Chicago, 1892, and in a celebratory portfolio volume, *The Growth of Industrial Art* (1892), published by the United States Patent Office, each oversize page depicting, in a series of drawings, the progress from primitive times of production by tools and utensils worked by hand to the modern era of machine production. Page after page shows weaponry, agricultural machinery, iron and steel furnaces, nails, railway cars, textile mechanisms, musical instruments, hydraulic motors, devices for the distillation of petroleum, steam engines, typewriters. Each item was produced, by the late 1880s, by processes of mechanization. As Thomas Schlereth and others have shown, the later nineteenth century was the new consumer era in which the good life became synonymous with the goods life as "department stores and mail-order houses turned local markets into national ones" (141). As the steady beat of Old Faithful underlay the new consumer abundance, that steam pulse throbbed in the production of middle-class American culture.

The steady beat of Old Faithful was reinforced, too, in the percussive prosody of verses in the *McGuffey's Eclectic Reader* series used in elementary schools nationwide from the 1870s into the 1920s. Prepared for each grade level, the readers contained moral stories encouraging respect for authority, inspirational speeches of statesmen and founding fathers, short fiction by authors such as Washington Irving and Nathaniel Hawthorne—and verses like the following by Eliza Cook, its message instilled with a heavy prosodic beat:

> Work, work, my boy, be not afraid;
> Look Labor boldly in the face;
> Take up the hammer or the spade,
> And blush not for your humble place. (qtd. Westerhoff, 59)

The clockwork beat was enhanced elsewhere in the rise of brass bands, and especially by the hugely popular marches of John Philip Sousa (1854–1932), who, despite composing numerous operettas, waltzes, songs, and other musical forms, is known principally for his 136 marches. "One could scarcely walk the distance of a city block without hearing a Sousa march being played on a piano or some other instrument" (Bierley, 10). The Sousa band appeared in hundreds of U.S. towns and cities—in the town parks in which Muir's own readers were said to saunter free of care—in concerts always featuring such Sousa marches as "Hail to the Spirit of Liberty," "The Invincible Eagle," "The Liberty Bell," in addition to "The Washington Post," "El Capitan," and best known of all, "The Stars and Stripes Forever," composed in 1896. Sousa was called the March King and "The Pied Piper of Patriotism" (Bierley, 15). A Chicago newspaper in 1896 observed, "When Sousa plays a march his arms swing in direct, soldierly, undeviating lines back and forth like military pendulums" (Bierley, 135).

One recognizes the demonstration of a relentless pulse and its enactment in the very performance of the conductor. The discipline is Foucaultian in the social message on uniformity, on metronomic precision, on a steady and unvarying tempo set by a godlike authority and followed without question. The popularity of march music especially promoted patriotism during the Spanish-American War, but its close association with militarist chauvinism ought not to obscure its late nineteenth- and early twentieth-century connection to the industrial rhythms modeled on a mechanistic ideal of tempos set with unvarying regularity. The March King, central to what Neil Harris has recently called "the culture of reassurance," worked in synchrony with Old Faithful.

Yet if Old Faithful's regular cadences were replicated in reassuring ways to the more affluent segments of U.S. society, so were the irregular and explosive eruptions of the geysers that eluded human prediction. Evidently the geyser basin of Yellowstone also aroused anxieties pertinent to the industrial system and thereby to its bodily identity. No other geyser approached Old Faithful in regularity of pulse. Its punctuality was offset by other geysers' "capricious[ness]" and "misbehavior," and some of the geyser names suggest the anxiety evoked by their very irregularity and turbulence: Hurricane, Restless, Spasmodic, Spiteful, Impulsive, Fitful, Spasm (Francis, 34; Hague, "Yellowstone," 523). Against Old Faithful, the very unpredictability of other geysers needs to be engaged, not solely in geophysical terms but, as with Old Faithful, in those of sociocultural issues in late nineteenth- and early twentieth-century America.

For Yellowstone's old identity as hell on earth was not quite effaced or even entirely repressed despite the vigorous efforts of its post-1870 spokespersons. The continuation of the old infernal identity has less to do with an inadequate campaign on behalf of the new Yellowstone Wonderland than it does with certain contemporary representations of industrial America. Ironically, just at the point when the cohort of photographers, painters, railroad executives, and publishers collaborated to identify Yellowstone as America's Wonderland, public discourse in the country was fashioning an infernal identity for industrial America. While the West was newly configured in edenic terms, the industrial Northeast and Midwest were assigned Yellowstone's old identity as hell on earth.

In fact, from the 1860s, fiction writers, journalists, and illustrators presented the new urban industrial order in terms of the infernal. Woodcuts and lithographs, for instance, in *Harper's Weekly Magazine* (November 1, 1873; July 7, 1888) showed tense laborers shoveling coal into beehive coke ovens as flames roil skyward, while other bare-chested workmen tend the fiery furnaces of the iron mill as flames backlight the night sky in a blinding blaze. Writers, too, produced these kinds of infernal images. Rebecca Harding Davis, in *Life in the Iron Mills* (1861), published in the *Atlantic Monthly*, described a "city of fires that burned hot and fiercely in the night . . . caldrons filled with boiling fire. . . . Fire in every horrible form." It was, she wrote, "like a street in Hell . . . like Dante's Inferno" (20, 27). Industrial Pittsburgh, just sixty miles north of Davis's Wheeling, was characterized in 1883 by a travel writer as "the great furnace of Pandemonium . . . the outer edge of the infernal regions" (Glazier, 332).

Such accounts of industrial, technologically driven America corresponded to the characterization of "American Nervousness," which, in 1881, George Beard attributed to an urbanizing American environment of traction railways, industrial machinery, electrification, steam engines, factories, the very locomotive rods and pistons moving the passenger railroad cars of the Northern Pacific, the Burlington Route, and the Oregon Short Line that brought visitors to Yellowstone. While Frederick Jackson Turner affirmed the westward path of civilization as "the steady growth of a complex nervous system," Beard blamed that same civilization for overtaxing the body's neural system in a world thought to engender a host of diseases, including consumption and neurasthenia, the etiology found in the fast-paced temporal pressures of cities and industrial plants and the age itself.

The tourists at Yellowstone came to feel awe at the sight of Old Faithful, but evidence indicates that visitors who produced travel texts on the park did so as inhabitants of an industrial, technological world. This is to say that their texts show a Yellowstone—and especially Old Faithful and the geyser basin—framed in an experience largely of industrialism and its conditions of production and labor. As Old Faithful became an icon of industrial America, the erratic surrounding geysers, boiling springs, and mud volcanoes were read as a statement on the industrial body under mortal threat. The geyser area was a reflective image of the industrializing United States.

Muir, as active agent in the production of a Yellowstone Wonderland, worked to allay anxieties about danger there. The mansion and its grounds are entirely hospitable to visitors. Addressing a middle-class reading public, Muir framed his park description in reassurances that "most of the dangers that haunt the unseasoned citizen are imaginary," that "overcivilized people" are subject to "irrational dread," for instance, of rattlesnakes and murderous Indians—"No scalping Indians will you see" ("Yellowstone," 51). "Fear nothing," he says, for "no town park you have been accustomed to saunter in is so free from danger as the Yellowstone" (57–58). Muir then tries to make the old hellish nicknames sound zany and fun, as though anticipating the later twentieth-century theme park. Names like "Hell Broth Springs," the "Devil's Caldron," and "Colter's Hell" are "so exhilarating that they set our pulses dancing" (58). Muir sets up a sympathetic pulsing of the geothermal and the arterial in the realm of rhythmic movement whose beat is emphatically more musical than mechanical. As partners, the visitors and the geysers have a ball.

Others, however, did not reproduce Muir's terpsichorean rhetorical strategy. Travelers' accounts through the 1880s–1910s continued to enforce a somber linkage between the geyser basin and the Inferno. By implication, their descriptions are shadowed by the presumed presence of demonic, monstrous bodies in hell. And their statements show the extent to which industrial-age America did not efface the old Yellowstone identity as "a place where hell bubbles up" but actually renewed it. They described "a seething caldron over a fiery furnace" emitting a "villainous smell" ("Washburn Expedition, 1," 434). One of the mud volcanoes bears "testimony to the terrible nature of the convulsion that wrought such destruction" (Langford, 354). A writer in *Scribner's Magazine* noted the "weird, uncanny, sulphurous, at times even dangerous" aspect of the geyser area (Hague, "Yellowstone," 516). Another said, "It seemed as if we were looking upon a panorama of the Inferno," and still another remarked that the air was "burdened with such sulphurous odors that at times it was rendered almost unfit for respiration" (F. King, 597; Owen, 193). A mother shepherding her seven children through a Yellowstone vacation in 1905 recalled that "like everybody else, we loved Old Faithful . . . feared Excelsior, admired the Giant and Beehive." But, she said, "the horrible rumbling as if an earthquake were imminent and the smell of brimstone made me eager to get my brood into the valley of safety beyond the Yellowstone" (Corthell, 1466). Even the scientists reverted to fraught language in description of the geyser: the Excelsior is "a violently boiling cauldron . . . its waters may be seen in violent ebullition" (Jagger, 324). Absent Old Faithful, and unable to join in the spirit of Muir's injunction to "fear nothing" and dance, texts from the 1870s, including Muir's, authorially link the geyser basin with the Inferno in affirming its volcanic geophysics. In 1896 Arnold Hague of the United States Geological Survey asserted that "all geologists who have visited [Yellowstone] concur that the 'great body' of rock and mineral is 'volcanic'" (Hague, "Age of Igneous Rocks of the Yellowstone," 447). Two years later, a geologist described the process: "Volcanoes developed throughout the entire Rockies. . . . Great masses of lava were intruded into the rocks. . . . Beds of volcanic ash testify to violent explosive volcanic activity" (Tarr, 1407). The novelist Owen Wister's hero, the Virginian, visits the geysers and smells a "volcanic whiff" (qtd. Sears, 169). One writer compared the probable eruptive force of the Yellowstone-area volcanoes with those of the widely publicized recent eruptions of Krakatoa (1883) and of Tarawera, New Zealand (1886) (Weed, "Fossil," 235).

U.S. visitors to Yellowstone were not encouraged to consider the likelihood of renewed volcanic activity. (Muir reassured them that "the fire times had passed away, and the volcanic furnaces were banked" [64].) The "glass road" of volcanic obsidian over which they rode in wagons and stage coaches to the geysers was considered a wonder, not a threat.

Yet readers of "The Yellowstone National Park" find even Muir drawn repeatedly to the subject of eruptive violence. Despite his assurance that destruction is creation and that the volcanic era is safely removed in the distant past, Muir's description of Yellowstone as a mansion with lawns, library, and artistic furnishings is repeatedly challenged—even threatened—by textual preoccupation with volcanic eruptions. Among constant reassurances that the park is wholesome, healthful and civil, Muir's reader encounters recurrent "hot lava beds," the subterranean "fierce furnace fire," deracinating "awful subterranean thunder," "volcanic fires . . . [spewing] immense quantities of ashes, pumice and cinders . . . into the sky," the "shocks and outbursts of earthquakes, volcanoes, geysers, storms" (37, 41, 45, 61–62, 70). Readers may see in the desultory repetition an essayist reproducing the very erratic eruptions of which he writes. Apparently unable to contain the volcanic past or the eruptive present in a single passage or section of the essay, Muir obsessively returns to description of the geysers' force time after time throughout the text. Discursively he enacts the very erratic and dangerous actions of the region's geomorphology. It is as if the Yellowstone mansion and estate and its occupants stood liable to be destroyed, to be buried in the molten lava of an American Pompeii.

Images of the Inferno in Muir and other writers indicate anxieties not allayed by reassurances that the fires are extinct. The spewing, hissing eruptions were proving otherwise. An 1897 "Editor's Study" column in *Harper's* cited a "lady" who considered the geyser area of Yellowstone as "the safety-valve of the United States." These function as "vent-holes of its internal fires and explosive energies." But for their relief, "the whole country might be shaken with earthquakes and blown up in fragments" (320). The lady reported it "not encouraging" to feel the hot crust underfoot and identified the subterranean area as a "terrible furnace."

The imagery of safety valve and furnace, together with that of the danger, destruction, and chaos of the Inferno, tends once again to collapse boundaries between Yellowstone and the industrial East and Midwest. Public discourse indicates that apart from the pleasures of Old Faithful, the Yellowstone visitors alighted at the geyser basin only to encounter a geophysical version of the very Inferno familiar to them from fictional and journalistic accounts of the material environment of industrial eastern and upper midwestern cities of the United States.

Yet this, perhaps, is the point—that just as Old Faithful provided reassurance about the health of the industrial order, so the erratic and frightening geyser basin was read as a geophysical text on sociocultural threats to the new industrial order. There is some evidence that such a threat was perceived in bodily terms referent to industrial workers who occupy "t' Devil's place," workmen who are "bad" and "desperate" enough to be condemned to hell (R. Davis, 20, 27). The heaving, spewing, violent, and capricious geysers and volcanoes replicate an industrializing scene periodically rife with social turmoil, including strikes and riots devolving from conditions of labor and wages. In this sense, the erratic, arrhythmic geysers are a homology of the bodies necessary to keep the industrial world in mechanistic synchrony, but which, at intervals, instead subvert its clockwork rhythms. One Homestead steelworker told Hamlin Garland in 1893, "The worst part of this whole business is this. It brutalizes a man" (qtd. Serrin, 62). Such brutalized bodies, perhaps versions of the swarthy, sooty, muddy industrial laborers' bodies—as Davis termed them, "filthy and ash-covered. . . . coarse and vulgar"—threaten the clockworks pulse of the industrial order. As erratic geysers, they "pulsate in rhythmic beats from the mighty heart of internal chaos" (R. Davis, 24; Townsend, 163). In *Life in the Iron Mills* they are "boisterous," but at Yellowstone infernally roiled enough to emit "sighs, moans, and shrieks" (R. Davis, 26; Sedgwick, 3573).

The sulphurous, heaving mud volcanoes, hissing steam vents, and explosive eruptions—in short, the Inferno—had a textual foreground, moreover, in the dire volcanic social vision recurrent in public discourse in the United States from the early nineteenth century and deeply engaged with the social body of nonelites. Political, religious, and educational figures had recurrently exploited volcanoes as a terrifying metaphor for the collapse of social order in the United States, as Fred Somkin has shown. Back in 1789, Fisher Ames of Massachusetts warned at a political convention that "a democracy is a volcano, which conceals the fiery materials of its own destruction" (24). In 1817, the *Columbian Orator* reprinted Yale president Timothy Dwight's description in *The Conquest of Canaan* of "a fiery Judgment Day marked by quaking, fire-belching mountains" (Somkin, 39). The possibility that slavery or some other issue might prompt riotous rupture of the social order led the Reverend Ephraim Peabody in 1846 to say that while "all may be smooth and fair on the surface," the "fires of a volcano are moving beneath the thin crust, and . . . in a moment they may burst through and lay the labors of centuries in ruins" (7). In 1855 the Reverend Richard Storrs voiced his fear that crime, slavery, vice, and Catholicism threatened the United States, which he feared slept "on the crater's edge" as "fiery floods threaten an overflow . . . more terrible than was felt by Pompeii or Herculaneum" (21). In a Fourth of July oration of 1842, Horace Mann speculated that the nation "is an active volcano of ignorance and guilt" (29).

The eruption of strikes and riots of the later nineteenth and early twentieth centuries also prompted description in volcanic terms. The "political and industrial battles" in Colorado from 1894 to 1904, for instance, led to the publication of a report from the U.S. Commissioner of Labor (1905): "The reading of that report leaves one with the impression that present-day society rests upon a volcano, which in favorable periods seems very harmless, but, when certain elemental forces clash, it bursts forth in a manner that threatens with destruction civilization itself" (Hunter, 303). Statements of this kind produce a volcanic social body correlative with the rumored hell on earth at Yellowstone, and thus the nineteenth-century United States becomes a continuum of volcanic geopolitics, one to be continued in the 1930s Depression, when a Homestead, Pennsylvania, coroner and detective-turned-burgess, John Cavanaugh, observed that "the entire lower Monongahela Valley and Pittsburgh has been resting on a [communistic] smoldering volcano, which has been ready to burst out at any moment" (qtd. Serrin, 176).

Possibilities for sociocultural "volcanic" explosion apparently intensified with the availability of the new explosives invented by Alfred B. Nobel in 1866 and developed in the United States by the Du Pont Corporation and others. Nobel's work enabled production of a stable explosive in which nitroglycerine was mixed with an inert filler, such as sawdust, then pressed into paper cylinders and set off with a detonator. Used in construction, mining, and civil engineering, it was lightweight and portable.

And like the explosive volcano, it served to express deep anxieties about hidden dangers of social disorder. Anybody in possession of a stick of dynamite became a potential one-person volcano. Josiah Strong's best-selling social critique, *Our Country: Its Possible Future and Its Present Crisis* (1885), described as "social dynamite" the "largely foreign" male population of "roughs . . . lawless and desperate men of all sorts" (132). Strong's "social dynamite" gained credence the following year, when some of the eight anarchists found guilty of detonating the bomb that killed a policeman in Chicago's Haymarket Riot spoke in the language of explosive social change. August Spies declared, "From Jove's head has sprung a Minerva—dynamite!" Revolutions, he added, result from certain "causes and conditions . . . like earthquakes and cyclones" (*Accused*, 7, 8). One may recall the Yellowstone visitor anxious about the earth hot under her feet as Spies's speech warned that laboring wage slaves would rise in revolt: "Everywhere, flames will blaze up. It is a subterranean fire. You cannot put it out" (10).

Spies's fellow anarchist, Albert P. Parsons, who denied using dynamite to cause the 1886 Haymarket Riot, nonetheless declared its efficacy as a "democratic instrument" and was quoted by one alarmed author as citing the "splendid opportunity . . . for some bold fellow to make the capitalists tremble by blowing up [the Chicago Board of Trade] building and all the thieves and robbers that are there" (McLean, 33).

The texts celebrating a clocklike Old Faithful and deploring the infernal adjoining geysers would seem hostile to the notion of dynamiting buildings or otherwise altering the social order in incendiary ways. Such texts were not produced by those laboring twelve hours daily in dangerous, debilitating, low-paying toil, but by those sufficiently affluent to buy rail and coach seats to the Rockies, to stay at hotels or to camp in the Wylie Company's system of tents, beds, and meals with campfires at the rate of five dollars per day, to take leave of a primary residence for weeks at a time. These, and not the self-described wage-slave laborers with anarchist views, were the visitors poised to applaud Old Faithful.

And these were the visitors who shuddered when, unexpectedly, one or another of the other geysers "burst forth again without warning, and even greater violence," who saw eruptions "pulsating in rhythmic beats from the mighty heart of internal chaos." For civil violence had abated but not

ceased in the decades following the Civil War, as verified in such events
as the deadly Great Railroad Strike of 1877 over the issue of hourly wages,
the Haymarket Riot of 1886 which started over the eight-hour workday,
the New Orleans race riots of 1866, the Homestead Strike of 1892, the
Pullman Strike of 1894, the miners' strike at Coeur d'Alene, Idaho, in
1899, the Colorado strikes and riots from 1894 to 1904—all of which
seemed to nativists dangerously explosive. Add to these the actual explosives, from the bomb thrown into Chicago's Haymarket to the carload of
dynamite detonated by striking miners to blow up the mine concentrator,
an area where waste was extracted from ores, at the Coeur d'Alene mine.

It is important to recognize that Yellowstone's visitors—camped with
their own "wagons, tents, and provisions," their "coffee pot, frying pan
and kettle," and "a buffalo robe to spread on a pile of fir, pine, or hemlock
twigs, with blankets for covering, [that] makes a bed which renders that
city pest, *insomnia,* an impossibility" (Logan, 160)—looked to Old Faithful to help them keep faith in an industrializing nation which was built,
some feared, on incendiary volcanic soil. Given these tourists' class position, the American body politic and the mechanistic body of the new industrial order must have seemed tenuous, contingent, and contested. Dr.
Osler's Wall Street bodily engine, driven relentlessly, would wear out with
aneurysms or cardiac failure at age fifty, "fit only to be scrapped," while
Old Faithful itself could break rhythm or, like other geysers, go extinct.[2]
The "immense quantities of ashes and cinders thrown into the sky" and
dimming the sun in "sulphurous clouds" could signal industrial progress
and prosperity or, on the contrary, cataclysmic destruction (Muir, "Yellowstone," 62). In the post-1870s decades, it was not at all clear whether
the America of the pulse of Old Faithful would become an enduring industrial-age Wonderland or manifest its long-term national, geopolitical
identity as "a place where hell bubbles up."

4

America's Moon: "A Dream of the Future's Face"

I believe this nation should commit itself, before the decade is out, to
landing a man on the moon and returning him safely to earth. . . . I believe we should go to the moon.

—JOHN F. KENNEDY, 1961

The trip to the moon had to serve as the embodiment of a new vision.

—NORMAN MAILER, *Of a Fire on the Moon*, 1970

And he liked the moon rock and thought . . . that she liked him. Yes . . .
Yet she was young, she had just been transported here, and there was
something young about her . . . there was something familiar as the ages
of the bone in the sweet and modest presence of this moon rock. . . .
Hanging man Aquarius, four times married and lost, moved out of
M[anned] S[pacecraft] C[enter] with the memory of the moon, new
mistress, two feet from his nose.

—NORMAN MAILER, *Of a Fire on the Moon*, 1970

For the uses of men we have been butchered
And crippled and shut up and carved open
under the moon that swells and shines
and shrinks again into nothingness, pregnant
and then waning toward its little monthly
death. The moon is always female . . .

—MARGE PIERCY, *The Moon Is Always Female*, 1974

In 1969, after Apollo 11 astronauts walked on the lunar surface, a white
male America claimed its own heavenly body, the moon. It did so within a

decade of John F. Kennedy's presidential call and of the publication of Norman Mailer's 1964 novel—*An American Dream*—titled after a core national myth. Kennedy's summons presumed a bipolar male world of contending superpowers, the United States and the Soviet Union, in which America defended its right to perpetuate the national dream in the atomic age. Both men, the politician and the writer, worked out of a masculinist worldview of unrelenting striving for mythic status achievable by male acts of physical courage. To fly in an experimental rocket projectile beyond earth's atmosphere to the moon was one such act by which national primacy could be claimed worldwide. Kennedy, a World War II naval hero and now commander-in-chief of the U.S. armed forces, initiated politically and militarily the project about which Mailer wrote, in a literary tradition governed by the nationalistic mandate of the Great American Novel. Both men drew upon the legacy of the frontier to define American manhood in contention with—in fact, in possession of—the American heavenly body, the moon, which Mailer claimed as his own new mistress.

As a body of Nature's nation, the moon was self-evidently vastly distant (c. 240,000 miles) from earth and the American mainland. The Apollo program, customarily considered in a cold war context, is also usefully situated within the late twentieth-century U.S. expansionist embrace of state territories. In 1959 the U.S. Congress and the American public had sufficiently overcome reservations about nonmainland territorial bodies to admit Alaska as the forty-ninth state (with its state slogan "The Last Frontier") and the islands of Hawaii as the fiftieth.

No interest group in the late 1950s was promoting a notion of statehood for the moon (or, for that matter, for certain other geographic bodies, such as the Mariana Islands' Guam, an unincorporated U.S. territory, or the Caribbean Puerto Rico, a Spanish-speaking, self-governing island commonwealth, both sites the legacy of U.S. imperialism).

But the idea of lunar possession was compatible with the instatement of lands so distant from the North American territory that modern aeronautic transport was the preferred means of connecting Americans to their newly united turf. Something antecedent to this had occurred in the nineteenth century, of course, when the distant western territories became states, Colorado in 1876, Idaho and Montana in 1889, Wyoming in 1890, to cite just a few, and were reached by road and rail. In 1871 Walt Whitman's *Democratic Vistas* predicted that Cuba and Canada would become states of the Union in an American world linked by electric communication. As the new national transit system of automobiles, trucks, and airplanes supplanted that of the railroad, air became the feasible way to unite the states. It sounded more like a transit plan than a futuristic fantasy when Arthur C. Clarke, in an Epilogue to the Apollo 11 astronauts' *First on the Moon,* said that "with any luck, the DC-3 of the space age should begin its career in the 1970s" (Armstrong, Collins, and Aldrin, 447).

The public, what's more, was long accustomed to televisual travel. Actual railroad cars and track that carried tourists west to Yellowstone had yielded, by the mid-twentieth century, to the television screens promising armchair voyages to distant lands. Lest the moon project seem parochially nationalistic, however, the texts advancing the "trip to the moon . . . as the embodiment of a new vision" claimed universality within national particularity (Armstrong, Collins, and Aldrin, 384–385). Indeed, the Apollo space program—named for the Greek god of light and knowledge—indicates in its very appellation a self-conscious aspiration for an enduring and transcendent classical mythology within the specific context of the cold war and U.S. globalism.

The centuries-long literary tradition of lunar embodiment, in addition, was now associated with an American tradition, the frontier, which gave new ideological and utilitarian meaning to the embodied moon. The identification of the Kennedy administration as the New Frontier conjoined the nineteenth-century frontier ethos with the moon project, which Kennedy called "among the most important decisions that will be made during my incumbency in the Office of the Presidency" (qtd. Logsdon, "Challenge," 2). Just as the idea of a western frontier governed the creation of Yellowstone and its geyser area as a new world of industrialization in the late nineteenth century, and just as Frederick Jackson Turner's frontier thesis gave ideological credence and coherence to that western project, so did the frontier provide the terms of the argument by which cold war America sponsored the space program and especially the moon flights. Technology, inevitably, dominated both frontiers, the steam technology of nineteenth-century rail and factory, and the new computer and propulsion technology of the space age.

A critique of this male project arose too, though this time not from disenfranchised workers protesting economic inequities in "storms" or volcanic eruptions of strikes and riots. Twentieth-century protest arose instead from feminists, whose analysis of patriarchy posed a sociopolitical challenge to the existing misogynist social order and, accordingly, to the lunar frontier.

The terms by which white male America claimed its heavenly body were thus challenged and redefined in new ways. Frontier nationalism and its concomitant male conquest of the lunar body were being critiqued by the new feminists. The female lunar body proved to be a contested site within the realm of cultural analysis. Within a U.S. nationalist domain, the terms by which white male, misogynist America claimed its heavenly body underwent radical critical revision via the new feminism. The Apollo lunar missions, when viewed through an emerging new feminist critique, were not regarded as an expression of valiant frontier values nor as a national imperative of Nature's nation, nor even in their Apollonian naming a reaffirmation of the classical lunar tradition.

The lunar pursuit of "a dream of the future's face," instead, was disclosed from a feminist viewpoint as a set of chauvinist heterosexual power relations recorded over a long history in the national literature (Mailer, *Fire on Moon,* 132). In the years of the Apollo flights, a spokesperson for the newer outlook, Annette Kolodny, was at work in the University of California libraries in Berkeley on a literary study of metaphoric responses to the American environment from the Renaissance era of exploration. Kolodny's doctoral dissertation, published as *The Lay of the Land* (1975), argued that from the seventeenth century, white Anglo-Euro male writers represented American territory—especially of the western frontier—as the female body of the mother, the sister, the concubine, with tangled relationships of infant suckling, fraternal incest, and male rape of a "virgin" land.

Kolodny closely read pastoral literature from the seventeenth to the twentieth centuries and found a recurrent, indeed obsessive pattern of New World ravishment. In her terms, Mailer's claim of a moon rock as his "new mistress" was but one contemporary example of pervasive male domination of New World women and the environment. Although Kolodny did not include lunar texts in her study, her demonstration of the sexualizing of the American frontier West was crucial to a feminist critique of male lunar "conquest." Indeed, it put the very term inside the punctuation marks of irony.

This critique was also conducted in feminist poetry, notably in *The Moon Is Always Female* (1994) by Marge Piercy, which rejects Maileresque lunar courtship as thinly masked butchery, the crippling and silencing of women under the very lunar presence—the lunar authority—that must be newly, urgently reclaimed for female autonomy. Tidal and menstrual power, the poet-novelist insists, summons women to recognize the "most basic right, the right to control our bodies, the right to control the life within us, to choose when and whether to give birth—not to be used in field or factory" (*Parti-Colored,* 60, 62). While male writers, preeminently

Mailer, worked to Americanize the classical Hecate, Luna, Artemis, Diana, and Phoebe in a male frontier context of the "winning of the moon," feminist critics and poets rejected the male project.[1] Instead, they embodied the moon for purposes of their own, principally for the restoration of a premodern female autonomy.

"Moon" texts, like those produced in response to the once-exotic American western landscape of the Yellowstone, are a disparate lot, including political science scholarship, government policy reports, poetry, fiction (for example, James Michener's best-selling *Space*), biography (for instance, of the German father of modern rocketry, Wernher von Braun), historical narratives, television news broadcasts, and articles in mass-market magazines, in addition to recorded transcripts of communication between astronaut crews and the NASA (National Aeronautics and Space Administration) Manned Spacecraft Center in Houston, Texas, together with one astronaut memoir to date (Buzz Aldrin's *Return to Earth*).

The formulation of the moon as a heavenly body to be claimed and possessed emerges in part from phrases scattered through these texts—of the moon as a "platinum lady," as Mailer puts it, and elsewhere as a "harsh mistress," as "Queen of the Night," as a "hospitable host" awaiting visitors. The feminist moon rises for a female cohort as a round "O!," as a "Hoop / of cool fire," as a "silver mirror in which we see / ourselves dimly but truly reflected," the first-person pronouns all referring to women (Piercy, *Moon,* 133). The legacy of moon lore and of science from Western classical antiquity through the Renaissance and beyond also suffuses these later twentieth-century American moon texts and contributes substantially to the gendering and the embodiment of the moon, providing the vocabulary for the debates on lunar incarnation.

New Frontier

Above all, the moon is a frontier incarnation, even if the ubiquitous usage of "frontier," as Patricia Limerick observes, has made the term "the flypaper of [the American] mental world," attaching itself to healthful diets, to the civil rights movement, heart transplants, innovations in music as well as a range of consumer products, including the fastening device Velcro (which proved a godsend for the Apollo 11 astronauts struggling to anchor all sorts of gear in a state of weightlessness) (Limerick, 21). Limerick, Richard White, and others have worked to show that "frontier" is, intellectually speaking, a "zone of cultural interpenetration and contested hegemony," meaning one in which several cultures, Anglo, Native American, and Chicano, have crossed borders and struggled for degrees of dominance. In popular usage, however, the term is shorthand for adventure and a dynamic U.S. future (Limerick, 21). The concluding phrase on "the unique glory of the trail-blazing flight of Apollo 11" in the Apollo astronauts' own *First on the Moon,* reinforces this latter idea of adventure, quest, dynamism (Armstrong, Collins, and Aldrin, 495). These are the associations James Michener doubtless sought to elicit in his best-selling docudrama of a novel, *Space* (1982), which associates the entire space program with American historical benchmarks of national unity, including the frontier of Daniel Boone (229).

It was the historian Turner whose "frontier thesis" both explained the expansionist nineteenth century and framed the multiple uses of the term in the twentieth. Turner is the *genius loci* of the West in which Old Faithful beat the industrial pulse of nineteenth-century America. His thesis informs the lunar frontier of the Apollo program as well. The latter part of the twentieth century, however, found an important successor to—or perhaps confrere of—Turner in the popular historicizer of the frontier, Walt Disney. "Frontier," writes the historian Davis Wrobel, "has become a metaphor for promise, progress and ingenuity," and Disney could not have said it more succinctly (qtd. Limerick, 21). Disneyland, it is important to recall, contained both Frontierland and Tomorrowland, positioning Davy Crockett and the rockets in an American synthesis that is simultaneously historicizing and ahistoricizing. Frontierland featured continuous gunfights, a white river packet boat, *The Mark Twain,* a playground called Tom Sawyer Island with a fort, log cabins, Indian war canoes, and high-sided "Mike Fink" keel boats of the kind shown in Disney's *Davy Crockett* movie and television series. Disney's western frontier was signified in the weekly adventures of Davy Crockett (played by Fess Parker) and popularized by the fad of children's coonskin caps.

Nearby was Tomorrowland, where visitors could approximate the feeling of weightlessness in a ride simulating interstellar travel. Tomorrowland included a rocket monorail, flying saucers, and a flight circle featuring the "76 TWA Rocket to the Moon." At the same time, Disney's mid-1950s television series on ABC featured animated versions of the simulated space vehicles and astronauts painted by Chesley Bonestell for *Collier's* magazine in 1951.

Reportedly, President Dwight D. Eisenhower so appreciated the Disney films related to space that he ordered copies for high-ranking military officers at the Pentagon (Patton, 40). Disney's *Man in Space* (1959), a

24. Disneyland's Tomorrowland (under construction), a 1955 TWA exhibit with a simulated rocket ride to the moon.

book adapted by Willy Ley for schoolroom use, compares rocketry to the
firing of a gun, implicitly the Colt .45 of the West, as represented by the
Jupiter-C launch from Cape Canaveral, which carried the first U.S. artificial satellite into orbit (7). It is perhaps not surprising that by July 1969,
astronaut Buzz Aldrin's wife, Joan, felt that the experience of watching
her husband and his partner on the moon on television was "like a Walt
Disney cartoon, or even a television show" (Armstrong, Collins, and
Aldrin, 340).

Representations of space exploration in figures of the American frontier
of the West became so commonplace that it is accurate to say that frontier
terminology provided the mythos for the United States' space effort.[2] The
Apollo 11 crew and their families had a moon map of informal names out
of the Old West: "Dry Gulch," "Apollo Ridge," "Twin Peaks," "Smoky
Ridge," "Boothill," "Sidewinder Rill" (Armstrong, Collins, and Aldrin,
22, 206). Pictorially, in addition, Chesley Bonestell's 1950s space paintings linked the lunar surface with the American West, for the artist was so
struck by his first sight of the Rocky Mountains that he "used Hollywood
techniques to make people believe in space the way painter Albert Bierstadt or photographer W[illiam] H[enry] Jackson made people believe in
the wonders of the West" (Patton, 40). If the actual lunar landscape better
resembled a slag heap by a steel mill, nonetheless the romantic version

popularized by the mass-market magazine and "imagineered" by Disney resembled a valley in the Rockies (Patton, 40).

Actual western topography, too, was shaped into an approximation of the moon's surface. For Apollo astronaut training, NASA and the U.S. Geological Survey cooperated in creating a simulacrum of the lunar landscape in an area of north central Arizona, in the volcanic area of the San Francisco Peaks, where a "lunar" landscape was fashioned with carefully detonated explosives of carbon nitrate—"three generations of craters, rays coming out from them, double-ring craters, blocky rim craters, everything" (Armstrong, Collins, and Aldrin, 216–218).

Although the training schedule of the astronauts prevented practice on the Arizona "lunar" surface, geologists in space suits roamed the area testing the complex tools designed for lunar fieldwork and practicing traversing the terrain in order to provide backup information as needed during the Apollo 11 flight. Thus the geologists played the part of astronauts on a simulated lunar surface of the U.S. western "frontier." (The 1972 NASA Apollo 17 mission report mentions the astronaut Ronald Evans's observation that small humps on the moon's far side resembled volcanic domes he had studied near Mono Lake, California [*Apollo 17,* 6].)

The American West, moreover, was already identified with the moon in the national monument called Craters of the Moon, located in a volcanic area in Idaho, roughly sixty miles in diameter, about one hundred statute miles southwest of Yellowstone National Park and lying at the foot of the White Komb Mountains on the edge of the Snake River plateau. The monument, now comprising 53,309 acres, was created on May 2, 1924, when President Calvin Coolidge declared it "a weird and scenic landscape peculiar to itself," his proclamation describing the area as containing "a remarkable fissure eruption together with its associated volcanic cones, craters, rifts, lava flows, caves, natural bridges, and other phenomena characteristic of volcanic action which are of unusual scientific value and general interest" (*Draft General Management Plan,* 100).[3]

Craters of the Moon interests us precisely because it was not a lunar simulacrum but thought to be a close approximation to actual lunar geomorphology. Geologists' theories that the moon was volcanic in origin lent credence to the view that the volcanic topography in Idaho was nearly identical to the moon's. The site was named and publicized, however, by neither geologists nor President Coolidge, but by a western booster as eager to promote tourism in Idaho as was Disney his California theme park. The designation of the Idaho acreage as lunar territory is attributable to Robert W. ("Bob") Limbert, a native Nebraskan who gave the area, previously known as the Valley of Craters, its new lunar name and tirelessly promoted the attractions of his adopted state, Idaho, in the era of railroad and automobile tourism.

Limbert was a naturalist, taxidermist, explorer, cowboy, photographer, and author who lectured widely in the 1920s–1940s.[4] His masculinist performances included screenings of hunting and fishing motion pictures, bird call imitations and exhibitions of "unbelievable feats of marksmanship" with rifle and revolver. Like the South Dakotans who brought Gutzon Borglum to their state to carve Mt. Rushmore in order to attract tourists, Limbert argued in numerous public lectures that "Craters of the Moon [was] destined in the near future to play an important part in attracting tourists . . . [and become] one of the nation's sightseeing playgrounds" (mss 80, box 1, folder 29).

Limbert's linkage of Idaho and the moon was a brilliant publicist's strategy undergirded by scientific volcanic theory prevalent up to the time of the Apollo missions.[5] Limbert's own bold U.S.-lunar analogue was set forth for broad-based consumption in his March 1924 *National Geographic* photo-essay, "Among the 'Craters of the Moon,' " an account of his third exploratory expedition in which he detailed a two-person, two-week trek with camera and packs. His article acknowledged evidence of Native American predecessors ("an old Indian trail"), listed such flora and fauna as wild onion and bears, and noted the presence of water. Limbert also tried to let readers join him vicariously, for example, "imagine yourself in some gigantic funnel of bright red and black" (307). He recounted harrowing moments but limited his adjectives to present himself as a dispassionate, if rugged, surveyor letting facts speak for themselves as he documented the various topographical features and their positionings.

The twenty-one photographs accompanying Limbert's text depicted volcanic craters, pits, broad barren swaths, lava stiffened to show its onetime violently roiling eruption. His expedition was described as a Rooseveltian male adventure of physical courage, thereby a plausible precursor to the moon voyages of the New Frontier.

The *National Geographic* essay which marked Limbert's beginning as publicist for Craters of the Moon was crucial in providing him a credential and speaker's platform of sorts. Having renamed the former Valley of Craters and having documented the area's geomorphology in the periodical of the National Geographic Society, Limbert was positioned to launch the campaign dear to his heart, publicizing Craters of the Moon so effectively that tourists would flock there and make its designation as a national park inevitable.

25. Limbert expedition to Craters of the Moon, 1924, showing volcanic folds
thought by scientists to resemble the lunar surface.

Limbert's lectures and speeches hinged on the lunar-western analogy.
His "Taking a Trip to the Moon (in Idaho)," which was presented repeatedly before "hundreds of organizations throughout America," opened
with an extended analogy linking the volcanic western terrain with that of
the moon: "If by some heavenly catastrophe a section of the moon, dead
silent and mysterious were hurled against the surface of the earth[,] would
it be worth visiting? Would it attract people to explore its gigantic crater
pits, its seas of frozen lava, its great dead volcanic mountains, with bot-
tomless pits and caverns of strange rock formation?" (mss 80, box 1,
folder 29). The sole response to this rhetorical opener was, of course, the
affirmative. Sometimes Limbert reversed the trajectory, asking audiences
to imagine a human being "hurled through space and landed on the
moon," the moon scientifically certified, he said, to resemble the site in
northwestern Idaho ("Valley of the Moon," mss 80, box 2, folder 10).

Limbert lectured frequently in Idaho and throughout the American
West and Midwest. He delivered at least sixty radio broadcasts in 1931,
and his articles appeared regionally and nationally in *World's Work*, *The
American Magazine*, *Sunset*, *Popular Science*, *Outdoor America*, *Outdoor
Life*, together with reviews of his talks in newspapers in Salt Lake City,

Chicago, Omaha (mss 80, box 2, folders 10, 11). Just as western tourism to Yellowstone and its Old Faithful geyser was promoted by railroads, so Limbert's commissioned brochure for the Union Pacific Railroad, *Unknown Places in Idaho,* informed prospective tourists of Union Pacific branch lines ready to take them for a "prolonged visit" to the featured Craters of the Moon, a site of "fantastic formations . . . an awe-inspiring experience" (mss 80, box 1, folder 37, pp. 8–10).

The idea that the lunar landscape already existed in the American West was thus transmitted through the efforts of Robert Limbert, aided by the identification of Craters of the Moon as a national monument administered by the U.S. Park Service, and also through the continuing geological scientific theory in support of similar volcanic origins of the moon and the Craters site. Unsurprisingly, a 1960 follow-up article on the Limbert expedition, also appearing in *National Geographic,* included testimony by an official of the Aero-Space Laboratories of North American Aviation, itself "concerned with designing equipment for landings on the moon by instruments, and, eventually, by men" (Belknap, 512). The official, Dr. Jack Green, declared the features of the Idaho site to be "especially interesting" because they were "nearly as well preserved as we might expect to find them on the moon" (516).

The American West thus not only prepared the public to understand the space program in frontier terms but provided an actual geomorphic lunar site. Western imagery also provided ideological energy for a spacework culture. In the 1970s and 1980s, Ray Williamson of the Office of Technology Assessment of the U.S. Congress collected narratives of space workers (engineers, scientists, and managers) and found that their frontier imagery formed an ideological justification for "an expanded U.S. presence in space." Williamson cites the terms producing the alliance between the late twentieth-century space program and the prior centuries of westward movement of U.S. expansion—"like forts in the early west," "the space frontier," "a new high frontier," "America's frontier for growth"—all terms deployed by professionals involved in the design and logistics of the U.S. space effort (256, 258, 259, 261).

Even the naming of a spacecraft, *Pioneer,* "conjures up the image of outer space as frontier" (Williamson, 256). The astronaut Neil Armstrong, the first human being to set foot on the moon, stated, "Space is the frontier," though his fellow astronaut Bill Anders, of Apollo 8, had been even more explicit: "To me, and I think to many Americans, there had always been a sense of exploration and a sense of the frontier . . . now space was our frontier" (Chaikin, 164; Armstrong, Collins, and Aldrin,

202). Political scientists, too, have advanced the idea of the space frontier, for instance in a book titled *Reaching for the High Frontier* (Michaud), an essay subtitled "The Forgotten Frontier" and emphasizing the notion of the moon as an exploitable resource for mining (Katz), and another piece describing the moon as a "power frontier" in the contest between the cold war superpowers, the United States and the Soviet Union (Fawcett, 357).

Some of those warning against the identification of the space program with a problematic frontier history inadvertently lend credence to the linkage. Folklorists, in particular, have warned against adherence to the notion of space-age "manifest destiny" from the woodsman and pioneer to the spaceman, with a corollary of the mandate of so-called civilized peoples to claim "open territory" occupied only by "savages" (Young, "Guest," 228). Bolstered by media representation, one folklorist observes, "The lore of the western frontier has been used to argue for the expanded exploitation and settlement of outer space" (Young, "Guest," 228). Yet this critique nonetheless sustains the terms by which the space age is conceived as a resumption of the frontier era. The reported position of Native Americans who "pity the Indians and the buffalo of outer space" refers to the repression and genocide of Indians by whites ironically but recapitulates that narrative all the same (Young, "Guest," 227–228, 271). It was probably a foregone conclusion that the chaplain of the *Hornet,* the Navy recovery vessel to which the Apollo 11 astronauts were hoisted after splashdown, would offer a prayer of thanks in which he referred to the national effort to "blaze new trails" (qtd. Mailer, *Fire on Moon,* 453).

Yet the male American frontier was also prime for the deconstructive critique of Kolodny's *Lay of the Land,* which inverted traditional terms of western heroism to reveal, instead, misogyny. *The Lay of the Land* looked back into American literary history from a late twentieth-century conviction of environmental spoliation and emergent feminism, and it resumed and redirected Henry Nash Smith's *Virgin Land: The American West as Symbol and Myth* (the title taken from Turner's reference to American "new worlds of virgin land") (Turner, 270). *The Lay of the Land* did not lift its gaze heavenward to include discussion of Norman Mailer, NASA or the American moon. Kolodny's project, however, exposed and critiqued the masculinist western frontier paradigm within which Mailer's and other American moon texts operated. It moved conceptually to expose the male heroism of *An American Dream, Of a Fire on the Moon,* Michener's *Space,* and the astronauts' own statements as a pattern of compulsive, hypermasculinist exploitation of the environment and of women.

This newer kind of argument, not surprisingly, opened the way for yet another new frontier as women, too, claim that fraught term in *Frontiers: A Journal of Women Studies*. *Frontiers* was conceived as a forum in which to dismantle Turner's "frontier that assumed an ethnocentric hierarchy from savagery to civilization" and committed itself instead to decentering that univocal frontier in order to "reconsider the contexts and consequences of histories that brought different peoples to occupy common territory" (Jameson, 10). A cofounder of the journal, Elizabeth Jameson, recalls that she "first thought about 'frontiers' from a feminist perspective in 1974 when the original Frontiers Collective met in Boulder" and that a colleague "suggested *Frontiers* to connote both our region and the new territory we were charting as feminists and as publishers." Jameson adds that the plural form of the terms was chosen "to connote the many arenas for women's achievement and empowerment" (Jameson, 6).

Heavenly Body

But what of the heavenly body, the moon, in its frontier incarnation? She will not appear as a lunar Annie Oakley or Calamity Jane but as a descendant of the western classical lunar Diana, the virgin goddess of hunting and childbirth, and variously named Artemis, Luna, Cynthia, Phoebe. This embodied and personified moon might seem an archaism in twenti-eth- and twenty-first-century American literature, especially in the masculine world of NASA and of the male writer drawn into its domain. Idaho's Robert Limbert only obliquely feminized the moon in public lectures seeming to augur NASA's interest in Craters of the Moon as an analogue to the lunar surface. "Were the daily papers to suddenly flash the news that an interesting piece of the moon, dead silent and cold, with its mysterious crater rings, its seas of frozen rock, and its rivers of hardened rock . . . [had] by some mighty catastrophe of nature been projected through space and landed in our northwestern United States," Limbert said, "it is certain that various expeditions under the leadership of competent scientists would at once be organized to explore its hidden mysteries" ("Our Next National Park," mss 80, box 1, folder 18).

Yet when Norman Mailer referred to a lunar "platinum lady" in *An American Dream* (1964, 12) and to "the moon! that pale sister of Creation" in his *Of a Fire on the Moon* (1970, 170), he deliberately renewed the tradition of classical lunar personification in a late twentieth-century American frontier context. Indeed, Mailer's fiction and journalism became an important source of American lunar incarnation in the late twentieth century. Mailer, self-identified as a macho figure, made an extensive effort on behalf of nationalist masculinity to embody the moon for the American literary tradition and its male authorial pantheon.

Mailer explicitly identifies himself as a *literary* man, invoking the tradition of belles lettres, for instance, in an extended comparison of the astronauts' knowledge of engineering to an English professor's familiarity with specialized studies of the British-American canon (*Fire on Moon*, 252–254). He continues the figuration of the moon that had become traditional in literary texts over centuries—the moon, for instance, whose "body [is] mysterious beyond measure," who "kept herself like a subject before the king—her face always presented, her back always hidden," whose "face" is a "self-portrait" (*Fire on Moon*, 282, 286, 292). As Mailer well knows, the lunar identity, unlike that of the geysers of the American West, had an exceptionally intricate foreground in Western cultural representation extending to ancient Greece and Rome, which a writer schooled in literary history would understand and be prepared to exploit in response to the contemporary American space project.

But the moon, too, had been a new world—a new kind of heavenly body—in the seventeenth century, as Marjorie Nicolson showed years ago. At that time, the new "optik tube," a 30x telescope, showed the terrain of the moon to be irregular, with elevations and declivities that perforce mandated a "new realism" in treatment of it. Several issues Nicolson has discussed are engaging for consideration of twentieth-century lunar literature, for instance the ways in which the classical Diana becomes accommodated to the new terrestrial information, the hypotheses on the probability of interplanetary civilization, and thus the plausibility of relativistically different cultures throughout the cosmos. Especially intriguing in a postcolonialist moment is the notion of imperial expansion which entered into the calculations on the viability of lunar habitation even in an eighteenth-century Britain, which entertained the possibility that the new lunar world would become a British colony (Nicolson, *World in Moon*, 48–49).

Particularly noteworthy here, however, is Mailer's and others' inherited legacy of a moon personified from the seventeenth century. Forgoing the impersonal pronoun, writers repeatedly represented the "heavenly body" both implicitly and explicitly as female and embodied. In 1610 Galileo declared "the body of the Moon" to be "a most beautiful and delightful sight," its surface "just like the face of the Earth itself" (Nicolson, *World in Moon*, 1). At the end of the century, another writer referred to the "Moons Face" (9). Francis Bacon cited the "moon and the other heavenly bodies" (16), while Johannes Kepler described "a certain bright heavenly body which we call the Moon" (17). The very term "body," as in "heavenly body," of course can refer to the entire material or physical structure of an entity and is subject to male or female designation. When the United States signed the United Nations General Assembly Resolution XVIII of 13 December, 1963, stating that "outer space and celestial bodies are not subject to national appropriation by claims of sovereignty, by means or use or occupation, or by any other means," it was endorsing, with eighty other nations, language put into circulation in Galileo's time (Fawcett, 359). The terminology of "the moon and other celestial bodies" was a stock phrase appearing some twenty-two times in the treaty (Fawcett, 361).

By the eighteenth century, most writers enforced the notion of a moon gendered as female, even though some (here, Francis Godwin) mixed gender reference, citing both the "Man in the Moon" and lunar parts that are "somewhat darker than the rest of her body." More typical, Abraham Cowley spoke of the "white moon" as the sun's mistress and another poet of "her monthly light" (Nicolson, *World in Moon,* 20, 21, 32). Legatee of Galileo's knowledge of the lunar surface is Jonathan Swift's "Progress of Beauty," which personified a female moon satirically beset by a blemished complexion:

> When first Diana leaves her bed,
> Vapours and steams her look disgrace,
> A frowzy, dirty-colored red
> Sits on her cloudy, wrinkled face:
>
> But by degrees when mounted high,
> Her artificial face appears
> Down from her window in the sky,
> Her spots are gone, her visage clears. (20)[6]

By the eighteenth century the moon was consistently female, both corporeally and especially facially. Although eighteenth-century studies of atmospheric conditions increasingly called into question the habitability of the lunar environment, texts of the seventeenth through the nineteenth centuries show a recurrent figural representation of the moon both embodied and female. Whether "she" was inhabited is secondary to consideration of the very she-ness of the moon. The convention of this gendering piques interest when, in a late twentieth-century text generally averse to personification, in this instance Michener's *Space* (1982), a German rocket scientist declares, "Look at the Moon, coming like a gray goddess in the east" (375).

The very infrequency of moments like this in Michener and other moon texts, to be sure, raises a problem about another body—the body of evidence. A reader seeking information about the space program in the standard accounts would be unlikely to notice figural references to lunar embodiment except as minor details. Is the moon really arguably, then, the frontier embodiment? Isn't it more accurate to say that its personification is at most the residue of an older Western cultural tradition, a mere rhetorical tracing from centuries of science reportage, poetry, narrative? Isn't there a suspicion that contemporary terms of embodiment ought to be regarded as mere residual particulates clouding the clear atmosphere of a scientized moon?

Transcripts of the Apollo 11 moon walk of the astronauts, for example, show no indebtedness to the literary-cultural lunar tradition of embodiment, for the diction is explicitly functional, informally conversational, efficient, utilitarian. Norman Mailer noted the "resolute lack of poetic immortality in the astronauts' communications with the earth," their "jargon . . . resolutely divorced from any language with grandeur to match the proportions of the endeavor" (*Fire on Moon,* 293, 274). Here is a portion of verbatim transcript of Neil Armstrong and Buzz Aldrin on the moon, July 20, 1969, as the two collected lunar samples while the NASA space center in Houston monitored their progress:

ALDRIN: I say, these rocks are rather slippery. . . . Very powdery surface where the sun hits. The powder fills up all the very fine porouses. My boot tends to slide over it very easily. . . . Say, Neil, didn't I say we might see some purple rocks?

ARMSTRONG: Find the purple rocks?

ALDRIN: Yes, they are small, sparkly . . . [*static*] . . . I would make a first guess, some sort of biotite. We'll leave it to the lunar analysts. . . . Now, let's move that [scoop] over this way. . . . The blue color of my boot has completely disappeared now into this—still don't know exactly what color to describe this other than grayish-cocoa color.   (Armstrong, Collins, and Aldrin, 328–329, 333)

In this passage, Armstrong and Aldrin are amateur geologists reporting on geophysical properties in an elementary way in accordance with the flight plan for Apollo 11. The exchange is self-evidently utilitarian. Their officially inspirational and patriotic moon moments, also planned, were quite separate from those of the tasks of sample gathering, flight, navigation, photography, experimental set-ups, and so on. At the time of the lunar sample gathering represented above, Armstrong had, as Mailer said, "joined the ranks of the forever quoted" with the line "That's one small step for a man, one giant leap for all mankind." Momentarily the two astronauts would unveil a plaque which read, in English, "Here men from the planet Earth first set foot upon the Moon, July, 1969 A.D. We came in peace for all Mankind" (Mailer, *Fire on Moon,* 399; Armstrong, Collins, and Aldrin, 321, 329).

The two would also manage to push an American flag, stiffened with wire to simulate the effect of a breeze, into a resistant lunar surface and would receive a call from President Richard M. Nixon declaring this to be "the most historic telephone call ever made. . . . Because of what you have done, the heavens have become a part of man's world" (Armstrong, Collins, and Aldrin, 332–333). In this official, nationally broadcast exchange, the words of the president and of the astronauts sound interchangeable ("all the people on this earth . . . truly one. . . . United States . . . men of peace of all nations . . . vision for the future"), and thus ceremonial rhetoric combines with rock talk at the level of Geology 101, all in the service of the mission, the national interest, and the advancement of knowledge (333).

The moon in representations such as those above is either a geologic entity or the staged occasion for the celebration of the officially designated human—read pioneer American—spirit. In fact, the deliberate *dis*embodiment and deromanticizing of the moon via NASA seems strategic by design, as Andrew Chaikin shows at the opening of his history of the Apollo program, *A Man on the Moon* (1994):

> When the moon rises beyond the Atlantic shore of Florida, full and luminous, it seems so close that you could just row out to the end of the water and touch it. In January 1967, the moon seemed to draw nearer by the day to the hard, flat beaches of Cape Kennedy. Seen from there it was no longer the governess of the tides, the lovers' beacon, the celebrated mistress of song; it was a target, a Cold War beachhead in the sky. It was NASA's moon. (10, emphasis omitted)

Here, on site, we see NASA's "Cold War beachhead in the sky" replace the personified "governess of the tides" and "celebrated mistress of song," which is to say that the female moon of a romantic and classical tradition is deliberately replaced by the moon of modern science and technology. The American moon of the later twentieth century will be neither "governess" nor "mistress" but a military objective in an actual, if undeclared, war. Indeed, the Apollo 8 astronauts who orbited the moon in 1968 stated that "the place looked like the deserted battlefield of the final war" (Chaikin, 109). "Like a military invasion," as a geologist associated with the Apollo program put it—"like a military invasion" with generals, troops, theaters of operations, and so on, and himself as an infantry captain (Chaikin, 406).

Scientific-technological study of the moon was conducted in the language of the earth sciences, not militarism, but such discourse further operated to replace the mythic Luna. Lunar samples would be indices of earth's own chemical evolution, and a science reporter summarized the theoretical debates to be settled by examination of the lunar samples of Apollo 11: "We should know whether or not the moon is 'alive,' with a hot, churning interior and current volcanic activity; or whether it is 'dead,' with no such activity" (Sullivan, 45). (The Apollo project validated the latter, "dead" moon theory.)

Pre-Apollo theories advanced by "leading" scientists, including a Nobel laureate, further demythified the moon by representing its constituent parts in the terminology of science. Back in 1952, in the magazine *Collier's*, the scientists Fred Whipple and Wernher von Braun wrote that "the principal aim of . . . [the] first lunar exploration will be strictly scientific," and they promised tests for gases such as xenon and krypton, for the presence of a magnetic field, for indications of a "lunar molten iron core" (Whipple and von Braun, 42). The two scientists promised that lunar samples would be collected, including dust, rock, lava, and drill-core minerals (44).

Scientists involved in the Apollo project also emphasized the importance of lunar samples, which were considered comparable to the meteorites named tektites, octahedrites, and hypersthene chondrites (Sullivan, 45). On earth, scientists awaited lunar samples to ascertain the possible presence of microorganisms, to date the cosmos by analyzing the rare lunar atmospheric gases (argon, helium, neon), to prove whether heat on the moon might be caused by radioisotopes, to learn the effects of twenty thousand years of solar wind bombarding the lunar surface, to use x-ray spectroscopy to learn the chemical composition of the moon, to study lunar crystals to reconstruct processes which formed the lunar seas. The mythic Luna, it goes without saying, had no part in these projects, which *Life* magazine described in its 1969 special edition, *To the Moon and Back,* with readers offered color photographs of the scientists in their high-tech laboratories.

And nonspecialist NASA reports, such as that of the 1972 Apollo 17 flight (which included for the first time a professional geologist, Dr. Harrison H. Schmitt), also characterize the lunar exploration as entirely scientific, as in this typical passage: "Careful study of the soil in the Lunar Receiving Laboratory on Earth showed that it was composed mostly (about 90 percent) of tiny orange-tinted glass spheres and fragments. The particles were mostly finer than about 50 microns (1/500 inch) and contained about ten times as much zinc as other lunar samples" (5). The Apollo 17 mission included the dedication of a moon rock to the world's youth via a NASA-sponsored International Youth Science Tour undertaken in cooperation with the State Department, the U.S. Information Agency, and the National Science Teachers Association. The lunar present and future were to belong solely to science.

This demythification of the female moon falls within a post-seventeenth-century Baconian scientizing of the natural world which Caroline Merchant terms the "death of nature." She shows that, commensurate with the development of capitalism, the scientific revolution succeeded in removing "animistic, organic assumptions about the cosmos." As she explains, the universe was increasingly regarded as "a system of dead, inert particles moved by external . . . forces" (*Death of Nature,* 193). Merchant emphasizes the scientific effacement of the cosmic female principle. By formulating the universe as a "mechanism of inert matter in motion, . . . the mechanists transformed the body of the world and its female soul" (195). In the twentieth century, thereby, NASA's scientized moon replaces La Luna.

Suppose, however, that in the light of the sci-tech discourse and the promotion of science education, we return to linger with NASA's "Cold War beachhead in the sky," which allegedly replaces the personified "governess of the tides" and the "celebrated mistress of song." At this point in the text, the governess-mistress is relegated to a superannuated realm of romance and of antique science, while NASA's new moon is defined as a modern beachhead in a nuclear-era military campaign of sophisticated rocketry. Indeed, the 1969 *Life* magazine special edition on Apollo 11 headlined: "So Long to the Good Old Moon" (O'Neil, n.p.).

Although the NASA projection of a cold war beachhead is said to replace the lunar governess-mistress, negation is not the same as effacement. The lunar governess and the mistress do not disappear from the reader's mind but only shift in hierarchical priority. They become background; in the American slang term, they are "history," meaning bygone and irrelevant. The NASA task will be to keep them there, to privilege and to protect its own semantic hierarchy in order to legitimate its new sci-tech and military moon. To do so, NASA must seem to arrest historical progress so that its moon prevails. The NASA moon, otherwise, might be understood only as part of an evolving, historical lunar identification.

Yet the astronauts themselves prove to be carriers of the older meanings, for it is evident that they were schooled in lunar ideas predating the NASA cold war beachhead they themselves were instrumental in establishing. To a remarkable degree, the astronauts were devotees not only of frontier ideas but specifically of Jules Verne's *From the Earth to the Moon* (*De la terre à la lune*, 1865). "Shades of Jules Verne!" exclaimed a *National Geographic* writer in a special issue, *Man's Conquest of Space* (1968), which declared Verne's *From the Earth to the Moon* to be "prophetic" (Shelton, 144, 40; see R. Miller, 53). Set in Baltimore, *From the Earth to the Moon* recounts the project of a post–Civil War gentlemen's Gun Club to raise the vast sum of over two million dollars to cast an enormous (twelve feet tall, nine feet wide) gun, named the Columbiad, able to fire a projectile containing three spacemen at the moon, and to observe the moment of impact through a mammoth new telescope constructed in the Rocky Mountains. (Verne had left his astronauts stranded in lunar orbit, and readers' protests prompted the sequel, *Around the Moon,* in which they are returned to earth.)

Club members of *From the Earth to the Moon* are promised they will be "Columbuses of this unknown world." The book anticipates the location of the rocket launch station at Cape Canaveral, for Verne's Columbiad gun is fired in Florida, causing an earthquake throughout the peninsula, the flames visible for one hundred miles offshore (125). Verne's text, in fact, was an important antecedent for the Apollo project, and his scheme for a direct moon rocket shot was carefully considered before being supplanted by the plan for staged, disposable rockets and boosters with a lunar orbit rendezvous.

The astronaut James Lovell of the Apollo 8 mission "devoured" Verne's tale in boyhood, and *First on the Moon,* the coauthored account by Apollo 11's Armstrong, Collins, and Aldrin, carefully traces similarities between their mission and that described in the century-old *From the Earth to the Moon,* including the trio of astronauts, the launch from Florida in December, the deluge of visitors converging to witness the historic event, the mechanical genius Verne ascribes nationalistically to Americans, the very naming of the spaceship *Columbia* (Chaikin, 65; Armstrong, Collins, and

Aldrin, 62–63). In a television broadcast from the moon, Neil Armstrong tutored the public about Verne's book: "This is the commander of Apollo 11. A hundred years ago, Jules Verne wrote a book about a voyage to the moon. His spaceship, Columbia, took off from Florida and landed in the Pacific Ocean after completing a trip to the moon. It seems appropriate to us to share with you some of the reflections of the crew as the modern-day Columbia completes its rendezvous with the planet earth and the same Pacific Ocean tomorrow" (Armstrong, Collins, and Aldrin, 401). The Apollo astronauts obviously found in Verne's tale a prophecy of their own efforts, one so nationally momentous that Armstrong broadcast a tutorial to some two hundred million Americans.

Yet *From the Earth to the Moon* taught its readers something else as well. Simply put, from Verne's own national tradition of *La Luna,* it taught them about a moon gendered as a female. Verne's moon proves to be uninhabited, indeed uninhabitable, but it is repeatedly gendered female as "Queen of the Night" and represented throughout Verne's text in feminine pronouns—for example, of "her mass, density and weight; her constitution, motions, distance, as well as her place in the solar system" and the point at which "she will be crossing the zenith," when "she is *new,*" "when she is in her *first* or *last* quarter" (20, 28, 32).

In this gendering, Verne in part subsumes an even older tradition of moon voyage texts, such as Johannes Kepler's *Somnium,* which rebuked the ancient world for mistaking "her," the moon, for "a Piece / Of red-hot iron" when she really proved to be fecund, and Elkanah Settle's *World in the Moon,* a spectacle in which one character, named Wildblood, when asked how he likes the new lunar world, replies, "As I do a Mistress the better for being a new one" (qtd. Nicolson, *Voyages,* 47–48, 79). Verne's female lunar precedents abound, and his knowledge of the tradition of such voyage narratives has been documented (Nicolson, *Voyages,* 243–249).

Although his fictional voice closely resembles newspaper reportage, Jules Verne, citizen himself of an imperialist nation, evidently also understood the undertone of sexual possession in the masculinist American territorial expansionism when he observed that "for the Yankees, they had no other ambition than to take possession of this new continent of the sky, and to plant upon the summit of its highest elevation the star-spangled banner of the United States" (34). Yet the lunar continent is the "Queen of the Night." Verne's Columbiad (which was the title of Joel Barlow's late eighteenth-century epic poem advancing the notion of an American empire spreading throughout the Americas) summons an image of Americans thrusting the flagstaff shaft into the lunar body, thus to conquer the "Queen of the Night."[7]

At this point it is useful to recall Stewart Guthrie's view that landscapes (in this case, moonscapes) suggest humanity, that the external environment is innately suggestive of the human being, and therefore that anthropomorphism is a persistent, involuntary cognitive process underlying environmental bodily figuration (117). From this framework, one returns to texts of the American space program with a rather different sensibility. One now appreciates not only the utilitarian voices and scripted ceremo-

26. NASA Apollo 11 rocket lifts off from earth, bound for the moon, August 1969.

27. Astronaut Neil Armstrong with wire-stiffened flag and flagstaff thrust into the surface of the moon, August 1969.

nial utterances but also the references to the moon as a "harsh mistress," to its "pockmarked face," its "forbidding face," its "face of pure Nature," its "ripening," its lunar parts "giving up their secrets," its dust "telling its own story," to the very "difficulty of tak[ing] the moon's pulse" (Chaikin, 303, 384, 104, 426, 110, 364, 367; Shepard and Slayton, 308). One feels receptive to the personification of a moon "here to tell us the story . . . forever lost on our planet" but able to "fool" the astronauts snarled in problems of mapping and siting (Chaikin, 281–282). One is less inclined to dismiss as aberrant certain statements of Neil Armstrong, who referred in a press interview to the "heavenly body" and, in his coauthored *First on the Moon*, personified the moon that "summoned life out of . . . the sea, and led it onto the empty land" (qtd. Mailer, *Fire on Moon*, 45; Arm-

strong, Collins, and Aldrin, "L'Envoi," in *First,* n.p.). Armstrong recalled
that the sun was "magnificent, but the moon even more so. . . . It seemed
almost as though it were showing us its roundness, its similarity in shape
to our earth, in a sort of welcome. I was sure it would be a hospitable host.
It had been awaiting its first visitors for a long time" (Armstrong, Collins,
and Aldrin, 324).

The moon is sexualized in such texts, too, as an object of heterosexual
male desire and conquest despite NASA's careful management of the image of the space program as male, familial, virile but nonerotic. The astronaut wives, for instance, are represented as unfailing in domestic duty,
their efforts at grooming and fashion serving values of domesticity, never
erotic allure. In a moment of erotic displacement, however, Neil Armstrong said, "It's a peculiar thing, but the [lunar] surface looked very warm
and inviting. It looked as if it would be a nice place to take a sunbath. It
was the sort of situation in which you felt like going out there in nothing
but a bathing suit to get a little sun" (Armstrong, Collins, and Aldrin,
306). In an era when nude bathing was taboo, the image of Armstrong
stripped to swim trunks sunbathing on a sensually warm lunar sur*face* resumes and expands Verne's Euro-American notion of the lunar female.

More explicit sexual expressions are also present in the American space
texts. The lunar mountains, slopes of "smooth bright forms" are "vir-
ginal," but astronaut Charles (Chuck) Conrad, preparing for the Apollo
12 flight, is reported to have laughed at *Playboy* pinups annotated "with
proper geologic terminology: 'Don't forget: Describe the protuberances' "
(Chaikin, 414, 264). The Apollo 15 project, which involved a level of
geological sophistication unprecedented in the program, prompted this
exclamation from a member of the U.S. Geological Survey: "Did you see
those guys [moon-walking astronauts David Scott and James B. Irwin] today? They . . . found that boulder, and they sampled the soil around the
rock, and then they rolled it over and got some of the soil underneath it!
Why, they did everything but fuck that rock!" (Chaikin, 421–422). Jules
Verne might smile, knowing better.

At this point we can revisit Michener's *Space,* a kind of print-form
docudrama account of the whole space program from the World War II
German V-2 rockets through the post-Apollo era of interplanetary exploration. *Space* for the most part resists reversion to the romantic literary
tradition but does include this erotic passage in which a former test pilot
and now naval officer contemplates applying for the astronaut program:
"He was . . . torn with longing: God, I want to fly again! I want to test every plane in the world. The Moon . . . He bit his lower lip until the pain

startled him: The Moon. I know every crater on the Moon. He remained by the ship's railing, tears of desire flooding his eyes" (401).

On one level, his ardent desire is to join test pilot comrades in the homosocial, macho world of high-intensity flying. The terms of that desire, however, are sexualized as the moon becomes the object of a desire so great it evokes a tearful flood, an inadvertent confirmation of lunar eros. Similarly, another pilot-turned-astronaut is shown worthy because "every muscle in his body wanted to keep flying upward" (269). The self as ejaculatory projectile serves as the defining credential in *Space*. The astronauts are physically consumed with lunar passion. Apollo will not be an occupation but a mission of obsessive, erotic desire. (In keeping with NASA's image management, Michener's astronaut wives are represented consistently as domestic partners responsible for household management and child care, their interest in personal appearance serving only the goal of respectability.)[8]

Michener's text also argues that the moon is ultimately so worthy of the sacrifice of human life that when one fictional astronaut dies in an accident on the lunar surface, both his widow and lover (a careerist Asian journalist, not a wholesome suburban American gal/woman) join together at the memorial service, implicitly because they rightfully yield to the consuming lunar passion that is greater than the worth of their mere mortal female flesh.

Platinum Lady and New Mistress: Norman Mailer's Moons

From the context within which Michener, the astronauts, and various journalists and spokespeople worked—a context of a centuries-old tradition of lunar personification and of a political New Frontier—emerged Norman Mailer's *American Dream* (1964), a bid to reclaim the moon in its very literary incarnation, to renew it in literary terms even as NASA and the scientists redefined it solely as the object of space exploration and scientific study.

No particular lunar interest is evident in the background of the U.S. Army veteran and Pulitzer Prize–winning novelist who first gained critical acclaim for his World War II antiwar novel, *The Naked and the Dead* (1948). Yet it is useful to recall that Mailer, as a literate and culturally savvy U.S. citizen, inhabited a media environment of space and lunar information and speculation that developed in the United States from the early 1950s. Over a two-year period, for instance, *Collier's*, which was at that time one of the nation's most widely read general-interest magazines, with a circulation of three million subscribers, published eight feature articles on the feasibility of space—including moon—travel. A full-scale media campaign accompanied the *Collier's* project, including appearances by Wernher von Braun on network news and morning programs (such as NBC's *Today* and CBS's *Gary Moore*) with viewing audiences approaching eight million. *Time* and *Life* also ran articles on space travel. Cornelius ("Connie") Ryan of *Collier's* developed the periodical series into two books, *Across the Space Frontier* (1952) and *Conquest of the Moon* (1953). As one historian writes, "Many men who eventually went to work in the U.S. Space program attribute their initial spark of interest to the pages of *Collier's*" (Liebermann, 142). In addition, as noted above, the Walt Disney three-part television production on space, *Man in Space, Man and the Moon,* and *Mars and Beyond* (1955–1957) helped to create a general public awareness of space in very positive terms.

Awareness also grew in ominous cold war terms, first in October 1957, when the Soviets launched Sputnik, an artificial satellite that circled the globe, and then, over three years later, when cosmonaut Yuri Gagarin orbited the earth in a Vostok spaceship, which one Washington newspaper called "a psychological victory of the first magnitude for the Soviet Union," moving John F. Kennedy to make the public pronouncement with which this discussion opened, one calling for the U.S. manned space flight to the moon within the decade (Logsdon, "Challenge," 149). Through the early 1960s, not only did Soviet space launches gain media attention but so did the American Mercury and Gemini programs, particularly Alan Shepard's sixteen-minute suborbital flight for the United States in Freedom 7 in the Mercury program and John Glenn's February 1962 encircling of the earth, an event covered extensively by newspapers, magazines, and television.

A writer of Norman Mailer's generation (b. 1923) would very much inhabit the later twentieth-century lunar media environment. Mailer took an undergraduate degree in engineering and became a journalist as well as a novelist (see Dearborn). He wrote for various politically leftist magazines in addition to *Esquire* and the newspaper the *Village Voice* (which he helped to organize). He wrote a series of magazine articles on John F. Kennedy, published in book form as *The Presidential Papers* (1963), and it is therefore unsurprising not only that he wrote *Of a Fire on the Moon* (1970) on the Apollo 11 project but also that his earlier *American Dream* should be framed by, arguably dominated by, the moon in its emphatically literary identity as La Luna.

Throughout other writings, Mailer exploited the moon in various ways, for instance in his account of the Republican and Democratic party conventions of 1968, *Miami and the Siege of Chicago* (1968), in which the moon functions as a stock figure of remoteness, of the nocturnal, of the exotic. The Chicago stockyards are "as empty as the railroad sidings of the moon" (87), while the postmidnight hours are of "the effulgence of a full moon" (127), and a psychedelic experience features "alleys of the mad where cockroaches drive like Volkswagens on the oilcloth of the moon" (139).

In *An American Dream,* however, a novel categorized in reviews as allegorical, Mailer personifies the moon as a dominating female presence in a first-person narrative told by the protagonist, Stephen Rojack, a mid-twentieth-century Renaissance man with his own television show, a best-selling book, a university professorship, and a term served in elective office in the U.S. House of Representatives. It is doubtless deliberate that in a novel named for a core national myth, Rojack introduces himself at the beginning as a World War II hero who once double dated with fellow congressman John F. Kennedy. The protagonist thus allies himself with the New Frontier and with its mission to land a man on the moon. In fact, the double date occurred on the night of a full moon, and Mailer's protagonist trumps Kennedy in lunar terms: "The real difference between the President and myself," Rojack says, "may be that I ended with too large an appreciation of the moon" (2).

That appreciation grew from a wartime night when, also "under a full moon," the soldier and soon-to-be hero Rojack killed four German soldiers whose deaths are recounted in detail (2–6). At the opening of the novel several years later, Rojack is experiencing the profound psychological crisis—a sort of posttraumatic stress—suppressed since that wartime night when he both confronted the "abyss" and began his "secret frightened romance with the phases of the moon" (2, 7). Rojack, we learn, is latently both murderous and suicidal. Within a few years of the publication of *An American Dream,* feminist critics would also cite him as proof of his creator's misogyny. Within the opening sequences, Rojack will strangle and shove from a New York high-rise window the body of his "Great Bitch" wife, Deborah, from whom he is separated and who, before her death, was an heiress and also the daughter-lover of Oswald Kelly (a New York–based, self-made multimillionaire and global power with ties to the CIA and Mafia). Mailer will demonstrate Rojack's sexual prowess as he twice copulates with his dead wife's German maid (as though World War II continues in sexual battle), survives a standoff with the New York ho-

micide detectives whose pathology report strongly implicates him as his
wife's killer, then finds solace in a new love with a southern jazz singer,
Cherry, whose Little Italy Mafia handlers and drug-crazed black jazzman
lover, Shago, also must be confronted *mano a mano* in Rojack's tests of
mental and physical power. Finally, Rojack will gain liberation in a walk
along a high-rise terrace balcony parapet as his father-in-law—and the
moon—both try to precipitate his fall. In that penultimate scene, Rojack's
unwillingness to retrace his steps along that baluster—an act certain to
cause his death—causes instead the death of his singer-lover, since her life,
in order to continue (according to the novel's metaphysics), must be paid
for by a double parapet walk that would surely kill Rojack.

An American Dream rejects the realist fictional worlds of Mailer's
contemporary, John Updike (Updike's *Centaur* aside), sustaining instead
the hypermasculinist ethos of Ernest Hemingway, whose male world is
framed in terms of war and contact sports. Yet *An American Dream* also
reverts to the grand metaphysics of a Melville. In Mailer, the American life
of an ethnic intellectual *arriviste* (Rojack is half Jewish) is a struggle for
the soul's self-possession in a world of competing demonic and godly
powers. Good and Evil, however, cannot be easily disentangled, nor can
Rojack always seek the light. At certain points, he says "yes to the Devil,
yes to the Lord" (133). Both appear in one another's guises, and Rojack's
quest is to free himself once and for all from the clutches of known and
confirmed evil, which was incarnate principally in his secretive and sadis-
tic dead wife.

In this world, the personified female moon is powerful and fully realized in the first of two scenes in which Rojack walks a narrow high-rise
parapet and risks falling to his death:

> So I stood on the balcony by myself and stared at the moon which
> was full and very low. I had a moment then. For the moon spoke
> back to me. By which I do not mean that I heard voices, or Luna and
> I indulged in the whimsy of a dialogue, no, truly it was worse than
> that. Something in the deep of that full moon, some tender and not
> so innocent radiance traveled fast as the thought of lightning across
> our night sky, out from the depths of the dead in those caverns of the
> moon, out and a leap through space into me. And suddenly I under-
> stood the moon. (11)

The scene establishes Mailer's rhetorical ground rules for Rojack's com-
munion with the moon. There will be no indication that the protagonist

hears hallucinatory voices, or that Mailer will succumb to crudely sub-literary allegorical techniques. From quantum mechanics and mysticism both, Mailer will bid to make credible the instantaneous and profound communication of the moon to a Rojack whose very nerve endings are cosmic antennae. Some five years later, Mailer explained the basis for this technique: "Metaphors arise [out] of a charged and libidinous universe with heavenly bodies which attract each other across the silences of space" (*Fire on Moon,* 224). Rojack thus can say, "That platinum lady with her silver light . . . was in my ear, I could hear her music: 'Come to me,' she was saying, 'come now. Now! . . . now is your moment. What joy in the flight' " (12).

The moon's invitation, however, appeals to Rojack's suicidal side. Rojack knows that while his body—"bones and all"—will "drop like a sack," he will simultaneously "fly," "soar," "rise" and "leap the miles of darkness to that moon." But at best the moon's message is out of phase with his life (12). Mailer expresses his protagonist's quandary in the appealing terms of the American work ethic: " 'You can't die yet,' said the formal part of my brain, 'you haven't done your work' " (13). Nonsense, replies the moon, "You've lived your life, and you are dead with it" (13). Subtly, in lunar terms the novel here pivots from the mystical to the murderous. The moon may be a "Lady . . . baleful in her radiance," but she is also a killer, the gravitational power of suggestion her lethal weapon.

At this point, Mailer shifts reader empathy to Rojack's energies of earthly self-preservation. "Let me not be all dead," he cries, and his imperative is the novel's very cry for life (13). The reader is now to be wholly supportive of the Rojack who pulls himself back over the balcony railing and gets on with the work of his life.

But what work? The imperatives of Mailer's plot have been summarized above, but throughout the novel one is impressed above all by Rojack's relentless need—his very compulsion—to confirm at every opportunity the very substance of his own body. His muscles, nerves, internal organs are minutely examined in terms of mass, gravitational field, and anatomical integrity. The climb up over the balcony when he resists the moon's call shows some of this:

> My right hand tightened in its grip, and I whipped half-around to the balcony, almost banging into the rail with my breast, my back now to the street and the sky. . . . I . . . slipped back over the rail, and dropped into a chair. I was sick. I assure you I was sick in a way I had never been before. Deep in a fever, or bumping through the rapids of

a bad nausea, one's soul could always speak to one. . . . Nothing but sickness and dung remained in the sack of my torso. (13)

This is the kind of bodily inscription that essentially makes up *An American Dream* from first to last. The wind "reaches to the forest of nerves on [Rojack's] gut," and he feels as if "his chest [is] separated from [his] groin," and his "skin lived on thin wire" while emotions pass like ghosts through "the aisles of [his] body" (15, 26, 40). In sexual congress, his toes "move in the wet with all the deliverance of snakes who have crossed the desert," but in the orgasmic moment, "there was an explosion, furious, treacherous and hot as the gates of an icy slalom with the speed of [his] heels overtaking [his] nose" (42, 46). His "bones are soup," he feels "the marrow oozing from his bones," his scrotum is a "charnel house," and his "body [is] like a cavern where deaths are stored" (244, 190, 44, 195).

These are examples selected virtually at random. One could readily find a different yet nearly identical assortment, for such figures are deployed relentlessly as if Mailer's main mission is to embody his protagonist, repeatedly to set forth images to realize Rojack's ("Raw Jock's") very bodily being, as if therein lies his identity. Indeed, *An American Dream* is about the embodiment of its hero in relation to the embodiment of the moon. As a literary lesson, it is tempting to believe that Newton's third law of motion—that for every action there is an equal and opposite reaction—is enacted in the novel in a case study of the body of its central character. Rojack's is a body in motion, active and reactive in excruciating physical detail.

The moon, on the contrary, represents the "lightness of being," to borrow Milan Kundera's term. It is threatening or, in Kundera's complete phrase, "unbearable," precisely because it represents a powerful weightlessness that the novel rejects as emasculating. As a "silvery whale," the moon is a feminized Moby Dick afloat in her lunar marine domain. (Mailer would elsewhere suggest that an astronaut might need "some of the monomania of Captain Ahab" [*Fire on Moon,* 331].) And the moon returns for the penultimate scene of a second parapet walk, this time on the balcony of Rojack's menacing father-in-law who, in private conversation with Rojack, confesses to incest with his daughter even as Rojack admits to killing her.

"Look at the moon, look up at the moon," says Rojack's inner voice as he walks that Upper East Side parapet with a renewed "desire to leave the balcony and fly" (259). The moon, a "princess of the dead," renews its "pale call," but readers are long aware of Rojack's compulsive need for bodily gravitational weight and so know he must and will not yield (indeed, he braves wind gusts and deflects the umbrella thrust by which his father-in-law tries to unbalance and tumble him to the street below). Mailer later wrote of the "weightlessness, that absence of gravity which space doctors worried might produce profound deteriorations of the organs and the flesh" in sustained space flight, of "muscles that go slack in weightlessness at a much accelerated pace" (*Fire on Moon,* 226, 250). Though astronauts reveled in their "weightless wonderland," that very state, gendered female in *An American Dream,* threatens a masculinity defined in terms of gravity, muscle mass, the very Archimedean ability to land an earthly knockout punch (Shepard and Slayton, 120).

Men's inability to live in that weightless lunar territory without unspeakably bulky constraints also rankled Mailer, who identified with male literary athleticism. The Apollo 11 astronauts in their space capsule and on the moon would look to him like "swaddled Eskimo children in baskets," each one like an "upright piano turned by movers on a corner of the stairs" (*Fire on Moon,* 371, 398). This from a writer representing proper astronautical masculine grace in Hemingwayesque terms of football quarterbacking, pole vaulting, boxing, fielding baseballs, downhill skiing, and so on (*Fire on Moon,* 12–13, 23, 27, 38).

Mailer's aversion to strong, outspoken women is a matter of record. His *Prisoner of Sex* (1971), which was largely a reaction against Kate Millet's *Sexual Politics,* rejected feminism in every guise while defending male coital vitality espoused in the fiction of his brethren Henry Miller and D. H. Lawrence as well as in his own. Mailer put women at contrary poles as beasts or goddesses, severed women's housework from males' "real" work, opposed childbearing to male heroism (19, 20, 27–28). Not surprisingly, in *An American Dream,* Rojack's dead wife looms threateningly large. She is "big," her hair "a huge mass," her Irish nose "large," her height in high-heeled shoes exceeding his by an inch (19). "I was afraid of her," says this Gulliver of his Brobdingnagian wife, Mailer all but stating outright what readers must know—that in relation to Deborah, Rojack has been literally a lightweight (25). Weight and weightlessness become the crux of *An American Dream,* which exposes the white American male's anxiety about his own disembodiment in a lunar atmosphere of virtual weightlessness. Disney had explained in his *Man in Space,* adapted for schoolroom use, that the firing rocket would make a man feel his weight was multiplied several times over, but that in space, free of the pull of gravity, he would move freely "without support from floors, wings, or rocket motors" (21). Some six years after the publication of *An American*

Dream, the astronaut Michael Collins would recall that on the Gemini 10 mission, he gave a "little" push with his fingertips and "sailed out the open hatch": "And when I tried to stop my movement I found that my body just kept on going. My hands came loose and I just sailed nose over teakettle into space" (Armstrong, Collins, and Aldrin, 224). Buzz Aldrin reports that the moon reduced his full-suit weight from 360 to 60 pounds (236). All this is Mailer's greatest dread, that the moon's gravitational field—one-sixth that of earth's—will prevail and render him a lightweight. Mailer shows the double bind: the novel's need for the personified moon equals Rojack's dread of her. The moon threatens to defeat its aspirant space-age conquerer.

Rojack therefore rejoices when his "limbs come alive" on that second parapet walk. Mailer can thus conclude this novel-journey where it began, in "the harbors of the moon," this time no German battlefield but the casinos of Las Vegas where Rojack wins at the gambling tables because his deceased new lover, Cherry, telepathically signals the winning bets. In a novelistic wish-fantasy, Cherry telephones Rojack from a lunar heaven where she and Marilyn Monroe are part of a sorority whose house "mother" is the moon herself (269). At the end, the macho Rojack is, as ever, at risk but given a new start, a new lease on life in the West, the territory most readily identified as frontier America and most vividly imagined, prior to the Apollo project, as terrain closely resembling that of the moon.

Mailer weighed in, so to speak, yet again on the moon in *Of a Fire on the Moon* (1970). In this second volume, Mailer appears not as a novelist but as a journalist, identified in the third person as Aquarius (Mailer's birth sign), whose task is to report the story of the Apollo 11 project in the style of the Sixties-era new journalism. Events are to be recounted with factual accuracy but subjectively, the author himself appearing as a participating character with clearly acknowledged biases, predilections, and personalized interpretations of events.

For a nontechnical audience, *Of a Fire on the Moon* meticulously explains the physics of rocketry and the digital binarism of the computer, the schedule of events in the Apollo 11 flight, the geologic theories of the origin of the moon—and thereby presents its era as arguably consonant with that of the development of the telescope and the new science in the early seventeenth century. But "Aquarius" is equally at liberty to speculate on whether there might be a "psychology of machines" and to comment critically on a corporate and plastic modern America and its deodorized WASP technocrats even as he continues the metaphysics of *An American*

Dream in which God and the Devil contend for supremacy. It is as new journalist that Mailer incarnates the NASA complex in male terms: Houston's Manned Spacecraft Center is the "brain," Cape Kennedy the "body," the launch complex "the bones and muscles of a Colossus" (52).

"Aquarius" also meditates on his own literary task. One problem was the impersonal, technocratic NASA language that Mailer himself had spoofed in scatological terms in *Why Are We in Vietnam* (1967) (48–49). Next was the astronauts' lack of a rudimentary sense of narrative shape. Because their work requires "constant and promiscuous concentration," they are "like narcissists, like children, like old people [exhibiting] a single-minded emphasis on each detail which arrived before them, large or small" (273). From so much foreshortened, indiscriminate data, Mailer must create formal coherence, and his ability to do so becomes a kind of "advertisement for [him]self."[9] In addition, the author of "The White Negro" and celebrant of hipsterism, a writer who repeatedly has plundered the black idiom to enrich his narratives, also worries that writing a book on the antiseptically technocratic Apollo 11 might have been a mistake. He admits that the project has "tormented" him and that he might have "blundered" in agreeing to write "a sex-stripped mystery of machines which might have a mind, and mysterious men who managed to live like machines" (*Fire on Moon*, 293, 436, 467). Like Henry Adams's *Education, Of a Fire on the Moon* is powered by the exploitable perplexity of an author-persona out of phase with a new world order and the human bodies representative of it.

Mailer's essential problem, however, is one of embodiment. Although "the trip to the moon had to serve as the embodiment of a new [American] vision," Mailer cannot endorse the bodies of the embodiment: "Man had become a Herculean embodiment of the Vision, but the brain on top of the head was as small as a transistorized fist, and the chambers of the heart had shrunk to the dry hard seeds of some hybrid future" (*Fire on Moon*, 384–385, 130–131). "Man" in this bodily identity is the desiccated and spiritually anemic white Anglo-Saxon Protestant, and the astronauts its replicant incarnation. Mailer, a Jew, recounts this exchange at a private dinner party in Houston, where over drinks "Aquarius" chats with a black professor:

> "You know," said the professor, "there are no Black astronauts."
> "Of course not."
> "Any Jewish astronauts?"
> "I doubt it."

The Black man grunted. They would not need to mention Mexicans or Puerto Ricans. Say, there might not even be any Italians. "Did you want them," asked Aquarius, "to send a Protestant, a Catholic, and a Jew to the moon?" (138–139).

That last query jabs satirically at the ethnic pattern of Mailer's war-novel rival, James Jones, whose *From Here to Eternity* served the "melting-pot" ideal in World War II terms. Mailer remarks that in the season of Apollo 11, the black man, whose culture is supposedly averse to technological precision, is altogether excluded while he, Mailer, can take a certain "pleasure" as a Jew who is at least nominally white. Presumably it did not occur to either man to recall the World War II precedent of the Tuskegee Airmen, the all-black squadrons of pilots trained at the Tuskegee Army Air Force Flying School to fly bomber escort aircraft, their proven success signaling blacks' eligibility for postwar flight training which, absent racial bias, could have enabled racial diversity in the Apollo crews (see Sandler). Presumably, in addition, it did not occur to Mailer or his acquaintance to broach the notion of a female astronaut, notably the supersonic civilian test pilot Jerrie Cobb, who had undergone NASA's physical and mental tests for astronauts and scored in the top 2 percent, thus qualifying her for the original 1962 Mercury astronaut group. She was excluded, however, through gender bias, especially that of John Glenn, who testified before a congressional committee that because males designed and built the spacecraft, males alone were entitled to fly them.

Ethnic, female, and nonwhite America, according to *Of a Fire on the Moon,* is alien to a moon project monopolized by WASPs—and not just any WASPs, for astronauts Shepard and Slayton reported NASA's reluctance to schedule Oklahoman Gordon Cooper for a space flight because of his "twang": "They did not want a redneck in orbit" (158). Class status or its simulation was a factor in eligibility for lunar conquest.

Mailer writes that the astronauts are heroes, saints, and adventurers but also "technicians," "robots," and "cogs of the machine" (313). Their space suits are the armor of a knighthood of Nixon's middle American "silent majority," the moon mission "only a chalice for the wounded bewildered heart of the Wasp" and a "code of honor for corporation executives hitherto bereft of pride" in a historical moment of Vietnam-era public antiwar demonstrations protesting the military-industrial complex (423, 385). Student demonstrators pelted the Apollo 11 astronauts with tomatoes at a postflight ceremony at Marquette University (Aldrin, 247).

As "Aquarius," Mailer is inevitably allied with the Sixties-era "Age of

Aquarius" promulgated by the hippie culture, including the rock opera *Hair,* one of whose songs celebrates the "dawning" of the Age of Aquarius. Although *Of a Fire on the Moon* repeatedly critiques youth, hippies, and new leftists, Mailer's greater antipathy is clearly targeted at the moon mission's "wild nihilism of the Wasp, that same laser of concentration and lack of focus on consequence" (440). (Readers of accounts of the Apollo project will recall the brilliant engineering conception for Apollo 11 by which equipment would be steadily jettisoned to eliminate weight in order to maximize chances for the astronauts' safe return—rocket engine stages, modules, lithium hydroxide canisters, armrests from the lunar module, TV camera and tripod, close-up camera, packaging materials and brackets, PLSS (personal life support system) backpacks, boots, all "trash" as flight director Deke Slayton called it, the very flag a detritus-producing design demonstrating to many the United States' flagrant history of environmental trashing of another female entity, mother earth [411].)

The chief offense, however, for an evident romantic like Mailer-Aquarius is that Apollo 11, the much-vaunted event of a lifetime, had proven to be dull, a one-day celebration without personal or national resonance. Mailer misses his opportunity to expand a point he has introduced, that the awkward bulk of the astronauts on the moon robbed them of the physical agility of athlete-heroes, while the television broadcast quality of the moon walk was so primitive that a viewing audience accustomed to vivid close encounters of global events felt a distinct dissociation. Nevertheless, when Mailer invokes Homer's Ulysses and Jason and the *Argonaut,* he indicates that America had missed its rightful epic, for "something was lacking, some joy, some outrageous sense of adventure . . . It was almost as if a sense of woe sat in the center of the [American] heart" (385, 386). Even if "the moon had been drawing us to her for years," even if "the plastic amphitheaters of NASA were nothing less than the intimations of her call," still NASA's unforgivable, cardinal sin was "in making the moon dull, the moon, that planet of lunacy and harvest lovers" (457, 410).

Mailer's loyalties, it is clear, lie instead with that moon which is "the platinum satellite of our lunacy, our love, and our dreams" (*Fire on Moon,* 152). In *An American Dream,* he had worked to wrest the moon of NASA from its scientific-technological identity and reinstate Luna in the contemporary moment. *Of a Fire on the Moon* continues the deliberate effort to revive and sustain the literary moon, to keep her alive for the enterprise of humanistic literature, lest she slip away into history, supplanted by the new moon as defined and "owned" solely by geologists, chemists, physicists, and engineers.

As if to demonstrate proper lunar passion, Mailer offers a sketch of his own lunacy, his marriage beginning and ending in full moons, his wife "unreachable when the moon was full . . . scream[ing] on nights of the full moon with a voice so loud she sounded like an animal in torment," while he himself, like the alter-ego Rojack, felt "the fullness of the moon in his own dread, his intimations of what criminality he might possess" (436–437).[10] This is the moon, Mailer speculates, which could be "a disguise of Heaven" or "the Infernal Shades" (457).

Mailer's production of lunar meanings is contiguous with those of prior centuries of Western texts. It comes from the conscious decision explicitly to revitalize a lunar tradition that might otherwise languish solely in muted or residual tracings as the NASA moon gained cultural supremacy. It presumes an American literary tradition gendered male. (Mailer even implies that he has, in effect, rescued the moon from suburban domesticity—from an identity as "the gray wife of the earth's edges," the astronauts thereby implicitly a trio of husbands made drab by their drab wives [379].) *Of a Fire on the Moon* works to reembody the moon in terms which *An American Dream*'s Rojack would well understand and approve. On his final page, Aquarius concludes his report with an account of his viewing of a moon rock—a "marvelous little moon rock"—through hermetically sealed, double-glass panes at the Manned Spacecraft Center in Houston (471). Aquarius views the rock, "gray as a dark cinder" and measuring just under $3'' \times 2''$, and he meditates:

> Yet she was not two feet away from him, this rock to which he instinctively gave gender as she—and *she*—was gray, gray as everyone had said . . . and rays ran out from the [pin-sized] craters, fine white lines, fine as the wrinkles in an old lady's face . . . and he liked the moon rock and thought . . . that she liked him. Yes. Was she very old, three billion years or more? Yet she was young, she had just been transported here, and there was something young about her . . . there was something familiar as the ages of the bone in the sweet and modest presence of this moon rock . . . hanging man Aquarius, four times married and lost, moved out of M[anned] S[pacecraft] C[enter] with the memory of the moon, new mistress, two feet from his nose. (471–472)

28. Apollo 11 astronauts Edwin (Buzz) Aldrin, Michael Collins, and Neil Armstrong examine moon rock retrieved during moonwalk of Apollo 11 mission and displayed at the Smithsonian Institution, September 1969.

In one sense, a passage like this, entwined with references to Mailer's four failed marriages, compulsively and chauvinistically personifies a small rock as a female lover and thus takes great literary risks. The passage calls forth the possibility of the author's outright slide into inadvertent self-parody. Alternatively, given the mention of John Donne's name among a pantheon of canonical forefathers earlier in the text, the passage may also show Mailer's deliberate venture into the kind of metaphysical conceit—for example, of lovers as compasses in Donne's "Valediction: Forbidding Mourning"—that shocked eighteenth-century belletrists but found great favor in the mid-twentieth-century literary hegemony of the metaphysicals' ally, T. S. Eliot (253). Further, Mailer's reference to the Protestant United States in which "America" supplanted the Virgin in people's hearts suggests the author's alliance with Henry Adams, whose *Education* paired spiritual and technological power in radically, improbably twinned metaphors of "the Dynamo and the Virgin."

Certainly the "platinum lady" of *An American Dream* and the "new mistress" of *Of a Fire on the Moon* show Mailer's deliberate renewal of the Western literary tradition of the lunar Diana, Phoebe, Cynthia, and Artemis. The protagonist Rojack's relation to the moon is adversarial, but Mailer's representations basically Americanize the classical lunar body. His inscriptions of the platinum lady and moon rock mistress express the arousal of male sexual dreads and desires and so reclaim the moon from its dispassionate NASA scientism even as they continue a centuries-long literary lunar tradition and Americanize it as a male project.

Yet the "sweet and modest" lunar female by which Mailer attempts a romantic reclamation of the moon is emphatically imprisoned on terra firma, sealed in, stripped nude, and on public view at the *Manned* Spacecraft Center. Terrestrial and tiny, the she-moon poses no challenge to terrestrial masculinity and so can be gendered and miniatured, then courted and claimed as mistress, for "she" is a specimen captured by men and by men's technology, brought back from the frontier by the astronaut frontiersmen to be displayed at the newer, twentieth-century version of P. T. Barnum's museum, the Smithsonian.

"Man has always been an explorer," observed the astronaut Michael Collins: "To me, there's a fascination in thrusting out and going to new places" (173). The phallic thrust may have struck Mailer as a literary banality, but the male prerogative and raison d'être were unquestionable. Perhaps Mailer's confession to a "simple masculine envy" of the astronauts ("he too wanted to go up in the bird") was as inevitable as his identification with these official heroes who had what fellow new journalist Tom Wolfe called "the right stuff" (*Fire on Moon*, 97). Mailer boasted that he, like an astronaut, "travel[ed] to the inner space of his brain to uncover the mysteries of the moon" (379). (In *Prisoner of Sex*, he asked, "What is a novelist but a general who sends his troops across fields of paper?" [153].) With all acknowledged ambivalence and aversion to the WASP Apollo lunar frontiersmen, Mailer-Aquarius joined that fraternity in pursuing the moon, his "dream of the future's face" (*Fire on Moon*, 132).

Mailer worked to wrest the female moon from the meshes of NASA's dull technologized and scientized moon, but his "platinum lady" and full-moon lunatic mate occupy the same territory. Both are found in the domain of patriarchy. Kolodny's *Lay of the Land* argues paradigmatically that the NASA-Mailer moons are really obversions of one another, both equally sexist and exploitive. Reframed by the new feminist or proto-ecofeminist argument, the masculine heroic becomes the misogynist, ironized "heroic." Accordingly, the ventures of the space-age frontiersmen become a blatant patriarchal act of lunar conquest, and the indelible print of the astronauts' bootsoles on the lunar sur*face* is a continuation of the American masculinist "lay of the land."

The Moon Is Always Female

Thus far, it appears that gender alone generates the oppositional terms by which the moon is embodied. This male-female division can appear to be naturalized within American culture, as if a male aggressive drive for domination became inevitable from the seventeenth century, with a feminist critique reframing that ethos in terms of misogyny just as inevitable as the twentieth century drew to a close. It is important, therefore, to recognize an alternative lunar personification within a heterosexual model of human relations. In 1968 a short story entitled "The Distance of the Moon" appeared in the Italian writer Italo Calvino's *Cosmicomics,* which was published in the United States in an English translation and offered sportive, fabulist narrative treatments of scientific facts and theories, including the theory that the moon had once been much closer to earth and pulled away as the earth's gravitational field weakened.

Like the other stories in *Cosmicomics,* "The Distance of the Moon" debates the imaginative terms by which science and technology make their totalizing truth claims. The story advances the values of fabulism, whimsy, and rhetorical figuration to evince the necessity of the imaginary. Calvino's lunar tale features raw moon milk dipped by the bucketful and refined for human consumption. The story nonetheless rebukes the West's technological utilitarianism (evident in the 1998 lunar orbital surveying machine named *Prospector*).

Unlike other later twentieth-century moon texts under consideration here, "The Distance of the Moon" is non-national by being prenational, the story set in an unspecified past when the moon's elliptical orbit swung her so close to earth that a ladder and a few acrobatic twists enable earthlings to climb aboard: "Climb up on the moon? Of course we did. All you had to do was row out to it in a boat and, when you were underneath, prop a ladder against her and scramble up" (3). Lunar adventures in the story center on the extraction of the milk ("very thick, like a kind of cream cheese") hidden beneath the scabby, scaly lunar terrain (5).

Calvino whimsically embodies the female moon in plot tensions tightening around a love triangle—the narrator's cousin, Deaf One, shown to be enamored of the Moon, while the (boat) Captain's Wife, a harpist, is enamored of the Deaf One, and the I-narrator is enamored of the Captain's Wife. Deaf One is the consummate lunar lover, playfully touching "naked and tender folds of lunar flesh . . . as if he wanted to impress his whole body into the Moon's pulp," to do "something secret meant to take place in the [Moon's] hidden zones" (7). And Deaf One's love has a gravitational pull of its own: "Once I even thought I saw the Moon come toward him, as he held out his hands" (5).

The climax of "The Distance of the Moon" takes place at the last moment when the Moon's distance from earth lets the milk excursion boats lift the visitors from the lunar surface before the moon withdraws to a distant orbit beyond human reach by ladder and climbing pole. The narrator and the Deaf One escape back to earth, but the Captain's Wife deliberately stays on. Knowing she cannot compete with the Moon for the Deaf One's love, she decides to win him by merging with the Moon. The narrator gazes up at her with lovesick yearning: "She was the color of the Moon; she held the harp at her side and moved one hand now and then in slow arpeggios. I could distinguish the shape of her bosom, her arms, her thighs. . . . I still look for her as soon as the first silver appears in the sky, and the more it waxes, the more clearly I imagine I can see her, her or something of her, . . . she who makes the Moon the Moon and, whenever she is full, sets the dogs to howling all night long, and me with them" (16).

Calvino's Moon is thus doubly female, and the fabulist tale is overtly one of heterosexual desire and love making. Unlike Mailer's "platinum lady" or his moon rock "mistress," however, Calvino's female Moon is no object of male conquest or of combat. His is not a story in which erotic desire mandates conquest. Unfulfilled and unfulfillable desire, instead, is a state to be embraced per se for its very poignant human intensity.

Calvino's Moon is to be loved selflessly, as Deaf One does: "He was unable to conceive desires that went against the Moon's nature, the Moon's course and destiny" (15). If the Moon was inclined to a new, distant orbit beyond the reach of her lover and suitor, then Deaf One would help her achieve her desires by nudging her spaceward in a world suffused with generosity and bounty across lines of sex and gender. "The Distance of the Moon" does not presume a binary world of sexualized winning and losing. Heartbreak is not a call to conquest and possession. The story demonstrates how a later twentieth-century text can embody the female moon in a heterosexual world free of hypermasculinism.

Feminist commitment, too, finds expression in a rethinking of the moon and of the ways in which its very female identity mandates its centrality to the lives of women themselves. "Women," wrote Mailer in *The Prisoner of Sex,* "had that unmentionable womb . . . dam for an ongoing river of blood whose rhythm seemed to obey some private compact with the moon" (60–61).

The feminist poet and novelist Marge Piercy apparently agrees with Mailer:

> In my spine a tidal clock tilts and drips
> And the moon pulls blood from my womb.

These lines, from "The Perpetual Migration," in a suite of poems based on the lunar calendar in Piercy's *The Moon Is Always Female* (1977–1994), appear to concur with Mailer's view (115). The bases for Piercy's positions, however, differ radically from Mailer's. He understands the lunar compact ultimately as a source of male empowerment and creativity. The Maileresque lunar lover-temptress jeopardizes men's lives or promises male sexual gratification. But either way, she exists essentially to serve male fears and desires.

Marge Piercy's moon, in contrast, serves as a vital source of female autonomy. She, too, rejects NASA's sci-tech moon and works to renew the literary Luna. Unlike Mailer, however, Piercy pledges a female allegiance to the moon in order to escape patriarchy and the practices of male misogyny, instead propounding and celebrating a governing sociopolitical and religious female principle.

Piercy, born in 1936, grew up in a white working-class family in Detroit, Jewish on her mother's side, Welsh-English on her father's. Though inhabiting the same lunar media environment as Mailer, one shaped by Disney and popular images of the moon in mass-market magazines, Piercy developed an interest in mother goddess religions while an undergraduate at the University of Michigan (B.A., 1957). Receiving an M.A. from Northwestern in 1958, Piercy began to publish poetry and fiction focused on inequities in America based on economics, race, class, and gender. This feminist writer credits storytelling by her mother and her maternal grandmother as a crucial source for her own work, whose overt political themes have evoked criticism for inattention to craft and praise for direct statement.

Piercy identifies Walt Whitman as a major influence, and his relevance to her feminism may best be seen in Camille Paglia's remark on Whitman's revival of "the cosmology of the ancient mother cults" (qtd. Shands, 5). Piercy's Judaism, similarly, is a source of female strength, as in Rosh Hodesh, a half holiday at the new moon, in which, in *Mars and Her Children,* she celebrates "How the full moon wakes you / The hunger

29. Tea tin featuring female moon. © 1997 Celestial Seasonings, Inc.

moon / [at the] Shabat moment" (qtd. Doherty, 37). Piercy has declared herself to be "passionately interested in the female lunar side of Judaism" (qtd. Shands, 8).

Piercy's moon is arguably configured in the resurgent, later twentieth-century goddess movement, a feminist rebellion against Western religions' male dominance and suppression of female sacred principles. The goddess movement furthers the reclamation of female sources of sacred authority. Carol Christ writes, "The suppression of female symbolism and female power by the canonical traditions of the West is being reversed as modern women lay claim to their own forms of spirituality and power" (*Laughter*, 47). Christ adds that "symbols of female sacrality are reemerging as women begin to reclaim their spiritual power" (47).

One part of the goddess movement is historical recovery, as indicated in Christ's chapter "The History of the Goddess" in *Rebirth of the Goddess*, and in the 1997 title *Women and Goddess Traditions in Antiquity and Today* (C. King). Such projects reveal ways in which the reproductive system of the female body was ramified into ritual and worship in the prehistoric era and subsequently devolved into cults of goddesses influential in politics, education, the military. The cult of the lunar Diana, for instance, was active in imperial Rome, with one of her shrines found at Aricia (C. King, 336–337, 344).

Correlative with historical recovery is the goddess movement's mandate to further the creation of sacred female symbols. Christ says, "Women must participate fully in the creation of symbols and theories," warning that celebration of the female body, sexuality, birth, and nurturance per se will not "magically" produce societal equality (*Rebirth*, 93). One study of the practices of the contemporary goddess movement remarks that "the world of communes, small groups, makeshift organizations, workshops, retreats, training schools, and mail-order courses is the social turf that feminist spirituality claims as its own" (Eller, 11). To which Piercy would add the activities of writing and the publication of essays, fiction, and poetry.

Piercy issues this manifesto on female bodily autonomy in "Right to Life" (1979):

> Priests and legislators do not hold
> shares in my womb or my mind.
> This is my body. If I give it to you
> I want it back. My life
> is a non-negotiable demand.
>
> (*Moon Is Always Female*, 97)

This feminist-era lunar body, then, would be neither Mailer's nor NASA's, but a self-possessed female body presiding over female lives. Just as feminist critics like Kolodny were rewriting the narrative of white male Americans' territorial ventures, so Piercy represents those feminists reclaiming the female lunar body for their liberation statements. (The song writer Laura Nyro, for instance, recorded "The Descent of Luna Rose," a song about the menstrual cycle.)

The female moon of feminist writers was thus inscribed as a source of restorative and continuing vitality for women's own lives irrespective of male yearnings or dreads. The moon embodied in the work of Marge Piercy is a prime case in point. *She* becomes a potent goddess empowering women's lives from a pre-Western point when women, as Piercy writes, "were more nearly equal and held considerable social and religious power." In her speculative novel *Woman on the Edge of Time* (1976), the hill women perform special ceremonies for ovulation, which all Piercy's women experience in synchrony with the lunar cycle. Piercy's prehistoric moon ever supersedes and transcends a history of women's "legislated and enforced bondage, mutilation, second-class citizenship described as biological destiny" (*Parti-Colored*, 60). Margarete Keulen comments, "The celebration of the menstrual cycle as part of the cycle of life exemplifies [in the novel] the value of women and their exclusive experiences in a feminocentric society" (96).

The sources of Piercy's lunar knowledge, then, deliberately differ from the sci-tech realm of the Apollo project and of Mailer's masculine literary patronymic. Her sources are neither geologic, physical, nor chemical, nor based solely in Western literature. It is noteworthy that Piercy, like Calvino, works from sources extraneous to those of the West, including the North American United States. She says, "The lunar calendar has really been an intimate part of my life since I moved between the ocean and the bay and had to become conscious of the tides." Piercy's literary lunar lineage is pointedly not canonically Western, neither Anglo-American nor trans-Mississippian but an eclectic mix of sources, including Robert Graves's work on goddess religions, fairy tales, folklore, and the Celtic, Native American, Greek, Roman, Norse, and Arthurian mythologies, in addition to the biblical, Talmudic, and Hasidic traditions (*Parti-Colored*, 60, 65, 74, 59).

Piercy's poems in *The Moon Is Always Female* (1972) are premised on the moon, not as Mailer's subordinate "satellite of our [male] lunacy" but as the central source of female identity:

The moon as reflection of our womanhood, our roundness, the moon as a controller of our menstrual cycle and the tides, the moon as patron of what is left of the wild and of the wild within us, ourselves as one among many furry mammals and part of the food chain on land and in the sea, and the moon as the triple goddess we turn to as a magnifying mirror to trace our lineaments, the powers within us, the powers we hope to touch in freedom and full lives (*Parti-Colored*, 77).

The lunar body in this feminist identity is mirrored in actual women's bodies. The moon and the woman are mutually reflexive personifications one of the other. Logically, then, no woman would rebel against lunar regulation, since moon and woman are in synch. Thus the poet writes, in "O!," the concluding poem of the lunar cycle of poems in *The Moon Is Always Female*, of women who "hunt for roots / in the sea where love rules and women / are free to wander / in the sweet strict seasons / of our desires and needs" (133). The lunar body rejects all utilitarian efforts to colonize it and instead authorizes feminist values of choice, independence, assertiveness, and agency.

The modern moon is, Calvino's narrator remarks, a "flat, remote circle," but of course this is not the case, as Calvino well knows (16). In media and commerce, for example, popular music and greeting cards sustain a tradition of lunar romanticism, as songs like "Moonlight and Roses" and "Moonlight Becomes You" recycle on radio, and artists from Elvis to Bill Monroe and Nanci Griffith sing "Blue Moon of Kentucky" and "Just Once in a Very Blue Moon."

The heavenly body late in the twentieth century, however, is also a contested site exhibiting unresolved sociocultural polarities—on masculinism versus feminism, on the humanistic versus the scientific and technological. In the late nineteenth and early twentieth centuries, the geyser Old Faithful exemplified Nature's nation at the frontier and validated a masculinist industrial order of factory production. So in the later twentieth century did the moon newly incarnate the male frontier venture in a moment of computer technology, rocketry, and televisual representation —also a moment of the entwined contraries of hypermasculinity and feminism. If the social upheaval of strikes and riots was signified in erratic geyser eruptions at Yellowstone, such conflict arguably found its counterpart in insurgent, later twentieth-century feminism, which challenged the terms of America's social and economic order and its gender-based power inequities via women's public street demonstrations and the courts.

The moon became one important body in this large conflict. For those who claimed lunar territory preeminently for science and technology, the NASA/Apollo moon functioned as nature which was subject to "conquest" through chemical, physical, and microbiological analysis. In this sense, it became the space-age, scientific, and technological western frontier of Nature's nation.

But as the Apollo astronauts exceeded gravity to reach the moon, politically engaged writers strove to exert a new kind of countergravitational pull at the closing decades of the millennium. Just as the NASA Apollo project could not entirely efface the centuries-long lunar identity as incarnate female, so writers sought to renew that very identity for contemporary sociopolitical power, Mailer to capture the literary moon for the realm of hypermasculinism, Piercy to free it for feminist and female sociopolitical and religious authority. The cultural debate converges only on one point: that the moon is always female.

III

Bon Aqua

5

Hot Springs: American Hygeia

Let me stand in my age with all its water flowing round me.

—MARGARET FULLER, *Summer on the Lakes, in 1843*, 1844

The tide itself was the greatest marvel, slipping away so noiselessly, and creeping back so softly over the flats, whispering as it reached the sands, and laughing aloud "I am coming!"

—LUCY LARCOM, *A New England Girlhood*, 1889

The touch of the sea is sensuous, enfolding the body in its soft, close embrace.

—KATE CHOPIN, *The Awakening*, 1899

Blessings on the Water Cure!

. . . . .

Borne upon the ocean's tides,
    Floating on the streams along,

. . . . .

Voices from the founts and rills,
    Are the notes which Hygeia sings;
And the light they flash meanwhile,
Is the splendor of her smile!

—K. ARVINE, *Water-Cure Journal*, 1851

At all times Hygia [*sic*] stands in this God-blessed valley stretching out her beautiful arms and wooing the afflicted. Her most precious of gifts is free to all who would take them . . . whoever will, let him partake of the waters of 'health' freely.

—*To the Hot Springs of Arkansas*, 1880

From the 1840s to the 1890s, American texts affirmed the paradox of water embodied, of liquid represented through the female human body. The epigraphs above affirm health and dynamic energy in aqueous incarnation, and each does so in female terms. In Margaret Fuller's travelogue of a western journey into America's lake country, the author identifies herself bodily ("let me stand") with the element from which "Venus was born" (82, 11). In Lucy Larcom's personal memoir, it is the feminine, soft whispering tide that beckons landlubber boys to prove their manhood.

Fiction and promotional texts also emphasize the succor of female bodies of water. In Kate Chopin's once-scandalous novel of a woman's developing social-sexual consciousness, the personified sea envelops a woman swimmer in its bodily embrace. In the journal of the water-cure movement, the smiling pagan goddess of health, Hygeia, acquires an evangelical identity. Accommodated to mid-nineteenth-century Protestant Christianity, she alleviates suffering with the smiles and songs audible in flashing "founts and rills," while in the promotional pamphlet for Arkansas's spa resort at Hot Springs, it is once again Hygeia who stretches out her beautiful arms to offer health in the form of nature's own healing waters, which is to say, in the form of her body. Each epigraph shows aquatic fluidity personified in both female and feminine terms, with sex and gender allied in the embodiment of water.

The nineteenth-century female body of water is remarkable, first, because of the water itself, as distinct from the terra firma that scholars and other observers have considered to be the site of gendered and sexualized personification. As Annette Kolodny has shown, from the era of exploration, New World geomorphic configurations elicited texts notable for sexist responses of male conquest, for example, of the Grand Tetons and numerous valleys, which were thought to mimic the female body in obvious mammary and yonic form.

Yet water has universally been identified with a female principle. Klaus Theweleit observes, "A river without end, enormous and wide, flows through the world's literatures . . . the women-in-the-water; woman as water, as a stormy, cavorting, cooling ocean, a raging stream, a waterfall." Theweleit surveys female identity as a "limitless body of water that ships pass through, with tributaries, pools, surfs, and deltas; woman as the enticing (or perilous) deep, as a cup of bubbling body fluids; the vagina as wave, as foam, as a dark place ringed with Pacific ridges; love as the foam from the collision of two waves, as a sea voyage, a slow ebbing. . . . To enter those portals is to begin a global journey, a flowing around the world" (283–284).

30. Hygia [*sic*], Water Goddess of Health, placed prominently on the title page of the hydropathic physician R. T. Trall's water-cure encyclopedia, 1851.

Global female aquatic identity notwithstanding, the female body of American waters has not been well understood—in fact, has not been particularly visible—although it too is integral to the geographics of Nature's nation. In geophysical and metaphysical terms, the body of waters has promised American health and healing in a tradition extending from the baths and spas of classical antiquity. America has been thought to manifest its health-giving environment especially in springs and pools but also in flowing streams.

The relative obscurity of America's female incarnate waters makes necessary a kind of primer here simply to map them. Unlike popular geomorphic bodies such as the Yellowstone geysers, Walden Pond, Mt. Rushmore, and even the moon, the female bodies of water are less familiar and need to be situated. (Even U.S. Park Service employees are apt to be unaware that Hot Springs, Arkansas, has a strong claim as the first national park.) Geographically, these female texts range widely, making continental claims from the south Louisiana sea-spa of Grand Isle to the upper midwestern lakes and streams of the Wisconsin Territory to the hot springs of Arkansas. Yet the task is not solely one of sighting, for the waters prove to be as contested as they are liminal—indeed, arguably contested precisely because they are liminal. Nineteenth-century discussions of the hygienic waters reveal a struggle for authority over their very identity. The record of the struggle is present in fiction, promotional pamphlets, middle-class magazines, newspapers, and scientific governmental reports, in which literary and scientific vocabularies coexist disjunctively and disclose certain interlocking arguments. These concern the waters' gender identity, their environmental meanings, and their environmental manifestations of domesticity and of subversive female energies. The very liminality of the waters evidently prompted debates and elicited gender-based anxieties, even as the healthy and the sick alike were summoned to partake of them.

Hot Springs, the American Spa

Hygeia became a naturalized U.S. citizen of sorts in 1832, when the U.S. Congress took cognizance of the salubrious powers of the Arkansas hot springs, which Timothy Flint termed "a great and increasing resort for invalids from the lower country" (qtd. Jones, 20). Congress accordingly set aside the Arkansas lands encompassing the warm springs and mineral springs as a federal reserve, making it the foundational United States national park.

In her American incarnation, Hygeia arguably could be located in any number of nineteenth-century sites in many states of the Union. Hot Springs, Arkansas, however, has a particular claim on Hygeian identity, to some extent because of its 1840s representation as the site where "nature calls from fortune's frown, / Her children of disease" (qtd. D. Brown, 28). More precisely, Hot Springs merits its claim as an "American spa" of Hygeian centrality because of its history as an official U.S. reservation of 2,529.1 acres set aside by an order of President Andrew Jackson in April 1832. The act designated four land sections "with the said [hot] springs, reserved for the future disposal of the United States [which] shall not to be entered, pre-empted or appropriated for any purpose whatsoever" (Shugart, vii). Dee Brown notes, "It was the first time the Federal Government chose to preserve land for recreational purposes," and the order predated the establishment of Yellowstone National Park by forty years (15).[1]

Until the 1870s, "recreation" was a term that could be applied only very loosely to the "Valley of Vapors," in which a steep, rocky hillside of some six hundred feet daily gushed forth 850,000 gallons of pure water averaging 143 degrees Fahrenheit. Apart from Native Americans, only venturesome whites such as hunters and trappers had seen it firsthand at the turn of the nineteenth century. Thomas Nuttall's Arkansas territory travel *Journal* of 1819 described "many thermal springs . . . boiling out of the side of the hill . . . and hot enough to boil eggs or fish." Nuttall observed "a kind of rude enclosure made around the spring, as a steam bath" (240). Yet even in the 1830s travel to the springs was still dangerous, an "obscure track . . . exceedingly rocky and difficult" (qtd. D. Brown, 17–18).

The early decades of the nineteenth century nonetheless show crude efforts to exploit the site via primitive lumber-and-canvas bath houses and rude cabins, notably Asa Thompson's 1830 bath house of "small log cabins with plank tubs" (*Arkansas,* 157). One visitor of 1832 observed only "four wretched-looking log cabins" in the area, and stage coaches from Little Rock took one and a half days until passenger train service was established in 1875 (Shugart, 1; D. Brown, 17–22).

By the late 1870s, however, Hot Springs largely mirrored the socioeconomic hierarchy of the nation, in that its hydro-therapeutic establishments ranged from the commodious Arlington Hotel, with its own bath house, to the shanties of the "Dugout pools" (Ral Hole, Corn Hole, Mud Hole), where indigents, both white and black, sought treatment without benefit of private physicians (and in segregated facilities).

The affluent whites to whom the increasingly sumptuous hotels, bath houses, and railroad passenger cars were marketed were invited to gaze en route from their Pullman car windows to see "kaleidoscopic landscapes— here a cotton, there a corn field, livened by their dusky laborers" (*Hot Springs . . . Carlsbad of America,* 5). By 1899 visitors to Hot Springs were enticed not only by plate-glass views of manual labor but by saddle horses "trained to easy gaits" and by "tennis grounds, golf links, baseball park, race course," and "popular concerts, by a carefully selected orchestra," while guests of the Pullman Hotel dining room could enjoy prime rib, saddle of lamb, and a dessert of banana ice cream (Stitt, 13, 21). Those "sportively inclined," according to *DeBow's Review* (1867), could play at "faro, rondo, coolo, roulette, monte, and keno" ("The Hot Springs of Arkansas," 92). The diet, accommodations, and recreation of indigent health-seekers went unrecorded, but the *Cutter's Guide* of 1884 listed a month's expenses at Hot Springs, including board and lodging, bathing, and physician's fees, as ranging from $47 to $150 (60).

Yet successive superintendents of the Hot Springs reservation recognized that the poor, too, had the right to seek health benefits from the thermal waters. By the mid-1880s some four hundred such persons daily sought hydrothermal relief. A superintendent's 1877 order to raze the shanty-tent camps of the poor was coupled with recommendations to build, first, a wood building known as the Free Bath House with a common tub, followed by a mid-1880s enlargement providing a separate women's area and pool, and then, at the turn of the century, a masonry building with individual tubs (D. Brown, 38–39). (In the 1920s, the Park Service transferred jurisdiction to the United States Public Health Service.) In addition, the plight of Union and Confederate veterans afflicted with debilitating injuries and illnesses moved a small group of influential men with Hot Springs connections to guide through Congress a bill establishing an Army and Navy Hospital, which opened in 1887. By 1893 a report to the secretary of the interior chronicled government expenditures devoted to "the operation of the bathing interests," which it declared to be in "effective condition" and Hot Springs itself well advanced toward its claim "accorded it by the Government as a national sanitarium" (Stevens, 1893, 12). Two years later a newspaper account proclaimed, "Hot Springs is the national sanitarium" ("At Pittsburg").

What could the health-seeker of the late nineteenth century expect to find? According to a vivid local-color sketch of "The Hot Springs of Arkansas" in *Harper's New Monthly Magazine* for January 1878, white middle-class visitors alighting from the train at the Hot Springs Station at first negotiated "the perspiring, shouting, excited crowds of hotel, boardinghouse, and doctors' runners, hackmen, and porters" (a crowd including drummers with handbills for doctors most likely to be quacks, warned *Harper's*) (194). Visitors then found themselves in a "city" whose streets were "half country road[s]" and "ranged with a heterogeneous collection of hotels, doctors' offices, stores, saloons, etc., while the bath houses stretch in long rows on the other side of the creek" (203).

Harper's portrayed the street scene as an exotic meeting of the eastern seaboard with the frontier. Eastern dandies and walking parties of ladies mixed with the "youthful hunter" just in from the country to sell his bagged game or the buck slung over his saddlebow. Emigrant wagons and horse-cars jostled with mule-drawn wagons of farmers haggling for the sale of their cotton crops. Hogs rooted and wallowed at will. And everywhere were the invalids, some appearing healthy, others on crutches ("The Hot Springs of Arkansas," *Harper's*, 194, 203, 202).

The newly arrived patients, once registered at their hotels or boarding houses, prepared to begin a course of daily baths typically prescribed by

31. The January 1878 issue of *Harper's New Monthly Magazine* featured scenes from Hot Springs, Arkansas, including the bath houses.

their home physicians in referral partnership with Hot Springs physicians. (The latter struggled constantly to maintain both lucrative caseloads and their reputations for professional legitimacy, as emphasized in the credentials listed on one doctor's card: "Dr. Jos. H. Leslie, Resident Physician and Surgeon. . . . Late Medical Director of the Western Commercial Travelers' Association, St. Louis, Mo., Local Surgeon Iron Mountain R.R.") In strong terms, the individual was cautioned to avoid self-treatment and in-

THE HOT SPRINGS OF ARKANSAS.

32. The same issue of *Harper's New Monthly Magazine* portrayed a creekside scene near the prestigious Arlington Hotel.

stead to submit to medical supervision in a course of treatment extending over periods of weeks, months, or even successive years.

Each day's bath, according to *Harper's*, was a "curious operation," in which, at mid-morning, each patient shouldered a blanket and, carrying a tin cup and coffee pot (for timely drinking of the hot waters), "saunter[ed]" to one of the bath houses. There, helped by "a negro bath-man" or "-woman," the patient was immersed in a hot bath (ninety to ninety-five degrees), with a three-minute hourglass set to the side as a timer. Leaving this bath, "according to the course prescribed," the patient then either "enter[ed] a box filled with the dense vapor which rises from the waters, or [sat] on the top of the vapor box . . . allowing the vapor to play all over the body." Meanwhile, the bather was simultaneously "drinking the hot water . . . from the nozzle of his coffee-pot, thus having at the same time internal as well as external application" (199). The entire procedure lasted eight to ten minutes, after which patients typically were rubbed down, dried, and dressed, whereupon they returned to their rooms to seek a half hour of bed rest.

As for the efficacy of the baths, *Harper's* claimed that "sluggish secretions are aroused, circulation is accelerated, and disease is thrown off" (199). The magazine recapitulated in brief the assertions of the medical-promotional literature that the baths cured or ameliorated diseases of "skin and blood, nervous affections, rheumatism, diseases of women" (195). Other promotions of the "national sanitarium" extended the list considerably. One early 1900s pamphlet contained testimonials of cures under headlines such as "Rheumatism in All Its Forms Cured," "Paralytics Restored," "Stomach Troubles Cured," "Cured of Eczema," "Nervous Prostration Cured," "Blind Restored to Sight" ("Hot Springs . . . Power of the Waters," 11, 25, 30, 32, 34, 35).

As the *Harper's* article indicates, journalistic representations were a major source of the Hot Springs identity, including its gendering and embodiment as female. Indeed, the female body of waters is America's own expression—as a mother expresses milk—of nutriments and healing sustenance. A *DeBow's Review* essay of 1867 situated Hot Springs in a classical aquatic context of "naiads and mermaids" and proclaimed that "Nature . . . has scattered here with lavish hand her richest endowments," notably "the hot springs . . . like gold tried in fire . . . and giving healing to the nations" ("The Hot Springs of Arkansas," *DeBow's,* 90, 87). The *Youth's Companion* (1885) similarly depicted the thermal baths as "this help which Mother Earth herself seems to provide . . . the pale sufferers . . . in this place where health pours out of the earth in living floods" (Trowbridge, 20, 19). Needless to say, these "living floods" are the very waters of life.

Hygeia also was deployed repeatedly in promotional pamphlets for— and in architectural features of—the bath houses. The Fordyce Bath House (now the visitors' center and headquarters of Hot Springs National Park) has an "art glass dome . . . worked into a design representing Neptune's daughter [and] mermaids . . . in a swirl of water" (*Fordyce Bath House,* 14).

As railroads such as the Missouri and Pacific Railway established profitable passenger service to Hot Springs, the rail lines issued promotional literature reinforcing the association of health with a female principle of nature that was bodily and aquatic. The legend of De Soto at the springs, for instance, was renewed in an 1893 railway pamphlet blithely legitimating the fiction: "Where historians fail, tradition steps in to supply the missing links." Tradition, in the pamphlet at least, linked female waters to the rejuvenation of a sick explorer-hero. Implicitly, just as De Soto revived when the "most charming" Indian maiden, Ulelah, brought him "cool water from the spring," so is the 1890s modern man of the age of stressful rail and steam invited to his own rejuvenation at "the Hot Springs of Arkansas—the Fountain of Youth of the Spaniards" (*The Hot Springs of Arkansas: An Historical and Legendary Account*, 23–27, 28).

To read the literature of the bath houses and the railroads was repeatedly to be reminded that Dame Nature expressed herself, "her arrangement of things," when she "caused . . . these springs of health-renewing mineral waters . . . to burst forth in the midst of this beautiful valley":

> Dame Nature planned the City of Hot Springs after her own unique methods. She planted fountains of living waters in the hills, and made them [the hills] her engineers. With the mighty power of persistent gentleness she chiseled out the avenues . . . and shaped the contour of the coming town. . . . She wound her streets in sinuous sweeps . . . [and] shaded hill and valley alike with her novelest and choicest forest trees, provided suitable sites for hotels, business houses, residences and bath houses, . . . and turned on the hot water. (*Hot Springs . . . Carlsbad of America*, 43–44)

We recall the Hot Springs promotional booklet quoted among the epigraphs that opened this discussion: "At all times Hygia [*sic*] stands in this God-blessed valley stretching out her beautiful arms and wooing the afflicted. Her most precious of gifts is free to all who would take them . . . whoever will, let him partake of the waters of 'health' freely" (*To the Hot Springs*, 26).

These female healing waters, however, were legitimated in the nineteenth century in large part through a scientizing of Hygeia. This is to say that the Hygeian Greco-Roman classical tradition, long allied with belles lettres, now also coexisted with the newer practices of medical and physical science. The coexistence of the classical and scientific identifications of Hot Springs and other aquatic entities was complementary and yet proved contentious. Discourses representing divergent epistemologies disclosed ambivalence over the legitimization of authority, over the production of meaning, and over power relations and the conundrum of female waters which were regarded as domesticated and yet as dangerously subversive too.

A wide range of texts on Hot Springs show this discordance. In 1867, *DeBow's Review* stated that "underneath these boiling waters is a depth of mystery deeper than the ken of human knowledge." The *Review* noted the futility of attempts to trace the origins of the hot springs by spade, pick, and blasting powder. The springs would always remain a "mystery of mysteries," concluded the essay, even when the "geological structure" was examined in a "scientific" light ("The Hot Springs of Arkansas," 90). The passage might have been written by Hawthorne.

Scientists, however, rejected any such notion of a Dame Nature as the female personification of the unknowable "mystery of mysteries." Increasingly through the nineteenth century, those self-identified as scientists—overwhelmingly male in number—represented Hot Springs as a congeries of chemical and geophysical phenomena whose cause was debatable within a professional, collegial cohort focused on chemical compounds, rocks, and minerals together with human physiology. For those of a scientific outlook, the medical application of the thermal waters motivated discussion in the context of allopathic medicine. Female figurations of Dame Nature and Hygeia, accordingly, were largely absent from texts produced in the form of treatises, surveys, governmental reports, and professional journal papers.

The author of *A Treatise on the Hot Springs of Arkansas* (1874), Algernon S. Garnett, provides a good case in point, identifying himself as a resident physician (M.D.), as a former professor of comparative anatomy, physiology, zoology, hygiene and dietetics, and as a member of the American Association for the Advancement of Science, the organization which has been termed "a polestar" in nineteenth-century American science (Bruce, 266). Garnett had been a Confederate surgeon aboard the *Merrimack* in the first naval battle of the ironclads, and after the war he formed the alliance sponsoring the establishment of the military hospital at Hot Springs (D. Brown, 40).

Garnett's monograph is interesting for its exhibition of the transit from the classical Hot Springs of Hygeia toward the scientized Hot Springs of the newer scientific-medical cohort. The *Treatise* is replete with references to international scientific debate on the nature and physics of water, microbiology, inorganic chemistry, the human physiology of spring water when ingested and applied dermatologically ("the skin possesses the property of absorbing both liquid and gaseous matter, and at a temperature of 75° to 80°F. absorbs with much facility" [10]), and on Charles Lyell's *Principles of Geology* and its relation to Arkansas's Hot Springs (22–24).

Yet Garnett adheres to a marked degree to the ideals of a classical education and to the Greco-Roman ideological origins of American democracy and republicanism—and thereby recalls the tradition of the baths of antiquity and of the panoply of female water goddesses and spirits. "Bathing was used by the Greeks before the time of Homer," he writes, "and Venus is described as fleeing, after her disgraceful amour with Mars had been published, to the groves of Pathos, where she was laved by the Graces" (17). Garnett then quotes a passage from the *Odyssey* in which Ulysses, in his visit to Circe, is bathed by "four hand-maidens . . . sprung from the fountains . . . and from the sacred rivers, which flow forth into the sea." The fourth handmaiden, says Ulysses, "having put me in a bath, she washed me and anointed me with rich oil" (17).

Garnett cites and quotes from this passage, solely, he says, in order to show that Greek baths of 1100 B.C. were "very similar to the fashion of the present day" (17). Cautioning that bathing models of decadent Rome must be rejected in nineteenth-century America, Garnett then expounds at length on the usefulness of the Roman bath as an exemplary hygienic and socially democratic practice, thereafter relinquishing classical antiquity altogether to address himself to contemporary scientific theories of therapeutic bathing (35–44). "The age of miracles has passed," he proclaims, implicitly including in that passage the era of Venus and Hygeia (44). (Lest one presume, however, that the ascendance of science over classical-romantic myth signals a hermeneutic advance per se, it is useful to notice the erroneous science and the grammatically hedged, scientizing rhetoric in which Garnett "explains" the efficacy of Hot Springs waters versus those merely heated on a stove: "It is *conceded* that water terrestrially heated is charged with a larger quantity of electricity than that which has had its temperature artificially raised, and upon this fact, I base, in part, the curative value of thermal waters" [37].)[2]

The scientized Hot Springs was by no means Garnett's alone. Even the standard annual guides to Hot Springs, the *Cutter's Guide,* produced by Charles Cutter between 1874 and 1917, contained thermal tables and chemical analyses of the waters as well as descriptions of hotels. The precision with which the water temperature of the individual springs was recorded, to the half degree, together with inorganic compounds per gallon carried out to three decimal places, expressed the ability of science literally to unearth New World geophysics, to set forth information obtainable by scientific instruments and by replicable, objective methods of inquiry and analysis. The feminized healing waters, typically described in the *Buckstaff Baths* pamphlet of 1912, could appeal to romanticized notions of "Nature . . . perfum[ing] the air with balmy refreshment to nourish her visiting children"; but the authority vested in the hot springs was also scientific—and by schooling and practice, therefore, a male enterprise.

This is to say that the complex history of Hot Springs includes not only the Native American legends and the classical tradition of Dame Nature, Hygeia, water nymphs, and Venus. As Garnett's *Treatise* indicates, it also extends into the nineteenth-century American scientific tradition of the geological and topographic surveys that were undertaken with the dual objectives of public enlightenment and the exploitation of natural resources concomitant with the expansion of the nation. Thomas Nuttall's Arkansas *Journal* of 1819 augurs this trend, showing the botanizing characteristic of the eighteenth-century *philosophes* and naming the chemical components of the hot springs area, the water "charged with an excess of carbonic acid, holding lime in solution, deposit[ing] a calcareous tufa" (177, 241). By the 1860s, as one historian of American science, Robert Bruce, has written, "geologists saw the chief use of their science to be pointing the way . . . to coal, oil, and mineral deposits" (122). These surveys bear directly on the identification of Hot Springs and other mineral waters as valuable for bodily and economic American health and on the ways in which Hygeia became a scientized body.

Preceded by the Coast Survey, which began in 1807, the many state surveys, including Arkansas's own, led by the state geologist, David Dale Owen, were conducted under geologists' leadership between 1830 and 1880 (Daniels, 194, 214; Bruce, 167). "In all states a major purpose was to locate, describe, and publicize such natural resources as building stones, shales, clays, slates, coal, and ores . . . [and] salt and mineral springs" (Daniels, 196). The surveys meshed well with antebellum Americans' tendency toward "descriptive science, which minimized the need of theoretical grounding" (Bruce, 94). Thus a scientist trained in one area might readily work in an area of study afield of his own. A chemist, for instance, might sometimes "analyze geological specimens" (94).

With salt and mineral springs as a salient objective of survey activity, it follows that any site found to have such springs in abundance stood to become a major, national health resort. Thus the formation of the sanitarium in Arkansas and its identity as the "American spa" or "national sanitarium." Development of the site, moreover, gained impetus from the dual identity of many nineteenth-century American physician-scientists, a remarkable number of whom "prefaced" scientific careers with M.D. degrees, viewing medical training to be the "best preparation for science." Bruce notes, "Of the leading scientists (listed in the *Dictionary of American Biography*) who were active at any one time between 1846 and 1876, one in seven had an M.D. degree" (40; see 90).

Given such schooling and the impetus of scientific study, it followed that the Hot Springs mineral waters would be subjected to repeated and detailed medical-chemical analyses and represented in prose intended to characterize the site as empirically operational as well as efficaciously medicinal. In fact, in 1858 *DeBow's Review* had published David Dale Owen's description of "the minerals and springs of Arkansas," an excerpt from Owen's first report of the Geological Survey of Arkansas. Owen, a physician as well as a geologist, acknowledged "evidence of an incandescent condition of the interior in the numerous hot springs which issue from the flanks of the mountain" ("flanks" the notably anthropomorphic term). He rejected certain theories purporting to account for the subterranean heating of the water and posited his own preferred (though erroneous) theory that the hot waters were "permeated by heated gases, vapors, and steam in their course to the surface" ("Minerals and Springs of Arkansas," 202).

"Judging from the curative properties of these waters," Owen expected chemical analysis to confirm the presence of "carbonate of potash and soda, as well as iodides and bromides of these bases, since, in most cases, glandular swellings and visceral obstructions seem to be removed and reduced by the use of these waters" (203). Owen asserted as demonstrable the "valuable remedial properties of the Hot Springs," especially "for cutaneous disorders, certain chronic forms of rheumatism, gout, neuralgia, mercurial complaints" (204).

Owen's report serves as a rough paradigm of others to follow. His recorded measurements of the temperatures of various of the springs, his naming of the manufacturer of his thermometer, and his chemical analysis and diagnostic-prescriptive guidelines for treatment at the hot springs were but a crude version of the scientific reports of his successors.[3] Within the scientizing tradition of Owen and his cohort, prospective health-seekers would not be invited into Hygeia's embrace so much as they would be attracted to a scientific bathing experience whose medicinal value was thought to lie in chemical-physiological interactions, for instance in the kind of electrical stimulation which Garnett's *Treatise* had worked to prove effective:

The peculiar sensations of the bath may be characterized as electrical and exhilarating. Upon immersion the patient becomes conscious of the electrical influence in the water, by very slight shocks, producing a most pleasant sensation; following this is a nervous, stimulating effect, especially noticeable by those whose vital energies have been relaxed or exhausted. The aged experience the sensation of complete rejuvenation, while those who have been debilitated by wasting disease feel a returning energy, like the pulsings of vigorous health. (*To the Hot Springs,* 19)

On the basis of this passage, together with texts by Owen, Garnett, and others, one might assume that nineteenth-century science vaporized Hygeia at her very own Hot Springs Valley of Vapors. We seem once again to be witnessing the scientific "conquest" of female nature in the post-Baconian transformation which Caroline Merchant terms the "death of nature" and Evelyn Fox Keller graphs as a belief system coding science in phallic terms as "hard" over and against the feminine sentiment "soft" (77). Merchant's work serves to locate Owen, Garnett, and their cohorts within a scientific tradition that legitimated the manipulation of a female nature within a framework of values based on power (*Death of Nature,* 193). This post-Baconian method "made possible the exploitation of the natural environment. . . . [Just as] woman's womb had symbolically yielded to the forceps, so nature's womb harbored secrets that through technology could be wrested from her grasp for use in the improvement of the human condition" (*Death of Nature,* 169, 189). As Keller explains, in this model the subject and object are "radically" divided and the "scientific mind is set apart from what is to be known, that is, from nature" (79).

By this argument, self-identified scientists exploited the Hygeian waters of Hot Springs, transforming them into a medicinal liquid whose mineral content was chemically asserted to be clinically efficacious. The language of science and medicine takes such preeminence that the female, animistic Hygeia is vanquished.

To be sure, in representations of Hot Springs, an epistemic disjunction is apparent between science and medicine, on the one hand, and Hygeia, on the other. In the gush of the hot springs, one hears the voices competing for epistemic authority and hears, as well, a national debate about the aquatic bodies of Nature's nation. When scientized, Hygeia is not only dissected but radically repositioned as a compound of hydrogen and oxygen whose additional chemical content is readily subject to analysis and whose location is a matter of debatable geological hypotheses. Hygeian chemical analysis is a demystification per se. It constitutes a bid to supersede the mentality of a classical identity and, de facto, to relegate that mentality to the status of cultural residue.

But this is not the full story here, as a careful look at publication dates of the diverse above-cited texts on Hot Springs reveals. For the sake of orderly discussion, I have dealt first with the representations of the thermal baths in terms of female figuration, then moved on to consider the involvement of scientists-physicians in rewriting Hot Springs from a different hermeneutic mentality.

From the late 1860s into the 1910s, however, the two kinds of discourses coexisted, the classical-literary-sentimental which embodied the Hot Springs as female, and the scientific-analytical which disembodied that figure in an ultimate molecular dissection. Both discourses were in simultaneous circulation and indeed often leached into each other within the same publication, whether in national magazines or promotional pamphlets or "literary and philosophical" periodicals committing some of their space to scientific matters (Daniels, 150). The double discourse, moreover, sometimes appeared in the same passage, as in this from a bathhouse booklet of 1894: "Chemical analysis shows that the mineral constituents amount to but eight and one-half grains per gallon, so the doctors are fain to ascribe the healing qualities of the water to its almost purity, aided by the beneficent and peculiar heat it brings from Dame Nature's bosom" (*Maurice Bath-House,* n.p.).

"Nature's bosom" and "chemical analysis" are intended to be partners in this text, not adversaries but an ontological complement. In this and similar passages to be found in bath-house pamphlets, in railroad publications, and newspaper and magazine articles, the healing hot waters of medical-chemical analysis promise improved health, cures for disease and disorders, and (given the previously quoted phrases on "rejuvenation" and "pulsings of vigorous health") a renewed cardiovascular and sexual potency to be achieved by electrical stimulation. The scientific analyses and tabulations of "chemical analysis" provided reassurance that applications of the most advanced medical knowledge awaited the health-seeker at Hot Springs. They purported to prove that the very geology of America, Nature's own nation, produced an exceptionally salubrious water whose intrinsic healthful agents could be revealed by science.

To account for the persistence of Dame Nature in a scientizing era, we might recall Stuart Guthrie's assertion that "landscapes . . . suggest humanity," which is to say that anthropomorphic urges factor significantly

33. Stained-glass ceiling in men's section of Hot Springs' Fordyce Bath House, 1910s, eroticizes the aquatic female body representing health and healing. Detail.

in human engagement with the natural world—that the external environment is innately suggestive of the human form. The image of "Dame Nature's bosom" is anthropomorphically pictorial. Its traditional associations provide reassurance that draws on the fluids of gestation and lactation, with the primary values those of nurturance and healing. The promise of sexual vigor is also implicit, as it is in the female water figures from Venus to Hygeia, whose place in classical antiquity guaranteed respectability but whose aquatic embodiment added a covertly sensuous and Venusian sexual appeal to healthful well-being. Science quantified and tabulated the aquatic salubrity that made Hot Springs the sanitarium of Nature's nation, while an anthropomorphic Hygeia embodied its sustaining mystique in the American New World. Just as twentieth-century astronauts and their devotees in the NASA Apollo project would exhibit anthropomorphic responses to the scientized and technologized moon, so in the preceding century did physicians and scientists disclose their own anthropomorphism in representations of a Hygeian Hot Springs.

The Greco-Roman reference to Hygeia on the part of men of science arguably serves one additional, sociological end, which is the credentialing of a scientist as a gentleman educated in the liberal arts tradition. The class status of scientists as gentlemen was arguably at least as dependent upon classical knowledge as upon scientific training, perhaps more so. Those like Garnett and Owen who were self-identified as medical or physical scientists or engineers had good reason not to rid their texts of anthropomorphic terms of embodiment. Their tables, graphs, and disinterested objectivity in descriptive prose went far to divest science and engineering texts of references to human bodies, but their female references were the inflections of gentlemen.

At Hot Springs, then, Hygeia and H_2O coexisted compatibly among

34. Angelic figure of Hygeia, a Christianized version of the pagan goddess, featured in an advertisement for Dr. R. T. Trall's water-cure encyclopedia, 1851. On either side, health-seekers bathe in her healing waters.

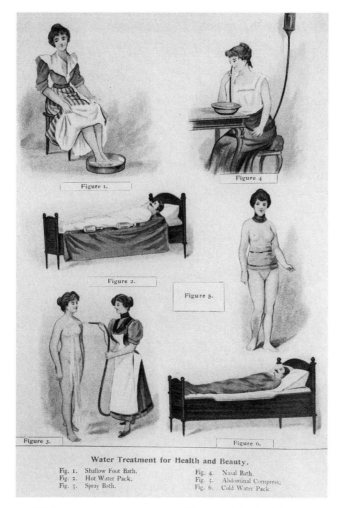

Water Treatment for Health and Beauty.

Fig. 1.	Shallow Foot Bath.	Fig. 4.	Nasal Bath.
Fig. 2.	Hot Water Pack.	Fig. 5.	Abdominal Compress.
Fig. 3.	Spray Bath.	Fig. 6.	Cold Water Pack.

35. Various water-cure treatments illustrated in Dr. Mary Melandy's *Perfect Womanhood for Maidens, Wives, Mothers,* 1901.

interested parties, each with a different agenda though with a common economic interest in the maximal attraction of paying visitors to the spa. From the state geologist to the writers of bath-house brochures and the on-site physicians, all were promoters of the Arkansan Hot Springs enterprise. The epistemic fault lines, if evident, were largely ignored. Elsewhere, however, through the nineteenth century the debate over the aquatic body of Nature's nation would erupt along lines of gender.

Rivers of Empire and "Vital Fluids" in Circulation

Given Hot Springs' status as a national park, given the ubiquity of U.S. waters gendered as female, one must ask why the very idea of female American waters is not generally well known, why it is not a part of the cultural mix of received knowledge, the kind of data routinely formed into American television quiz show or board-game questions? Why is the American Hygeia not on par—or in parlance—for instance, with the Mississippian Father of Waters?

It is probable that since the nineteenth century, the female bodies of water have been overshadowed, not only by ignorance of their geographic locales but by readers encouraged to respond most fully in print and in the classroom to grand male aquatics. The problem of obscurity is evidently not solely aquatic. While fairly recent studies relegate Hot Springs to a page or two, entire volumes have been devoted to the most visually dramatic of water sites, notably Niagara Falls, whose representational responses were widely published and standardized in masculinist terms of the sublime by the 1830s. As John Sears observes, Edmund Burke's concept of sublimity, set forth in *A Philosophical Enquiry into the Origin of Our Ideas of the Sublime and Beautiful* (1757), became the paradigm for nineteenth-century visitors' emotional response to the Falls: "The early travel accounts and guidebooks are full of Burkean rhetoric about the astonishing height, enormous volume, stupendous force, and eternal sound of the Falls" (14). Sublimity so dominated visitors' response to the Falls that the concept and its vocabulary had degenerated by the 1830s into a cliché (Sears, 12, 14–15).

Water, of course, is a salient feature in nineteenth-century American literature, though the references are principally to male-identified oceans and to the "rivers of empire," as Donald Worster titles his study of the history of water in the American West. One thinks at first, not of Margaret Fuller or Kate Chopin or of a Hot Springs health spa or of water cures, but of the oceans in Richard Henry Dana Jr.'s *Two Years before the Mast* (1840, 1869) or Melville's *Moby-Dick* (1851), or of Henry David Thoreau's wilderness-identified *Walden* (1854) or of Twain's Mississippi in *The Adventures of Huckleberry Finn* (1884) or *Life on the Mississippi* (1883), or perhaps of John Wesley Powell's *Exploration of the Colorado River of the West* (1875). Frederick Jackson Turner wrote, "On the tide of the Father of Waters, North and South met and mingled into a nation" (29). In the canonical texts, males embark upon treacherous waters to face tests of physical and metaphysical courage. On the Great Lakes, which

Melville identifies as an honorary ocean with an "ocean-like expansive-ness" and oceanic "noblest traits," the poet Henry Wadsworth Longfellow set his popular verse epic *The Song of Hiawatha* (1855), in which a hero proves his mettle in combat against a great sea creature. The poem exalts its Lake Superior setting "By the shores of Gitche Gumee, / By the shining Big-Sea Water" in which Hiawatha, the hero sworn to "cleanse the earth of all that harms it," battles to the death the great sturgeon, the King of Fishes (*Moby-Dick,* 347; *Song of Hiawatha,* 171, 179–181).

It is useful to recall, in addition, the significance of inland canals, which George Washington himself supported in a business investment promoting canal construction between the Potomac and Ohio Rivers. Visionary plans for an American transcontinental network of canals appear in the early nineteenth-century epic poem by Joel Barlow, *The Columbiad* (1806), which represents them in Herculean terms as a vast body's circulatory system. "System of Canals," Barlow jotted in a notebook (1802), "& the activity it would give to Commerce, compared to the veins & arteries & the circulation of the blood. . . . Canals . . . vein the green slopes . . . and plant new ports in every midland mound." Barlow's canals serve the project of federal governmental "power," as Washington's plan for inland navigation served what the president termed "a new empire" (qtd. F. Smith, 88; see Tichi, 148, 147). The canals are conceptually male, and Melville's tribute to the white "American born" brains and to the *auslander* brawn that built the "American Canals" serves as the mid-century's assent to such male engineering projects as the Erie and Chesapeake and the Potomac Canals (*Moby-Dick,* 216, 347).

Crucial issues in these texts range from the consolidation of governmental power (as in *The Columbiad*), to initiation rites of a civilizing Native American hero (Hiawatha), to attempted flight from stifling civility to wild woodland (Thoreau), to survival and morality in a slave-holding America (Huck), to youth-unto-adult self-fashioning (the cub pilot Clemens), to spiritual-psychological restoration of health within a revenge plot (Dana and Melville's Ishmael). Whatever the thematic crux, the Herculean canal, "Big-Sea Waters," the planet's open oceans, and the mighty Mississippi and Colorado are unquestionably represented as commensurate in importance with the trials of the American males for whom these waters constitute both staging area and métier of heroic struggle. Lucy Larcom recalled that in her New England coastal town, it was difficult to dissuade boys from going to sea, that "land-lubber" was a term of utmost opprobrium, and that "the spirit of adventure developed in [young men] a rough, breezy type of manliness" (94).

Noncanonical texts, such as memoirs and popular journalism, apparently also assign male identity to American waters and thus support the male canon in this regard. The Indian-derived "Father of Waters" is embodied as a riparian patriarch in Julius Chambers's *Mississippi River* (1910), which recounts the author's 1872 voyage southward, following his doctor's prescription for health, as his subtitle says, "*Twenty-seven Hundred and Seventy-Five Miles from Source to Sea.*" Another text is the sensationalist *The Johnstown Horror!!!, or Valley of Death, Being a Complete and Thrilling Account of the Awful Floods and Their Appalling Ruin* (J. Walker, 1889). This latter, written and marketed for a popular audience, calls the flood waters the German male "erl king," a spirit of mischief and evil, in its narrative of the flood, in which the city of Johnstown, Pennsylvania, was destroyed in less than fifteen minutes when a defective dam at the Conemaugh River burst during a period of unusually heavy rainfall in 1889. The dam released more than a half million cubic feet of water, which surged toward the town and caused one of the worst disasters in U.S. history, with over two thousand fatalities.

The Johnstown Horror, of course, deals with a single public event, while Chambers's memoir is a personal travelogue. The opening passages of both, however, establish the male identity of the powerful bodies of water. *The Johnstown Horror* does so in reference to the engulfing erlking of German legend, while Chambers's *Mississippi River* opens in proclaiming the metaphor of the "Father of Running Waters" (xv). Paternity and patriarchy combine in both terms, the one foreign, the other domestic, the one inimical to both author and his readers, the other embraced in masculine terms as the male memoirist takes gendered pride in the possibility that his health will be restored by his river journey on foot and by canoe.

Both *The Mississippi River* and *The Johnstown Horror,* however, embody the headwaters as female. Precedent for this rhetorical model had been set by Barlow's *Columbiad* (1806), which echoes Shakespeare's *Richard III* in describing the geologic parturition of the Potomac River: "from rock-ribb'd lakes I forced my birth" (140–141). *The Columbiad's* Potomac, allied with George Washington and the new capital city of his namesake, is figured as the son of maternal lakes. Far upstream, at the source, are the maternal "rock-ribb'd lakes" from which the Washingtonian Potomac "force[s]" its birth and then matures downstream, as if in a scenario from the Greco-Roman mythology pervasive in the poem. *The Columbiad* contains both male and female bodies of water in a mother-son relation, with each party aquatically separated.

The memoirist Chambers and the popular journalist of the Johnstown

Flood followed Barlow's precedent in assigning female identity to the quieter headwaters. Chambers, citing the explorations of Henry Schoolcraft at the northernmost sources of the Mississippi, affirms the Chippewa legend of a young woman, Itasca, buried under sand hills in the midst of a godly struggle: "The rills that flow from the rocks and sand, forming the lake, are made by the tears of Itasca weeping for home and friends" (118). Another of those lakes is named "Julia Lake . . . formed in the shape of a heart," and the memoirist himself goes on to give to a Mississippi source—a "lakelet," which he discovers—the name "Dolly Varden," compounding the female identity with "lakelet" and "pretty little stream" (104, 150, 152).

The Johnstown Horror operates nearly identically in its gendering. The enormity of the flood is first expressed in comparison to "Niagara . . . falling upon an ordinary collection of brick and wooden houses" (22). Otherwise, as noted, the raging flood is an erlking, "a demon" venting "hellish glee" and destructive as "a bolt of Jove" (20, 23). The originating source of the Johnstown Flood, however, is female:

> Away up in the misty crags of the Alleghenies some tiny rills trickle and gurgle from a cleft in the mossy rocks. The dripping waters, timid perhaps . . . hug and coddle one another until they flash into a limpid pool. A score of rivulets from all the mountain side babble hither over rocky beds to join their companions. Thence in rippling current they purl and tinkle down the gentle slopes . . . now pausing for a moment to idle with a wood encircled lake, now tumbling in opalescent cascade over a mossy lurch, and then on again in cheerful, hurried course down the Appalachian valley. (18)

Intermittently, says the text, a "Pennsylvania Dutchman coaxes the saucy stream to turn his mill wheel" (18). The "saucy stream" is entirely girlish from its origin in the yonic "cleft in the mossy rocks." Throughout the passage, the source of the flood is innocently coquettish. *The Johnstown Horror* dissociates the "unleashed" male water power from its female origins. The flood narrative, like the memoir, assigns male identity to the major waterway but insists that the originating, compelling, quieter waters, the rills and rivulets and lakes and lakelets, are female.

The flood narrative and Mississippi memoir, thus doubly gendered, redirect us back to the classic male canon. *The Johnstown Flood* and Chambers's narrative serve as guides in a search for occluded—yet present—female waters.

We might begin with the opening of *Moby-Dick,* which offers diverse examples of revivifying waters. In "Loomings," we meet the morbidly depressed Ishmael who takes readers on a tour of marine sites to which whole populations resort for mental health, for example, to the Battery on the southern tip of Manhattan and so up from the Lower East Side to Broadway and the docks along the Hudson (93–94, 704).

But Ishmael also takes readers inland in the tradition of American landscape painting, specifically that of Mount Washington Valley "Saco" art of northern New England (paintings such as Thomas Cole's 1827–28 *Lake Winnipesaukee* and Sanford Robinson's 1854 *Mount Washington from the Saco*). From Ishmael, we learn that a "magic stream" is a crucial component of these artists' formula for pastoral landscape paintings. Mandatory to the composition is the image of the shepherd whose eye is fixed on "the magic stream before him" (95). To Melville's critical eye, these popular pastoral paintings are a sentimental "tranced" bundle of narcoleptic clichés (and thus allied with the feminine sentimental forms of representation). In the actual geography represented in such paintings, which is to say the real American countryside of "some high land of lakes," the American rural dweller nonetheless finds necessary "magic" in the dale with its "pool in the stream." This pool is the occasion for quiet reflection, for Melville-Ishmael believes it induces reverie, since "meditation and water are wedded forever" (94).

Wedded domesticity, the hallmark of the female sphere, is also a pronounced feature of Huck's and Jim's sensualist raft life on the Mississippi in *The Adventures of Huckleberry Finn.* As Huck says of the pair, "We said there weren't no home like a raft . . . when we got her out to about the middle, we let her alone, and let her float wherever the current wanted her to go; then we lit our pipes, and dangled our legs in the water . . . we was always naked, day and night" (128–131). In these terms, Huck and Jim have a companionate "marriage."

The move toward feminized waters is also explicit in *Hiawatha,* in which the aqueous female is explicitly present, though subordinate in rank to the male "Big Sea Water." After reading of a maiden with eyes like "two blue lakes among the rushes," readers meet Minnehaha, who will marry Hiawatha in Longfellow's symbolic union of the native American hero with American nature which is emphatically female—and aquatic. Minnehaha's feet are "rapid as the river," her "tresses flowing like the water":

> And he named her from the river,
> From the waterfall he named her, . . .
> Minnehaha, Laughing Water . . . (pp. 163–164, 172)

36. *Lake at Franconia Notch, White Mountains,* by Albert Bierstadt, n.d. Oil on paper. J. Ackerman Coles Bequest, 1926. The Newark Museum / Art Resource, N.Y.

Minnehaha is destined to become Hiawatha's heterosexual beloved because she is the very incarnation of female nature. She is no "squaw" (as Thoreau dubbed Walden Pond on one occasion) but the fleet-of-foot and ever mirthful feminine water who is unfailing in her good cheer and thus the appropriate marital helpmeet for the hero (*Walden*, 295). Conversely, given the metaphors by which Minnehaha is personified, any stream flowing briskly with an audible splash becomes, by virtue of those attributes, female.

Ironically, to extend this "divining rod" a bit further into the traditional nineteenth-century American canon, the female-as-water can be inadvertently legitimated even when canonical texts operate strategically to delegitimate her. Hawthorne provides a good case in point. At least twice he exploited the link between the female and the aquatic, and in tones more of Melville's scorn than of Longfellow's blithe endorsement. In *The Scarlet Letter* (1850), in "The Forest Walk," Hester and Pearl sit on a mossy heap in "a little dell" with "a brook flowing through the midst" (203). The novel closely examines the brook's flow, at first like a hydrologist poring over a stream table. Hawthorne's next move is anthropomorphic, the stream personified as a specific symbol of the friendless little girl, Pearl, "babbl[ing] . . . like the voice of a young child that was spending its infancy without playfulness" (204). In addition, the brook implicitly is identified as an incessantly gossipy, "loquacious" adult female who whispers tales from the heart of the male forest of "giant trees" and publicly transmits or "mirror[s] its revelations on the smooth surface of a pool" (204).

Hawthorne revisits the notion of a female-identified pool in his tale of a failed utopian community, *The Blithedale Romance* (1852), which continues his hostile development of the female body of water in the episode of the drowning—and posthumous rape—of Zenobia, the sensual fictional authoress whose luxuriant hair, like Hester's, is largely hidden from view but is ornamented by a single exotic hothouse flower emblematic of her superabundance of "bloom, health, and vigor" (16). A character thought to be based on Margaret Fuller, the powerfully female Zenobia arguably exceeds Hawthorne's efforts to contain her as a costumed "work of art" (164). Immersing her in the misery of unrequited love, Hawthorne stages her suicide by drowning, specifically in a pool fed by the river in which the Blithedale Yankee caretaker recalls boyhood fishing.

Hawthorne has a literary critical point to make. Discovered by three men in a punt, Zenobia's body shows her "dark hair streaming down the current" and limbs "swaying in the current" as if in grisly anticipation of Longfellow's personification of Minnehaha (234). Deposited on the river bank, the body proves to be contorted, rigid, even mutilated—here, the rape—by the metal hay-rake used to locate it in the pitch black water in the light of a "large and oval" moon (232). Hawthorne uses this graphic scene to critique both the passionate Zenobia and the sentimental literary convention represented by her death. He is contemptuous of the woman's foolish decision to commit suicide in the trite, affected, picturesque way of storied broken-hearted maidens "seeking peace in the bosom of the old, familiar stream . . . where, in childhood, they used to bathe their little feet, wading mid-leg deep, unmindful of wet skirts" (236–237).

From the novel's viewpoint, Zenobia's exit from life follows the despised sentimental female formula perpetuated by the "damned mob of scribbling women"—though Hawthorne adapts that very convention in his critique. It is important to recognize, however, that the tradition which Hawthorne so vividly scorns locates female identity in water, that is, in the very stream, the pool, the brook and freshet composing the woman's natural element. The female cycle of life is not ashes to ashes but water to water. And that element is also the site of mystery, "keeping its own secrets from the eye of man, as impenetrably as mid-ocean could"

(232). Ultimately the river pool gives up Zenobia's corpse but not her body of secrets.

These feminized waters, as we see, are both present and yet simultaneously obscured in such texts as Longfellow's, Melville's, Twain's, and even Hawthorne's. Arguably, it was in the male writers' interest to downplay them, to allow them the status of motif but not theme, to inscribe in *sotto voce* the waters that otherwise might compete for equal attention with—or gain supremacy over—the tumultuous aqueous episodes in *Moby-Dick,* or the rough-hewn river sequences in Twain, or even Longfellow's once-popular verse epic accounts of heroic deeds along the Great Lakes. Female bodies of water are thus present yet subdued in the very texts that otherwise celebrate male aquatic heroism.

Another possibility must also be considered, namely, that of the social subversiveness inherent in water's liminality. The very fluidity of the babbling brook seems to rankle Hawthorne. It is the liminal quality that Victor Turner describes as "neither here nor there" but "betwixt and between the positions assigned and arrayed by law, custom, convention, and ceremonial" (*Ritual Process,* 95). Such liminality has been identified with the status of nineteenth-century American women who potentially can subvert the existing structure of power relations because they "represent the possibility of life outside the community, and the possibility of the dissolution or alteration of political structures" (Norton, 132). The river pool that gives up Zenobia's corpse but not her body of secrets opens the possibility of liminal political subversion fomented in sites of aquatic submersion. Bodily, the implication is that women's corporeal-aqueous self harbors subversive energies.

The real-life Zenobia, Margaret Fuller, assayed and supported this sociocultural subversion in a *Dial* sketch and in her *Summer on the Lakes, in 1843* (1844), the latter a volume of autobiography, travelogue, social criticism, and anthropology. When she claimed her place "in my age with all its water flowing round [her]," New England's foremost female intellectual, the editor of the Transcendentalist magazine *The Dial* and the doyenne of famed Conversations with a circle of women, emphatically claimed her place in the sociocultural currents and eddies of her time.

Early on in *Lakes,* the sojourners, including Fuller and her traveling companions, James Freeman Clarke and his sister, Sarah Ann Clarke, depart from a visit to Niagara Falls, where Margaret finds she prefers the river's whirlpool to the "thundering" Falls, being drawn instead to the "slight circles that mark the hidden vortex [which] seem to whisper mysteries the thundering voice above could not proclaim" (and thereby providing Hawthorne his very terms of aquatic anxiety) (5). Then we hear the travelers' conversation, doubtless re-created from notes, on a steam-boat during a heavy rain. Fuller offers a debate on the gendered, socio-political nature of earth and water. (Fire and air, the other two classical elements, are acknowledged but not deployed in the debate.) Earth is fig-ured as the site of the precious metals that are excavated to drive com-merce and to measure the status of the centuries-long idolatry of empire. Earth is thus the realm where "all things glitter, and nothing is gold; all show and no substance," where the gold is coined and stamped with royal signifiers of empire, the mere "hieroglyphics of worship" (10–11). (Lucy Larcom similarly observed that "avarice and self-seeking ambition always find their true level in muddy earth" [84].)

Water, on the contrary, is, first of all, the "gentle element" (10). "From water Venus was born," and it is "the mother of Beauty, the girdle of earth, and the marriage of nations" (11). Its very liquidity lends itself to Art, which is for Fuller the pinnacle of culture and society. Intrinsically, water converts "coarse utilities" of maritime commerce, both salt and fresh, into the picturesque: "All trades, all callings, become picturesque by the water's side, or on the water. The soil, the slovenliness is washed out of every calling by its touch. All river-crafts, sea-crafts, are picturesque, are poetical. Their very slang is poetry" (11).

The *Lakes* discussion is gendered insofar as its earthly terms of argu-ment are linked with male realms of industry, of kings and empire, of a capitalist market economy. The discussants acknowledge the irony of their complicity in this commerce, since it largely flourishes via fishing and marine and freshwater shipping and transport, including the travelers' own ("*J.* Have you paid for your passage? *M.* Yes! And in gold, not in shells or pebbles") (11). Water, however, is the element that effaces evi-dence of coarse trade and transmutes it into Art. This is water secondarily of the male "Triton" but primarily of the origin of Venus (10). The me-dium of poetry and painting is intrinsically the medium of Venus's birth.

Fuller expresses the reality she finds in those waters in lakescapes like this one from Milwaukee:

> The bank of the lake is here a bold bluff, eighty feet in height. From its summit, you enjoyed a noble outlook on the lake. A little narrow path wound along the edge of the lake below. I like this walk much. Above me this high wall of rich earth, garlanded on its crest with trees, the long ripples of the lake coming at my feet. Here, standing in the shadow, I could appreciate better its magnificent changes of color, which are the chief beauties of the lake-waters. (68)

This quietly pleasing scene functions as a not-so-subtle tribute to Fuller's own taste. In full view of the tree-garlanded, eighty-foot bluff, her chosen stance on the "little" path allows the "long" ripples (presumably geometrically proportionate to the height of the bluff) to approach her. In the cool shadow, the visual advantage of "magnificent" changes of color on the water is hers to enjoy and thereby the reader's to imagine in full confidence that the author has chosen the optimal vantage point for herself and her reading audience. Fuller is the beneficiary but also the compositor of the scene. Hers is the educated, aesthetic eye best qualified for siting and compositional representation.

And the fact of the water itself is not incidental but crucial. Significantly, Fuller rejects the traditional male posture of conquest or command from atop a "snowy peak"—for example, of Mt. Washington, antecedent to Mt. Rushmore—which offers "a commanding view of the landscape" (81). "It would be vain," she writes in verse, "from glittering heights the eyes to strain." Instead: "Let me stand in my age with all its waters flowing round me. If they sometimes subdue, they must finally upbear me" (82). (Fuller's death by drowning off the New England coast upon her return from participation in the Italian revolution of 1848 makes her stance in the "water flowing round" her grimly allegorical.)

By the time she embarked on her journey to the lakes, Fuller had already published an aesthetic-political female aquatic proclamation in the *Dial*. Her "Leila" (1841) is an impassioned, romantic portrait of a suprahuman female figure shown to command and suffuse the elements of earth, air, fire—and especially water. Leila is deified for her "mystery," for her "elemental powers of nature" and her "boundlessness, of depth below depth" (462). She is celebrated and explained by an apparently male narrator, who professes complete devotion, awe, and a fearlessness which he acknowledges to be unusual among mortals confronting the very notion of such a superwoman. Leila is the "overflow of the infinite," transcendent of "sex, age, state, and all the barriers behind which man entrenches himself from the assaults of Spirit" (462, 463). A mere earthling can seek her in her element, a lake:

> In the centre of the park, perfectly framed in by solemn oaks and pines, lies a little lake, oval, deep, and still it looks up steadily as an eye of earth should to the ever promising heavens which are so bounteous, and love us so, yet never give themselves to us. As that lake looks at Heaven, so I look on Leila. At night I look into the lake for Leila.

If I gaze steadily in the singleness of prayer, she rises and walks on
its depths. (463)

Fuller's figure of a lake as earth's eye, of course, prefigures Thoreau's same
image of Walden Pond, though the Walden personification is androgy-
nous while Fuller's is overtly and aggressively female. As the narrator says,
Leila is the "vasty deep" and her purpose is to "circulate as the vital fluid,"
while "rivers of bliss flow forth at [her] touch" (463, 464, 466). Visually,
too, Leila is a water power: "Leila, with wild hair scattered to the wind,
bare and often bleeding feet, . . . divining rods in each over-full hand"
(466).

One can envision Fuller's Leila rendered in white marble by the leading
mid-nineteenth-century American sculptors, such as Hiram Powers or
Randolph Rogers, or perhaps by Chauncy B. Ives, who represented the
ancient water spirit *Undine* (c. 1855) as rising from the sea covered in
veils. Yet Ives's figure is contained by her veils, just as Powers's *Greek Slave*
(c. 1843) stands in chained demure humility, while Fuller's Leila, on the
contrary, would not be subject to restraint because she embodies cosmic,
elemental, unrestrained power. The subversion which this fearless aquatic
female principle represents is nothing less than a personal-social transcendence of earthly life as it is known. Politics, economics, and existing social
arrangements will be utterly transformed in the imminent epoch of her
domain. Allied with Venus, the messianic Leila is poised to lead the world
to new parturition. She is the quintessential agent of Transcendentalism.

Fuller thus proclaims ecstatic vitality amid the very flow whose hidden
mystery is so troubling to Hawthorne that he drowns the female in it—
not just any female but the Fullerian embodiment of femaleness at its
most vital. Nineteenth-century American texts can be viewed in this regard as a fight over gendered water rights: Hygeia versus H_2O; the oceanic
and imperial riparian versus the mysterious pool and stream; the commercial versus the artistic; his drowning pool versus her aquatic buoyancy;
Moby-Dick versus Leila. These tensions and gendered binarisms are present, and they appropriately prompt considerations of identity, agency,
narrative contestation, and preeminence.

"Turbid and Swollen" Flood Waters

When the focus shifts solely to the female body, however, more informa-
tive and richly problematic issues can surface. Hot Springs Hygeia's beau-

tiful arms, the Chippewa Itasca Lake, Minnehaha's genial liquidity, Zenobia's aquatic mystery, Leila's "depth upon depth" can direct us toward the consideration of ways in which female physiology lends itself to aquatic environmental embodiment.

Female anatomy, physiology, and morphology are incontestably important in the designation of environmental waters of Nature's nation. The language in which the environmental meanings is coded reverts to anatomical functions that are particular to women, to the fluids of fertility, of gestation, of lactation. Since the concern is so often for health, or hygiene, of both the social and the personal body, the major criterion of value pertains to nurturance, rejuvenation, and healing. As these benefits are understood to be inherent to certain American bodies of water, the key words of health pertain by extension to issues of bodily function. The fluids of fertility, of nurture, of inclusive protection are definitively those of the female body, and they coalesce in the idea of water as the prime agent of health. These fluids constitute the hygienic body of waters.

Yet hygiene seems dependent upon aquatic quietude, a trait hardly attributable to waterways subject to recurrent flooding. What, then, of torrential waters whose floods cause bankside havoc? Does the hygienic female principle fall into abeyance when the subject turns to flood? Do female waters in turbulent full flood default to a male identity? Do the male "rivers of empire" displace the female?

It is tempting to think so, perhaps for reasons related to "who built America," to cite the title of an American social history project (Gutman et al.). The Beecher sisters' *American Woman's Home* (1869) naturalized male responsibilities for material culture: "To man is appointed the outdoor labor—to till the earth, dig the mines, toil in the foundaries . . . all the heavy work" (19). Given that the American built environment through the nineteenth century was largely a male project, through work such as forest clearance, barn raisings, road building, and factory construction (if not operative work), it seems unlikely that forceful, even violent waters imperiling all this would be assigned a female identity. To invert the proposition, one could say that it serves a masculinist ethos to identify the most physically energetic of waters as male. To do otherwise would be to cede enormous power to a female principle.

When the memoirist Chambers says of the effort to contain a flooded Mississippi, "No braver struggle between man and nature was ever made," it is understood that "nature" here is not female, much less feminine (211–214). Chambers's statement belongs to a patriarchal culture that could hardly accommodate female waterways identified with destruction

on a scale that defeats human (male) effort, whether in the ruinous cyclical floods of the river-valley farms settled and owned or rented by men or,
in the case of Johnstown, in the freak flood which flattened the houses
built by male carpenters and construction workers, and which destroyed
the very hallmark of the new industrial order, the Cambria Iron Works, in
a town whose economic prosperity was based on coke, steel, and iron.

Periodically throughout the eighteenth and nineteenth centuries, floods
disrupted and ruined domestic life in both agricultural and industrial settings, and the 1861 Humphreys *Report on the Physics and Hydraulics of the
Mississippi River,* termed "one of the classics of hydrological data," chronicles "Great Floods" of the Mississippi from 1798 through 1859, especially
marking those of 1828, 1844, 1849, 1850, 1851, 1858, and 1859 (F.
Smith, 416; Humphreys, 167–183). Because the built environment so
badly damaged or destroyed by these floods was largely a male effort, the
ascription of such power to female agency would have been psychologically unconscionable in any genre, from narrative fiction to an engineering report.

Nor would the largely female ethos of middle-class domestic gentility
be served by female gendering and embodiment of flood waters. Fuller's
Leila is an agent of transcendence, not of catastrophe. (In fact, Fuller's
own resistance to the notion of a female flood is apparent in her pejorative characterization of the inexorable arrival of immigrants to the western plains as a "torrent of emigration [which] swells very strongly"
[*Lakes,* 70].)

Such an unwritten taboo against, say, a Mississippi gendered as the
"Mother of Waters" does not mean, however, that the grand waterways in
full flow escape female identification. These embodied female waters are
actually present in full flood despite the neat paradigm of the *Columbiad,*
and despite the embrace of the English translation of "Father of Waters"
and the description of the Johnstown Flood as an erlking. This is to say
that waters that are turbulent and torrential are not always transsexualized
as males via the rhetorical strategies of birth *(The Columbiad)* or metamorphosis *(The Johnstown Flood).* They are also at times imaged as female.
In their female incarnation, however, the fierce waters are radically problematic and require cunning rhetorical moves in efforts to maintain the
patriarchal order.

To see how texts negotiate the turbulent, flooding female bodies of water, we begin with John James Audubon's *Delineations of American Scenery
and the American Character* (a volume of extracts reprinted from his *Orni-
thological Biography,* 1831–1839). *Delineations* is a miscellany of travel

sketches written between 1808 and 1834, and focused principally on the great river valleys of the Mississippi and Ohio. The sketches were interspersed with Audubon's numerous projects in descriptive ornithology (his best-known book being *Birds of America* [1827–1838]), and they adopt the convention of personification of the natural world as one of female "Nature" who "display[s] all her loveliness," who "open[s] her graceful eyelids" at dawn, "arrayed in all that was her richest and purest," and yet who, as a storm comes on, assumes an "angry aspect, seem[ing] to be breathing for a moment, before collecting her energies, to inflict some signal punishment on guilty man" (220, 226, 237).

With nature framed in female terms in dress and also in emotional expression from mild equanimity to anger, readers encounter Audubon's chapter "A Flood," a most graphic description opening with his remark that "many of our larger streams, such as the Mississippi, the Ohio, the Illinois, the Arkansas and Red River" are seasonally subject to "the most extensive overflowings of their waters" (29). Audubon then describes "the enormous mass of [Ohio and Mississippi] waters . . . booming along, turbid and swollen to overflowing" (29). Fences and dwellings are "unable to resist its violence . . . the dreadful effects of such an inundation" (30). The water, he writes, "rushes out and overspreads the whole of the neighboring swamps," and "so sudden is the calamity, that every individual, whether man or beast, has to exert utmost ingenuity to enable him to escape from the dreaded element" (30). Audubon continues to describe the flood waters as "swollen," "covered with yellow foam," an "impetuous mass of foaming and boiling water" which, when it recedes, leaves "a deep deposit of muddy loam" and which exudes "disagreeable" and "noxious exhalations" (32, 33).

The "Flood" chapter does not contain female pronouns or directly personify the waters as Dame Nature. Yet the terms of the natural world are established in the text as female, against whom the river valley population must work to repair and raise the "artificial barriers," the levees: "In spite of all exertions, however, the crevasse opens, and water bursts impetuously over the plantations, and lays waste the crops" (32). Logically, this scene pits nature against herself, her nurturant maternalism against her deluge. That is, nature divides against herself as long as gender is thought to be the sole criterion of reference.

In Audubon, however, the category of class intervenes to prevent any acknowledgment of internal discordance in the text. Simply put, his Dame Nature is more of a lady than a woman. "Arrayed in all that was her richest and purest," she is dissociated from the bodily function that would implicate her directly in the devastating flood afflicting the valleys in a seasonal cycle. Audubon's *Delineations* discloses one rhetorical strategy by which powerful, turbulent waterways are gender-implicit but, in representation, stop short of a clear-cut homologic relation to the female body.

For that link, we must turn to Melville, who broached the point explicitly in his short story "The Tartarus of Maids" (1835), in which pale, white female operatives toil in a paper mill, while outdoors, at one side of the factory building, the "Blood River . . . boiled . . . redly and demoniacally" (p. 1987).

Melville's Blood River is customarily interpreted as symbolic of the monthly wash of menstrual blood of the virtually imprisoned mill operatives-maids. The text demonizes this river, the menstrual flow becoming as threatening as the pale maidens are innocuous. The story positions the female figures—the maids who work inside a factory characteristic of the new industrial order—as demure innocents. The narrative separates them from their bodily function, which is represented by the boiling river of blood outdoors. Melville expresses a certain empathy for the maids, as Audubon conveys his reverence for a gentrified Dame Nature. "The Tartarus of Maids" respects the categorical genteel, just as Audubon's *Delineations* reveres the gentry.

Both texts therefore dissociate the females whose class position commands authorial allegiance from the fearsome, macro-environmental havoc of female bodily function. Class position in Melville's and Audubon's texts becomes a strategic opportunity by which the lady or maid remains innocent of aquatic destruction, while the bodily function of the woman, meanwhile, can be presented as demonstrably dangerous.

That womanly function is, quite literally, a disorder, a dangerous disturbance of the proper order of things. As such, it begs for correction. Lexically, the terms of that correction accord with the criteria of two professions seldom in the nineteenth century considered to be cognates: medicine and engineering. Yet mainstream nineteenth-century allopathic medicine and civil engineering are the areas of expertise conjoined in the prevention and remediation of disorders of female fluidity, both riparian and gynecological.

From this perspective, both the female body and those bodies of water apt to flood can be said to occupy the same subject position. Defined as disorderly or pathologic, both are in prime position for intervention by male expertise. The peril that both pose is, in and of itself, a summons to organized effort at the restoration of order via control measures. Just as the boiling, demoniac Blood River implies the need for the engineer's dams and levees, so the female reproductive system, prone to menstrual flooding, requires gynecological intervention. It is not surprising, therefore, to find in the professional literature a convergent and complementary vocabulary from medicine and also from earth science and engineering. As we shall see, the convergent vocabularies of medicine and of civil engineering indicate that riparian and gynecologic-obstetrical management were congruent activities.[4]

One must remember the nineteenth century's foundational principles in which women's disorders were thought to center in the precarious physiology of the womb and reproductive organs. From the allopathic medical perspective, a woman's lifetime constituted a series of health crises from puberty through reproductive years and menopause. Allopathic medicine emphasized females' physiological precariousness and their tendency to suffer mental and physical breakdowns. Allopathic practitioners, such as Hot Springs' Algernon Garnett, treated ladies (and doubtless maids too) but worked to control female physiology through crisis management, providing interventionist treatments in gynecology and obstetrics.

Nineteenth-century allopathic medical literature structured women's bodies in a pathologic vocabulary that proved homologically applicable to the nation's waterways, and vice versa. The geographic-hydrological literature addresses problems of periodic American river valley floods—for example, of the Mississippi—in female pronouns referent to the rivers and their originating sources. As we noticed in a review of the Hot Springs texts, certain terminology from developing specialized fields of medical study overlaps with that of scientific-technical literature. It is not surprising to find vocabularies of medicine joined with those of hydrology and geology, especially when waters overflow their channels.

Flood control, in this sense, becomes the mission coextensively of the engineer as well as of the gynecological practitioner, with fluidity itself the synecdoche for the female body. Flooding was—and remains at the turn of the twenty-first century—a crossover term for the menstrual dysfunction of menorrhagia. Defined throughout the nineteenth century as "a large quantity of the menses," it was described in gynecological literature of the time as "flooding" and "a full stream" (Hollick, 178, 181; Melandy, 100).

As the image of flooding suggests, aqueous health is a matter of management by outside agents, such as engineers and medical doctors, since fluidity can be excessive, pathological. The "mechanics of fluids," to cite the title of Luce Irigaray's essay on the long-standing "argument" between female fluidity and male logic and rationality, is thus operant from disciplines of medicine and engineering. Hygeia sometimes coexists in uneasy relation to her menorrhagiac sister. At the same time, flood control is the environmental version of the medical government of menses.

Given the destructive effects of floods, the lexicon of environmental terms that cross-reference women's physiology is pejorative. This vocabulary is based, first, on the recurrent personification of American lakes and rivers in such terms as "water body" or "terrestrial water bodies." These combine with references to a female nature (for example, "sister" lakes) to frame a discourse of environmental problems that are cast in negative terms—terms that prove to be interchangeable with those in contemporary nineteenth-century texts on gynecology and obstetrics or midwifery (Russell, *Lakes,* 2, 3).

Indeed, a vocabulary of female pathology was concurrently promulgated throughout the nineteenth century in the gynecological-obstetrical literature of allopathic medicine. One woman physician recommended a hard bed, elevated and warmed feet, and a nonstimulating diet as treatment for "flooding," a recurrent term in the allopathic literature, as is "gushing" and phrases on "blood that flowed in a stream" (Melandy, 100; Churchill, 449; Ashwell, 112, 105; Elliot, 223, 224). Another condition diagnosed as leucorrhoea, or "the whites," is named among "several varieties of discharges . . . caused by an increased secretion of the mucus lining of the . . . generative organs," and "discharge" is also a common term across numerous obstetrical-gynecological texts (Melandy, 198; Dewees, *Treatise,* 123; Ashwell, 105).

Menorrhagial and hemorrhagial women exhibit "congestions," "excessive flow," and "frequent recurrence of the discharge" (Emmet, 174; Hodge, 65, 66). The literature refers to "oozing" and to an "immoderate flow" of a uterine discharge that "cannot readily escape" (Davis, 163; Dewees, *Treatise,* 123, 134). A prize-winning study by the distinguished physician Mary Putnam Jacobi refuted the standard medical notion that menstruating women needed a great deal of rest, yet employed standard phrases from medical literature on "the oozing of blood," "sluggish" blood circulation, and the "defects of the genital canal," including a medical colleague's phrase on blood "dammed up towards the ovaries" of celibate women (202, 222, 223, 214).

Because the medical terms replicate those found in texts on environmental waters, there is a certain interchangeable vocabulary of riparian and female function.[5] Rivers and lakes are presented as exhibiting the very pathological symptoms of women's reproductive health crises. There are the "swollen" streams and tributaries contributing to "great floods," including the Mississippi River headwaters area (Russell, *Rivers*, 22, 232, 233; qtd. Humphreys, 76). Waters are "turbid" and "discharge" themselves (Humphreys, 94, qtd. 197). Streams flow "sluggishly" and need to rest (Russell, *Rivers*, 37). They require "drainage" (Russell, *Rivers*, 259). In *Man and Nature*, one environmentally pathological symptom is "the augmented swelling of the lakes" (303). Low-water shoals and flood tides expose an "ooze" and "slime" (288, 291, 295). The soil of Tuscany, says the aptly named Marsh, "when thoroughly saturated with water, . . . flows like a river [and] becomes pasty, almost fluid" (352). Yet engineering interventions constituting "the most brilliant achievements of modern engineering" have drained the malarial "stagnating water," thereby "regulating the flow of the surface waters" into and through engineered conduits (353).

George Perkins Marsh's *Man and Nature* presents a socially hierarchical paradigm governing this analogic vocabulary of bodies of water and bodies of women. The paradigm accords high status to male technical-scientific expertise and authorizes experts' intervention in the on-site domain of knowledge, be it of a human body or a body of water. Essentially, Marsh posits a "civilized man" who is superior to nature, being of a "more exalted parentage" and a "higher order of existence than those born of her womb and submissive to her dictates" (36–37, 29). Mother Nature and her offspring thus occupy a world that is definitively subordinate to—and consenting to—the interventionist dictates of sapient "civilized man." That man might be an officer in the Army Corps of Engineers or a physician. Marsh's text, which endorses a male engineering mentality, comes very close to reproducing the allopathic theory of health when Marsh commends "the success with which human guidance has made the operations of nature herself available for the restoration of her disturbed harmonies" (353).

These crossover vocabularies from medicine and science-technology are comparable but not identical. Some terminology from hydrology and gynecology evidently is too overtly comparative. The literature on lakes and rivers does not refer to floods as hemorrhages, nor are gynecological dams for the stanching of blood flow called levees. Bodily lesions are not called crevasses, the dreaded term referent to the failures of levees during high water. This being said, it appears nonetheless that in the nineteenth century a remarkable common lexicon conjoins the female body with the North American system of waterways, especially insofar as those waterways were thought to obstruct transport or threaten onshore damage. The matching terms from engineering and medicine indicate that the forceful waterways apt to flood or flow torrentially became a female-identified lexical trace element of violently subversive female presence, one requiring interventionist control.[6]

Kate Chopin and the "Voice of the Sea"

By the end of the nineteenth century, the ample American record of public discourse on every aquatic entity from seas to rivers, springs to ponds, rills, freshets, and so on afforded multiple interpretive opportunities, including a new feminist statement based upon the Hygeian model. This Hygeian body of Nature's nation, as we have seen, had been celebrated in the various "charming" lakes, lakelets, and springs of, for example, Longfellow's "laughing waters" or Fuller's "gentle element" or the Humphreys report's "little streams, all of which have their sources in beautiful, gushing springs of clear cold water" (64).

While those waterways apt to disrupt human socioeconomic arrangements prompted the lexicon of female pathology, the quieter waters thought to constitute the health-giving female bodies of waters were allied with the nineteenth-century idea of woman as domestic caregiver. As one historian of the water-cure movement remarks, the female body figured centrally in American hydropathy, which "directly utilized several key components of water's symbolic nature," including its "ability to soothe, cool, relax, and stimulate" (Cayleff, 19). Water cure, moreover, fostered an emancipationist feminist ideology that "stressed woman's right to increased choices, opportunities, and rewards" (Cayleff, 18).

The goddess of health accordingly flourished in nineteenth-century America in the burgeoning spa resorts at numerous mineral springs and in the medical-health movement of water cure or hydropathy. The water-cure movement alone fostered the development of establishments from Maine to San Francisco, and cures typically were offered in bucolic settings commensurate with the ideals of the quieter waters eulogized in so many texts as the "gentle element," the "charming stream," the "fountains of . . . beauty, health, and wealth," and so on (Cayleff, 75–108; Donegan, 185–197).[7]

One such spa was located on the Louisiana Gulf, where the female body of water emerged in the work of Kate Chopin (1851–1904). This writer of fictional sketches and stories, set in her mother's Creole Louisiana and her cotton-trader husband's New Orleans, is most appreciated in later twentieth-century literary studies for *The Awakening* (1899), a novel set in New Orleans and in the spa resort of Grand Isle, Louisiana. Chopin interests us here because her work bears directly on issues of female aquatic embodiment present in the Hot Springs texts and continued from the 1840s in Margaret Fuller's "Leila" and *Summer on the Lakes*. *The Awakening* is crucial to a discussion of the aquatic body of Nature's nation because, at the very end of the nineteenth century, Chopin exploited feminist themes of aquatic subversion within an argument based upon the notion of Hygeian succor. In addition, Chopin vastly expanded the aquatic territory which constitutes the female body, bypassing the springs and lakelets to claim female embodiment of the vast sea.

Chopin's *Awakening* is a latecomer to the American literary canon, having been rediscovered in the late 1960s following decades of oblivion to which the novel was consigned from the date of its publication, when the book and its author were denounced as immoral and insurrectionist. *The Awakening* is the story of the intellectual-sexual awakening of Edna Pontellier, a young New Orleans matron summering at Grand Isle with her husband and sons as she comes to understand the extent of women's constraints in patriarchal society. Realizing a selfhood in which she would give her life but not her self for her two children, and sexually drawn to a young Creole man while at Grand Isle, Edna returns to the city in quiet rebellion against the hypocritical social rituals that lubricate her husband's business dealings ("that outward existence which conforms, the inward life which questions" [57]).

Realizing that her relation to her husband is largely proprietary on his part, and determined to cultivate a talent for art by focusing her energies on painting, Edna rejects her marriage as one that "masquerade[s] as the decrees of fate" and moves from her French Quarter household into a small cottage (62). Her intellectual-sexual awakening, however, leads not to a gratifying new life but to frustration and depression. The novel concludes with her return to Grand Isle in the off season, where, on the beach, she disrobes and swims out to sea, failing to turn back when fatigued and thus drowning in what many readers regard as a suicide.

Examined in critical studies from numerous viewpoints over nearly thirty years, *The Awakening* discloses issues in its author's literary career, its formal design, its place in the American local-color tradition, its role in the feminist New Woman movement, and so on. More recently, the novel has been interpreted according to its identification with water, specifically with Aphrodite. In Sandra Gilbert's reading, Edna's final swim is not a suicide but enacts a regeneration myth in which she is born of and renewed by her sea bathing. Gilbert calls our attention to Chopin's image of Edna as "Venus rising from the foam," to a decorative "naked Venus" in the novelist's drawing room, and to the scenes in *The Awakening* in which "Edna's last swim . . . is a death that points toward a resurrection, . . . a Venusian Easter" (*Awakening*, 172; Gilbert, 32, 31).

To revisit *The Awakening* here is to extend Gilbert's insights within the tradition of the female body of water of Nature's nation. It is to encounter a feminist argument in which the vast sea of the century's male canon is newly identified as a female bodily entity whose very gender claims subvert a masculinist ethos. Chopin's sea is both *of* woman and *for* her.

The Awakening belongs in the context of nineteenth-century hydrotherapy. First, notice that Chopin's setting, Louisiana's Grand Isle, is in many ways a typical American spa in combining recreation with the promotion of health. The ingredients of the summertime spa resort are all there—the hotel and cottages, the bath houses along the white beach, the bathing suits, wicker rockers, seasonal books, hammocks, sunshades, palm leaf fans, games of lawn croquet and billiards, the evening entertainments of "music, dancing, and a recitation or two," and swimming (68).

The novel highlights the health-spa dimension by repeatedly referring to health concerns important to the nineteenth century. Chopin reminds readers of the threat of fevers—Edna's children's and, later on in the autumn, Edna's own. A progressing pregnancy (of a friend of Edna's, Adele Ratignole) is by medical definition a health crisis, the bouillon tea prepared to counteract its fatigue an oft-prescribed tonic, while Edna's own mental health increasingly becomes cause for concern to her husband and a family friend who is a physician (and to herself, though for diametrically opposed reasons). We learn of an apparently healthy summer visitor, a young woman, who "died between summers" (53). Infant clothing is being sewn to protect against winter's "deadly cold" drafts (52). The sight of a wound or scar "sickens" Edna (130). Chopin writes, "The Creole woman does not take any chances which may be avoided of imperiling her health" (66).

Edna, a Kentuckian by birth and upbringing, is not a Creole, as the novel makes abundantly clear. Yet in terms of nineteenth-century hydrotherapy, she is very much a health-seeker. Sea bathing and swimming were an important part of the hydrotherapy movement, with John Bell's *Of Baths and Mineral Waters* (1831) an authoritative treatise cited repeatedly throughout the century in later hydrotherapy texts. Bell notes the testimony of women sea bathers exhilarated by dashing breakers and finds "the exercise of *Swimming* . . . [to provide enjoyment and] the consciousness of security when bathing on the sea shore" (176). "Swimming is for most persons an active exercise—by which respiration and muscular

movements are greatly accelerated . . . [and] best tolerated by the san-
guine, the vigorous, and the robust among the healthy," and by those "la-
bouring under febrile excitement among the invalids" (179, 181). For
"the young and healthy, . . . the sense of refreshment [is] . . . incontestable
proof of the salubrity of the practice," while those who are fevered "ought
to visit the beach . . . [at] the time of increased heat and flushing" (189,
182).

Those optimal beneficiaries of swimming—the vigorous and the fevered—sound like an odd pairing, but in nineteenth-century terms they
reveal Chopin's strategy in noting Edna's "splendid body" and her repeated feverishness (72, 128, 130, 139). The text thus readies its protagonist for the ultimate swim in which she is to be "enfold[ed] in . . . the soft,
close embrace" of the sea.

First, however, Edna must learn to swim, to enter the water as her fellow spa vacationers do, "walk[ing] into the water as though into a native
element" (73). She does so in the moonlight, shouting for joy "as with a
sweeping stroke or two she lifted her body to the surface of the water." To
learn to swim in this sea is to gain the "power . . . to control the working
of her body and her soul . . . [and] a feeling of exultation overtook her" as,
"intoxicated with her newly conquered power," Edna "swam out alone"
(73, 74). In accordance with Bell's advisory on sea bathing, Edna finds
swimming invigorating (99).

Chopin, meanwhile, works to personify the sea as female with its "seductive odor" and "everlasting voice . . . like a mournful lullaby" (56, 49).
The sea will ultimately enfold Edna in its embrace, and so the novelist
must undertake the task of marine personification. As all readers notice,
the sea's voice becomes crucial to this process: its "sonorous murmur
reache[s] Edna like a loving but imperative entreaty" (56). One passage
further incarnates the female vocative sea (and reappears, nearly verbatim,
toward the novel's conclusion): "The voice of the sea is seductive; never
ceasing, whispering, clamoring, murmuring, inviting the soul to wander
for a spell in abysses of solitude; to lose oneself in mazes of contemplation" (57, 176). Chopin writes, "The voice of the sea speaks to the soul.
The touch of the sea is sensuous, enfolding the body in its soft, close embrace" (57; cf. 83). Chopin creates a partnership of the sea and the female
moon, whose "mystic shimmer . . . cast a million lights across the distant,
restless water" (70).

Edna's final swim, free of the heavy wet bathing suit (which could
weigh up to forty pounds in the 1890s), has been interpreted by many
readers as the suicidal act of a woman whose new consciousness has only

served to move her from romantic illusion to the abyss of a culturally and psychologically unlivable existence. According to this view, the social arrangements of Edna's world provide her no channels for energy informed by thought, and therefore the resulting isolation, the "ennui," and obsessive "hopelessness" can be seen to prompt her self-destruction (152, 145).

In the context of nineteenth-century hydrotherapy, however, and in the female aquatic tradition of Nature's nation, *The Awakening*'s conclusion must be understood much more as a homecoming. "Invited" by the waves, Edna feels "like some new-born creature, opening its eyes in a familiar world that it has never known" yet has fantasized as a child swimming strokes in an ocean of Kentucky bluegrass (175, 60). Now at last the Edna who was orphaned in childhood at her mother's death is embraced by an insistent maternal sea whose voice, if mournful, is nonetheless a lullaby as it sings, whispers, insists on welcoming, albeit seductively, the free, naked, powerful body of its daughter in pleasure and succor. Edna can now swim the actual sea, reentering the natural element she inhabited before memory itself.

The sea in *The Awakening* emphatically enlarges the female body of water beyond its literary predecessors. Chopin pointedly does not show Edna learning to swim (much less conclude her earthly life) in a creek, a spring-fed pond, or a little pool of "Laughing Waters." Hers is not a "Summer on the Lakes," nor is her Gulf analogous to Mark Twain's Mississippi "Father of Waters" which flows along Chopin's own hometown, St. Louis, its current loaded with all kinds of debris as inventoried in *Life on the Mississippi* and *The Adventures of Huckleberry Finn*. Chopin's embodied sea, like the waters of Fuller's "Leila," is pure, powerful, and transcendental. Like the Hygeian Hot Springs and the crystalline waters of the water cure, it is the healing element on a grand scale, a scale arguably enabled by the American-British New Woman movement of the 1890s that expanded the female domain by reconceiving women's identity and worldly status. The movement's support of sexual freedom, economic autonomy, and self-gratification through work outside the home involved women such as Chopin, who were largely white and middle class and sufficiently secure, or so it seemed, to be outspoken, iconoclastic, and independent. The sea in *The Awakening* is territorially vast because the New Woman movement enlarged the female sphere conceptually and operationally.

At the turn of the twentieth century, Kate Chopin thus extended the spatial dimensions of the American Hygeia tremendously. *The Awakening* feminized the entire sea as a maternal body. While in New Orleans, Edna glimpses the "masts of ships and the big chimneys of the Mississippi steamers," vessels that revert to the male marine and riparian "smoke and soot" commercial world given nineteenth-century literary expression in Melville, Dana, and Twain (113). Chopin's sea, on the contrary, is clean, even hygienic as the body of Nature's nation. Its undertow is but a serpentine grip at the ankles, its turbulence the dynamic of female consciousness on the rise, its demeanor feminine and virtually domestic as the waters "ripple" like cream, break in "little foamy crests," are "whipped . . . into froth," and "curl" as "foamy wavelets" (109, 73, 59, 175).

None of the pathology of female flooding makes its way into the world of *The Awakening*. None of the hurricanes that would be personified as women for decades in the twentieth century roil Chopin's Gulf to threaten havoc for mariners or for onshore lives and property. Chopin opposes the "ocean's roar" to the "whisper" of the sea and thus genders her Gulf feminine in opposition to the oceanic male even as she claims vast aquatic female acreage (82, 83). She continues Fuller's portrayal of the "gentle element" from which "Venus was born" and closes the nineteenth century with female aquatic grandeur, with Edna's final swim a move to the maternal body, both *mer* and *mère*.

6

Love Canal: Hygeia's Crisis

[Chemicals] pass mysteriously by underground streams until they emerge and, through the alchemy of air and sunlight, combine into new forms that kill vegetation, sicken cattle, and work unknown harm on those who drink from once pure wells.

—RACHEL CARSON, *Silent Spring,* 1962

The swale theory seemed to be holding up. [Dr. Paigen] said residents who lived on the historically wet areas should be relocated . . . immediately. . . . I can't tell you what it was like on some days. It was hot, and the air would just hang there. The fumes were thick. They made your eyes water, or you coughed. Someone described it as similar to trying to breath underwater. . . . In the summer, you knew you were living on a chemical dump.

—LOIS GIBBS, *Love Canal—My Story,* 1982

A quagmire of sludge . . . oozed from [Love] canal's every pore.

—MICHAEL BROWN, "Love Canal and the Poisoning of America," 1979

After years of breathing "underwater" summer after summer, the Niagara Falls housewife-turned-neighborhood-activist Lois Gibbs was "very excited" to learn of the "swale theory" in September 1978, when a New York Department of Health task force held a public meeting in her community of Love Canal, a part of the city of Niagara Falls, New York (Levine, 89). Swales, as Lois was learning, referred to natural drainageways by which underground liquids can flow and form subterranean ponds. The liquids in this case were water mixed with toxic industrial chemicals, a wetlands of death and illness on which Lois, her family, and her neighbors lived in the 1970s. The swale theory seemed to clear up the great mystery of how the community's illnesses—clusters of cancer, asthma, birth defects, neurological problems—could cut across streets and even whole blocks. It suggested that the route of debilitation was the hidden swale path and ponds.

Lois Gibbs, at twenty-six, did not see herself as a legatee of the tradition of the American Hygeia. She identified herself instead as a housewife and mother who worried about her son's seizures, which began when he entered their neighborhood's 93rd Street School. Her concern became focused when she read reporter Michael Brown's articles in the Niagara Falls *Gazette* in August 1977 on the history of the canal, prompted by investigations of the Department of Environmental Conservation for New York into problems of fish contamination in Lake Ontario, and then realized that her son's school was located over canal-area land. It sharpened when she sought her chemist brother-in-law's translation of arcane chemical terminology into lay language and learned of the potential health damage threatened by the substances in the canal, such as Dioxin, thought to be the most toxic compound ever produced. It strengthened as Gibbs began to suspect that her son's seizures had their etiology in the canal's chemicals but then found officials at every level to be resistant to an exploration of that connection. It matured over months and years of do-it-yourself political effort in which the shy, nonpolitical Gibbs forced herself to go door to door in the neighborhood, organize neighbors, itemize their health problems, approach officials and experts, talk to reporters, and speak out at public meetings. She became a leader in a cause that gained national attention in the news media, in large part because she developed an effective on-camera persona, beginning with an outcry, "You're murdering us!" in a public meeting with New York State officials in August 1978 (Levine, 34; Gibbs, 26–32).

Throughout the work on the Love Canal crisis, the high school–educated Gibbs consistently exploited her identity as housewife, not as environmental activist. Her 1982 book, *Love Canal—My Story,* claimed to be one of "a housewife who went to Washington" (xiii). Her as-told-to account of the environmental crisis in her community chronicles her efforts, together with those of her neighbors, to document their area's high instances of illness ranging from respiratory and neurophysiological disorders to cancer, to learn just which underground contaminants lay beneath their modest suburban homes, and to mount an ultimately successful campaign to make the state of New York and the federal government, including the president, responsible for evacuating 790 of the 850 Love

Canal families, literally moving them to safer ground. According to her coauthor, the clinical psychologist Murray Levine, Gibbs learned "about law, politics, toxicology, and engineering," learned to deal with "bureaucrats, scientists, professors, lawyers," and ultimately learned "to face down governors, senators, and mayors" in order to rescue her family and neighbors from their environmentally contaminated Love Canal community (qtd. Gibbs, xiv).

In a larger context, the moment was propitious for the activist work of a Lois Gibbs, in part because American environmental crises had been widely publicized for over a decade. Anyone watching television news or subscribing to a newspaper or news magazine learned something about the contamination of earth and water in post–World War II America. In 1965, the U.S. Health Service held public hearings on Lake Erie's deterioration, which television newscasters termed the "North American Dead Sea" (Vogel, 55). In 1969, a rupture at a Union Oil Company drilling station off the coast of Santa Barbara, California, in an underwater area called the Torrey Canyon, released a thick crude oil slick over four hundred square miles of the Pacific and forty miles of beaches and covered thousands of seabirds and sea otters. Media images of hapless oil-covered animals appeared in print and on television. In that same year, Lake Erie was featured when a section of Cleveland's Cuyahoga River, a tributary of the lake, burst into flames fed by oily sludge.

Environmental expertise became an important part of public discourse in the name of education and warning in these years. Rachel Carson's *Silent Spring* (1962) became a cornerstone of public education about the contamination of earth, air, and inland waters and seas when cold war nuclear detritus and pesticide sprays entered the ecosystem. In *The Quiet Crisis* (1963), Stewart Udall, the secretary of the interior in the Kennedy administration, argued that the post–World War II production of automobiles and other consumer goods had diverted public attention from stewardship of the land and threatened to substitute the gross national product for a proper "land ethic" (188–191). Others, such as the biologists Paul Ehrlich and Barry Commoner, foretold an imminent "ecotastrophe." Commoner, a professor at Washington University, St. Louis, was featured on the cover of *Time* (February 2, 1970) and was called the "Paul Revere of Ecology," implying that he was signaling an upheaval of revolutionary scope (Vogel, 59).

Federal legislation was passed in response to data showing that the "quiet crisis" was actual: the 1963 Clean Air Act, the 1965 Motor Vehicle Air Pollution Control Act, and the 1967 Air Quality Act all reinforced the necessity of a national, not merely local or statewide, level of regulation. In 1972, over President Richard Nixon's veto, Congress passed the Federal Water Pollution Control Act (FWPCA), which called upon the Environmental Protection Agency to set rigorous standards for industrial and municipal discharges into the nation's waterways. On April 22, 1970, Americans by the millions attended public events to observe the nation's first Earth Day, which one speaker, Senator Gaylord Nelson, a Wisconsin Democrat, hoped might mark "the birth date of a new . . . ethic that rejects the frontier philosophy . . . and accepts the idea that even urbanized, affluent, mobile societies are interdependent with the fragile, life-sustaining systems of the air, the water, the land" (qtd. Vogel, 51).

Through all this, Lois Gibbs still did not identify herself as a conservationist, a term applicable during much of the century to privileged whites, not to blue-collar families like her own. She had not read Rachel Carson's *Silent Spring,* the best-selling exposé of pervasive environmental contamination by pesticides, the "elixirs of death" moving through "surface waters and underground seas" (15–51). She did not see herself as the inheritor— much less the reinvigorator—of the Hygeian tradition from the nineteenth century. Gibbs never traveled to take the waters at upstate New York's Saratoga Springs. Living minutes from Niagara Falls, she did not seek out Margaret Fuller's *Summer on the Lakes* as a foremother's guide to the Falls' "slight circles that mark the hidden vortex [which] seem to whisper mysteries the thundering voice above could not proclaim" (5). Gibbs was not a proponent of the water cure, which had largely died out in the opening decades of the twentieth century. There is also no evidence that she knew Kate Chopin's *Awakening* or any of the other nineteenth-century American texts that represent water in female bodily terms. Nor, in the late 1970s and early 1980s, did Gibbs play a conscious role in the development of the new, feminist ecological thought that would become known as ecofeminism and that changed the paradigm by which female aquatic bodies once again could legitimate the notion of an American Nature's nation. Nature's nation, in Gibbs's terms, meant a peaceful neighborhood and a house with a grassy yard in which children could play barefoot in the summertime.

The self-styled canal housewife nonetheless became a major participant in the Hygeian twentieth century, one of environmental crisis and ecofeminist activism in the context of aquatic bodies of water. As an environmental activist who focused on an aquatic site in the cause of familial health and well-being, Gibbs inevitably became an inheritor of the nineteenth-century Hygeian tradition in which water signifies healing and nourishment incarnated in the female body. Her Hygeian identity was mandated by her focus on the aquatic entity of Love Canal, which itself was figured as the afflicted, malignant body of a sickened Nature's nation, a human body oozing sludge from every pore and in dire need of cleansing and healing.

Love Canal

Love Canal's early history locates it firmly in the nineteenth-century version of the Hygeian tradition, though its origins lie in the male world of heavy industry and, in literary tradition, in the canals promoted by George Washington for the furtherance of the empire and identified by Joel Barlow and Herman Melville as male power projects. In the early 1890s, in the Niagara Falls village of LaSalle, workers broke ground at either end of William T. Love's projected industrial canal. Located between the upper and lower parts of the Niagara River, the canal site promised advantages both for industry and for residential life. At that time, the politically well-connected entrepreneur, Love, was implementing his vision of a three-thousand-foot navigable power canal filled with waters diverted from the Niagara River. The three-hundred-foot drop was to be used to generate electricity for industry and to provide free electrical power for a residential community to be named Model City. "Love wanted workers to have easy access to ideal housing in nice neighborhoods" (Irwin, 145).

Although a few Model City houses were built by the shore of Lake Ontario, Love's project fell victim to the mid-1890s depression and to the discovery that alternating current enabled electrical generation at sites distant from water-power sources. Abandoned, the sixty-foot-wide, ten-foot-deep canal entered into the tradition of healthful American waters which were identified through the nineteenth century as female. No longer an industrial waterway for the generation of electrical power, the canal became a site consonant with gentle female waters. "Embedded in an area of orchards and farms," the abandoned canal was "watered by riverlets and creeks stemming from Niagara" (Levine, 9). As we know, the riverlets or rivulets, creeks, springs, freshets, and so on formed a well-established pattern in which the aquatically embodied goddess of health is thought to provide human well-being manifest in Nature's nation and to afford it to all who seek her succor. We recall the mid-nineteenth-century advocate of the water-cure health regimen who wrote, "Voices from the founts and rills, / Are the notes which Hygeia sings."

These were not the notes sung by the riverlets and creeks of William Love's canal as the twentieth century progressed. The new identity was cast in negative terms of toxicity. The male world of industrial production, technology, and business reinserted itself, literally, into the canal, which became a waste dump site. It was as if Hygeia had become Rappaccini's daughter, a version of Nathaniel Hawthorne's young woman poisoned by her own mad-scientist father and toxic to any who might come into contact with her.

By 1905, in fact, the scientists and engineers whose hermeneutics worked to redefine Hygeia as a vestige of a nostalgic classicism were serving a succession of chemical companies that located manufacturing plants at Niagara Falls. In 1942, fifteen years after LaSalle was annexed to the city of Niagara Falls, the Hooker Electrochemical Company (a subsidiary of the Occidental Petroleum Company), a manufacturer of products such as dyes, perfumes, and solvents, received permission from an agency of the city to dump waste products into the canal, which, until then, had been "a pleasant place for outdoor play, swimming, and fishing" (Levine, 10).

The Hooker wastes included alkalis, fatty acids, caustics, and chlorinated hydrocarbons, dumped in metal or fiber barrels or poured into the trench as sludge or liquid. The canal was considered an "excellent" dump site for these materials because the area was sparsely populated, because dumping was not prohibited by law, and because the canal was large and lined with thick walls of nonporous clay (Levine, 10). Eyewitness testimony, though undocumented by records, has indicated that the U.S. Army also used the canal as a dump site (Levine, 25, 53).

By 1953, then, a minimum of 21,800 tons of chemical waste had been discharged into the canal and nearly filled it. Although the older residents told newspaper reporters that the airborne chemical vapors choked them, killed their grass, burned the paint off their houses, caused fires, and, on contact with the skin, injured the chemical workers exposed to the substances they themselves were dumping, still the canal might have remained one of thousands of similar unremarked-on sites of toxic contamination in the United States because, by 1953, it was covered over with earth and grasses and resembled a long, broad field. Indeed, in the 1970s, real estate agents would promote the notion that a recreational park would one day be developed in the area.

Perhaps this benign, pastoral appearance contributed to the decision of the city of Niagara Falls, which was hard pressed for space, to build on this site the elementary school that was attended in the 1970s by the children of Lois and Harry Gibbs and their neighbors. As the Gibbses and others learned, in April 1953, for a token one-dollar payment, the Hooker Company had deeded sixteen acres of land, including most of the canal, to the city, which then erected an elementary school on six of those acres. Two- and three-bedroom modest homes, some guaranteed with federally backed FHA or GI mortgages, were built in the early 1970s and sold for $18,000 to $23,000, their backyards bordering land extending from both sides of the canal. The homeowners' children could be found "playing at recess and after school hours on the playground and the adjoining fields, all over the old canal site" (Levine, 12).

Adeline Levine's *Love Canal: Science, Politics, and People* (1982) chronicles the signs of trouble, unheeded at first: the strong odors in humid or rainy weather, the chronic irritation to the feet of barefoot children at play, the spontaneous explosion of rocks thrown or dropped from the canal field, the seepage of oily black sludge into a basement whose owner kept a sump pump running constantly. Such occurrences were dismissed by all parties, residents and city officials alike, as relatively trivial, the material fact of the school itself reassuring to residents as a symbol of safety

37. Aerial view of Love Canal, 1980, showing surrounding neighborhoods.

and stability, though by 1969 "inspectors reported that the conditions were hazardous with holes in the surface of the field, formed by rusting barrels collapsing, and chemical residues left on the surface after the rainwater had evaporated" (14–15).

Heavy rain- and snowfall in the mid-1970s exacerbated these problems. Foul waters pooled in the Love Canal homeowners' backyards and made them useless. "Decades-old chemical barrels were deteriorating; chemicals were moving through underground waterways and through the soil to the yards and basements and vaporizing into the air in people's homes and yards" (Levine, 15). In July 1978, state officials gave residents of the area mimeographed sheets containing values of the chemicals found in their basements and other rooms when tested: benzene, toluene, benzoic acid, lindane, trochloroethylene, dibromoethane, benzaldehydes, methylene chloride, carbon tetrachloride, and chloroform (Levine, 24). The raw data were not interpreted for the residents; indeed the data, according to the officials, were uninterpretable.

By then the officials and Love Canal residents were snarled in a process that grew increasingly acrimonious and frustrating, although one that ultimately became politically successful for residents who achieved their goal of government-financed relocation, with a lend-lease arrangement between the federal and state governments enabling the state of New York to buy the contaminated properties from the homeowners and free them to move elsewhere without going bankrupt. President Jimmy Carter himself shook Lois Gibbs's hand onstage at the Niagara Falls Convention Center on October 10, 1980, commending Gibbs and her grassroots organization for "keeping the matter of Love Canal alive for such a long time." He also credited her with hastening the creation of the Environmental Protection Agency's Superfund, which was designed for high-priority, emergency cleanup of environmentally contaminated areas such as her own neighborhood (Levine, 207–208).

From a sociological perspective, Love Canal can be seen as a case of mutual mistrust between officials and residents (and one exposing intramural strife among residents and among city and state agencies as well). Authorities involved in data gathering, testing, and programmatic planning came to regard the Love Canal residents as unrealistic in their expectations, irrational, even paranoid, while residents saw these officials as secretive, duplicitous, obstructionist, and indifferent to their plight. *Love Canal: Science, Politics, and People* meticulously recounts that history.

A study of the environmental identities of Nature's nation, however, requires a different discursive direction. It requires, first, examination of the basis for a radical shift from the nineteenth-century female aquatic body of health to its diseased twentieth-century counterpart. The nineteenth-century Hygeian body, which was thought to confer health and healing to all willing to imbibe or immerse themselves in it, was superseded in the later twentieth century by the toxic body. Hot Springs gives way to Love Canal, a body known to be wounded and malignant, a corpus of sickness and death. There is an ironic inversion here. Congress under President Andrew Jackson had set aside the Hot Springs area in 1832 as a federal reserve so that citizens could ever afterward seek health from drinking and bathing in the Arkansan natural hot springs. In 1980, however, Congress and President Carter inverted that Jacksonian order of things when they intervened to help evacuate citizens from a onetime pleasant aquatic site turned toxic dump through systematic human contamination. In 1980 Love Canal too became a kind of federal reservation, not gated with ornamental patriotic eagles as at Hot Springs but fenced and posted with warning signs—as *Time* magazine put it, "a national skull and crossbones" ("Canal Cleanup").

In significant part, the positioning of Love Canal as a national site of environmental toxicity is attributable to Lois Gibbs's skills as publicist in the persona of homemaker. Early on, her chemist brother-in-law served as her media consultant, instructing her to make important statements when the television cameras were on and when the print reporters were in the room taking notes at the beginning of meetings. "Where's [New York governor Hugh] Carey?" she shouted at a meeting of local, state, and county officials. "I'd be here if I was governor! . . . You're treating us like the *Titanic!* Women and children first!" (qtd. Levine, 37). Adeline Levine records that from May 17 to June 16, 1980, 544 newspaper articles appeared on Love Canal in area papers, including the *New York Times.* The story was featured in radio and television news spots virtually daily, and several national television programs were "devoted partly or wholly" to the Love Canal problem, including *Today* (May 22), *The MacNeil-Lehrer Report* (May 22), *Sixty Minutes* (May 25), and *CBS Sunday News* (May 25). An hour's broadcast of the *Phil Donahue Show* aired on June 19, when the producers brought forty Love Canal residents, including Gibbs and the mayor of Niagara Falls, to Chicago for a taping, the program thereafter shown around the country in different time slots. *Good Morning America* aired several segments on Love Canal during the first two weeks of June, as well, and several documentaries featured the Love Canal problems, including one on PBS's *Nova* (July 25) and CBS's *A Plague on Our Children* (August 12) (Levine, 171–172).

Gibbs's media and political skills thus cannot be underestimated in considering why this particular site gained its national and international identity as the homology of American environmental sickness—why, for instance, that role did not devolve instead upon Woburn, Massachusetts, whose town wells were found to have been chemically contaminated by corporate entities of Beatrice Foods and W. R. Grace and which received considerable media attention beginning in September 1979. Woburn, too, had a potential principal female spokesperson in Anne Anderson, the mother of a leukemia victim and an early activist in the Woburn cause. But although Anderson spoke to the media, she did not mobilize her community or work to shape its story in order to bring redress through political means.[1] As for Gibbs, "when television news cameras were trained on her regularly, she learned to make her points within fifteen seconds" (Levine, 32).

Gibbs's very effectiveness in political organizing and media encounters must not obscure her importance within the bodily terms of Nature's nation. Her leadership, in fact, is particularly crucial because Love Canal, encompassing the canal itself and the homes situated on it, operates as an extension of the sheltering female body. Gibbs's self-identification as housewife and homemaker is central here. In *Love Canal—My Story*, she reports making curtains, preparing meals, helping her husband turn their basement into a finished room, and then feeling great conflict and dismay when her political activities—which were conducted on behalf of her family's well-being—seriously disrupted its domestic life.

These are not trivial but self-defining activities and feelings, and they both coalesced and loomed larger when Gibbs and her neighbors formed their Homeowners Association, a designation legally significant for tax and mortgage reasons but connotatively weighted by the links of its name to domesticity and thereby to the sheltering female body itself. The very idea of the homemaker as the leading voice of this environmental crisis may seem accidental, a kind of vox populi of statistical probability in decades in which the working-class household income of one wage earner could support the at-home American wife. Yet Elaine Scarry has formulated the bodily significance of this phenomenon in an analogy between the body and its material expression, the sheltering room. The room, she says, "expresses the most benign potential of human life," being "an enlargement of the body" which keeps the individual it houses "safe and warm" (38). Like the body, Scarry continues, it houses the individual "in the same way the body encloses and protects the individual within." Further, "like the body, its walls put boundaries around the self, preventing

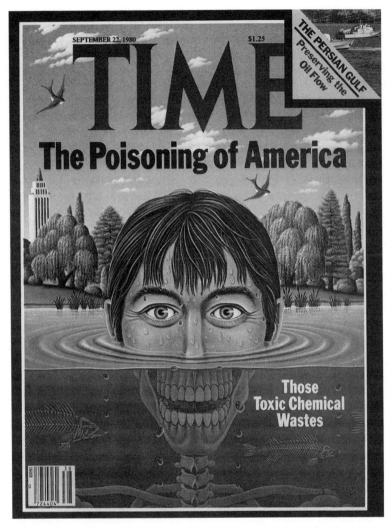

38. *Time* magazine cover of September 22, 1980, showing lethal toxicity of apparently placid waters.

undifferentiated contact with the world, yet in its windows and doors . . . it enables the self to move out into the world and allows the world to enter" (38).

Each Love Canal house was such a room, an enlargement of its home-maker's maternal body. The boundaries between that body and the outside world, however, were violated by the permeation of toxins from the canal. The home itself, with doors and windows closed, afforded no protection from the outside, which was itself verifiably, if invisibly, toxic. In this metaphoric extension, drywall and uterine wall form an analogue, but fail equally in their critical function. Whether pregnant or postpartal, the maternal body can afford no protection against the insidious toxins which, as we know, "were moving through underground waterways and through the soil to the yards and basements and vaporizing into the air in people's homes and yards."

The aquatic legacy devolving upon Gibbs and her homemaker neighbors was nonetheless Hygeian. By definition these women bore the responsibility for the domestic well-being of their children and spouses. The social radicalism of the Sixties was not their mentality. "A Hard Rain's A-Gonna Fall," the counterculturist Bob Dylan's song about poison "flooding [the] waters," was not Gibbs's or her homemaker-neighbors' anthem. They were heirs of the hetero-normative domestic advice dating from the Beecher sisters' *American Woman's Home* (1869) and *Godey's Ladies Book* to the 1950s–1970s versions, *Good Housekeeping, Redbook, McCall's,* and the *Ladies' Home Journal,* representative of a culture that included nuclear-family sitcoms such as *Leave It to Beaver* and *Ozzie and Harriet* and the cooking school of *Betty Crocker's Cookbook,* a best-seller in the 1950s when Lois Marie Conn Gibbs and her women neighbors were growing up. In 1978 one Love Canal resident posted on her front fence a "recipe" that used her role as homemaker to make its point:

LOVE CANAL RECIPE:
1. MIX 82 CHEMICALS
2. PLACE IN CANAL FOR 25 YEARS
YIELD: SICKNESS + DEATH (Swan, 48)

In 1960, when *McCall's* cited "the All-American housewife," the term projected an ideal adult female identity, one incorporating responsibilities for the promotion of family health (N. Walker, 189).

In the larger sense, then, the aquatic Hygeian body was helpless and/or toxic. Masquerading in the later 1950s and 1960s as a pastoral greensward, the failed industrial project turned from a supposedly healthful site into a swale of sickness and death. The contamination of the homes in its area, correlatively, turned the material expression of the health-giving maternal bodies—that is, the very houses—into pathological sites. Both the canal and the contaminated homes became a grisly inversion of Hygeian waters and domesticity. Print and visual media produced these pathological meanings in bodily descriptions of the canal as a "wound that never heals," as a "festering" problem producing a "psychological" and also physical "scar" and "bleeding" into basement walls. It is a "malignant growth" and a "malignancy tending to produce death or deterioration" as "of a tumor." As Michael Brown wrote, "A quagmire of sludge . . . oozed from the canal's every pore" (Smart, 30; Griffin, 26, 28; Kadlecek, 41; Brown, "Love Canal and the Poisoning of America," 34, 36; Tallmer, 35; Wexler, 30, 31; Austin, 21).

Love Canal is here first and foremost a body. It is the incarnation of Nature's nation, but despoiled. It is a body scarred, gravely wounded, infected and infectious, and mortally ill from a malignant tumor. It has no self-healing properties. Its gestational function is one of sepsis. This bodily Love Canal is the synecdoche of the nation's environmental crisis. It is the environmental Typhoid Mary of the era of chemical contamination.

More than that, Love Canal's metaphoric figuration as a malignancy codes it with a complex of sociocultural meanings, according to Susan Sontag's *Illness as Metaphor* (1979), which was published amid the Love Canal crisis. Sontag's late-1970s examination of the socially pathologic meanings of cancer decodes the journalists' descriptors of Love Canal as a "malignant growth" and as a "malignancy tending to produce death or deterioration" as "of a tumor."

As an analyst of pathological images, Sontag observed that diseases of uncertain origin, such as cancer, "have the widest possibilities as metaphors for what is felt to be socially or morally wrong" (61). "Any disease that is treated as a mystery and acutely enough feared will be felt to be morally . . . contagious" (6). Like tuberculosis, which lent itself to a complex of sociocultural meanings through the nineteenth century especially, cancer is a "master illness" used to "express a sense of dissatisfaction with society, . . . a profound disequilibrium between individual and society" (72–73). Cancer, Sontag argues, is felt to be obscene in the root definition of the term, "ill-omened, abominable, repugnant to the senses" (9).

Sontag connects cancer metaphors to specific contemporary cultural conditions of the 1960s–1970s. Characterization of the disease as a chaotic or uncontrolled growth, for instance, links it to late capitalism's dependence upon an economy of "irrational indulgence of desire" (63). It is the disease in which the body consumes itself, consumerism run amok. Yet cancer, Sontag finds, is also figured in terms of warfare—terms of invasion, of defense, of battle—and the cold war and war in Vietnam become implicated, the former in particular because cancer was considered to be an alien invasion (65–67, 13).

Sontag, a public intellectual with an ambiguous relationship to the post-1960s feminist movement, did not engage issues of gender, but her study invites such inquiry (see Wiseman). To what extent, one asks, were social anxieties about cancer also a displaced, masked set of anxieties about feminists' disruption of a patriarchal social order in the United States? To what extent, accordingly, might we find phrases from the lexicon of cancer in other cultural areas identified as female? Notions of malignancy as uncontrolled growth are to be found, for instance, in 1970s consumerism, which was largely gendered female even in the hetero-normative households whose incomes depended upon males. The uncontrolled growth in "irrational indulgence of desire" thus implicates women as agents of economic havoc in an economy that nonetheless requires such indulgence. And female-identified consumer products were themselves publicized as cancer-causing agents. Such manufacturers as the Hooker Company produced carcinogens which entered bodies not only from waste dumps but via food, cosmetic, and pesticide products, from breakfast bacon to hair dye to kitchen shelf paper treated with pesticides.

In a male-female binary, moreover, the female body is other, its very alienness mandating conquest. Cancer, Sontag says, is figured not only as the "biggest enemy" but also as the "furthest goal," and she notes that John F. Kennedy's promise to land American men on the moon was matched symmetrically by Richard Nixon's promise to "conquer" cancer. The female, sexualized moon of conquest can be paired here with a subtextual cancerous female, especially as articles on cancer appeared in mainstream magazines through the 1970s.[2] Along with smoking-related lung cancer, female breast cancer gained particular public attention, the breast itself arguably positioned as the synecdoche of the female body in public discourse ranging from Hollywood films and advertisements to the La Leche League's advocacy of breast feeding.

It extends as well to the literary representation in Philip Roth's *The Breast* (1972), a novel featuring a male professor of literature who is metamorphosed, in a Kafkaesque turn, into a female breast. The literary lineage of Kafka's "Metamorphosis" affords Roth the formal expression of gender anxiety evoked by the insurgent women's movement, which induced in Roth a fantasy of his hapless sexual metamorphosis. Add to this the Boston Women's Health Collective's best-selling *Our Bodies, Ourselves* (1971), the popular self-help manual that focused entirely on women's mental and bodily health, including nutrition and reproduction. The growth of the women's movement from the late 1960s, with its agenda for redrawing the social and political map of America, accounts in part for the principal topographic metaphors of cancer, which "spreads," and "proliferates," a disease "whose outreach," Sontag noticed, "is the whole body" (15–16, 11).

The problematic "spread[ing]" American body is emphatically female. The post-Sixties women's movement literally made women's bodies figure large in a public sector vastly broadened by television. Feminists' public demonstrations and street marches sociopolitically increased the presence of female bodies in the public domain. That larger presence promised— or threatened—to grow, perhaps uncontrollably, the growth per se patho- logical. The bodily female symbol of succor and nourishment, the breast, thus became an engulfing monstrosity in Roth's novel and was rhetorically implicated in the dire terms of cancer in journalism. This is not, by any means, to dismiss the gravity of statistics on any cancer. It is to say that in the United States, the gender anxiety prompted by social dislocations of the late Sixties women's movement led to a pathological inscription of the embodied female. She threatened to evade control, her cells, her very body to proliferate and loom ever larger. The anticancer political-medical initiatives, cast in terms of war and conquest, must be recognized in part as reactive, as a campaign to defeat and contain the expansive female body.

Ecofeminism and Its Prologues

Love Canal thus signifies more than a downward slide from purity to con- tamination, health to mortal illness. Regarded solely as the twentieth-cen- tury inversion of the preceding tradition of aquatic female health and well-being, Love Canal becomes the most lamentable environmental end game. Opposed to the Hot Springs spa, the canal shows Nature's nation degraded to its antithesis. The congeries of meanings devolving from terms of malignancy, moreover, give the site the greatest moral-political urgency in terms of gender-based discord. The terms implicate a late-capi- talist nation recently at war in Southeast Asia and chronically fighting a cold war with the Soviet Union. They further extend to the dislocations prompted by an aggressive feminist movement politically engaged to ex- pand women's rights and women's presence nationally and internationally, if necessary in a new battle of the sexes.

Sontag broached the linkage between society, cancer, and the natural world as gendered female: "For the more sophisticated, cancer signifies the rebellion of the injured ecosphere, Nature taking revenge on a wicked technocratic world" (70). Here the female body has become malignant through male violation, and yet the male oncology establishment is enjoined at the highest, presidential level to "conquer"—or reconquer—the very body that its science-engineering cohort has made malignant. From the patriarchal vantage point, malignancy is the pathology to be understood and surmounted lest that malignancy, in its wild cell-by-cell uncontrolled growth, transform the body politic into female form, the very metamorphosis being women's revenge.

Sontag's access route into subtextual readings must not obscure the late 1960s–1970s active critique of environmental depredation as induced by Western ideologies. The environmental historian Caroline Merchant's *Death of Nature* (1980) argues that a Baconian seventeenth century "developed the power of language as political instrument in reducing female nature to a resource for economic production" (165). Others accounted for the crisis within the Judeo-Christian tradition and implied possibilities for redress. According to "The Historical Roots of Our Ecological Crisis," the widely reprinted 1967 essay by the historian Lynn White, Jr., the crisis resulted from a misreading of Genesis and from a failure to consider St. Francis as a model of human harmony with the natural world. By White's and Merchant's arguments, a fundamental misunderstanding of the obligation of earthly stewardship, coupled with a modern capitalist industrial system, can be seen as the predictor of the Hooker Company's conduct, indeed that of all chemical companies whose spurious patriarchal authority reifies or feminizes the natural world in order to dominate and exploit it economically.

All these critiques signaled the apparent demise of Hygeia in later twentieth-century America. The toxicity of Love Canal, framed within a critique of late capitalism, seemingly leads to the ideological end—a dead end—of a Hygeian Nature's nation. The goddess of health would seem to prove mortal after all, her mythic self slain by historical events. The very terms of the myth of Hygeia, in fact, seem to anticipate the end of the myth. Once the pure, healing waters are poisoned and in turn become poisonous, the Hygeian myth cannot be sustained. In this regard, Love Canal apparently marks the terminus of the female aquatic version of Nature's nation.

Yet a newer mythic formulation was ascendant largely in the 1970s—ecological feminism, or ecofeminism, which posed an alternative paradigm by which the mythos of the aquatic body of Nature's nation was reinvigorated both in response to, and in spite of, the relentless public record of environmental contamination. Arguably a part of the larger, international green movement whose history Roderick Nash has traced in *The*

Rights of Nature and which Vera Norwood identifies as "utopian," eco-feminism introduced a conceptual vocabulary by which the twentieth-century female aquatic body was redefined, not as the malignant, patho-logic inversion of her predecessors but as a body empowered, enlarged, and globally exemplary (Norwood, 262).

It must be recalled that women were not absent from aquatic conserva-tion in the early twentieth century. In 1908, for instance, a group of seven Louisiana women formed the Women's National Rivers and Harbors Congress, a kind of auxiliary to the National Rivers and Harbors Con-gress. The women's group, which allied with other conservation groups, grew to thirty thousand members representing thirty-nine states and ter-ritories by 1910, pressing for conservationist morality expressed in an agenda including clean shores and streams and the preservation of Niag-ara Falls (Merchant, *Earthcare,* 120–122). Such efforts were part of a larger network of affiliated women's conservation groups, including the Audubon movement, which "promoted legislation aimed at halting pollu-tion, reforesting watersheds, and preserving endangered species" (Mer-chant, *Earthcare,* 109).

Later twentieth-century ecofeminist thought, however, rejected alli-ances with male environmentalist projects. To begin with, ecofeminism rejected the notion of a corrective rereading of Genesis, St. Francis not-withstanding. It posited as illegitimate a male tradition of adversarial as-sault upon nature. Its mandate, instead, was the supersession of this masculinist era of assault by a female-based model of enduring ecological equanimity. The very 1974 coinage of the term *ecofeminisme,* generally credited to the French feminist Françoise d'Eaubonne, called for "egalitar-ian management of a world to be reborn . . . a planet in the female gen-der" (Mellor, 44). The movement mandated environmentalism as female.

Ecofeminist terms, if applied to Love Canal, frame the crisis not as a Hygeian terminus but as a dire, yet remediable, condition resulting from "anthropocentric illusion," in the words of Elizabeth Dodson Gray (2–8). Her phrase, intended to provoke radical revisioning of the human relation to the natural world, refers to a centuries-long, Western hierarchy situat-ing males at the pinnacle with nature subordinated at the very bottom. Gray advocated a newer environmental paradigm articulated in texts such as her own *Why the Green Nigger?—Re-Mything Genesis* (1979), its pro-vocative title a deliberate eco-shock meant to expose the systematic op-pression and degradation of the natural world within a white patriarchy.

Ecofeminism, then, has sought in Gray's terms to remythologize the natural world and its relation to humans even as it warns, in Rosemary

Radford Ruether's phrase, against "ecological band-aids" proffered by business and industry (200). Ruether's title, *New Woman, New Earth* (1975), asserted the possibilities of a feminist millennium, while in the polemical work *The First Sex* (1971), the feminist Elizabeth Gould Davis denounced men as "the enemy of nature" and eulogized women as "the ally of nature" whose "instinct is to bend, to nurture, to encourage healthy growth, and to preserve ecological balance" (335, 336).[3]

In the years of Lois Gibbs's involvement in the Love Canal crisis, Davis and Gray and others, notably Ynestra King and Susan Griffin, were at work both to expose and to reject the basis for a hierarchic and adversarial man-nature relation which they found to be environmentally pathologic and thus dangerous or deadly to all living things. They argued that there was an analogy between male oppression of women and environmental assault. At the same time, they reformulated a new paradigm—one of ecology—reliant on propositions of "coordination and symbiosis" (Gray, 70). The new paradigm is itself reliant upon a presupposed female " 'natural' affinity with the natural world" and sometimes poses the Goddess as its source of strength, while its keywords tend to emphasize wholeness and remediation—for example, "reweaving the world" and "healing the wounds" (Mellor, 45; see Plant; Diamond and Orenstein).[4] Merchant sums up the impetus of the movement: "A revolution in symbol structures could help to transform the patriarchal-technological culture. . . . In a new age of consciousness, the Earth as symbol of life, beauty, and spiritual fulfillment could regenerate respect for nature and reunify all human beings with other organisms and the planet" (*Earthcare*, 141). (Ecofeminism's reversion to "symbol structures," however, would soon reveal that its strength was also its vulnerability, as critics pointed out that pre-existing socioeconomic structures were left essentially unchanged by ecofeminist terms.)

Since our interest here concerns precisely those ways by which a seemingly defunct environmental myth—of Hygeia—is revived and renewed at a critical historical juncture, one must notice that each chapter of *Why the Green Nigger?* opens with a personal meditation or anecdote on water (on tides, a hurricane, swimming). It is important that in *Woman and Nature* (1978), Susan Griffin posits a woman who is daily "closer to herself" as "the moon swells and tides wash over the rock" where she lies (168). Ecofeminism claimed bodies of water as crucial to its project. Resurrecting Margaret Fuller's 1841 suprahuman water deity, "Leila," ecofeminism rewrites the aquatic bodies. It does so over and against both the pathologic and the traditionally feminine. The ecofeminist paradigm nullifies the nineteenth-century designation of relatively small bodies of water as marginal "Laughing Waters" and "saucy" streams, springs, lakelets, and so on. It rejects the status of such bodies as mere auxiliary aquatic maidens or as mothers of riparian sons, or as helpmeets to heroes whose bravery is exhibited on the open seas of male high adventure. Finally, ecofeminism lifts the censure from forceful female waters decried in the previous century as obstetrically-gynecologically pathological (as when such waters flood, leaving discharge, ooze, slime, and so on).

Regarded within this newer model, Love Canal is not simply the finale of a discredited ideology or the terminus of a Hygeian Nature's nation. Nor is it an aquatic "Typhoid Mary" or a synecdoche for a national sociopolitical malignancy cast in female subtextual terms. It belongs, instead, to a newer paradigm of ecofeminist waters susceptible to healing. It matters, in this model, that chemicals in Love Canal contaminate the Lake Ontario fish as they contaminate the residents' bodies, since both inhabit a complex but encompassing ecosystem. It matters, above all, that the body of a "wounded" and "bleeding" and even "malignant" canal is thought susceptible to "healing."

First-generation ecofeminism, espoused in certain male-authored texts as well as in those of women, repositions Love Canal in remediative terms even as it remodels the aquatic Nature's nation. As indicated, the newer paradigm joins the canal to all aquatic bodies worldwide. In addition, it claims female identity for vast bodies of water and argues the integrity of all biosystems, based on presumptive female traits of essentialist affinity with nature. These are the "re-mything" claims that enable a renewal of the aquatic bodies of Nature's nation in the later twentieth century.

Such claims are legitimated in large part by antecedents and contemporary examples in public discourse. In order for Hygeia to be reinvigorated within the purview of Nature's nation, it is necessary not only that the new paradigm emerge, but that it prove ideologically consonant with the premise of Nature's nation. American space, additionally, must manifest its inherent benevolent ethics in terms of the female human body. The instatement of the new paradigm, moreover, is only possible when the older one becomes susceptible to a critique of the kind posed not only by investigative scholars and analysts but by those enactive texts—poems, narratives, essays—which show a superseding paradigm moving into place more or less prior to its discursive articulation.

The antecedents become the foreground of the new paradigm, just as contemporary examples reinforce it. This is to say that certain texts must be shown to reject the older paradigm and to exhibit an ecofeminist version of the female aquatic body even before the movement theorized its position argumentatively. And contemporary examples demonstrate the viability of the ecofeminist position. Indeed, American environmental writing shows an important, but as yet unacknowledged, basis by which ecofeminist thought could legitimate itself in a twentieth-century Hygeian Nature's nation.

We might briefly reach back, first, to the mid-nineteenth century to find a precocious vignette of the ecofeminist bodily paradigm. Once again we are situated in upstate New York, not in the Niagara Falls area but in the lake country around Cooperstown, which is the center of Susan Fenimore Cooper's *Rural Hours* (1850), itself a female naturalist-diarist's book of hours, a miscellany of social commentary and naturalist observation, including the figuration of bodies of water. Cooper's observations begin with the traditional feminine stream but take an unconventional direction:

> If there be only a quiet brook running through a meadow in some familiar spot, the eye will often turn, unconsciously, in that direction, and linger with interest upon the humble stream. Observe, also, that the waters in themselves are capable of the highest degree of beauty. . . . Give [such waters] full sway, let them spread themselves into their widest expanse, let them roll into boundless seas, enfolding the earth in their embrace. (75)

Beginning with a "quiet brook running through a meadow," presumably in her own New York home area, Cooper traces the course of this "humble stream" which, multiplied over vast spaces, "spread themselves into their widest expanse," then "roll into boundless seas, enfolding the earth in their embrace" (75). Such waters, says Cooper, are "capable of the highest degree of beauty," the very word "beauty" clearly feminizing this aquatic global embrace. The streams, widening into lakes and rivers, extend their arms into the sea which in turn enfolds the entire earth. The most remote humble brook becomes an arm of the sea embracing the world.

This great surrounding sea, as we recognized earlier, was claimed at the turn of the twentieth century in Kate Chopin's *Awakening*, with the protagonist Edna Pontellier enfolded in the maternal sea. *The Awakening* claimed the entire sea as a maternal female body welcoming her daughter home. Chopin's grand marine claim, which resumes and expands Susan Cooper's *pensée*, makes the Gulf of Mexico, along the third coast of the

United States, the female sea, which is undefiled either by steam technology's effluents or by the detritus of transport vessels. Chopin's Gulf of Mexico is an early version of the 1970s ecofeminist ideal, both vast and pure, and it is perhaps not coincidental that Chopin's largely forgotten 1899 novel should be rediscovered and enter the American literary canon in the 1970s, years of feminist, including ecofeminist, insurgence. Chopin, in fact, not only resumes Susan Fenimore Cooper's notion of a "sea around us" but points toward the conceptual title of Rachel Carson's best-selling second book, *The Sea around Us* (1951). The preposition "around" is crucial here, the sea indeed enfolding, as Cooper had indicated and as Chopin had demonstrated in her protagonist's homecoming immersion.

To be sure, the patriarchal tradition of the roiling, heaving seas and of the Mississippian "Father of Waters" continued in numerous literary texts of the twentieth century. In the Jerome Kern–Oscar Hammerstein II Broadway musical *Showboat* (1927), the song "Old Man River" upholds the Mississippi's patriarchal identity despite Paul Robeson's decades-long, increasingly angry interpretation of the lyrics that describe the "niggers" all working with bodies "wracked" with pain. Late in his career, Robeson managed to turn "Old Man River," his signature song, into a song of protest, but the Mississippi itself nonetheless retains its patriarchal identity.

The high seas, too, continued in the twentieth century to be test sites for male courage and adventure. In reprise from such titles as *Moby-Dick* and *The Song of Hiawatha,* one finds Thor Heyerdahl's *Kon-Tiki* (1950), its subtitle *Across the Pacific by Raft* referring to the 4,300 nautical miles the Norwegian Heyerdahl and his crew covered in one hundred one days from Peru to Tahiti to test the possibility that migrant peoples centuries earlier had balsa-rafted across the Pacific to settle in Polynesia. Herman Wouk's 1951 *Caine Mutiny* and Nicholas Monsarrat's *Cruel Sea,* together with *The Old Man and the Sea* (1952), Ernest Hemingway's Nobel Prize–winning novella, continued the nineteenth century's American literary emphasis on the sea as a test of male physical courage.

Yet this older paradigm was under challenge in several directions, not only expansively seaward, as in Susan Cooper and Kate Chopin, but also inwardly, to change the terms of the conventionally feminine, genteel quiet waters of the stream or creek. The feminine domain of "saucy" waters, even those turning punitive at the stroke of an authorial pen (compare Hawthorne's Zenobia), was radically redefined, for instance, in Annie Dillard's *Pilgrim at Tinker Creek* (1974). This Pulitzer Prize–winning Thorovian meditation on nature, metaphysics, and philosophy is loosely structured upon *Walden* though set in the author's Blue Ridge Virginia home.

Certain sentences and images in *Pilgrim* seem of a piece with the representations of Hygeian quieter waters of the nineteenth century. "The creeks are the world with all its stimulus and beauty," writes Dillard of a creek she embodies in traditional female terms of succor as a "haven," and bodily as a "breast" (5, 87). Certain portraits of the creek are spiritually feminine:

> Live water heals memories. I look up the creek and here it comes, the future, being borne aloft as on a winding succession of laden trays. . . . If you look up the creek, . . . your spirit fills. . . . It has always been a happy thought to me that the creek runs on all night, new every minute, . . . as a closed book on a shelf continues to whisper to itself its own inexhaustible tale. (101, 69)

The Pittsburgh-born Dillard seems in such statements to rework the genteel side of the Hygeian self as it devolved from the early twentieth-century movement called nature study, with its intellectual base in Protestant theology and natural history. Popularized by Anna Botsford Comstock and Liberty Hyde Bailey, the movement promoted a sympathetic understanding of nature for children increasingly raised in urban settings far removed from agrarian America. "Comstock's *Handbook for Nature Study* (1911) taught the methods by which every elementary-age child in the country could learn to love nature." It sought to instill a "love of the beautiful," "a sense of companionship with life out-of-doors, and an abiding love of nature" (Lear, 14). Nature study would seem to be the intellectual channel from nineteenth-century aquatic femininity directly to Annie Dillard.

Yet *Pilgrim at Tinker Creek* proves to be a Calvinist sermon in which water, fire, and blood mix as if they are elemental humors. This is a meditation pervaded by the aquatic cognate—blood—which opens *Pilgrim* in an account of the author's tomcat leaving her body marked with bloody paw prints as she slept and recalling Tinker Creek–area Indians whose arrows were grooved to channel blood from wounds. "I come down to the water to cool my eyes," says Dillard, "but everywhere I look I see fire . . . and the whole world sparks and flames" (11). Fire and water interplay in a fierce, violent nexus. Allying with male American exploration, Dillard hearkens to the Lewis and Clark expedition when "setting the prairies on fire was a well-known signal that meant, 'Come down to the water.' " Admitting that such signal was "extravagant," she embraces this extravagance as her own. *Pilgrim* claims "power" in a "hoop of flame that shoots the rapids in the creek" and becomes "the arsonist of the sunny woods" (77).

In *The Adventures of Huckleberry Finn* (1884), Mark Twain had spoofed his century's conventional representation of the stream as a site of maidenly drowning in a sketch of a "picture of a young woman in a long white gown, standing on the rail of a bridge all ready to jump off" (112–113). Dillard, however, positions herself repeatedly on a bridge spanning Tinker Creek, not to support Twain's satire, much less to follow the old script for female self-destruction, but to "stalk nature" as an aggressive "collector" of its aquatic being (84; see Albanese, 163–171). "I am an explorer," she writes, "and I am also a stalker. . . . I am the arrow shaft . . . and this book is the straying trail of blood" (13). In *Pilgrim*, we are very far from the paper mill maidens of Herman Melville's "Tartarus of Maids," their blood boiling at a distance from the factory interior where the genteel maidens toil. Reflecting back a quarter century after the initial publication of *Pilgrim*, Dillard writes that, above all, she wished her project to be "bold" (281).

Dillard need have no qualms, for no reader dare seek comfort at the "breast" of Tinker Creek. Early on, she recalls observing a feeding frenzy of sharks off the coast of Florida. "The sight held awesome wonders: power and beauty, grace tangled in a rapture with violence" (10). That moment, a reader feels, is Dillard's blueprint for a text in which beauty and grace, the program of a nineteenth-century Hygeian, are by themselves inadequate to a newer feminist Tinker Creek authenticated by dimensions of power and violence.

Other nineteenth-century aquatic bodily norms were also undergoing remarkable change and thereby auguring ecofeminism as a political movement that might potentially enlist male adherents and contributors.[5] It is useful to recognize the terms by which males could abandon patriarchy and enter into the female ecological world. The role played by religion and philosophy in this green movement has been documented by Nash in *The Rights of Nature* (87–160). Our focus, however, is literally corporeal, examining the human bodily terms by which males might identify themselves as ecofeminist. Not surprisingly, *Why the Green Nigger?* applauds Ronald Glasser's statement in *The Body Is the Hero* (1976): "The fluids in our bodies mimic the primeval seas in which we began. . . . We still carry those seas within us" (18–19). Such a statement, a reprise of Rachel Carson's observation that "there is an ecology of the world within our bodies," universalizes the body over eons and elides both gender and sexual difference (*Silent Spring*, 189).

Even in the mid-1950s, a well-regarded male anthropologist–nature writer, Loren Eiseley, evinced a striking sex-gender crossover in which he figured his own body in female terms of gestation. Just as Annie Dillard embraces traditional male traits (such as power and violence) for her *Pilgrim* persona, so Eiseley shows male reembodiment solely in female terms. This occurs in a 1957 essay, "The Flow of the River," in *The Immense Journey*, in which Eiseley recounts a personal experience of floating down the Platte River along the prairies of his native Nebraska.

The shallow Platte, for most of the year, is "a rambling, dispersed series of streamlets," and is known to be " 'a mile wide and an inch deep,' " says Eiseley, who admits his terror of the water from a near-drowning in childhood (12–13). With great trepidation, he decides to float along the channel. An adult nonswimmer, he first stands quietly in the water, then lies back to float, face to the sun, soon aware that he is "streaming over ancient sea beds" and floating over broken axles of prairie schooners and other evidence of American pioneers' crises.

The anthropologist genders the Platte as female, a "river calling to her children," and in the episode of his river float, Eiseley actually takes on the identity of the gestative female body himself: "I *was* water and the unspeakable alchemies that gestate and take shape in water" (13). The moment passes so quickly, one might say floats by so swiftly, that the reader might easily miss its radical import. Although gestation is figured alchemically and is therefore allied with men's secrets from the Middle Ages, Eiseley's self-identification is starkly and clearly maternal. Floating on the maternal river, he becomes a maternal aquatic body, something like aquatic *matrushka* dolls in which mother figures encapsulate smaller versions of themselves. Eiseley, like Dillard, refers to Thoreau for literary positioning and evidently to claim a male lineage in nature writing with a strong claim to scientific observation. He does not extend the moment of maternal bodily identity, though the moment stands in the published text, an indication of a paradigm shift in the making.[6]

Mother Sea and the Voice of the River

Revised sexually, racially, geographically, and in terms of gender identity, the American waters are newly defined in a paradigm shift that enables the renewal of the female body of Nature's nation. Tinker Creek and the Platte River become aquatic sites of female authority and of sexual-gender redefinition. Because these waters are doubly liminal, both substantively fluid and also fluid in sociopolitical representations, Love Canal can be reframed as a body open to healing and renewal, a body not permanently infectious and cancerous but potentially transformable from toxicity and malignancy to health.

Vitally important to the new paradigm, however, is the expansion of the Hygeian domain from springs and rills to the oceanic, all while retaining the definitive aquatic purity. Indeed, the ocean, which is incomparably vast and all-encompassing, doubles back to reclaim the small streams with which it connects—as from the Atlantic through the St. Lawrence Seaway to Lake Ontario and thus to Love Canal—and vice versa. Oceanic agency flows, in short, both ways. While Susan Cooper and Kate Chopin initiated this aquatic relationship, two other writers in the twentieth century, Marjory Stoneman Douglas (1890–1998) and Rachel Carson (1907–1964), far more extensively than their predecessors, advanced the notion that Hygeian aquatic purity and oceanic vastness are crucial to any appropriate conception of the environment, above all its aquatic ecology. It is doubtful that either Douglas or Carson would have wished to see her name enrolled among the ranks of 1970s ecofeminists (each might have said pigeonholed instead of enrolled), but the projects of both women writers are so central to the later twentieth-century Hygeian Nature's nation that they must be considered here.

Students of the history of conservation in the United States know of both Douglas's and Carson's identification with twentieth-century environmentalism. Douglas served on the 1927 committee to establish Everglades National Park, and her book *The Everglades: River of Grass* (1947) is credited with saving the Florida Everglades from complete destruction by real estate developers and agribusiness. Carson's *Silent Spring* (1962) arguably ushered in the era of awareness of the dangers of chemical pesticides to the environment. Douglas's *Everglades* "changed forever the way Americans look at wetlands," which were previously dismissed as useless swamps, while Carson's *Silent Spring* documented the "chain of evil" of man-made pollutants contaminating the "air, earth, rivers, and sea" (Byers; Vogel, 51).

Both Douglas and Carson claimed autobiographic allegiance to the sea. Douglas, raised in Taunton, Massachusetts, near the Narragansett Bay, recalled the pleasures of day sailing with an uncle and the exhilaration and excitement of "sunlight on the waves of . . . [a] little lake nearby" (*Voice,* 44). Her male ancestors were sea captains, and in *Voice of the River,* she wrote, "I think the sea was in my blood. From the beginning, I've had a constant interest in the sea. . . . I was a saltwater person" (65, 111). (When World War I broke out, Douglas joined the U.S. Naval Reserve.)

Carson, like Douglas, was aquatically oriented, having grown up along the banks of Pittsburgh's Allegheny River within earshot of its riverboats and paddle-wheelers. Later, in college, she studied aquatic specimens on field trips to the area's quarries, pools, and creeks (*Always, Rachel,* 7; Lear, 8, 32, 33, 45). Reportedly, the sea became her vocation in a defining moment in her Pittsburgh college dormitory room during a fierce thunderstorm, as Carson read lines from Alfred, Lord Tennyson's 1834 "Locksley Hall," concluding: "For the mighty wind arises, roaring seaward, and I go." Years later, Carson wrote, "That line spoke to something within me, seeming to tell me that my own path led to the sea—which then I had never seen—and that my own destiny was somehow linked with the sea" (Lear, 39–40). In her mid-forties, Carson wrote, "I loved the sea with a purely vicarious love long before I had seen it" (*Always, Rachel,* 7). Carson's books about the sea—*Under the Sea Wind* (1941), *The Sea around Us* (1949), and *The Edge of the Sea* (1955)—were, of course, foundational for *Silent Spring.*

Both writers also had strong mentors at home and in college. Carson's mother, Maria Carson, was to be her daughter's primary editor until near the end of Maria's life. Passionate about botanizing, bird watching, and nature study, Maria guided and encouraged Rachel's interest in the natural world, its flora and fauna, a role later assumed in loco parentis by Rachel's college professor of biology. Douglas, too, recalled a formative, indelible college geography course that led her to grasp what she termed "environmental geography" (*Voice,* 75). Her keen interest in the natural environment evidently quickened in her post–World War I young adulthood when, recently divorced, she went south to become a reporter for her father's fledgling *Miami Herald,* writing daily "about Florida as landscape and as geography" from the moment of her arrival at the edge of the "cool, blue and green . . . marvelous [Biscayne] Bay, . . . with the wind coming off the sea in the slanting early morning sunlight" (*Voice,* 127, 96).

A self-styled "skeptic and dissenter," Douglas claimed her environmental mentality was adopted from her lawyer-editor father, Frank Stoneman, who attempted to use his newspaper editorials to stop Florida's governor Napoleon Broward from draining the Everglades. "Father had very strong opinions about draining the Everglades even then [in 1910], though there wasn't much scientific information" (*Voice,* 50, 75, 98–99). Douglas was convinced that the multimillion-acre Everglades, inhabited by "spectacular" birds, ought to be a national park and not drained (*Voice,* 190).

Both Carson and Douglas also gendered the vast waters female. Like Carson, who declared the sea "mother sea" in *The Sea around Us,* Douglas too tended to embody the vast waters as female in her autobiography and a range of other writings, including short stories set in Florida of the 1920s–1940s (*Voice*, 1; see *Nine Florida Stories*). Douglas's nonfiction *Hurricane* (1958) locates the origins of female-named hurricanes in breathing sea waters which give "birth" to the storms, which "feed" on warmth and moisture, and, as offspring of the sea, "surge" over land to reconfigure its topography (11, 12, 14, 23, 33; see *Nine Florida Stories*). Destructive of fish, wildlife, and humans, the hurricane nonetheless "gives us life" (9). Douglas also personified herself as the voice of the "pale, seemingly illimitable waters" over some "seven hundred fifty or so square miles" (*Everglades*, 9).

Both Douglas and Carson were also self-identified as literary writers (see Gartner, 40–41). Both employed techniques characteristic of creative nonfiction prose, employing similes, metaphors, rhythms meant to be mimetic of the aquatic currents. Carson said of *The Sea around Us*, "If there is poetry in my book about the sea, it is . . . because no one could write truthfully about the sea and leave out the poetry" (qtd. Lear, 219). The nonpoetic response to marine life is thereby disqualified as inauthentic. The poetic inheres in the sea, and the writer is by definition the transcriber. Douglas's own statements are similar, for instance her declaration that *The Everglades: River of Grass* was her "best writing," her "most ambitious and important project," one that so "consumed" her for the rest of her life that she vocatively embodied herself in the title of her autobiography, *Voice of the River* (1987) (*Voice*, 190).

It is helpful to encounter a brief passage from each. Douglas writes in *The Everglades: River of Grass*:

> There are no other Everglades in the world. . . . Their vast glittering openness, wider than the enormous visible round of the horizon, the racing free saltness and sweetness . . . under the dazzling blue heights of space. . . . The miracle of the light pours over the green and brown expanse of saw grass and water, shining and slow moving below, the grass and water that is the meaning and the central fact of the Everglades of Florida. It is a river of grass. (*Everglades*, 5–6)

And from Carson's *Sea around Us*:

> And yet he [humankind] has returned to his mother sea only on her own terms. He cannot control or change the ocean as, in his brief tenancy of earth, he has subdued and plundered the continents. . . .

In the course of a long ocean voyage . . . as never on land, he knows
the truth that his world is a water world, a planet dominated by its
covering mantle of ocean, in which the continents are but tran-
sient intrusions of land about the surface of the all-encircling sea.
(*Sea*, 15)

It can be said of Douglas's Everglades as of Carson's Mother Sea that "its
genesis, its lure, and its life had been the preoccupation" of the "precise"
and "ardent" authorial mind (Hynes, 29). Their parallel biographical
routes to such stylizing of nature nonetheless require acknowledgment
that Carson's commitment to the natural world and to its poetic-scientific
transcription is the more pronounced matter of record.[7] The methods of
both writers, however, were strikingly similar: they consulted leading experts and translated technical knowledge into laypersons' terms in literary
style.

Douglas and Carson differ in Hygeian emphasis. Carson personifies
the sea as a presiding "Mother" demonstrating domestic values, while
Douglas resumes Kate Chopin's emphasis on marine purity. Carson's female domestication is essential for an ecofeminist re-mything of a Hygeian Nature's nation, just as Douglas's insistence on, and validation of,
aquatic purity is essential to the ecofeminist utopianism that renewed
Hygeia in the latter part of the twentieth century.

It is intriguing to note that Douglas had no plan to write an Everglades
book (just as Carson did not "elect" to write *Silent Spring* but was "chosen" to do so by pressure from alarmed, conservation-minded individuals
and one jarring court case over herbicidal spraying [Hynes, 30–31]). Pondering an offer to contribute a book to a series entitled Rivers of America,
Douglas mused on the possibilities of linking the Miami River with the
Everglades as she studied a horticultural map of the Everglades: "If it's
running water and it comes curving down . . . toward the Ten Thousand
Islands, and if there are ridges on either side, maybe the ridges are an east
bank and a west bank . . . and maybe this really is a river" (*Voice*, 191).
Douglas accepted the contract on a "writer's whim" and soon sought out
the state hydrologist for research on the groundwater of southeastern
Florida (*Voice*, 190–191).

Aquatic purity, which was Kate Chopin's emphasis in *The Awakening*,
became a major preoccupation in *The Everglades: River of Grass*. Douglas
challenged the traditional male ideology of empire as formulated in Florida governors William S. Jennings's and Broward's plan to "knock a hole
in a wall of coral" to drain the Everglades—in Broward's term, "millions

of acres of swamps"—and thus create the "Empire of the Everglades" (*Everglades,* 313, 312).

Douglas's book was published at a crucial juncture. The drainage program of which she wrote, inaugurated in the early 1900s, gained particular impetus in 1947, when, following two successive hurricanes, Congress allocated two hundred million dollars to the Army Corps of Engineers to design and construct a system of canals, levees, and pumping stations to protect Florida agricultural interests, notably the sugarcane growers, together with businesses and residential areas, from flooding. The corps project, however, destroyed bird and animal habitats as it drained the Everglades, its freshwater flushed into the sea at the rate of 1.7 billion gallons daily.

The Everglades: River of Grass, published in the same year as Congress's allocation to the Corps of Engineers, pitted the "Empire of the Everglades" against the "River of Grass" as Douglas confirmed the identity of the Everglades as an actual river and recorded the "reckless" drainage efforts of 1905 and 1909 in terms of defilement: "The first humus-laden dark water began to creep unnoticed down the clear current of the lovely river, staining the bright bottom sands . . . the dark-stained water worked its way over the clear sands, staining the bay bottom. . . . It seemed as though the frontier boiled up in a long, slow climax of violence. . . . The river and the bay were slowly darkened and fouled. The glitter, the whiteness, the play of light, the stimulus of the sun, the sense that a great city was building here [in Miami] made it impossible now for people to check ills daily growing greater" (323, 314, 316, 319, 333). *The Everglades* configures the Florida land boom and its criminal corruption of the 1920s as a consequence of the fouling of the pristine waters. Those responsible include women, but the onus is on the greedy, imperial males, foremost among them the aptly named Napoleon Bonaparte Broward.

Douglas's project did not take an ecocentric position. *The Everglades,* like her short stories, includes homo sapiens among the species of flora and fauna, separating humans who accommodate themselves benignly to the natural world from those who are destructive and predatory, including the 1890s millinery industry which killed birds for plumage and the early twentieth-century drainage projects that resulted in a lowered water table and in sweet water turned brackish as it thereby mixed with tidal saltwater. The glaring, smoky fires in the drying, drained areas of the Glades turned the "river of grass and sweet water" into a "river of fire," evidence of "greed and ignorance and folly" (*Everglades,* 375). The fires are portentous, an augury of the apocalyptic destruction to come if, at the "Eleventh

Hour," human behavior fails to change (see 349–357). Douglas, in fact, can be included in the tradition of those writers foreseeing "ecotastrophe" (see Killingsworth and Palmer).

She also belongs to the Hygeian tradition renewed in the later twentieth-century ecofeminist paradigm. Douglas resumes Kate Chopin's emphasis on aquatic purity and its alliance with a female principle. For Douglas, the absolute standard of value is aquatic purity. It is the highest criterion of worth. The medium of the healthy habitat is water pure and undefiled. This self-styled "Voice of the River" speaks for the quintessential Hygeian aquatic ideal.

In places, Rachel Carson's own phrases sound interchangeable with Douglas's and in fact could be lifted from *The Awakening,* as when Carson writes, "The distant voice of the sea was hushed almost to a sigh" (*Sea-Wind,* 13). In accordance with Chopin, Carson's contribution to the shift toward an ecofeminist paradigm is the insistence on marine maternity and its governance of all earthly life. Personification was for her an important narrative device (as when she traced the life cycle of a mackerel named Scomber in *Under the Sea-Wind*), and the ocean is Carson's greatest personification, a figure of utmost maternal grandeur.

Evidence suggests that Carson worked mentally to immerse herself in the medium of which she wrote. Government service with the Fish and Wildlife Service provided her expertise in fishery biology via library research and visits to Fish and Wildlife laboratories and field stations. Though Douglas admits to a mere twenty or so visits to the Everglades prior to beginning work on *The Everglades,* it was Carson's constant practice to encounter marine life first-hand, whether in a Georges Bank commercial fishing trawler whose deep-water nets yielded myriad species cast upon the deck, or whether walking the beaches, day or night, in Maine or on the Maryland shore or in the Carolina Low Country, taking notes by flashlight. By 1948 she defined herself as "a marine biologist . . . whose consuming interest happens to be the ocean and its life" (qtd. Lear, 154). She worked consciously to "get the feel of a world that was entirely water" (qtd. Lear, 102).

Carson's oceanic premise, the maternal sea, is a nurturative essence that is constant and continual. Although the oceanic "face is always changing," though the aquatic "pulse and tempo" vary as do her "moods," the maternal economy, the very physiology of the ocean, is figured in bookkeeping terms as a balanced ledger: "It is all a part of the ocean's system of balances, by which she pays back to one part of her waters what she had latterly borrowed for distribution to another" (*Sea,* 29, 75, 123, 146). Thus

Carson can cite the "rushing torrents" and "turgid flood" without the pejorative connotations of nineteenth-century texts (106). Her floods are normalized within the oceanic female body. They are reliably cyclical, not aberrant. "The permanent currents of the ocean are, in a way, the most majestic of her phenomena" (135). Carson wrote to the oceanographer William Beebe, "I am much impressed by man's dependence upon the ocean, directly, and in thousands of ways unsuspected by most people." She continued, "These relationships, and the belief that we will become even more dependent upon the ocean as we destroy the land, are really the theme of [my] book [*The Sea around Us*]" (qtd. Lear, 161).

Carson's maternal ocean, as Vera Norwood has demonstrated, is radically domestic. *The Edge of the Sea*, for instance, invites readers to peer under water "clear as glass," with a "ceiling," a mirror, and soft decorator colors of "pale apricot" and a "carpet [of] green sponge" (3). As Vera Norwood says, Carson's science is ever accurate, but her "description also calls upon images of home—[for] we peer through glass windows at a comfortable carpet, a lovely ceiling, and a tenant [the "elfin starfish"] regarding herself in the mirror" (*Made*, 151–152). As Norwood states, "Such images . . . deny any separation of individual homeplaces from the environment. Metaphors of home extended beyond the insulated, domestic round of 1950s' culture to include all of nature, while individual human homes took on meanings linking them to their environment" (151–152). Norwood rightly positions Carson within the American radical tradition, given that she "publicly questioned the methods and goals of a powerful elite composed mostly of professional men" and thereby "threatened to disrupt the social contract that placed women at home and men at the helm" ("Rachel Carson," 316, 317). Robert Gottlieb concurs in reflecting that "in a period when the question of pollution was only just beginning to receive significant public attention, Carson argued that public health and the environment, human and natural environments, were inseparable" and thereby created "a new environmental consciousness" (84).

Carson's contribution to an ecofeminist paradigm thus lies both in her instatement of a governing maternal ocean and in her rejection of a social Darwinist model of nature in favor of one of sheltering domesticity. The contrast is clear if we briefly revisit a late nineteenth-century text, Israel C. Russell's *Rivers of North America* (1898), which represents river development as a function of social Darwinist laws: "Those most favored capture the waters of their less favored neighbors and wax stronger at the expense of the weak" (319). Carson rejected this formulation and equally repudiated the literary naturalist writers' commitment to a world governed by impersonal forces. Instead, her narrative of sea life "conveys an overall sense of calm" because "everything is as it should be: the pattern of an ancient, sometimes violent, but endless cycle comforting in its certain repetitions" (Lear, 103).

That reassurance of perpetually comforting cycles, it must be noted, was based upon values of a placid middle-class domesticity that is both normative and ahistoric. Formulating the sea world as a comfortable furnished home, Carson takes no cognizance of long-standing environmental problems, natural or man made, resulting from the socioeconomic class disparities of the kind seen in Melville's paper mill or in Rebecca Harding Davis's iron mill, where workers sicken in foul air. As a middle-class protagonist in Don DeLillo's novel *White Noise* (1985) observes, "Society is set up in such a way that it's the poor and the uneducated who suffer the main impact of natural and man-made disasters" (114).

Neither Carson's sea books nor *Silent Spring* takes cognizance of the "poor and uneducated" who are especially so affected. The natural world of Carson's sea books, omitting a human presence, affords no glimpse of class-based environmental injustice over time. *Silent Spring* itself presumes a nationwide, materially comfortable American middle class under chemical assault only since the cold war. Carson's indictment of the experts and elites responsible for post–World War II environmental contamination does not acknowledge the longer American history of such elites' disregard for the welfare of those victimized by toxic environments for which the elites were responsible and from which they stood to gain economically in industrial America. In Carson, it is as if America's environmental problems are solely middle class and originate in the aftermath of World War II.

Silent Spring is thus not prefaced by a meditation on the human impact of the very environmental degradation which Carson's biographer traces to her childhood sight of the Allegheny River Valley's "relentless engines of [twentieth-century] industry, leaving scars on the land, pollution in the air, and debris in the river" (Lear, 8). Carson reportedly felt "embarrassment" in her youth at "the foul smell of the [riverbank] glue factory," supplanted years later by the acrid fumes of sulphur from the coal and coke business, a supplier to Pittsburgh's largest electrical utility company (Lear, 9, 54). "The fouling of the Allegheny River went on year-round. . . . The river looked as dirty as it smelled" (Lear, 55). Perhaps because her family's hilltop overlook of the Allegheny River Valley distanced her from the sight of those living below, Carson's "embarrassment" failed to prompt a historical framing of *Silent Spring*.

Toxic Discourse

Silent Spring, moreover, subverts Carson's matrilineal Mother Sea in ways the author may have failed to appreciate, for it is one of numerous texts in a subgenre which Lawrence Buell terms "toxic discourse," a "discourse of toxicity."[8] Carson's production of such discourse, as we shall see, serves to subvert the ecofeminist, twentieth-century Hygeia just at the point of her renewal. It is as if an observer of the vicissitudes of Hygeia in the twentieth century experiences a kind of whiplash: to discover the formulation of Carson's great matriarchal sea is also to recognize the extent to which Carson makes that Mother Sea vulnerable to matricide. This is to say that the very figure who empowered and feminized the sea in ecological texts also framed an ecofeminist paradigm that leaves the sea—indeed, all waters— subject to destruction by forces gendered as male.

Toxic discourse, which unsettles the ecofeminist neo-Hygeia of a recuperative Love Canal, is, Buell finds, a "discourse of allegation" that serves sociopolitical purposes and can "montage into [the] gothic" (Buell, 640, 659, 656). Buell traces its American literary roots to Hawthorne's "Rappaccini's Daughter" and to Upton Sinclair's *Jungle* (1906), an antecedent text of industrial toxicology. While such titles as Dillard's *Pilgrim at Tinker Creek* and Eiseley's "Flow of the River" contribute to an ecofeminist "re-mything" of the American Hygeia, a toxic discourse operates in the reverse direction to thwart that re-mything, as we shall see.

In the later twentieth century, toxic discourse proliferated in various texts, including Thomas Pynchon's *Crying of Lot 49* with its dire acronym of a W.A.S.T.E. system operating in southern California, together with such titles as *The Late Great Planet Earth* (1970) and *Toxic Nation* (1993), and the songwriter Neil Young's "After the Gold Rush," a reference to the industrial capitalist world in which Mother Nature is "on the run" in the waning twentieth century.

Don DeLillo's novel *Underworld* (1997), which explicitly updates Pieter Bruegel's *Triumph of Death,* provides an excellent case in point, with its passages on the contamination of waters (50–51, 574). Nuclear poisons prevail in DeLillo's American world of ancillary pathologies, "TB, AIDs, beatings, drive-by shootings, measles, asthma, abandonment at birth" (239). In *Underworld,* it is not the naturalist's spiritual reverie but gangland-style murder that can take place "where the river goes into the bay" or "where the lagoon lies silent . . . and there are marshes and inlets" (90). A leading character, who imagines his father, in Vietnam war–era

slang, "wasted," grows up to have a career based on "waste containment."
His co-worker stands at the shoreline observing the Fresh Kills landfill on
New York City's Staten Island:

> This was the reason for his trip to New York. . . . Three thousand
> acres of mountained garbage, contoured and road-graded. . . . Barges
> unloading, sweeper boats poking through the kills to pick up stray
> waste, . . . a maintenance crew working on drainpipes . . . that were
> designed to control the runoff of rainwater. Other figures in masks
> and butylene suits were gathered . . . to inspect isolated material for
> toxic content. It was science fiction and prehistory, garbage arriving
> twenty-four hours a day, . . . the gulls diving and crying. . . . The
> landfill showed . . . smack-on how the waste stream ended. (184)

In an epiphany, the main character realizes that his career in waste management actually has been spent in the logistics of the American psyche,
and in retirement, he and his wife take "long walks along the drainage canal" that recurs as a motif throughout the novel, a satiric comment on the
vanished, gentle recreational waters of the lover of nature (807).

Carson proves to be a foremother of DeLillo's and others' toxic discourse, despite her omission of class-based environmental issues, her trun-
cation of history, her eulogistic treatment of the sea, and the radical female domestic terms in which she casts ecological well-being. Carson, in
fact, set the terms for the mentality of *Underworld*, indeed for all contemporary narratives of environmental contamination. "The sea was her central character," as one scholar observes of Carson, and "she, its epic biographer" (Hynes, 29). Yet *Silent Spring*, as a foundational text of toxic
discourse, inadvertently problematizes the Mother Sea by working to discredit its actual authority. In so doing, it thwarts the renewed American
Hygeia.

It is in *Silent Spring* that Carson arguably subverts her own epic character, the female sea, and initiates the discourse that ultimately operates to
invalidate the Hygeian Nature's nation. First, we must recognize Carson's
own myth-making. Her Mother Sea, as portrayed in *The Sea around Us*,
has governed for "eons," her origins "shadowy," her "primeval birthdate
proximate with that of the earth, two billion years" (5, 6, 7). In the succeeding millennia "she" has distributed "the earth's water supply," including rivers, streams, and underground seas (*Silent Spring*, 40–42). Although Carson attempts a chronology of geologic time, Mother Sea for all

intents and purposes is atemporal, outside and transcendent of the vicissitudes of human history. Since no human beings occupy the world of Carson's sea books, her Mother Sea rules and reigns over an ecocentric world.

Yet *Silent Spring* introjects dire modern-day human events into this atemporal marine maternal world of "enveloping seas," and these events prove to be heuristically deconstructive of the ecofeminist Hygeia (*Silent Spring*, 39). As Buell says, "Carson explicitly played on . . . [nuclear-era] anxieties by branding the pesticide industry 'a child of the Second World War' and by representing pesticides' consequences with the imagery of war: weaponry, victimage, extermination, corpses, massacre, conquest" ("Toxic," 649–650). The terms are not only bellicose but primary. They are Carson's key words. Cold war pesticides constitute "an appalling deluge of chemical pollution . . . daily poured into the nation's waterways," and the "surface-moving waters" have become "rivers of death" (*Silent Spring*, 40, 44, 129–152). Thus the "enveloping seas," Mother Sea herself, is wrested from mythic status and enters the dynamic history of the cold war years. In *Silent Spring*, a historicizing anthrocentrism enters the realm of virtually mythic, female, atemporal ecocentrality.

Because these two worlds are gendered, moreover, the mythically ecocentric Mother Sea is assaulted by cold war–era contaminants which are male. Carson's is but one of numerous texts that consistently "masculinize" ecological opposition, which is figured as corporate, military, and governmental assault (Buell, "Toxic," 652). The discourse of toxicity shows the government, corporations, and military all functioning to foul and contaminate both earth and waters within a twentieth-century nuclear culture. In toxic discourse, a masculinized entity that is androcentrally powerful dominates the realm of the ecocentric Mother Sea and thereby its Hygeian body.

We need not venture far to see this pattern at work in the reporting of aquatic environmental mishaps at the turn of the twenty-first century. In February–March of 1999 an oil tanker, the *New Carissa*, ran aground at Coos Bay, Oregon, spilling at least seventy thousand gallons of oil into the sea, with the Coast Guard and Navy rushing to skim and pump the oil from the sea and from the ship's hold before storm wave action ruptured the hull, which was towed out to sea in pieces and sunk with a naval artillery bombardment and a torpedo fired from a nuclear-powered submarine.

Meanwhile, newspaper photographs of Coos Bay, displayed on the Internet in those months, showed volunteers working to rescue wildlife, while a hotline opened for reporting sightings of oiled birds on the state's beaches. Numbers of oiled birds and animals killed or rescued were tabulated and published. This scenario of the oil spill is in fact familiar, from the technological (tanker, helicopters) to the domestic (volunteers cleaning birds). The corporate transgressor is gendered male, the rescuers female, even if the corporate spokesperson is often a woman (the "soft" face of the phallic corporation) and the volunteer rescuers include men and boys.

Indeed, the Coos Bay episode occurred almost on the ten-year anniversary of the 1989 Exxon *Valdez* accident, when the Exxon Corporation supertanker ran aground and spilled eleven million gallons of oil into Alaska's Prince William Sound, ruining Aleut villagers' subsistence living and killing 250,000 seabirds, 2,800 sea otters, 300 harbor seals, 250 bald eagles, and about 22 killer whales. Newspapers from the *New York Times* to *USA Today* ran anniversary stories on the state of the Prince William Sound ecosystem ten years after the accident (see Verhovek). Exxon officials and consultants were quoted as reporting good progress toward ecological restoration, while others, including marine biologists and area residents, emphasized the continuing damage to the Bay of Alaska.

These reports frame the division between the corporation and the others (villagers, ecologists) in gendered polarity. The *USA Today* photograph, for instance, positions the *Valdez* in oil-fouled water with flanking superimposed photographs of two women, a Native American and a marine biologist, who emphasize that neither marine nor human lives have recovered despite appearances to the contrary (Straus, B1). The very layout of the newspaper montage supports the gendered nature of toxic discourse, the tanker surrounded by spilling oil a sign of the male corporate world, the photographs of those expressing ecological concern and indictment female. In fact, the Exxon vice-president for environment and safety inadvertently contributed to the gender division of toxic discourse by stating that, despite Exxon's accidental damage to the Alaskan coastal environment, "Mother Nature . . . has remarkable powers of recovery, and the natural order does reestablish itself" (Verhovek, A8).

Nature here, however, is represented as a passive victim, an identity reinforcing traditional forms of female oppression (see Merchant, *Earthcare,* 139, 142). These political valences have been exposed by analysts of environmentalism. Gottlieb notes that the antitoxics movement, which is fundamentally feminist in its approach and outlook, has lacked a theoretical framework or long-term vision and has been weakened by internal discord among ecofeminists, whose differing agendas Merchant has described (Gottlieb, 207–234; Merchant, *Earthcare,* 139–165). In a paradigm structured upon female environmental vulnerability to male assault, the eco-feminist Hygeia is repeatedly wounded and weak.

As for Marjory Douglas's *River of Grass*, the Army Corps of Engineers was once again summoned to the Everglades in 1999, this time, according to the *New York Times*, "as an act of restitution for its earlier folly." Its new "stated purpose [was] to recapture the freshwater that is now wastefully flushed out to sea" by creating reservoirs, pumps, and weirs to infuse the South Florida aquifer with freshwater now lost through drainage. The editorial voice proclaims that "surely, this time around, the Everglades deserves its due" ("Equity in the Everglades," A18). In terms of toxic discourse, the corps is, of course, the male entity, the restoration of the Everglades dubious by virtue of that fact alone.

Love Canal inevitably is configured within this gendered binary of toxic discourse originated by Rachel Carson. The canal, in these terms, is not rehabilitative but doomed—at best in remission—because the agencies of decontamination are governmental, military, and corporate, all of them male. True, the first-wave ecofeminist paradigm augured well in remything terms for the rehabilitation of Love Canal. And the U.S. Environmental Protection Agency routinely uses the term "cleanup," a word with domestic overtones of good housekeeping. Following the federal government's Love Canal decontamination program, the area was renamed Black Creek Village (just as the Exxon *Valdez* was renamed the *SeaRiver Mediterranean*), and in 1997, refurbished houses were sold at below-market rates to buyers for whom the burden of the canal's notorious history was outweighed by their eagerness to own a home. The account in *U.S. News and World Report* nonetheless rejects Hygeian ecofeminism in favor of toxic discourse when it calls Love Canal "the world's most infamous hazardous-waste dump" under a heading that reads "6 Rooms, Toxic Canal Vu" (Sept. 15, 1997: 67). At the turn of the twenty-first century, the mythic agency of Mother Sea is thwarted by the toxic discourse of *Silent Spring*, and Hygeia remains a body in crisis.

Notes
References
Credits
Index

Notes

Introduction

1. These "changes in the land," to borrow William Cronon's term, elicited anxieties that not only Miller but also Leo Marx and Barbara Novak documented some time ago. The concept of an inherent Nature's nation has been extended in more recent years, notably in Myra Jehlen's *American Incarnation* (1986), a study focused principally on fictional form but which backdates Miller's chronology of the Nature's nation paradigm. Whereas Miller located its origin in nineteenth-century American texts, Jehlen finds its antecedent in European source texts of a projected America in which history is transformed into geography, "time into space." Instead of growth, there is an unfolding of a "permanent inherent nature" (10). Jehlen explains, "The Europeans who became Americans conquered and developed in their own image a territory of whose existence their forebears had been ignorant. In that way they were quintessential aliens—yet they described their national origin and growth as an impulse of the land itself" (6). The spatial dimension of the land meant that the United States became defined "primarily as a place" (6). The new world as nature thus would—rather, will—unfold but is, a priori, intact and whole. *Place* is of signal importance. If America shifts time into space, its spatial identity becomes its national identity. The nation becomes defined by its very geomorphology. Caroline Merchant reminds us that the word "nation" is derived from the Latin word *nascere* (to be born), and "hence the state was born from the state of nature" ("Reinventing Eden," 138).

2. Elsewhere I have shown the cultural obsession with the idea of American environmental reform over two centuries. See *New World, New Earth: Environmental Reform in American Literature from the Puritans through Whitman* (1979).

3. Joining all sites in *Embodiment of a Nation* is their status as identifiers of

the nation, though in recent years scholarship on national identity has focused on print forms, not on place. Geography and geomorphology have been subordinated to print, as in Benedict Anderson's *Imagined Communities,* which argues that print texts, especially newspapers, promote nationalism via a capitalist vernacular, and more recently Priscilla Wald and Dana Nelson have extended this discussion, analyzing the vexed issue of personhood and citizenship through scrutiny of an intratextual world of fictional narratives, court cases, magazine publications of the Young America movement, political speeches, and medical, political, and ethnographic texts.

Yet another school of thought has allied itself more closely with material culture and art studies. Lauren Berlant and Russ Castronovo address the nineteenth-century American culture of monumentalism, while John Bodner has examined the role of public commemoration in citizenship.

4. Guthrie surveys anthropomorphism in art and architecture too, not only in folklore, in forked tree limbs fashioned to emphasize their kinship to human form, but in foliage masks in Greek and Roman decorative carving, and in striations in stone that enable artisans to carve and position columns or other forms to present petric anthropomorphic objects to advantage in such structures as the cathedral. From Dürer to Dalí, artists have inscribed human faces or bodily forms in natural formations, for example, in clouds or mountains. And though personification is pervasive in European literature, including allegory, through the Middle Ages and into the eighteenth century, and though it is also present in the poetry of the eighteenth century as well as in prose descriptions of natural events and of landscapes, students of these literary forms have failed to point out their anthropomorphic origins (122–151).

5. Guthrie argues in *Faces in the Clouds* that "God or gods consist in seeing the world as humanlike" and that anthropomorphism results (as Mircea Eliade, Clifford Geertz, and others have argued) from the symbol-making function of language, "which makes possible culture as the basis of human thought and action, which in turn makes viable our modern biological form, *Homo sapiens*" (178, 198). " 'Condemned to meaning,' " as Merleau-Ponty put it, human beings semiotically acquire thought and action in a relentless, ubiquitous search for signs and symbols (198). Guthrie cites Paul Ricoeur's view that human beings engage in symbolism "both consciously and unconsciously, while awake or asleep, neurotically or creatively in speech and writing, in the arts and sciences, with or without insight into its possibilities and implications," and he notes Ricoeur's concurrence with Wilhelm von Humboldt's statement that "man *is* language" (qtd. Guthrie, 198). Much the same position is put forward across disciplinary fields, from the classicist Gilbert Murray's statement that the gods are "as a matter of course anthropomorphic" to Claude Lévi-Strauss's statement that "religion consists in a *humanization of natural laws*" and in the "anthropomorphization of nature" (Murray, 9; Lévi-Strauss, 221). Guthrie formulates an unconscious process expressed as a syllogism: "Perception is interpretation, interpretation is the provi-

sion of meaning, and the form with the greatest meaning is that of humans" (140).

6. Recent scholarship on the human body is crucial to this inquiry. Since the 1980s, scholars such as Catherine Gallagher, Donna Haraway, Lynn Hunt, Mary Jacobus, Thomas Laqueur, Richard Sennett, and Mark Seltzer have demonstrated that the anatomical history of the human body is integral with its broader history in terms of gender and sexuality, material culture, social and self-discipline, law, economics, politics, and social culture.

1. Mt. Rushmore

1. These phrases are 1991 essay titles by Rex Alan Smith and Albert Boime.

2. See, for instance, Amy Kaplan and Donald Pease, eds., *Cultures of United States Imperialism* (Durham: Duke University Press, 1993).

3. Historians of sculpture must recognize the influences of Auguste Rodin and Michelangelo Buonarroti on sculptural form in which the emergence from compositional stone is salient. Borglum studied the work of Rodin at the Ecole des Beaux Arts, Paris, just as Rodin had traveled to Italy to study Michelangelo.

4. Susan Fenimore Cooper, in *Rural Hours* (1850), similarly proclaimed the "majesty," "grandeur," and "sublimity" of mountains which she said were misnamed, however, for mere male mortals in "honest broadcloth, close buttoned to the chin," the contrast between topography and name "reminding one rather unpleasantly of that between the mountain and the mouse" (75, 306–307).

5. Phrenology's complicity with racist hierarchical attitudes is amply exhibited in O. S. Fowler's text *Human Science, or, Phrenology*—for example, "All Indian heads and skulls the Author ever saw, and he has seen them literally by the thousands, have an extreme development of Destruction, Secrecy, Caution, Firmness, Devotion, Observation, Size, Form, and Locality, with Full Eventuality, and moderate Causation, Kindness, Beauty, and Friendship. This combination of Faculties indicates just such traits as Indians generally possess. Their extreme Destruction would create that cruel, bloodthirsty, and revengeful disposition common to that race, which makes them turn a deaf ear to the cries of distress, and steels them to such acts of barbarity as they are wont to practice and in torturing the hapless victims of their vengeance. . . . Exceptions . . . of course exist, especially among their chiefs. Red Jacket had a large frontal and coronal lobe, especially a high, bold forehead, and towered equally above his peers in hard sense. [Cherokee] John Ross has a superior head and character. So has Red Cloud" (180, 181).

The African-American head fares no better than the Indian. "The African race, as found in America, furnish another instance of the striking correspondence between their known character, and their phrenological developments. They generally possess large Ambition and Perceptives, as seen in the length of their heads from nose to crown, large Devotion and Tune, Hope, Caution, and love, but less Destruction and Force. Hence their love of hilarity, song, and dance, without much wit, as well as their rapid increase. Their larger Tune and Expression than Causality would create exactly such composition as we meet with in negro songs, doggerel rhymes glowing with vivacity and melody, and containing many words and repetitions, with but few ideas. Their Friendship would make them extremely attached to their families and the families of their masters, and pre-eminently social. Their excessively large Ambition would create in them that fondness for dress and show. . . . Their large Spirituality accounts for their beliefs in ghosts and supernatural events so often manifested among them" (184–185).

The edition quoted above is from 1873, though mid-nineteenth-century readers of the Fowlers' *Phrenology Proved, Illustrated, and Applied* (1849) would have encountered virtually the same passages on Native Americans and Africans (29–32).

6. Contrast this with Henry David Thoreau's figuration of the head-hands, which allies him with the ethos of hard physical work that is physically muscular, even animal-like in its habits: "The intellect is a cleaver; it discerns and rifts its way into the center of things. I do not wish to be busy with my hands any more than is necessary. My head is hands and feet. I feel all my best faculties concentrated in it. My instinct tells me that my head is an organ for burrowing, as some creatures use their snout and forepaws, and with it I would mine and burrow my way through these hills . . . and here I will begin to mine" (*Walden*, 98).

Thoreau rejects drudgery but embraces work, his intellectual faculty a self-styled cleaver, the very blade whose metallic sharpness requires deftness and muscular force for operation. The head (both "hands and feet") is motive power coupled with the physical ability to grasp, scoop, dig—in short, to sink a shaft in kindred relation to burrowing animals. Thus Thoreau's similarity of image is only apparent in comparison to Emerson's Napoleonic will to power.

7. It is noteworthy that Emerson was subject to phrenological analysis; he was represented in O. S. Fowler's compendium on the subject as "a perfect model of th[e] writing organism." Says Fowler, "We have no one pure *thought* author who excells him in the condensed energy, the breadth and pith of his thoughts, and the logical and forceful style in which he presents them" (*Human Science*, 265).

2. Walden Pond

1. A cautionary note is in order, lest Henry Steele Commager appear to be an obtuse apologist for the status quo, which he was not. In 1975, following the decade-long Vietnam War and the Watergate political scandal that led to the resignation of President Richard Nixon and apparent public ennui in the face of corruption, Commager asked, "How did we get from Independence Hall to

Watergate, from Yorktown to Vietnam, from Washington to Nixon . . . from *The Federalist Papers* to the White House [Watergate] Transcripts?" (*Jefferson,* xviii, xix). He cited benchmarks of American democratic principles in order to measure the nation's political downward slide, evident in the United States' blockage of a United Nations relief mission for the children of North Vietnam, official lawlessness, "the use of surveillance, wiretapping, security checks, censorship," and public torpor in the face of "duplicity, mendacity, corruption, and turpitude without parallel in our history" (*Jefferson,* xix).

Commager's anguish was that of a scholar who deplored the McCarthy witchhunts and the loyalty oaths endorsed by President Harry Truman. His dismay was that of a historian who understood the ideological deceptions of a capitalist state that "gave an illusory nourishment to millions of frustrated and ambitious men and women" via business propaganda, court decisions, and advertising exalting "the worst instincts of jealousy, snobbery, and fear, and reduc[ing] competition to its most primitive form" (231).

Commager, however, had removed himself from the kind of sociohistorical criticism practiced by leftists such as Dwight Macdonald and I. F. (Izzy) Stone (1907–1989), who became a contributing editor of the *New York Review of Books* but earned his reputation as the editor and publisher of *I. F. Stone's Weekly,* a newsletter which reached a readership growing from five thousand to seventy thousand over a nineteen-year period, 1953–1972. In the early 1960s Stone had written extensively of the failure of presidential leadership in its timidity in the aftermath of violence in the South. He noted, "The sickness of the South is the sickness of every ruling class in history. These always see conspiracy rather than suffering as the mainspring of every upsurge by the oppressed" (*Time of Torment,* 148).

Whereas Commager equivocated on the issue of slavery in the Jeffersonian era, claiming it to be "one of the ironies of Jefferson's career" that his agrarian democratic policies also nourished slavery, Stone rejected such rhetorical devices and spoke plainly of "the great heroes of the party of the common man" as "Gracchus type, upper-class leaders of lower-class upsurge . . . men of comfortable fortune and privileged position" (Commager, *Jefferson,* 55; Stone, *Polemics,* 7). Unlike Commager, who positioned the Rushmorean figures on an Olympus to be emulated by successors, Stone saw grave political flaws extending to the late eighteenth century. His Lincoln is the Great Equivocator who did nothing to extend the vote, his Theodore Roosevelt "a premature Fascist, an American Mussolini before his time" with "his cult of war and masculinity, his imperialist adventures in Latin America and his naive racism" (23).

2. The Sixties bookshelf includes diverse titles both delegitimating traditional authority and providing new sources of insight for personal empowerment and social change. Texts customarily cited include Jack Kerouac's *On the Road* and *Dharma Bums,* which began the "rucksack revolution." Ken Kesey's *One Flew over the Cuckoo's Nest* became a gloss on authoritarianism embodied in the figure

of Nurse Ratchet, construed by the protagonist, Chief, as a machine mechanism, just as Joseph Heller's *Catch-22* (begun in 1953, published in 1961) conflated the militarist and bureaucratic state, its title naming the double bind trapping the Yossarian-Everyman and -woman.

The Sixties bookshelf included Carlos Castaneda's *Don Juan, Black Elk Speaks,* Paul Goodman's *Growing Up Absurd,* Robert H. Rimmer's *Harrod Experiment, The Whole Earth Catalogue,* Walter H. Clark's *Chemical Ecstasy: Psychedelic Drugs and Religion,* the women's health book *Our Bodies, Our Selves,* Alan Watts's numerous books on Eastern mysticism, together with the alternative or underground press. Newspapers distributed free of charge weekly by the tens of thousands in major urban locales sprang up on both coasts and made their way inland, including the San Francisco *Oracle,* the Berkeley *Barb,* the *Los Angeles Free Press,* the *East Village Other* (New York), *Great Speckled Bird* (Atlanta), *Big Us* (Cleveland), *Daily Planet* (Miami), *Fifth Estate* (Detroit), and scores of others (see Leamer, Glessing, Peck). Estimates of readership nationally varied widely but appear to have averaged about three million, principally youth indifferent to mainstream journalism and identified with messages of dissent (Glessing, 120, xv).

3. Malcolm X's "graduate school" was the library at Norfolk (Massachusetts) Prison, where he read widely in historical texts bearing on imperial and colonial acts against dark-skinned peoples. He would doubtless have enjoyed incorporating in his speeches the work of Franz Boas, the pioneering figure in anthropological study who, working at Columbia University in the earlier twentieth century, discredited the "science-based" belief so prevalent in the nineteenth century that the shape of the skull bore a direct relation to behavior, thought, temperament, and intelligence. Boas was a pivotal figure in repudiating hierarchical racialization in the United States. His *Mind of Primitive Man* (1911) rejected as specious the importance of anthropometric measurements purporting to prove the validity of racial hierarchies. By 1915 Boas wrote that "many students of anthropology recognize that no proof can be given of any material inferiority of the Negro race; that without doubt the bulk of the individuals composing the race are equal in mental aptitude to the bulk of our own people" ("Introduction," vii–viii). In articles in the *Yale Quarterly Review* (1921) and *The Nation* (1925), Boas continued to argue the importance of cultural factors over heredity in human development.

4. In terms of racial, countercultural division, it is also useful to recall that by the late 1960s, well after the southern voter registration drives and freedom rides that prompted white beatings of blacks who attempted to register to vote or to exercise their right of free expression, white hippies, too, endured physical assaults, typically by police units, and they endured threats of, and actual, blows to the head. Following a May 1969 Berkeley police roundup of retail shoppers and street protesters alike, Robert Scheer, editor of the leftist *Ramparts* magazine, was imprisoned at the Santa Rita Rehabilitation Center, the prison workhouse of Alameda County, California. Scheer reported his incarceration in a sidebar in an issue of *Ramparts* in which he recounted the guards' threats and violence (" 'Hey,

you fuckin' hippie queer, . . . get up against the wall.' Whack.'" [51]). Most of the threats focused on the head: "All right, you creeps . . . the last guy out gets his head cracked open. . . . Move your head and I crack it open. . . . Creep, I split heads. . . . Move your asses, creeps, run to the mess hall or heads get split" (Scheer, 50, 51).

5. R. E. L. Masters and Jean Houston cite their long-term objective as the development of psychedelic drugs to treat mental illness, including alcoholism (5, 7). Their findings were based upon a combined fifteen years of research principally with two psychedelic drugs, LSD-25 and peyote, administered in dosages of one to two micrograms per kilogram of body weight of the subject. *The Varieties of Psychedelic Experience* reports on 206 first-hand observations of drug sessions and on interviews with 214 additional subjects "who have been volunteer subjects, psychotherapy patients, or who have taken the drugs on their own" (5). Masters and Houston emphasize those in their subject pool were free of psychiatric illness.

They enumerate the effects of psychedelic drugs as follows: "Even the briefest summation of the psychological effects of . . . [the] potent psycho-chemicals that alter and expand human consciousness . . . would have to include the following: Changes in visual, auditory, tactile, olfactory, gustatory, and kinesthetic perception; changes in experiencing time and space; changes in the rate and content of thought; body image changes; hallucinations; vivid images—eidetic images— seen with the eyes closed; greatly heightened awareness of color . . . depersonalization and ego dissolution; dual, multiple, and fragmented consciousness . . . in general, apprehension of a world that has slipped the chains of normal categorical ordering" (5). Masters and Houston classify psychedelic experience, ranging from the more superficial, which they call the aesthetic, to the intrapsychic symbolic and ultimately to the religiously mystical (toward which they are explicitly skeptical, though respectful of colleagues in the field of theology who themselves would certify some subjects' experiences as authentically religiously mystical).

6. In *Walden,* Thoreau's lexicon of Western and Eastern references from classical antiquity, accessible primarily to those of privileged education, militates against the countercultural goal of classless democracy. An elitist vocabulary similarly pervades a text much admired by counterculturists, Aldous Huxley's *Island* (1962), set in an unspecified site called Pala in Oceania, its inhabitants taught to live by the Golden Rule in relation to Nature and ecology and to seek the Buddhist "Clear Light" attainable in a state of altered consciousness.

Huxley's representation of a psychedelic epiphany relies heavily on references to orchestral music and its technical terms, just as *Island* reverts to benchmark figures of Western civilization (including Savonarola, Voltaire, Spinoza, Rabelais, Goethe, Gibbon) (313–314, 138, 56, 71, 87, 89, 129, 137). The "highbrow" realm of the class-based sacred becomes the counterculture's despised elitism, and thus despite the drug culture's admiration for Huxley (Leary, Metzner, and Alpert dedicate their *Psychedelic Experience* to him), *Island* shows the inadvertent subversion of the democratically green political agenda to which the counterculture was committed.

7. *Varieties of Psychedelic Experience* had pondered the issue of radical, imminent social change, assaying the revolutionary potential of the new consciousness, asking whether psychedelic drug use meant that "a significant number of presently productive individuals will, if exposed, abandon their posts as bank presidents, manufacturers, clergymen, engineers, physicists, educators, in favor of writing blank verse or pondering the riddle of the cosmos" (62). Such an outcome, the authors concluded, was "extremely unlikely," given the Western traditions on which U.S. mainstream society was based, meaning that the Sixties "revolutionary doctrine" would at most effect minimal social change, while structures of established authority—military, corporate, educational, legal, and so on—would sustain their traditional forms of power.

8. It is noteworthy that in *Howl,* Ginsberg attempted a psychedelic representation combining the popular material culture of "neon" and of "blinking traffic light" with the "shuddering lightning in the mind . . . seeking visionary indian angels . . . in supernatural ecstasy," but as a longtime student of Zen Buddhism, Ginsberg took seriously the idea of mystic, angelic light (10, 12).

9. I am grateful to Joe Hopkins of United Airlines for providing company information on the planning and design of the UA terminal.

3. Pittsburgh at Yellowstone

1. A succinct account of the exploration of the Yellowstone region and its development as a national park can be found in Sears, 158–163.

2. In 1996 it was reported that "over the last quarter-century, there has been a marked change in the eruptions" of Old Faithful, which now averaged eruptions every seventy-seven minutes, possibly because nearby geothermal well drilling had changed subterranean pressures (see Brooke).

4. America's Moon

1. The Greek and Roman goddess of the moon had three faces, according to lunar phase: Hecate was dark; Artemis or Diana was waxing; Luna or Selene was full.

2. Lunar terminology cast in frontier terms was peculiarly American. In fact, lunar naming had proceeded from the time of Galileo but had, by World War I, become so complicated and confused that regularization was required (and was accomplished only as of 1961 when the International Astronomical Union set basic rules).

3. Additional land was added to the monument area in President Herbert

Hoover's and John F. Kennedy's subsequent proclamations of 1930 and 1962—though in 1941, President Franklin D. Roosevelt signed a proclamation exempting from the monument a strip of land for the construction of an Idaho state highway, enabling motorists easier access to the area (*Draft General Management Plan*, 103–105).

4. Sources on Limbert are cited according to manuscript cataloguing in the Limbert Collection, Albertsons Library, Boise State University, Boise, Idaho.

5. In 1924 the geologist Harold T. Stearns of the U.S. Geological Survey wrote that "the Craters of the Moon region received its name because of the similarity of its topography to that of the surface of the moon as seen through a telescope," adding that the comparison to the "barren, rugged, black surface dotted thickly with pits and craters" was not highly exaggerated (362). In 1960 the geologist Jack Green of North American Aviation observed that while astronomers adhered to the theory that moon craters were caused by the impact of meteors, "some geologists, including me, think they are volcanic in origin because the shapes of the craters we see through telescopes closely resemble the volcanic basins we call calderas." Admitting that calderas are not found at Craters of the Moon, he nevertheless noted that many "features [there] closely resemble things we see in the dark areas of the moon—in the 'seas' " (qtd. Belknap, 512, 516).

6. A new representation of the "blemished" moon appears in the Apollo mission literature of the 1960s. Apollo 8 astronauts Frank Borman, Bill Anders, and James Lovell, the "first men to see the moon with the naked eye from sixty miles off the surface" reported its appearance like "clouds and clouds of pumice stone," "a dirty beach," "a battlefield, hole upon hole, crater upon crater . . . completely bashed" (Armstrong, Collins, and Aldrin, 203).

7. Jules Verne, as Marjorie Nicolson has shown, was himself the vehicle of a tradition of lunar voyage narratives, for instance that of Cyrano de Bergerac, *The Government of the World in the Moon* (1650), in which a female moon can drink the marrow of animals. (The narrative's voyager crash lands into a lunar Eden, "face plastered with an Apple" [Nicolson, *Voyages,* 162].)

8. Accounts of astronauts' marital circumstances can be found in Wolfe, *The Right Stuff.*

9. Mailer's *Advertisements for Myself* (1959) is a collection of autobiographical-confessional essays.

10. Mailer's "criminality" occurred with the stabbing of his wife, Beverly, with a knife, in 1960, an event not recorded in *Of a Fire on the Moon.*

5. Hot Springs

1. Arkansas and the Hot Springs area, it must be noted, had been occupied from about the first century, for the area of the hot water springs had been found by indigenous peoples who utilized the area's novaculite, a rock, useful for

chipped-stone tools. Notable groups in the area included the Quapaw (called the Arkansea) and Cahinnio tribes and the Caddo people, comprising many confederated tribes. The Choctaw "filtered into Arkansas during the 1700s and early 1800s" (Blaeuer, 9). Legends of intertribal use of the springs for medicinal purposes—for example, of the Quapaws coming "to bathe in the hot water and [plaster] themselves in mud to bake out the aches of arthritic joints"—abound but cannot be verified (qtd. Blaeuer, 15).

Popular accounts, too, served to historicize the area, including a 1939 De Soto Commission Report that supported the notion that Hernando De Soto rested and relaxed at Hot Springs in 1541 during his North American explorations of 1539–1543. This Eurocentric story is specious (Blaeuer, 12–13). The area began to be systematically surveyed when President Thomas Jefferson commissioned William Dunbar and Richard Hunter to explore this part of the Louisiana Territory, which became the property of the United States with the signing of the 1803 Treaty of Paris.

Because the U.S. government failed to pass legislation on the administration of the Hot Springs site in 1832, the springs were claimed by private citizens whose conflicting legal claims were mired in the courts until 1877, when the courts ruled against the claimants, whereupon the federal government reconfirmed the boundaries of the reservation, authorizing a survey, settling remaining justifiable land claims, and appointing a superintendent. At this point, "the area rapidly changed from a rough frontier town to an elegant spa city, with building, landscaping, and engineering projects proceeding apace" (Shugart, viii).

2. The discovery of trace elements of radium in Hot Springs water early in the twentieth century moved scientists and promoters of the area to proclaim that radioactivity was surely the heretofore elusive curative substance in the thermal waters.

3. Owen's legacy is to be found, for instance, in the report of the chemist J. K. Haywood, whose 1902 analysis of the spring waters for the Department of the Interior included separate analyses of the chemistry of forty-six different springs whose elements are identified in tables to the ten thousandth part per million. In a listing of mineral compounds, Haywood also states which illnesses and disorders are medically considered to be responsive to Hot Springs bath treatment, for example, "*Magnesium carbonate and bicarbonate.*—These two substances are mild laxatives and are perhaps the best of all carbonates and bicarbonates in correcting an acid condition of the stomach and curing sick headache caused by constipation. They are valuable in breaking up deposits in the bladder" (27). Haywood's reader can then proceed to his tables of chemical qualitative analysis to discover which springs are rich in these compounds, such as No.5, Avenue Spring, or No.8, Crystal Spring (36, 39).

4. In fact, in order to appreciate the degree of this congruence in the scientific-technical literature, it is useful to notice the extent of nineteenth-century rhetorical personification of American riverways. Both a massive engineering report on the Mississippi River and a geographic survey of North American rivers

identify a small headwaters creek as one of the "infant streams . . . truly the infant Mississippi" (qtd. Humphreys, 66; Russell, *Rivers,* 303). Such texts typically personify the river in terms of a life cycle from infancy to old age. A geographer in 1898 wrote in the parlance of his discipline that streams have a period of "youth" and "follow a long period of development and adjustment . . . throughout the[ir] lives" (Russell, *Rivers,* 32, 255, 37, 254). The "young" Colorado River has had a "precocious youth," we learn, but has "accomplished a Herculean task, and is still working with the energy of youth" (Russell, *Rivers,* 274, 283). Streams may "invade" territory, grow "sleepy," or be "joyous" (Russell, *Rivers,* 40, 263, 275). There is "rivalry" between "neighboring" streams, which can be "choked," though ice-bound lakes can make a "sudden escape" from dams and can exert a "genial influence" (Russell, *Rivers,* 255; *Lakes,* 11, 23, 38, 39). "Late in life," rivers "carve out their own fortunes and influence their surroundings" (Russell, *Rivers,* 302).

Even scientific-technical texts that strive to minimize personification exhibit it, as in the Humphreys report, which quotes diverse texts attributing human qualities to the river. The Mississippi "touches" high land, is "beset" by rapids, gives way in its channel "so reluctantly," then "bursts out from its cavernous reservoir, and, leaping down over the huge masses of rock below, here commences its long journey to unite with other tributaries in making the Mississippi the noblest river in the universe" (Humphreys, 95, 56; qtd. Humphreys, 67, 34). The Mississippi and other bodies of water have "a long and varied experience to relate" (Russell, *Rivers,* 260).

A prominent early conservationist text also participates in this thoroughgoing personification. George Perkins Marsh, a Vermonter, is considered one of the fathers of the American conservation movement for his *Man and Nature, or, Physical Geography as Modified by Human Action* (1864), which surveyed and decried the global environmental damage caused by human action, prompting Marsh's call for human remediation of the earth and its waters. The diction of *Man and Nature,* in a chapter-long survey of the global "Waters," configures a lake as a "body of water," islands which are "washed" by the sea, while spongy earth must "imbibe" additional moisture or, if too dry, be reduced to "barrenness" (295, 289, 307, 305). Rivers "divide themselves into several arms" and enter the sea "by different mouths" (340). It is feared that a lake would join with inland waters to "swallow up" soil, while drilling causes the "abstraction of fluids from the bowels of the earth" (295–296, 374).

Rivers and lakes, though masculine, are intermittently feminized, too, in the personifying terms present in these scientific texts. In the Mississippi headwaters region, Cass Lake "embosoms" four islands (Humphreys, 67–68). The Humphreys report, while commenting on "the moderating influence of [certain] lakes upon the floods of the river," cites "the works nature herself has established" (qtd. Humphreys, 39–40). A geographer observes that "the lakes in [the] desert regions have a different general history from their sisters whose banks are fringed with green vegetation" (Russell, *Lakes,* 90, 93).

5. It is indicative that the Humphreys report, which summarizes several hy-

draulics studies potentially important to the management of the Mississippi River, also includes one "relating to the circulation of the blood," and that the report is itself a document of the kind termed a "scientific investigation . . . in the direction of predicting when floods are to be expected, thus allowing opportunities to counteract their destructive effects" (Humphreys, 211; Russell, *Rivers*, 233).

6. Luce Irigaray's "The 'Mechanics' of Fluids" is helpful here, beginning with her observation that "the properties of fluids have been abandoned to the feminine" and that "fluids have never stopped arguing against the longstanding relationship of males' 'solid mechanics and rationality' " (116, 113). Examination of the properties of fluids, Irigaray observes, shows that "this 'real' may well include . . . *a physical reality* that continues to resist symbolization and/or that signifies the powerlessness of logic to incorporate in its writing all the characteristic features of nature" (106–107). Working from a post-Freudian psychoanalytic model, Irigaray theorizes a masculinist linguistic and mathematical effort to annihilate fluidity, which nonetheless evades linguistic structures of logic. One result of Irigaray's thesis that "women diffuse themselves according to modalities scarcely compatible with the framework of the ruling symbolics" can be shown to operate in the vocabulary of female fluidity in nineteenth-century obstetrics and hydrological engineering (with such women physicians as Mary Melandy and Mary Jacobi presumably trapped in a false consciousness because of the socialization of their medical training).

7. The popularity of spas and hot springs nationwide may be gauged by the presence of 196 of them in California alone in 1892, with another 110 listed elsewhere in the United States (W. Anderson, 277–281). It is noteworthy that a few miles above the junction of Gardiners and Yellowstone Rivers is a group of basins known as Diana's Bathing Pools.

6. Love Canal

1. Woburn, Massachusetts, a site of aquatic contamination, received considerable publicity during the Love Canal crisis but never achieved the national status accorded to Love Canal. In September 1979 the *Woburn Daily Times* first reported the contamination of wells supplying water to the west-of-Boston community ("Lagoon of Arsenic Discovered in N. Woburn"), whereupon the *Boston Globe* and the *New York Times* featured the story, quoting Anne Anderson, the mother of a leukemia victim, a son, Jimmy, who soon succumbed to the disease. The Woburn problem took the form of a nationally publicized lawsuit by a group of Woburn citizens against Beatrice Foods and W. R. Grace, the corporations owning the plants tried for causing death and disease by dumping toxic chemicals that contaminated the town's groundwater (Harr, 38–50). The Woburn case gained renewed public attention in Jonathan Harr's 1995 *A Civil Action* and in a

1999 Hollywood film of the same title, starring John Travolta as the lead attorney for the Woburn families. It is significant that the affected Woburn families chose to seek redress in court rather than exert political pressure through grassroots organization of their own. The spokesman for the affected Woburn families thereby became their attorney, not the figure of the mother whose child died of leukemia.

2. A review of the *Reader's Guide to Periodical Literature*, 1970–1979, shows some 39 articles on cancer in *Newsweek*, 23 in *Time*, 11 in *U.S. News and World Report*, and 10 in *Reader's Digest*. Among magazines for women, *McCall's* published 17, *Good Housekeeping* 21, *Ladies' Home Journal* 4, *Vogue* 7, and *Harper's Bazaar* 14. Of those listed above, 42 concerned breast cancer. Public consciousness of breast cancer was also raised by publications such as George Crile Jr.'s *What Women Should Know about the Breast Cancer Controversy* (1973), whose author appeared on nationally televised programs such as *Not for Women Only*, *Today*, and *The David Suskind Show*.

3. Ecofeminism has been subject to substantial revisionism since the 1970s, with critics arguing that its identification of the earth with a female principle is inadvertently complicitous with patriarchy, destructively univocal, and erroneously essentialist. Recent critics emphasize that the very term "ecofeminism" is susceptible to widely varying interpretation, though two scholars, Caroline Merchant and Karen J. Warren, have posited a foundational ecofeminist position. In 1996 Merchant stated, "Cultural ecofeminism analyzes environmental problems from within its critique of patriarchy and offers alternatives that could liberate both women and nature" (*Earthcare*, 5). Similarly, Warren argues that the promise of ecological feminism is that "it provides a distinctive framework both for reconceiving feminism and for developing an environmental ethic which takes seriously connections between the domination of women and the domination of nature" ("Power," 19, emphasis omitted). For late twentieth-century ecological feminist argument, see Warren's two edited compilations, *Ecological Feminist Philosophies* (1996) and *Ecofeminism: Women, Culture, Nature* (1997).

4. Politically, some feminists have taken a Marxist-socialist perspective. Mary Mellor writes that this group, based mainly in Europe and Australia, "drew upon more social constructionist and radical political perspectives, mainly eco-anarchism, but also socialism/Marxism." She adds that "United States ecofeminists, even from a theological background, have adopted a socialist politics" (45). Mellor provides a meticulous record of the debates within ecological feminism, including arguments against essentialist positions such as Elizabeth Gould Davis's, which have been rejected as naive and romantic, inadvertently reinforcing women's traditional social roles. Caroline Merchant, too, cautions that the female symbolic structures employed to transform the patriarchal-technological culture are "double-edged" in that women and nature can be rendered as "passive and submissive" (*Earthcare*, 142).

5. The ecofeminist objective of economic justice for racial minorities disproportionately affected by environmental contamination opens a consideration of

Nature's nation from racial and ethnic perspectives. Though beyond the scope of this project, such work is needed and would surely include the Native American Mississippian "Father of Waters" as a nonwhite aquatic body reidentified by the African-American poet of the Harlem Renaissance, Langston Hughes, in "The Negro Looks at Rivers," as a "muddy bosom . . . all golden in the sunset." Hughes's poem is autobiographically centered in the riparian ancestry of the Euphrates, the Congo, and the Nile but culminates in the Mississippi (Lewis, 257). The counterpart of the female Love Canal, accordingly, might be examined in the racialized degradation of such areas as Gary, Indiana, as chronicled in Andrew Hurley's *Environmental Inequalities: Class, Race, and Industrial Pollution in Gary, Indiana, 1945–1980* (1995) and in Robert Gottlieb's discussion of ethnicity as a factor in the quest for environmental justice (235–269).

6. The cosmologist James Lovelock, in *Gaia: A New Look at Life on Earth,* proposed the Gaia principle, which views the world as a superorganism. The theory, named for the female personification of the earth in Greek mythology, was denounced by Lovelock's scientist colleagues as a primitivist reversion to Goddess mythology. The preface of Lovelock's subsequent *Ages of Gaia: A Biography of Our Living Earth* reports this quandary over gender reference: "No feminist will complain if I use the pronoun, she, for Gaia, but no [scientific] journal will publish my paper if I do" (xiii).

7. Both Douglas and Carson were self-identified as writers even in childhood. Both, for instance, submitted stories and essays to the prestigious *St. Nicholas* juvenile magazine, which transmitted the values of the nature study movement to its readers. An essay of Carson's appeared in *St. Nicholas,* while Douglas managed to publish a crossword puzzle in its pages. Both were encouraged to think of themselves as writers by teachers from elementary school through college, and both read avidly (including Joseph Conrad, though Carson became keenly interested in other authors whose subjects were seafaring and the ocean—such as Herman Melville and Robert Louis Stevenson [Lear, 21]).

Carson's absorption in her mother's passion for "botanizing, bird-watching, and nature study" led her biographer to suggest that love of nature functioned as displaced childhood-adolescent intimacy, while Douglas produced a pamphlet urging the establishment of Fairchild Garden, a tropical botanical garden in south Florida (Lear, 13, 26; Douglas, *Voice,* 176). Both also attended women's colleges, Douglas at Wellesley, Carson at the Pennsylvania College for Women in Pittsburgh (later renamed Chatham College). Both also resigned from stultifying positions (Douglas from her reporter job at the *Miami Herald,* Carson from the U.S. Fish and Wildlife Service) in order to become full-time professional writers published in such magazines as the *Saturday Evening Post* and *Ladies' Home Journal* (Douglas) and *Atlantic Monthly,* the *New Yorker, Collier's, Reader's Digest, Holiday, Field and Stream, Vogue,* and *Woman's Home Companion* (Carson).

Carson and Douglas differ in one crucial respect. Douglas credited her father's journalistic rigor for her own passion for factual accuracy, while Carson's facts came directly from years of scientific training in marine biology, including a summer stint at the Marine Biological Laboratories at Woods Hole, Massachusetts, and an M.A. (1932) and doctoral training at Johns Hopkins University. The 1930s Depression, her father's death, and male sexist biases against women in the sciences redirected her toward writing as a source of income. The "old desire to write" began to "reassert itself," and in 1935 Carson began to write freelance nature articles for magazines and secured a full-time position writing educational materials for the U.S. Bureau of Wildlife and Fisheries, subsequently renamed the U.S. Fish and Wildlife Service (Lear, 77).

8. Buell argues that toxic discourse "insists on the interdependence of ecocentric and anthropocentric values" and that it "underscores the point that environmentalism must make concerns for human and social health more central and salient than it traditionally has [done]" (639–640). His use of the term is thus different from its usage in this discussion, in which it refers to representations of environmental toxicity.

References

The Accused, the Accusers: The Famous Speeches of the Eight Chicago Anarchists in Court. Chicago: Socialist Publishing Society, n.d.

Albanese, Catherine L. *Nature Religion in America from the Algonkian Indians to the New Age.* Chicago: University of Chicago Press, 1990.

Albert, Judith Clavir, and Stewart Edward Albert, eds. *The Sixties Papers: Documents of a Rebellious Decade.* New York: Praeger, 1984.

Alcott, Louisa May. *Work.* 1873. Reprint. New York: Penguin, 1994.

Aldrin, Edwin E., Jr. *Return to Earth.* With Wayne Warga. New York: Random House, 1973.

Alger, Horatio. *Ragged Dick* and *Struggling Upward.* 1868, 1890. Reprint. New York: Penguin, 1985.

Amory, Cleveland. *The Last Resorts.* New York: Harper & Brothers, 1952.

Anbinder, Tyler. *Nativism and Slavery: The Northern Know Nothings and the Politics of the 1850s.* New York: Oxford University Press, 1992.

Anderson, Benedict. *Imagined Communities.* Rev. ed. London and New York: Verso, 1991.

Anderson, John, and Stearns Morse. *The Book of the White Mountains.* New York: Minton, Balch & Co., 1930.

Anderson, Quentin. "Thoreau on July 4." *New York Times Book Review,* July 4, 1971: 1, 16–18.

Anderson, Terry H. *The Movement and the Sixties: Protest in America from Greensboro to Wounded Knee.* New York: Oxford University Press, 1995.

Anderson, Winslow. *Mineral Springs and Health Resorts of California.* San Francisco: Bancroft, 1892.

Apollo 17, the Most Productive Lunar Expedition. Washington, D.C.: National

Aeronautics and Space Administration. NASA Mission Report MR-12, 1977.

Arkansas: A Guide to the State. Compiled by Workers of the Writers' Program of the Work Projects Administration in the State of Arkansas. New York: Hastings House, 1941.

Armstrong, Katherine. "Work Indoors and Out: The Flowers of Yellowstone Park." *The Independent*, 50, no. 2578 (May 1898): 562.

Armstrong, Neil, Michael Collins, and Edwin E. Aldrin, Jr. *First on the Moon*. With Gene Farmer and Dora Jane Hamblin. Boston: Little, Brown, 1970.

Armstrong, Tim. *Modernism, Technology, and the Body: A Cultural Study*. Cambridge and New York: Cambridge University Press, 1998.

Ascher, Barbara L. "Winter Dreams: New York City." *New York Times*, November 21, 1999. Reprint. *New York Times on the Web*, November 30, 1999.

Ashwell, Samuel. *A Practical Treatise of the Diseases Peculiar to Women*. Philadelphia: Lea and Blanchard, 1845.

"At Pittsburg." *The Daily (Hot Springs) Democrat*, 1, no. 39 (March 29, 1895): 1.

Audubon, John James. *Delineations of American Scenery and the American Character*. New York: G. A. Baker, 1926.

Austin, Ian. "The United States' Toxic Deadlock." *Maclear's*, 98, no. 17 (April 29, 1985): 21.

Baldy, J. M., ed. *An American Text-Book of Gynecology*. Philadelphia: W. B. Saunders, 1896.

Banta, Martha. *Taylored Lives: Narrative Productions in the Age of Taylor, Veblen, and Ford*. Chicago: University of Chicago Press, 1993.

Bard, Samuel. *A Compendium of the Theory and Practice of Midwifery*. New York: Collins & Co., 1817.

Barlow, Joel. *The Columbiad*. 1806. Reprint. Washington, D.C.: Joseph Milligan, 1825.

Barnes, Clive. "Lawrence and Lee Cull Action from a Night." *New York Times*, November 2, 1970: 66.

Barthes, Roland. *Reading Degree Zero*. 1953. Reprint. New York: Hill and Wang, 1968.

Barwell, Richard. *On Aneurism: Especially of the Thorax & Root of the Neck*. London: Macmillan, 1880.

Bederman, Gail. *Manliness and Civilization: A Cultural History of Gender and Race in the United States, 1880–1917*. Chicago: University of Chicago Press, 1995.

Beecher, Catherine E. *A Treatise on Domestic Economy*. 1841. Reprint. New York: Source Book Press, 1970.

Beecher, Lyman. *Lectures on Political Atheism and Kindred Subjects; Together with Six Lectures on Intemperance*. Boston: John P. Jewett & Co., 1852.

Belknap, William, Jr. "Man on the Moon in Idaho." *National Geographic Magazine*, 118, no. 4 (October 1960): 504–525.

Bell, John. *On Baths and Mineral Waters.* Philadelphia: Henry H. Porter, 1831.

Bennett, David H. *The Party of Fear: From Nativist Movements to the New Right in American History.* Chapel Hill: University of North Carolina Press, 1988.

Bercovitch, Sacvan, and Myra Jehlen. *Ideology and Classic American Literature.* Cambridge and New York: Cambridge University Press, 1986.

Berlant, Lauren. *The Anatomy of National Fantasy: Hawthorne, Utopia, and Everyday Life.* Chicago: University of Chicago Press, 1991.

Bierley, Paul. *John Philip Sousa: American Phenomenon.* Englewood Cliffs, N.J.: Prentice-Hall, 1973.

——— *The Works of John Philip Sousa.* Westerville, Ohio: Integrity Press, 1984.

Blaeuer, Mark. " 'Didn't All the Indians Come Here?': Separating Fact from Fiction at Hot Springs National Park." Working Paper. Hot Springs National Park, 1998.

Boas, Franz. *The Mind of Primitive Man.* New York: Macmillan, 1911.

——— "Introduction." In *Half a Man: The Status of the Negro in New York,* by Mary White Ovington. New York: Longmans, Green, 1915.

——— "The Problem of the American Negro." *Yale Quarterly Review* 10 (1921): 384–395.

——— "What Is Race?" *The Nation* 28 (1925): 89–91.

Bodner, John. *Remaking America: Public Memory, Commemoration, and Patriotism in the Twentieth Century.* Princeton: Princeton University Press, 1992.

Boime, Albert. "Patriarchy Fixed in Stone." *American Art,* 5 (January–February 1991): 143–167.

Bonta, Marcia Myers. *Women in the Field: America's Pioneering Women Naturalists.* College Station: Texas A & M Press, 1991.

Boraiko, Allen A. "Storing Up Trouble . . . Hazardous Waste." *National Geographic Magazine,* 167, no. 3 (March 1985): 319–351.

Boyle, T. Coraghessan. *The Road to Wellville.* New York: Penguin, 1994.

Brewster, James N. "Love Canal: Redefining Disaster." *Christian Century,* 99, no. 25 (August 4–11, 1982): 829–830.

Bromell, Nicholas K. *By the Sweat of the Brow: Literature and Labor in Antebellum America.* Chicago: University of Chicago Press, 1993.

Brooke, James. "Time Trouble for Geyser: It's No Longer Old Faithful." *New York Times.* National Edition. February 5, 1996: A6.

Brown, Dee. *The American Spa: Hot Springs, Arkansas.* Little Rock: Rose Publishing Company, 1982.

Brown, Michael. *Laying Waste: The Poisoning of America by Toxic Chemicals.* New York: Pantheon, 1980.

——— "Drums of Death." *Audubon,* 82, no. 4 (July 1980): 120–133.

——— "Love Canal and the Poisoning of America." *The Atlantic,* 299, no. 6 (December 1979): 33–47.

Bruce, Robert V. *The Launching of Modern American Science, 1846–1876.* New York: Knopf, 1987.

Bryant, Bunyan, and Paul Mohai, eds. *Race and the Incidence of Environmental Hazards: A Time for Discourse.* Boulder and San Francisco: Westview, 1992.

Buckstaff Baths. Hot Springs, Ark., 1912.

Buell, Lawrence. *The Environmental Imagination: Thoreau, Nature Writing, and the Formation of American Culture.* Cambridge: Harvard University Press, 1995.

——— "Toxic Discourse." *Critical Inquiry,* 24, no. 3 (Spring 1998): 639–665.

Burgett, Bruce. *Sentimental Bodies: Sex, Gender, and Citizenship in the Early Republic.* Princeton: Princeton University Press, 1998.

Burroughs, John. *Camping and Tramping with Roosevelt.* Boston: Houghton Mifflin, 1907.

Bushrod, W. James. *American Resorts, with Notes upon Their Climate.* Philadelphia: F. A. Davis, 1889.

Byers, Stephen W. "Don't Mess with Her Wetlands." *New York Times Magazine* (January 10, 1999): 46.

Calvino, Italo. "The Distance of the Moon." In *Cosmicomics.* Translated by William Weaver. San Diego and New York: Harcourt Brace, 1968.

"Canal Cleanup." *Time,* 120, no. 4 (July 26, 1982): 13.

Carson, Gerald. *Cornflake Crusade.* New York: Rinehart, 1957.

Carson, Rachel. *Always, Rachel: The Letters of Rachel Carson and Dorothy Freeman, 1952–1964.* Boston: Beacon Press, 1995.

——— *The Edge of the Sea.* Boston: Houghton Mifflin, 1955.

——— *The Sea around Us.* New York: Oxford University Press, 1951.

——— *Silent Spring.* 1962. Reprint. Boston: Houghton Mifflin, 1987.

——— *Under the Sea-Wind: A Naturalist's Picture of Ocean Life.* New York: Simon and Schuster, 1941.

Castronovo, Russ. *Fathering the Nation: American Genealogies of Slavery and Freedom.* Berkeley and Los Angeles: University of California Press, 1995.

Cayleff, Susan E. *Wash and Be Healed: The Water-Cure Movement and Women's Health.* Philadelphia: Temple University Press, 1987.

Chaikin, Andrew. *A Man on the Moon: The Voyages of the Apollo Astronauts.* New York: Viking, 1994.

Chambers, Julius. *The Mississippi River and Its Wonderful Valley: Twenty-Seven Hundred and Seventy-Five Miles from Source to Sea.* New York: Putnam's, 1910.

Chapman, Robert. *American Slang.* New York: Harper & Row, 1987.

Chapple, J. A. V. *Science and Literature in the Nineteenth Century.* London: Macmillan, 1986.

Christ, Carol P. *Diving Deep and Surfacing: Women Writers on Spiritual Quest.* Boston: Beacon Press, 1980.

——— *Laughter of Aphrodite: Reflections on a Journey to the Goddess.* San Francisco: Harper & Row, 1987.

———— *Rebirth of the Goddess: Finding Meaning in Feminist Spirituality.* Reading, Mass.: Addison Wesley, 1997.

Christian, Eugene. *Little Lessons in Corrective Eating.* 1914. Rev. ed. New York: Corrective Eating Society, 1916.

Christie, John Aldrich. *Thoreau as World Traveler.* New York: Columbia University Press with the cooperation of the American Geographical Society, 1965.

Christie, John, and Sally Shuttleworth, eds. *Nature Transfigured: Science and Literature, 1700–1900.* Manchester and New York: Manchester University Press, 1989.

Churchill, Fleetwood. *On the Theory and Practice of Midwifery.* Philadelphia: Blanchard and Lea, 1863.

Clay, Charles. *The Complete Handbook of Obstetric Surgery.* Philadelphia: Lindsay and Blakiston, 1874.

Cleaver, Eldridge. *Soul on Ice.* 1968. Reprint. New York: Dell, 1991.

Clendening, Logan, ed. *Source Book of Medical History.* 1942. Reprint. New York: Dover, 1960.

Cobb, Lawrence Wells. "Henry Steele Commager." *Dictionary of Literary Biography.* Vol. 17: *Twentieth-Century American Historians.* Edited by Clyde N. Wilson. Detroit: Gale, 1983.

Cohen, Allen. "The *San Francisco Oracle:* A Brief History." In *Voices from the Underground: Insider Histories of the Vietnam Era Underground Press.* Edited by Ken Wachsberger. Vol. 1, 131–164. Tempe, Az.: Mica's Press, 1993.

Cohen, Michael P. *The Pathless Way: John Muir and the American Wilderness.* Madison: University of Wisconsin Press, 1984.

Colbert, Charles. *A Measure of Perfection: Phrenology and the Fine Arts in America.* Chapel Hill: University of North Carolina Press, 1997.

Colburn, David R., and George E. Pozzetta. "Race, Ethnicity, and Political Legitimacy." *The Sixties: From Memory to History.* Edited by David Farber. Chapel Hill: University of North Carolina Press, 1994: 119–148.

Collette, Will. "Citizen's Clearinghouse for Hazardous Wastes." *Environment,* 29, no. 9 (November 1987): 44–45.

Collier's, March 22, 1952: 22–36, 38–39, 65; October 18, 1952: 51–58, 60; October 25, 1952: 38–40, 42, 44–48; February 28, 1953: 40–48; March 7, 1953: 56–63; March 14, 1953: 38–44; June 27, 1953: 33–35, 38, 40; April 30, 1954: 21–29.

Combe, George. *Notes on the State of North America during a Phrenological Visit.* 3 vols. Edinburgh: Maclachlan, Stewart, 1841.

Combs, James. "Celebrations: Rituals of Popular Veneration." *Journal of Popular Culture,* 22 (Fall 1989): 71–77.

Commager, Henry Steele. *The American Mind: An Interpretation of American Thought and Character since the 1880s.* New Haven: Yale University Press, 1950.

———— *Jefferson, Nationalism, and the Enlightenment.* New York: Braziller, 1975.

Comstock, Theodore B. "Engineering Relations of the Yellowstone Park." *American Journal of Science* (November-December 1878): 460–461.

Cooper, Susan Fenimore. *Rural Hours.* 1850. Reprint. Syracuse, N.Y.: Syracuse University Press, 1968.

Corthell, N. E. "A Family Trek to the Yellowstone." *The Independent,* 58, no. 2952 (June 29, 1905): 1460–1467.

Cronon, William. *Changes in the Land: Indians, Colonists, and the Ecology of New England.* New York: Hill and Wang, 1983.

Cronon, William, ed. *Uncommon Ground: Rethinking the Human Place in Nature.* New York: Norton, 1996.

Cutter, Richard. *Cutter's Guide to the Hot Springs of Arkansas.* Battle Creek, Mich.: Gage, 1884.

Dale, Peter Allan. *In Pursuit of a Scientific Culture: Science, Art, and Society in the Victorian Age.* Madison: University of Wisconsin Press, 1989.

Dale, Stephen M. "Through Yellowstone on a Coach." *Ladies' Home Journal,* 21, no. 9 (August 1904): 5–6.

Dana, Richard Henry, Jr. *Two Years before the Mast.* 1840, 1869. Reprint, 1869 edition. New York: Signet, 1964.

Daniels, George H. *Science in American Society: A Social History.* New York: Alfred A. Knopf, 1971.

Davies, John. *Phrenology: Fad and Science.* New Haven: Yale University Press, 1955.

Davis, Edward P. *A Treatise on Obstetrics for Students and Practitioners.* Philadelphia: Lea Brothers, 1896.

Davis, Elizabeth Gould. *The First Sex.* New York: Putnam, 1971.

Davis, Rebecca Harding. *Life in the Iron Mills.* Edited by Tillie Olsen. 1861. Reprint. New York: Feminist Press, 1972.

Dean, Robert J. *Living Granite: The Story of Borglum and the Mount Rushmore Memorial.* New York: Viking, 1949.

Dearborn, Mary V. *Mailer: A Biography.* Boston: Houghton Mifflin, 1999.

DeLillo, Don. *Underworld.* New York: Scribner, 1997.

A Description of the Summer and Winter Health and Pleasure Resorts and Points of Interest Located on and Reached by the Missouri and Pacific Railroad and Iron Mountain Route. St. Louis: Woodward and Tiernan, 1890.

Dewees, William P. *A Compendious System of Midwifery.* Philadelphia: Blanchard and Lea, 1853.

———— *A Treatise on the Diseases of Females.* Philadelphia: Blanchard and Lea, 1853.

Diamond, Irene, and Gloria Feman Orenstein, eds. *Reweaving the World.* San Francisco: Sierra Books, 1990.

Dillard, Annie. *Pilgrim at Tinker Creek.* 1974. Reprint. New York: HarperCollins, 1998.

Disney, Walt. *Man in Space: A Tomorrowland Adventure.* Syracuse, N.Y.: Singer, 1959.

Doherty, Patricia. *Marge Piercy: An Annotated Bibliography.* Westport, Conn.: Greenwood Press, 1997.

Donegan, Jane B. *"Hydropathic Highway to Health": Women and Water-Cure in Antebellum America.* Westport, Conn.: Greenwood Press, 1986.

Douglas, Marjory Stoneman. *The Everglades: River of Grass.* 1947. Reprint. Sarasota, Fla.: Pineapple Press, 1997.

—— *Hurricane.* 1958. Reprint. Covington, Ga.: Mockingbird Books, 1976.

—— *Nine Florida Stories by Marjory Stoneman Douglas.* Edited by Kevin M. McCarthy. Jacksonville: University of North Florida Press, 1990.

—— *Voice of the River.* With John Rothchild. Sarasota, Fla.: Pineapple Press, 1987.

Dowd, Maureen. "Leaders as Followers." *New York Times,* January 12, 1997: E17.

Draft General Management Plan Environmental Assessment, Craters of the Moon National Monument, Idaho. Denver: United States Department of the Interior/National Park Service: Denver Service Center, 1991.

Dreiser, Theodore. *The Financier.* 1912. Reprint. New York: Meridian, 1995.

Durell, Fletcher. *A New Life in Education.* Philadelphia: American Sunday-School Union, 1894.

Early, Eleanor. *Behold the White Mountains.* Boston: Little, Brown, 1936.

Eastman's White Mountain Guide. Concord, N.H.: Eastman, 1876.

Echols, Alice. *Daring to Be Bad: Radical Feminism in America, 1967–1975.* Minneapolis: University of Minnesota Press, 1989.

"Editor's Study." *Harper's New Monthly Magazine,* 94, no. 560 (January 1897): 320–325.

Ehrlich, Paul. "Eco-Catastrophe." *Ramparts,* 8 (September 1969): 24–28.

Eiseley, Loren. *The Immense Journey.* 1957. Reprint. New York: Time-Life Books, 1981.

Eller, Cynthia. *Living in the Lap of the Goddess: The Feminist Spirituality Movement in America.* Boston: Beacon Press, 1995.

Elliot, George T., Jr. *Obstetric Clinic.* New York: Appleton & Co., 1868.

Emerson, Ralph Waldo. "The American Scholar." In *Selections from Ralph Waldo Emerson,* 63–80. Edited by Stephen E. Wicher. Boston: Houghton Mifflin, 1957.

—— *Collected Works.* Vol. 2: *Essays,* first series. 1841. Reprint. Cambridge: Harvard University Press, 1979.

—— *Essays and Poems.* New York: Library of America, 1996.

—— *Lectures and Biographical Sketches.* Boston and New York: Houghton Mifflin, 1888.

—— *Natural History of Intellect.* Boston: Houghton Mifflin, 1904.

—— *Selections from Ralph Waldo Emerson.* Edited by Stephen E. Wicher. Boston: Houghton Mifflin, 1957.

——— *Society and Solitude.* 1870. Reprint. In *The Complete Works of Ralph Waldo Emerson.* Vol. 7. Boston: Houghton Mifflin, 1912.

Emmet, Thomas Addis. *The Principles and Practice of Gynecology.* Philadelphia: Henry O. Lea, 1879.

Epps, Archie, ed. *Malcolm X's Speeches at Harvard.* New York: Paragon House, 1991.

Epstein, Samuel S., Lester O. Brown, and Carl Pope. *Hazardous Wastes in America.* San Francisco: Sierra Club Books, 1982.

"Equity in the Everglades." *New York Times.* National Edition. March 8, 1999: A18.

Fawcett, J. E. S. "The Politics of the Moon." *World Today,* 25 (1969): 357–362.

Feher, Michel, Ramona Naddaff, and Nadia Tazi, eds. *Fragments for a History of the Human Body.* Part One. New York: Zone, 1989.

——— *Fragments for a History of the Human Body.* Part Two. New York: Zone, 1989.

——— *Fragments for a History of the Human Body.* Part Three. New York: Zone, 1989.

Fenton, John H. "A Proposal to Shift Control of Area to State Is Opposed." *New York Times,* July 22, 1967: 16.

Ferber, Edna. *Saratoga Trunk.* New York: Doubleday, 1941.

Fite, Gilbert C. *Mount Rushmore.* Norman: University of Oklahoma Press, 1952.

Fitzgerald, F. Scott. *The Great Gatsby.* 1925. Reprint. New York: Scribner, 1953.

Floyer, John. *Psykhroloysia, or, The History of Cold-Bathing.* London: W. Innys and R. Manby, 1732.

Fordyce Bath House. St. Louis: Woodward, c. 1915.

Foucault Reader. Edited by Paul Rabinow. New York: Pantheon, 1984.

Fowler, O[rson] S. *Human Science, or, Phrenology.* Philadelphia, Chicago, and St. Louis: National Publishing Co., 1873.

Fowler, O[rson], and L. N. Fowler. *Phrenology Proved, Illustrated, and Applied.* New York: Fowlers and Wells, 1849.

Francaviglia, Richard. "Reflections from the Road: The Search for Main Street USA." *Chronicle of Higher Education* 43 (March 21, 1997): B8.

Francis, F. "The Yellowstone Geysers." *Littell's Living Age,* 153 (5th ser., vol. 38), no. 1972 (April 8, 1882): 31–36.

Fuller, Margaret. "Leila." *The Dial: A Magazine for Literature, Philosophy, and Religion,* 1, no. 4 (April 1841): 462–467.

——— *Summer on the Lakes, in 1843.* 1844. Reprint. Urbana and Chicago: University of Illinois Press, 1991.

Garnett, Algernon S. *A Treatise on the Hot Springs of Arkansas.* St. Louis: Van Beek, Barnard & Tinsley, 1874.

Gartner, Carol B. *Rachel Carson.* New York: Ungar, 1983.

General Management Plan Environmental Assessment—Draft: Craters of the Moon

National Monument, Idaho. Denver: Department of the Interior, National Park Service, 1991.

Gibbs, Lois Marie. *Love Canal—My Story.* As told to Murray Levine. Albany: State University of New York Press, 1982.

Gilbert, Sandra M. "Introduction" to *The Awakening,* by Kate Chopin, 7–33. New York: W. W. Norton, 1984.

Gill, Sam. "Mother Earth: An American Myth." In *The Invented Indian: Cultural Fictions and Government Policies,* 129–143. Edited by James A. Clifton. New Brunswick, N.J.: Transaction, 1990.

Gilman, Charlotte Perkins. "Our Brains and What Ails Them." In *Charlotte Perkins Gilman: A Nonfiction Reader.* Edited by Larry Ceplair. New York: Columbia University Press, 1991.

Gilmore, Michael T. *American Romanticism and the Marketplace.* Chicago: University of Chicago Press, 1985.

Ginsberg, Allen. *Collected Poems, 1947–1980.* New York: Harper and Row, 1984.

——— *Howl and Other Poems.* Introduction by William Carlos Williams. San Francisco: City Lights Books, 1956, 1959.

Gitlin, Todd. *The Sixties: Years of Hope and Days of Rage.* New York: Bantam, 1987.

Glasser, Ronald J. *The Body Is the Hero.* New York: Random House, 1976.

Glazier, Willard. "Pittsburg." In *Peculiarities of American Cities,* 332–347. Philadelphia: Hubbard Brothers, 1883.

Glessing, Robert J. *The Underground Press in America.* Bloomington: Indiana University Press, 1970.

Goldberg, Carey. "Thoreau, or at Least the Next Best Thing, Is Alive and Well." *New York Times,* August 10, 1999. Reprint. *New York Times on the Web,* November 30, 1999.

Goodell, William. *Lessons in Gynecology.* Philadelphia: D. G. Brinton, 1879.

Gorn, Elliott J. *The Manly Art: Bare-Knuckle Prize Fighting in America.* Ithaca, N.Y.: Cornell University Presss, 1986.

Gottlieb, Robert. *Forcing the Spring: The Transformation of the American Environmental Movement.* Washington, D.C.: Island Press, 1993.

Gottwald, Norman K. "Hippies, Political Radicals, and the Church." *Christian Century,* 84 (August 16, 1967): 1043–1045.

Gray, Elizabeth Dodson. *Why the Green Nigger?—Re-Mything Genesis.* Wellesley, Mass.: Roundtable Press, 1979.

Green, Harvey. *Fit for America: Health, Fitness, Sport and American Society.* New York: Pantheon, 1986.

Griffin, Melanie L. "The Legacy of Love Canal." *Sierra,* 73, no. 1 (January–February 1988): 26–28.

Griffin, Susan. *Woman and Nature: The Roaring inside Her.* 1978. Reprint. New York: Harper & Row, 1980.

Grogan, Davis, and Christopher Phillips. "The Ziolkowskis Are Honoring Chief

Crazy Horse, by Blasting Out a Mountain of a Sculpture." *People Weekly,* 32, no. 23 (December 4, 1989): 105–110.

Guthrie, Stewart Elliott. *Faces in the Clouds: A New Theory of Religion.* New York: Oxford, 1993.

Gutman, Herbert, et al. *Who Built America: Working People and the Nation's Economy, Politics, Culture, and Society.* 2 vol. New York: Pantheon, 1992.

Haer, John L. "The Psychedelic Environment: A New Psychological Phenomenon." *Journal of Popular Culture,* 3 (1969): 260–266.

Hague, Arnold. "Age of Igneous Rocks of the Yellowstone." *American Journal of Science* (June 1896): 445–456.

———— "The Yellowstone National Park." *Scribner's Magazine,* 35, no. 5 (May 1904): 513–527.

Hales, Peter. *William Henry Jackson and the Transformation of the American Landscape.* Philadelphia: Temple University Press, 1988.

Harr, Jonathan. *A Civil Action.* New York: Vintage, 1996.

Harris, Emmylou. *The Ballad of Sally Rose.* 1986. Warner Bros. 25205-2.

Harris, Neil. "John Philip Sousa and the Culture of Reassurance." In Harris, *Cultural Excursions,* 198–232. Chicago: University of Chicago Press, 1990.

Havig, Alan. "Presidential Images, History, and Homage: Memorializing Theodore Roosevelt, 1919–1967." *American Quarterly,* 30 (Fall 1978): 514–532.

Hawthorne, Nathaniel. *The Blithedale Romance.* 1852. Reprint. New York: Penguin, 1986.

———— "The Great Stone Face." In *The Centenary Edition of the Works of Nathaniel Hawthorne.* Vol. XI, 26–48. Columbus: Ohio State University Press, 1974.

———— *The Letters, 1853–1856.* In *The Centenary Edition of the Works of Nathaniel Hawthorne.* Vol. XVII. Columbus: Ohio State University Press, 1987.

———— *The Marble Faun.* 1860. Reprint. New York: A. L. Burt, 1902.

———— *Memoir of Nathaniel Hawthorne.* London: Henry S. King, 1872.

———— *The Scarlet Letter.* 1850. Reprint. New York: Penguin, 1983.

Hayden, F[erdinand] W. "The Hot Springs and Geysers of the Yellowstone and Firehole Rivers." *American Journal of Science and the Arts,* 3rd ser., vol. 3, no. 15 (March 1872): 161–176.

———— "The Yellowstone National Park." *American Journal of Science and the Arts,* 3rd ser., vol. 3, no. 16 (April 1872): 294–297.

Haywood, J[ohn] K[erfoot]. *The Hot Springs of Arkansas: Report of an Analysis of the Waters of the Hot Springs on the Hot Springs Reservation, Hot Springs. Garland County, Ark.* Washington, D.C.: Government Printing Office, 1902.

Heard, Alex. "Mount Rushmore: The Real Story." *New Republic,* 205, no. 3 (July 15–22): 16–18.

Heller, Joseph. *Catch-22.* 1961. Reprint. New York: Scribner, 1996.

Henderson, C. Hanford. "Through the Yellowstone on Foot." *Outing,* 34, no. 2 (May 1899): 161–167.

Henke, James. *I Want to Take You Higher: The Psychedelic Era, 1965–1969.* San Francisco: Rock and Roll Hall of Fame and Museum, 1997.

Herndl, Carl G., and Stuart C. Brown. *Green Culture: Environmental Rhetoric in Contemporary America.* Madison: University of Wisconsin Press, 1996.

Herndl, Diane Price. *Invalid Women: Figuring Feminine Illness in American Fiction and Culture, 1840–1940.* Chapel Hill: University of North Carolina Press, 1993.

Herndon, Dallas T. *Centennial History of Arkansas.* Chicago and Little Rock: S. J. Clarke, 1922.

Higham, John. *Strangers in the Land: Patterns of American Nativism, 1860–1925.* New Brunswick, N.J.: Rutgers University Press, 1955.

Himes, Chester. *If He Hollers, Let Him Go.* 1945. Reprint. New York: Thunder's Mouth Press, 1986.

"The Hippies: An Inquiry into the Roots and Meaning of Youthful Disaffection." *Horizon,* 10, no. 2 (1968): 4–30.

"The Hippies: Philosophy of a Subculture." *Time,* 90 (July 7, 1967): 18–22.

Hippler, Bob. "Fast Times in Motor City." In *Voices from the Underground: Insider Histories of the Vietnam Era Underground Press,* 9–36. Edited by Ken Wachsberger. Vol. 1. Tempe, Az.: Mica's Press, 1993.

Hodge, Hugh L. *On Diseases Peculiar to Women.* Philadelphia: Blanchard and Lea, 1860.

Hoge, James O. "Psychedelic Stimulation and the Creative Imagination: The Case of Ken Kesey." *Southern Humanities Review,* 23 (1969): 253–260.

Hollick, Frederick. *The Diseases of Woman, Their Causes and Cure Familiarly Explained.* New York: Burgess, Stringer, 1847.

"Hopi Way." *The Illustrated Paper.* Mendocino, Calif.: n.p., 1967.

Horkheimer, Max, and Theodor Adorno. *Dialectic of Enlightenment.* 1944. Reprint. New York: Continuum, 1993.

Horsman, Reginald. *Race and Manifest Destiny: The Origins of American Racial Anglo-Saxonism.* Cambridge: Harvard University Press, 1981.

"Hot Springs, Arkansas, and the Miraculous Health-Giving Power of the Waters." Myerson, St. Louis, n.d.

"Hot Springs, Arkansas." *Frank Leslie's Illustrated Newspaper,* 70, no. 1801 (March 22, 1890): 158–163.

Hot Springs, Arkansas: The Carlsbad of America. 3d ed. St. Louis: Woodward & Tiernan, 1894.

"The Hot Springs of Arkansas." *DeBow's Review.* After the War Series, 4, nos. 1–2 (July–August 1867): 86–94.

"The Hot Springs of Arkansas." *Harper's New Monthly Magazine,* 56, no. 332 (January 1878): 193–210.

The Hot Springs of Arkansas: An Historical and Legendary Account. St. Louis: Missouri and Pacific Railway Co., 1893.

Hot Springs Daily News, 18, no. 121 (July 23, 1896): n.p.

Hot Springs Illustrated Monthly, 3, no. 1 (May 1879): 3.

Houriet, Robert. *Getting Back Together.* New York: Avon, 1971.

Humphreys, A. A. *Report on the Physics and Hydraulics of the Mississippi River.* Philadelphia: Lippincott, 1861.

Hunter, Robert. *Violence and the Labor Movement.* New York: Macmillan, 1922.

Hutch, Richard A. *Emerson's Optics: Biographical Process and the Dawn of Religious Leadership.* Washington, D.C.: University Press of America, 1983.

Huxley, Aldous. *Island.* 1962. Reprint. New York: Harper and Row, 1972.

Hynes, H. Patricia. *The Recurring Silent Spring.* New York: Pergamon, 1989.

Indianhead, 1, no. 4 (August 18–31, 1967).

Irigaray, Luce. "The 'Mechanics' of Fluids." In *This Sex Which Is Not One,* 105–117. Trans. Catherine Porter. Ithaca, N.Y.: Cornell University Press, 1985.

Irwin, William. *The New Niagara: Tourism, Technology, and the Landscape of Niagara Falls, 1776–1917.* University Park: Pennsylvania State University Press, 1996.

Jackson, Donald Dale. "Gutzon Borglum's Odd and Awesome Portraits in Granite." *Smithsonian,* 23 (May 1992): 64–75.

Jacobi, Mary Putnam. *The Question of Rest for Women during Menstruation.* New York: G. P. Putnam's Sons, 1886.

——— "Shall Women Practice Medicine?" In *Mary Putnam Jacobi: A Pathfinder in Medicine,* 367–390. Edited by the Women's Medical Association of New York City. New York: Putnam's, 1925.

Jagger, T. A. "Some Conditions Affecting Geyser Eruption." *American Journal of Science,* 4th ser., 5, no. 29 (May 1898): 323–333.

James, William. *The Varieties of Religious Experience: A Study in Human Nature.* New York: Longmans, Green, 1902.

Jameson, Elizabeth. "Frontiers." *Frontiers: A Journal of Women Studies,* 17, no. 3 (1996): 6–11.

Jamison, Andrew, and Ron Eyerman. *Seeds of the Sixties.* Berkeley and Los Angeles: University of California Press, 1994.

Jarrasse, Dominique. *Rodin: A Passion for Movement.* Paris: Terrail, 1995.

Jeffers, Robinson. *The Collected Poetry of Robinson Jeffers.* Vol. 3. Edited by Tim Hunt. Stanford: Stanford University Press, 1991.

Jefferson, Thomas. "Jefferson to Henry Lee, May 8, 1825." In *The Writings of Thomas Jefferson.* Vol. X, 343. Edited by Paul Leicester Ford. New York: G. P. Putnam's Sons, 1899.

Jehlen, Myra. *American Incarnation: The Individual, the Nation, the Continent.* Cambridge: Harvard University Press, 1986.

Jones, Billy M. *Health-Seekers in the Southwest, 1817–1900.* Norman: University of Oklahoma Press, 1967.

Jumonville, Neil. *Henry Steele Commager: Midcentury Liberalism and the History of the Present.* Chapel Hill: University of North Carolina Press, 1999.

Kadlecek, Mary. "Love Canal—10 Years Later." *The Conservationist,* 43, no. 3 (November-December 1988): 40–43.

Katz, James E. "National Space Policy: The Forgotten Frontier." *Policy Studies Journal,* 10 (1982): 465–479.

Keller, Evelyn Fox. *Reflections on Gender and Science.* New Haven: Yale University Press, 1985.

Kellogg, John Harvey. *Plain Facts for Young and Old.* Burlington, Iowa: Segner & Condit, 1881.

——— *Rational Hydropathy.* 3d rev. ed. Philadelphia: F. A. Davis, 1906.

Keniston, Kenneth. *Young Radicals: Notes on Committed Youth.* New York: Harcourt Brace & World, 1968.

Kerouac, Jack. *The Dharma Bums.* 1959. Reprint. New York: Penguin, 1976.

Keulen, Margarete. *Radical Imagination: Feminist Conceptions of the Future in Ursula LeGuin, Marge Piercy, and Sally Miller Gearhart.* Frankfurt: Peter Lang, 1991.

Keyes, Donald D., ed. *The White Mountains: Place and Perceptions.* Hanover, N.H.: University Press of New England, 1980.

Killingsworth, Jimmie. *Whitman's Poetry of the Body: Sexuality, Politics, and the Text.* Chapel Hill: University of North Carolina Press, 1989.

Killingsworth, Jimmie, and Jacqueline S. Palmer. "Millennial Ecology: The Apocalyptic Narrative from *Silent Spring* to *Global Warming.*" In *Green Culture: Environmental Rhetoric in Contemporary America,* 21–45. Edited by Carl G. Herndl and Stuart C. Brown. Madison: University of Wisconsin Press, 1996.

King, Carol, ed. *Women and Goddess Traditions in Antiquity and Today.* Minneapolis: Fortress, 1997.

King, Frank B. "In Nature's Laboratory: Driving and Fishing in Yellowstone Park." *Overland Monthly,* 2d ser., 1, no. 174 (June 1897): 594–603.

King, Martin Luther, Jr. *The Essential Writings and Speeches of Martin Luther King, Jr.* Edited by James M. Washington. New York: HarperSanFrancisco, 1991.

King, Ynestra. "Feminism and the Revolt of Nature." *Heresies,* 13 (Fall 1981): 12–16.

Kinsey, Joni Louise. *Thomas Moran and the Surveying of the American West.* Washington, D.C.: Smithsonian Institution Press, 1992.

Koch, J. "Discovery of the Yellowstone National Park." *Magazine of American History,* 11, no. 6 (June 1884).

Kolodny, Annette. *The Lay of the Land: Metaphor as Experience and History in American Life and Letters.* Chapel Hill: University of North Carolina Press, 1975.

Langford, Nathaniel P. "The Folsom-Cook Exploration of the Upper Yellowstone in the Year 1869." *Contributions to the Historical Society of Montana,* 5 (1904): 349–369.

Larcom, Lucy. *A New England Girlhood.* 1889. Reprint. New York: Corinth, 1961.

Lask, Thomas. "College Seminar Honors Thoreau." *New York Times,* May 15, 1967, 54.

Lawrence, Jerome, and Robert E. Lee. *The Night Thoreau Spent in Jail.* New York: Hill and Wang, 1970.

Lawton-Peebles, Robert. *Landscape and Written Expression in Revolutionary America.* New York: Cambridge University Press, 1988.

Le Conte, Joseph. "Geysers and How They Are Explained." *Popular Science Monthly,* 12, no. 6 (1878): 401–417.

Leamer, Lawrence. *The Paper Revolutionaries: The Rise of the Underground Press.* New York: Simon and Schuster, 1972.

Lear, Linda, ed. *Rachel Carson: Witness for Nature.* New York: Henry Holt, 1997.

Leary, Timothy. *Confessions of a Dope Fiend.* New York: Bantam, 1973.

——— *Psychedelic Prayers after the Tao te ching.* New Hyde Park, N.Y.: University Books, 1966.

Leary, Timothy, Ralph Metzner, and Richard Alpert. *The Psychedelic Experience: A Manual Based on The Tibetan Book of the Dead.* New Hyde Park, N.Y.: University Books, 1964.

Lebeaux, Richard. *Thoreau's Seasons.* Amherst: University of Massachusetts Press, 1984.

——— *Young Man Thoreau.* Amherst: University of Massachusetts Press, 1977.

Leonard, Ira M., and Robert D. Parmet. *American Nativism, 1830–1860.* New York: Van Nostrand Reinhold, 1971.

Levine, Adeline. *Love Canal: Science, Politics, and People.* Lexington, Mass.: D. C. Heath, 1982.

Lévi-Strauss, Claude. *The Savage Mind.* Chicago: University of Chicago Press, 1966.

Lewis, David Levering, ed. *The Portable Harlem Renaissance Reader.* New York: Penguin, 1995.

Liebermann, Randy. "The *Collier's* and Disney Series." In *Blueprint for Space: Science Fiction to Science Fact,* 135–146. Edited by Frederick I. Ordway and Randy Liebermann. Washington, D.C.: Smithsonian, 1992.

Limbert, R[obert] W. "Among the 'Craters of the Moon.'" *National Geographic Magazine,* 45, no. 3 (March 1924): 303–328.

Limerick, Patricia. "The Persistence of the Frontier." *Harper's,* 289 (October 1994): 21–23.

Lindbergh, Anne Morrow. *Earth Shine.* New York: Harcourt, Brace & World, 1966.

Lipsitz, George. "Who'll Stop the Rain?: Youth Culture, Rock 'n' Roll, and Social Crises." In *The Sixties: From Memory to History,* 206–234. Edited by David Farber. Chapel Hill: University of North Carolina Press, 1994.

Logan, Mrs. John A. *The Home Manual: Everybody's Guide in Social, Domestic, and Business Life*. Chicago: H. J. Smith, 1889.

Logsdon, John M. "The Challenge of Space: Linking Aspirations and Political Will." In *Blueprint for Space: Science Fiction to Science Fact*, 147–154. Edited by Frederick I. Ordway and Randy Liebermann. Washington, D.C.: Smithsonian, 1992.

———— *The Decision to Go to the Moon: Project Apollo and the National Interest*. Cambridge: MIT Press, 1970.

Longfellow, Henry Wadsworth. *The Song of Hiawatha*. In *Longfellow's Poetical Works*. New York: A. L. Burt, 1901.

"Love Canal Revisited: Still More Questions." *Newsweek*, 101, no. 22 (May 30, 1983): 41.

Lovelock, James. *The Ages of Gaia: A Biography of Our Living Earth*. 1988. Reprint. New York: Norton, 1995.

MacDonald, William W. "Life and Death of the Hippies." *America*, 119 (September 7, 1968): 150–155.

Mackenzie, James. *The Study of the Pulse, Arterial, Venous, and Hepatic, and of the Movements of the Heart*. New York: Macmillan, 1902.

Mailer, Norman. *An American Dream*. 1964. Reprint. New York: Holt, 1987.

———— *Miami and the Siege of Chicago*. New York: New American Library, 1968.

———— *Of a Fire on the Moon*. Boston: Little Brown, 1970.

———— *Prisoner of Sex*. Boston: Little, Brown, 1971.

———— *Why Are We in Vietnam?* New York: Berkley, 1968.

Malcolm X. *The Autobiography of Malcolm X*. With Alex Haley. 1964. Reprint. New York: Ballantine, 1973.

———— *Malcolm X Speaks: Selected Speeches and Statements*. 1965. Reprint. New York: Pathfinder, 1989.

———— *Speeches at Harvard*. Edited by Archie Epps. New York: Paragon House, 1991.

Mann, Horace. *An Oration, Delivered before the Authorities of the City of Boston, July 4, 1842*. Boston, 1842.

Mansnerus, Laura. "Timothy Leary, Pied Piper of Psychedelic 60's, Dies at 75." *New York Times*, June 1, 1996: 1, 11.

Marchand, Roland. *Creating the Corporate Soul: The Rise of Public Relations and Corporate Imagery in American Big Business*. Berkeley and Los Angeles: University of California Press, 1998.

Marine, Gene. "America the Raped." *Ramparts*, 7 (December 1968): 72–74.

Marling, Karal Ann. *The Colossus of Roads*. Minneapolis: University of Minnesota Press, 1984.

Marsh, George Perkins. *Man and Nature, or, Physical Geography as Modified by Human Action*. 1864. Reprint. Cambridge: Harvard University Press, 1965.

Marx, Leo. *The Machine and the Garden: Technology and the Pastoral Ideal in America*. New York: Oxford University Press, 1964.

———— "Pastoralism in America." In *Ideology and Classic American Literature*,

36–69. Edited by Sacvan Bercovitch and Myra Jehlen. Cambridge and New York: Cambridge University Press, 1986.

Masters, R. E. L., and Jean Houston. *The Varieties of Psychedelic Experience.* New York: Holt, Rinehart and Winston, 1966.

The Maurice Bath-House, Baden-Baden. Hot Springs, Arkansas, c. 1894.

Maya Lin: A Strong Clear Vision. Written and directed by Frieda Lee Mock. Produced by Frieda Lee Mock and Terry Sanders. Santa Monica, Calif.: Sanders & Mock Productions/American Film Foundation, 1995.

McCay, Mary. *Rachel Carson.* New York: Twayne, 1993.

McKinsey, Elizabeth. *Niagara Falls: Icon of the American Sublime.* New York: Cambridge University Press, 1985.

McLean, George N. *The Rise and Fall of Anarchy in America.* Chicago and Philadelphia: R. G. Badoux, 1888.

Meigs, Charles, trans. *A Treatise on the Diseases and Special Hygiene of Females, with Additions,* by Colombat de l'Isere. Philadelphia: Lea and Blanchard, 1850.

Melandy, Mary. *Perfect Womanhood for Maidens, Wives, Mothers.* Boston: James H. Earle, 1901.

Mellor, Mary. *Feminism and Ecology.* New York: New York University Press, 1997.

Melville, Herman. *Benito Cereno.* In *Billy Budd and Other Stories,* 159–258. New York: Penguin, 1986.

——— *Moby-Dick.* 1851. Reprint. New York: Penguin, 1986.

——— "The Tartarus of Maids." In *The Harper American Literature.* Vol. 1, pp. 1984–1993. Edited by Don McQuade et al. 2d ed. New York: HarperCollins, 1987.

Merchant, Caroline. *The Death of Nature: Women, Ecology, and the Scientific Revolution.* 1980. Reprint. San Francisco: HarperSanFrancisco, 1989.

——— *Earthcare: Women and the Environment.* New York: Routledge, 1996.

——— "Reinventing Eden: Western Culture as a Recovery Narrative." In *Common Ground: Rethinking the Human Place in Nature,* 132–159. Edited by William Cronon. New York: Norton, 1995.

Michaud, Michael A. G. *Reaching for the High Frontier: The American Pro-Space Movement, 1972–84.* New York: Praeger, 1986.

Michener, James. *Space.* New York: Ballantine, 1983.

Miller, David C. *Dark Eden: The Swamp in Nineteenth-Century American Literature.* New York: Cambridge University Press, 1989.

Miller, Perry. *Errand into the Wilderness.* Cambridge: Harvard University Press, 1956.

——— *Nature's Nation.* Cambridge: Harvard University Press, 1967.

Miller, Ron. "The Spaceship as Icon: Designs from Verne to the Early 1950s." In *Blueprint for Space: Science Fiction to Science Fact,* 49–68. Edited by Frederick I. Ordway and Randy Liebermann. Washington, D.C.: Smithsonian, 1992.

Miller, Timothy. *The Hippies and American Values.* Knoxville: University of Tennessee Press, 1991.

Mills, C. Wright. *White Collar: The American Middle Classes.* 1951. Reprint. New York: Oxford University Press, 1977.

"The Minerals and Springs of Arkansas." *DeBow's Review,* n.s., 1, no. 2 (August 1858): 199–205.

Mitchell, S. Weir. "Through the Yellowstone Park to Fort Custer." *Lippincott's Magazine of Popular Literature and Science,* 25 (June 1889): 688–704.

Montgomery, Scott L. "Monumental Kitsch: Borglum's Mount Rushmore." *Georgia Review,* 42 (Spring 1988): 252–261.

Morse, Stearns, ed. *Lucy Crawford's History of the White Mountains.* 1845. Reprint. Hanover, N.H.: Dartmouth Publications, 1966.

Morton, Peter. *The Vital Science: Biology and the Literary Imagination, 1860–1900.* London: George Allen & Unwin, 1984.

Mrozek, Donald J. *Sport and the American Mentality.* Knoxville: University of Tennessee Press, 1983.

Muir, John. *Our National Parks.* 1901. Reprint. Madison: University of Wisconsin Press, 1981.

——— "The Wild Parks and Forests of the West." *Atlantic Monthly,* 81, no. 483 (January 1898): 15–28.

——— "The Yellowstone National Park." In *Our National Parks,* 37–75. 1901. Reprint. Madison: University of Wisconsin Press, 1981.

——— *The Yosemite.* 1912. Reprint. Madison: University of Wisconsin Press, 1986.

Murray, Gilbert. *Five Stages of Greek Religion.* Garden City, N.Y.: Doubleday, 1955.

Nabokov, Peter. "The Peyote Road." *New York Times Magazine,* March 9, 1969: 30–31, 129–133.

Nader, Ralph, and Ronald Brownstein. "Beyond the Love Canal." *The Progressive,* 44, no. 5 (May 1980): 28–31.

Nash, Roderick. *The Rights of Nature: A History of Environmental Ethics.* Madison: University of Wisconsin Press, 1989.

Nelson, Dana. *National Manhood: Capitalist Citizenship and the Imagined Fraternity of White Men.* Durham: Duke University Press, 1998.

Neushul, Peter. "Love Canal: A Historical Review." *Mid-America: An Historical Review,* 69, no. 3 (October 1987): 125–138.

Newfield, Christopher. *The Emerson Effect: Individualism and Submission in America.* Chicago: University of Chicago Press, 1996.

Nicolson, Marjorie Hope. *The Breaking of the Circle: Studies in the Effect of the "New Science" upon Seventeenth-Century Poetry.* New York: Columbia University Press, 1960.

——— *Mountain Gloom and Mountain Glory: The Development of the Aesthetics of the Infinite.* 1959. Reprint. New York: W. W. Norton, 1963.

——— *Voyages to the Moon.* New York: Macmillan, 1948.

———— *A World in the Moon: A Study of the Changing Attitude toward the Moon in the Seventeenth and Eighteenth Centuries.* Northampton, Mass.: Smith College Studies in Modern Languages, 1935.

Norton, Anne. *Alternate Americas: A Reading of Antebellum Political Culture.* Chicago: University of Chicago Press, 1985.

Norwood, Vera. *Made from This Earth: American Women and Nature.* Chapel Hill: University of North Carolina Press, 1993.

———— "Rachel Carson." In *The American Radical.* Edited by Mari Jo Buhle, Paul Buhle, and Harvey J. Kaye. New York: Routledge, 1994.

Novak, Barbara. *Nature and Culture: American Landscape and Painting, 1825–1875.* New York: Oxford University Press, 1980.

Nuttall, Thomas. *A Journal of Travels into the Arkansas Territory during the Year 1819.* Edited by Savoie Lottinville. Norman: University of Oklahoma Press, 1980.

O'Neil, Paul. "So Long to the Good Old Moon." *Life.* Special Edition: *To the Moon and Back.* 1969.

Osler, William. *The Principles and Practice of Medicine.* New York: D. Appleton & Co., 1895.

———— *William Osler's Collected Papers on the Cardiovascular System.* Edited with introduction by W. Bruce Fye. Birmingham: University of Alabama Press, 1985.

Otter, Samuel. *Melville's Anatomies.* Berkeley and Los Angeles: University of California Press, 1999.

Ovington, Mary White. *Half a Man: The Status of the Negro in New York.* New York: Longmans, Green, 1915.

Owen, W. O. "The First Bicycle Tour of the Yellowstone Park." *Outing,* 16, no. 3 (June 1891): 191–195.

Owings, Loren C. *Quest for Walden: The "Country Book" in American Popular Literature.* Jefferson, N.C.: McFarland, 1997.

Patton, Phil. "To the Moon, Chesley." *Esquire,* 117 (January 1992): 40–42.

Paul, Sherman. *The Shores of America: Thoreau's Inward Exploration.* Champaign-Urbana: University of Illinois Press, 1958.

Peabody, Ephraim. *A Sermon Delivered before the Boston Fraternity of Churches, April 2, 1846.* Boston, 1846.

Pease, Donald. *Visionary Compacts: American Renaissance Writings in Cultural Context.* Madison: University of Wisconsin, 1987.

Peck, Abe. *Uncovering the Sixties: The Life and Times of the Underground Press.* New York: Pantheon, 1985.

Piepmeier, Alison. *Woman Goes Forth to Battle with Goliath: Mary Baker Eddy, Medical Science, and Sentimental Invalidism.* Nashville: Center for Clinical and Research Ethics, Vanderbilt University, 1998.

Piercy, Marge. *Mars and Her Children.* New York: Knopf, 1992.

———— *The Moon Is Always Female.* New York: Knopf, 1994.

———— *Parti-Colored Blocks for a Quilt.* Ann Arbor: University of Michigan Press, 1982.

———— *Woman on the Edge of Time.* New York: Knopf, 1976.

Plant, Judith, ed. *Healing the Wounds: The Promise of Ecofeminism.* London: Green Print, 1989.

"The Poisoning of America." *Time,* 116, no. 12 (September 22, 1980): 2, 58–69.

Poovey, Mary. *Making a Social Body: British Cultural Formations, 1830–1864.* Chicago: University of Chicago Press, 1995.

Porter, Caroline. *Seeing and Being: The Plight of the Participant Observer in Emerson, James, Adams, and Faulkner.* Middletown, Conn.: Wesleyan University Press, 1981.

"Postal 'Hippie' Art Is Going Over Big with Hippies Here." *New York Times,* July 16, 1967, 51.

Practical Guide to Yellowstone National Park, Containing Illustrations, Maps, Altitudes, and Geyser Time Tables. St. Paul, Minn.: F. Jay Haynes, 1890.

Raeburn, Paul. "University Presses: Walden Pond vs. the Mall." *New York Times,* October 24, 1999: Book Review, 14.

Rand, Ayn. *The Fountainhead.* 1943. Reprint. New York: Signet, 1993.

Reich, Charles. *The Greening of America.* New York: Random House, 1970.

Richardson, Robert D. *Emerson: The Mind on Fire—A Biography.* Berkeley: University of California Press, 1995.

Riesman, David, with Nathan Glazer and Reul Denny. *The Lonely Crowd.* 1950. Reprint. New Haven: Yale University Press, 1969.

Rimmer, Robert H. *The Harrad Experiment.* 1966. Reprint. Buffalo, N.Y.: Prometheus Books, 1990.

Robinson, Harriet. *Loom and Spindle, or Life among the Early Mill Girls.* Kailua, Hawaii: Press Pacifica, 1976.

Rollins, Alice Wellington. "The Three Tetons." *Harper's New Monthly Magazine,* 74, no. 444 (May 1887): 869–890.

Roosevelt, Theodore. *An Autobiography.* 1913. Reprint. New York: Da Capo, 1985.

Roszak, Theodore. *The Making of a Counter Culture: Reflections on the Technocratic Society and Its Youthful Opposition.* New York: Doubleday, 1969.

Rothstein, Edward. "Modern Hunts for the Great White Whale Leave Ahab Adrift." *New York Times,* October 16, 1999: A19.

Ruether, Rosemary Radford. *New Woman, New Earth: Sexist Ideologies and Human Liberation.* 1975. Reprint. Boston: Beacon Press, 1995.

Ruland, Richard, ed. *Twentieth-Century Interpretations of Walden.* Englewood Cliffs, N.J.: Prentice-Hall, 1968.

Russell, Israel C. *Lakes of North America.* New York: Ginn, 1895.

———— *Rivers of North America.* New York: Putnam's, 1898.

Sandler, Stanley. *Segregated Skies: All-Black Combat Squadrons of World War II.* Washington, D.C.: Smithsonian Institution Press, 1992.

"Saving Thoreau's Pond: Rock Stars (Who Else?)." *New York Times,* August 14, 1990: A14.

Sayre, Nora. *Sixties Going on Seventies.* Rev. ed. New Brunswick, N.J.: Rutgers University Press, 1996.

Scarry, Elaine. *The Body in Pain: The Making and Unmaking of the World.* New York: Oxford University Press, 1985.

Schama, Simon. *Landscape and Memory.* New York: Knopf, 1995.

Scheer, Robert. "A Night at Santa Rita." *Ramparts,* 8 (August 1969): 50–51.

Schiebinger, Londa. *Nature's Body: Gender in the Making of Modern Science.* Boston: Beacon Press, 1993.

Schlereth, Thomas J. *Victorian America: Transformations in Everyday Life, 1876–1915.* New York: HarperCollins, 1991.

Schmeckebier, L. F. "Our National Parks." *National Geographic Magazine,* 23, no. 6 (June 1912): 531–539.

Schmitt, Brad. "Brad about You: A Long, Strange Trip to the Park." *The Tennessean* (October 11, 1997): 3A.

Schumacher, Michael. *Dharma Lion: A Critical Biography of Allen Ginsberg.* New York: St. Martin's Press, 1992.

Schweitzer, Glenn E. *Borrowed Earth, Borrowed Time: Healing America's Chemical Wounds.* New York: Plenum, 1991.

Sealts, Merton, ed. *Melville as Lecturer.* Cambridge: Harvard University Press, 1957.

Sears, John F. *Sacred Places: American Tourist Attractions in the Nineteenth Century.* New York: Oxford University Press, 1989.

Sedgwick, Henry D. "On Horseback through the Yellowstone." *The World's Work* (June 1903): 3569–3576.

Seltzer, Mark. *Bodies and Machines.* New York: Routledge, 1992.

Serrin, William. *Homestead: The Glory and Tragedy of an American Steel Town.* New York: Vintage, 1993.

Sessions, Francis C. "The Yellowstone Park." *Magazine of Western History,* 6, no. 5 (September 1887): 433–445.

Setterberg, Fred, and Lonny Shavelson. *Toxic Nation: The Fight to Save Our Communities from Chemical Contamination.* New York: John Wiley & Sons, 1993.

Shaff, Howard, and Audrey Karl Shaff. *Six Wars at a Time: The Life and Times of Gutzon Borglum, Sculptor of Mount Rushmore.* Sioux Falls, S.D.: Center for Western Studies, 1985.

Shands, Kerstin W. *The Repair of the World: The Novels of Marge Piercy.* Westport, Conn.: Greenwood, 1994.

Shelton, William R. *Man's Conquest of Space.* Washington, D.C.: National Geographic Society, 1968.

Shepard, Alan, and Deke Slayton. *Moon Shot: The Inside Story of America's Race to the Moon.* With Jay Barbree and Howard Benedict. Atlanta, Ga.: Turner, 1994.

Shew, Joel. *The Hydropathic Family Physician.* New York: Fowlers and Wells, 1855.

———— *Midwifery and the Diseases of Women.* New York: Fowlers and Wells, 1852.

Shugart, Sharon. *The Hot Springs of Arkansas through the Years.* Hot Springs, Ark.: Department of the Interior/National Park Service, 1996.

Silent Spring Revisited. Edited by Gino J. Marco, Robert M. Hollingworth, and William Durham. Washington, D.C.: American Chemical Company, 1987.

The Sixties Papers: Documents of a Rebellious Decade. Edited by Judith Clavir Albert and Stewart Edward Albert. New York: Praeger, 1984.

Skinner, B[urrhus] F. *Walden Two.* 1948. Reprint. New York: Macmillan, 1976.

Smart, Tim. "Love Canal: A New Cleanup Plan Stirs Old Fears." *Business Week,* no. 3014 (August 31, 1987): 30.

Smith, Frank E. *The Politics of Conservation.* New York: Pantheon, 1966.

Smith, Rex Alan. "Shrine of Democracy." *American History Illustrated,* 26 (March 1991): 26–41.

———— *The Carving of Mount Rushmore.* New York: Abbeville, 1985.

Smith-Rosenberg, Carroll. "Domesticating 'Virtue': Coquette and Revolutionaries in Young America." In *Literature and the Body: Essays on Populations and Persons,* 160–184. Edited by Elaine Scarry. Baltimore: Johns Hopkins University Press, 1988.

Snow, C[harles] P[ercy]. *Two Cultures and the Scientific Revolution.* Cambridge and New York: Cambridge University Press, 1959.

Somkin, Fred. *Unquiet Eagle: Memory and Desire in the Idea of American Freedom, 1815–1860.* Ithaca, N.Y.: Cornell University Press, 1967.

Sontag, Susan. *Illness as Metaphor.* New York: Farrar, Straus and Giroux, 1978.

Sousa, John Philip. *Marching Along: Recollections of Men, Women, and Music.* Introduction by Paul Bierley. 1928. Rev. ed. Westerville, Ohio: Integrity Press, 1994.

Spurzheim, J[ohann] K[asper]. *Phrenology, in Connection with Physiognomy.* Boston: Marsh, Capen & Lyon, 1833.

Stearns, Harold T. "Craters of the Moon National Monument." *Geographical Review* V, 14, no. 3 (July 1924): 362–373.

Stern, Madeleine B. *Heads and Headlines: The Phrenological Fowlers.* Norman: University of Oklahoma Press, 1971.

Stern, Sol. *"Trouble in Paradise." Ramparts,* 8 (November 1969): 22–28.

Stevens, Robert R. *Report on Hot Springs Improvements to the Secretary of the Interior.* Washington, D.C.: U.S. Government Printing Office, 1893.

———— *Report on Hot Springs Improvements to the Secretary of the Interior for the Fiscal Year Ended June 30, 1895.* Washington, D.C.: U.S. Government Printing Office, 1895.

Stewart, Omer C. *Peyote Religion: A History.* Norman: University of Oklahoma Press, 1987.

Stitt, H. S. *The Hot Springs of Arkansas and Its Great Hotels, the Arlington and Eastman.* St. Louis: Woodward & Tiernan, 1898.

Stone, I[sidor] F. *In a Time of Torment, 1961–1967: A Nonconformist History of Our Times.* Boston: Little, Brown, 1989.

—— *Polemics and Prophecies, 1967–1970.* Boston: Little, Brown, 1989.

Storrs, Richard. *Home Missions: As Connected with Christ's Dominion.* New York, 1855.

Stowe, Harriet Beecher. *Uncle Tom's Cabin.* 1852. Reprint. New York: Penguin, 1981.

Straus, Gary. "Exxon's PR Mess Still Isn't Cleaned Up." *USA Today,* March 4, 1999: 1B–2B.

Strauss, Neil. "Disneyland for Deadheads." *New York Times.* National Edition. January 6, 1998: B1, B6.

Strong, Josiah. *Our Country: Its Possible Future and Its Present Crisis.* New York: American Home Missionary Society, 1885.

Sullivan, Walter. "Knowledge Promises to Be Main Boon of Manned Lunar Landing." *New York Times,* July 17, 1969: 45.

Swan, Joan. "Uncovering Love Canal." *Columbia Journalism Review,* 17, no. 5 (January-February 1979): 46–51.

Tallmer, Matt. "Hooker's Other Love Canals." *The Progressive,* 45, no. 11 (November 1981): 35–37.

Tarr, Ralph S. "Geology of the Yellowstone Park," I and II. *The Independent,* 50, nos. 2607 and 2609 (November 17 and December 1, 1898): 1406–1408, 1572–1576.

Taubman, Howard. "On Stage, Thoreau Speaks to Today." *New York Times,* December 23, 1970: 16.

Theweleit, Klaus. *Male Fantasies.* Vol. 1: *Women, Floods, Bodies, History.* 1977. Reprint. Minneapolis: University of Minnesota, 1987.

Thompson, Hunter S. *Fear and Loathing in Las Vegas: A Savage Journey to the Heart of the American Dream.* New York: Random House, 1971.

Thomson, W. Hanna. *Brain and Personality.* New York: Dodd, Mead, 1907.

Thoreau, Henry David. *Cape Cod.* Edited by Joseph Moldenhauer. 1886. In *The Writings of Henry D. Thoreau.* Princeton: Princeton University Press, 1988.

—— The Illustrated *A Week on the Concord and Merrimack Rivers.* Edited by Carl F. Hovde, William L. Howarth, and Elizabeth Wetherell. Princeton: Princeton University Press, 1983.

—— *The Portable Thoreau.* Edited by Carl Bode. New York: Penguin, 1975.

—— *Walden.* 1854. Reprint. Edited by J. Lyndon Shanley. Princeton: Princeton University Press, 1971.

—— "Walking." In *The Portable Thoreau,* 592–630. Edited by Carl Bode. New York: Penguin, 1975.

Tichi, Cecelia. *New World, New Earth: Environmental Reform in American Litera-*

ture from the Puritans through Whitman. New Haven: Yale University Press, 1979.

Tindall, George Brown, and David E. Shi. *America: A Narrative History.* 3rd ed. New York: W. W. Norton, 1984.

To the Hot Springs of Arkansas, America's Baden-Baden. St. Louis: St. Louis, Iron Mountain & Southern Railway Co., 1880.

Toomer, Jean. *Cane.* 1923. Reprint. New York: Liveright, 1975.

Torgovnick, Marianna. "Politics of the 'We.'" In *Eloquent Obsessions: Writing Cultural Criticism.* Edited by Marianna Torgovnick. Durham: Duke University Press, 1994.

Townsend, Mary Trowbridge. "A Woman's Trout-Fishing in Yellowstone Park." *Outing,* 30, no. 2 (May 1897): 163–165.

Trachtenberg, Alan. *Reading American Photographs: Images as History, Mathew Brady to Walker Evans.* New York: Hill and Wang, 1989.

Trall, Russell Thatcher. *The Hydropathic Encyclopedia.* Vols. 1–2. New York: Fowlers and Wells, 1854.

Traub, James. "Our Local Correspondents: Get Rudy." *New Yorker,* October 14, 1996: 46–49.

Trowbridge, J. T. "The Satin-Wood Box." *Youth's Companion,* 58, no. 3 (January 15, 1885): 16–21.

Trudeau, G[arry] B. *I Have No Son.* New York: Popular Library, 1973.

Turner, Frederick Jackson. *The Frontier in American History.* 1920. Reprint. New York: Dover, 1996.

——— "The Significance of the Frontier in American History." In *The Frontier in American History,* 1–38. 1920. Reprint. New York: Dover, 1996.

Turner, Victor. *Ritual Process: Structure and Anti-Structure.* Ithaca, N.Y.: Cornell University Press, 1977.

Turner, Victor, and Edith Turner. *Image and Pilgrimage in Christian Culture.* New York: Columbia University Press, 1978.

Twain, Mark. *The Adventures of Huckleberry Finn.* 1884. Reprint. New York: Penguin, 1984.

——— *Life on the Mississippi.* 1883. Reprint. New York: Penguin, 1984.

——— *Roughing It.* 1872. Reprint. New York: Signet, 1962.

Udall, Stewart L. *The Quiet Crisis.* New York: Holt, Rinehart, and Winston, 1963.

Unknown Places in Idaho. Union Pacific Railroad, n.d.

Van Zandt, Peter. "Obituary: Laguna's Oaks." *Indianhead,* 1, no. 4 (August 18–31, 1967): 4.

Vecsey, Christopher. "American Indian Environmental Religions." In *American Indian Environments: Ecological Issues in Native American History,* 1–37. Edited by Christopher Vecsey and Robert W. Venables. Syracuse, N.Y.: Syracuse University Press, 1980.

Venturi, Robert, Denise Scott Brown, and Steven Izenour. *Learning from Las Ve-*

gas: The Forgotten Symbolism of Architectural Form. Cambridge: MIT Press, 1972.

Verhovek, Sam Howe. "Across 10 Years, Exxon Valdez Casts a Shadow." *New York Times.* National Edition. March 6, 1999: A1, A8.

Verne, Jules. *From the Earth to the Moon.* 1865. Reprint. New York: Airmont, 1967.

Vogel, David. "The Politics of the Environment, 1970–1987." *Wilson Quarterly,* 11, no. 4 (Winter 1987): 51–83.

Wachsberger, Ken, ed. *Voices from the Underground: Insider Histories of the Vietnam Era Underground Press.* Vol. 1. Tempe, Az.: Mica's Press, 1993.

Wald, Priscilla. *Constituting Americans: Cultural Anxiety and Narrative Form.* Durham: Duke University Press, 1995.

Walker, Eugene H. "Tracing the Source of Walden Pond's Waters." *Man and Nature,* December 1971: 11–20.

Walker, James Herbert. *The Johnstown Horror.* Philadelphia: H. L. Warren, 1889.

Walker, Nancy, ed. *Women's Magazines, 1940–1960.* New York: Bedford/St. Martin's, 1998.

Walls, Laura Dassow. *Seeing New Worlds: Henry David Thoreau and Nineteenth-Century Natural Science.* Madison: University of Wisconsin Press, 1995.

Warren, Karen J. "The Power and the Promise of Ecological Feminism." In *Ecological Feminist Philosophies,* 19–41. Edited by Karen J. Warren. Bloomington: University of Indiana Press, 1996.

Warren, Karen J., ed. *Ecofeminism: Women, Culture, Nature.* Bloomington: Indiana University Press, 1997.

———— *Ecological Feminist Philosophies.* Bloomington: University of Indiana Press, 1996.

"The Washburn Yellowstone Expedition, Nos. 1 and 2." *Overland Monthly,* 6, nos. 5–6 (May–June 1871): 431–437, 489–496.

Washington, Booker T. *Up from Slavery.* 1901. Reprint. New York: Penguin, 1986.

Water-Cure Journal, 11, no. 1 (January 1851): 1–24; vol. 11, no. 3 (March 1851): 57–80.

Watts, Alan. *This Is It, and Other Essays on Zen and Spiritual Experience.* 1960. Reprint. New York: Vintage, 1973.

———— *Zen and the Beat Way.* Boston: Charles E. Tuttle, 1997.

Watts, Steven. "Walt Disney: Art and Politics in the American Century." *Journal of American History* 82 (June 1995): 84–106.

Weber, Alfred, Beth L. Lueck, and Dennis Berthold, eds. *Hawthorne's Travel Sketches.* Hanover, N.H.: University Press of New England, 1989.

Weed, Walter. "Fossil Forests of the Yellowstone." *School of Mines Quarterly,* 13, no. 3 (April 1892): 230–236.

———— "Geysers." *School of Mines Quarterly,* 11, no. 4 (July 1890): 289–306.

West, Rick. "Saving Disney from Itself." *Harper's*, 294 (January 1997): 20–21, 66–68.

Westerhoff, John H., III. *McGuffey and His Readers: Piety, Morality, and Education in Nineteenth-Century America*. Nashville: Abingdon, 1978.

Wexler, Mark. "Poison Dumps: Malignant Neglect." *National Wildlife*, 18, no. 5 (August–September 1980): 30–31.

Whipple, Fred, and Wernher von Braun. "Man on the Moon: The Exploration." *Collier's*, 130 (October 25, 1952): 38–48.

White, Lynn, Jr. "The Historical Roots of Our Ecological Crisis." *Science*, March 10, 1967: 1203–1207.

White, Richard. " 'Are You an Environmentalist or Do You Work for a Living?': Work and Nature." In *Uncommon Ground: Rethinking the Human Place in Nature*, 171–185. Edited by William Cronon. New York: Norton, 1996.

The White Mountains: Place and Perceptions. Edited by Donald D. Keyes. Durham: University of New Hampshire Press, 1980.

Whitman, Walt. *Leaves of Grass*. Edited by Sculley Bradley and Harold W. Blodgett. 1965. Reprint. New York: W. W. Norton, 1973.

Wilcock, John. "Human Be-in." *International Times*, 8 (February 13–26, 1967): 2.

Wilkinson, Norman B. *Lammot Du Pont and the American Explosives Industry, 1850–1884*. Charlottesville: University of Virginia Press, 1984.

Williams, Vernon J., Jr. *Rethinking Race: Franz Boas and His Contemporaries*. Lexington: University of Kentucky Press, 1996.

Williams, William Carlos. *Paterson*. 1946–1958. Reprint. New York: New Directions, 1963.

Williamson, Ray A. "Outer Space as Frontier." *Parables of the Space Age: Western Folklore*, 46 (October 1987): 255–267.

Wilson, John. *Health and Health-Resorts*. Philadelphia: Porter and Coates, 1880.

Wiseman, Susan. " 'Femininity' and the Intellectual in Sontag and Cixous." In *The Body and the Text*, 98–113. Edited by Helen Wilcox, Keith McWatters, Ann Thompson, and Linda R. Williams. New York: St. Martin's, 1990.

Witcover, Jules. *The Day the Dream Died: Revisiting 1968 in America*. New York: Warner, 1997.

Wolfe, Tom. *The Electric Kool-Aid Acid Test*. New York: Bantam, 1968.

——— *The Kandy-Kolored Tangerine-Flake Streamline Baby*. New York: Noonday, 1965.

——— *The Right Stuff*. New York: Bantam, 1980.

Woodford, John. "Massaging the Blackman." In *Voices from the Underground: Insider Histories of the Vietnam Era Underground Press*. Vol. 1, 81–98. Edited by Ken Wachsberger. Tempe, Az.: Mica's Press, 1993.

Woodring, Paul. "A View from the Campus: Was Thoreau a Hippie." *Saturday Review*, 50, no. 68 (December 16, 1967): 68.

Worster, Donald. *Rivers of Empire: Water, Aridity, and the Growth of the American West.* New York: Pantheon, 1985.

Yablonsky, Lewis. *The Hippie Trip.* New York: Pegasus, 1968.

"Year of the Commune." *Newsweek,* 74 (August 18, 1969): 89–90.

"Yellowstone Park as a Summer Resort." *The Nation,* 71, no. 1839 (September 27, 1900): 248–250.

Young, M. Jane. "Guest Editor's Introduction." *Parables of the Space Age: Western Folklore,* 46 (October 1987): 227–233.

———— "Pity the Indians of Outer Space." *Parables of the Space Age: Western Folklore,* 46 (October 1987): 269–279.

Young, Neil. "After the Gold Rush." *Trio II.* Asylum Records 62275-2.

Zinn, Howard. *A People's History of the United States, 1492–Present.* New York: HarperCollins, 1999.

Credits

1. State of California as muscular arm. Artist Filip Pagowski, 1998.

2. Athlete as embodied map. *Sports Illustrated* cover, December 2, 1996.

3. *Erosion No. 2: Mother Earth Laid Bare,* by Alexander Hogue, 1936. The Philbrook Museum of Art, Tulsa, Oklahoma.

4. Mt. Rushmore, South Dakota. Photograph by Jamie Adams.

5. Mt. Rushmore during construction, 1938. Library of Congress.

6. *The Mount Washington Road.* Illustration by Henry Fenn, for William Cullen Bryant, ed., *Picturesque America*, vol. 1 (New York: D. Appleton & Co., 1872).

7. Ceramic phrenology model. Author's collection. Photograph by Jamie Adams.

8. *The Image Peddlar,* by Francis W. Edmonds, c. 1844. © Collection of The New-York Historical Society, Detail.

9. *The Old Man of the Mountain.* Illustration by Henry Fenn, for William Cullen Bryant, ed., *Picturesque America*, vol. 1 (New York: D. Appleton & Co., 1872).

10. Sony advertisement using Mt. Rushmore, 1996. Courtesy of Sony Electronics Inc.

11. President George H. W. Bush. Photograph by Joe Marquette, 1990. © Bettmann/CORBIS.

12. Mt. Rushmore, U.S. postage stamp.

13. Ceramic cranial flower pot. Author's collection.

14. *Doonesbury* comic strip, 1972. © G. B. Trudeau. Reprinted with permission of Universal Press Syndicate. All rights reserved.

15. Henry David Thoreau, U.S. postage stamp, 1967.

16. Walden Pond. © Bettmann/CORBIS.

17. Disneyland Main Street Electrical Parade. Photograph by Jamie Adams.

18. Civil Rights Memorial, designed by Maya Lin, Montgomery, Alabama. © Kevin Fleming/CORBIS.

19. Yellowstone National Park. Library of Congress.

20. *The Grand Cañon of the Yellowstone,* by Thomas Moran. U.S. Department of the Interior Museum.

21. Industrial chimneys of Pittsburgh, detail from postcard, 1910s. Author's collection.

22. Old Faithful geyser. Library of Congress.

23. Industrial "geyser" field of Pittsburgh, postcard, 1910s. Author's collection.

24. Tomorrowland at Disneyland Park. © Bettmann/CORBIS.

25. Craters of the Moon, 1924. Limbert Collection, Boise State University Library.

26. NASA Apollo 11 rocket. National Archives.

27. Neil Armstrong on the moon. National Archives.

28. Apollo 11 astronauts Edwin (Buzz) Aldrin, Michael Collins, and Neil Armstrong. National Archives.

29. Tea tin featuring female moon. © 1997 Celestial Seasonings, Inc. Photograph by Jamie Adams.

30. Water Goddess of Health, engraving from R. T. Trall, *Hydropathic Encyclopedia* (New York: Fowlers and Wells, 1851). Courtesy of The Newberry Library, Chicago.

31. Scenes of bath houses, Hot Springs, Arkansas, from *Harper's New Monthly Magazine,* January 1878.

32. Creekside scene near the Arlington Hotel, Hot Springs, Arkansas, from *Harper's New Monthly Magazine,* January 1878.

33. Stained-glass ceiling in Fordyce Bath House, Hot Springs, Arkansas. Detail. Photograph by author.

34. Angelic figure of Hygeia, engraving from advertisement for R. T. Trall, *Hydropathic Encyclopedia,* in *The Water-Cure Journal,* 1851. Courtesy of The Newberry Library, Chicago.

35. Water-cure treatments illustrated in Dr. Mary Melandy, *Perfect Womanhood for Maidens, Wives, Mothers* (Boston: James H. Earle, 1901).

36. *Lake at Franconia Notch, White Mountains,* by Albert Bierstadt, n.d. Oil on paper. J. Ackerman Coles Bequest, 1926. The Newark Museum / Art Resource, N.Y.

37. Love Canal, 1980. The Library of the State University of New York, Buffalo.

38. "The Poisoning of America." James Marsh, artist. *Time* cover, September 22, 1980. © Time Inc.

Index